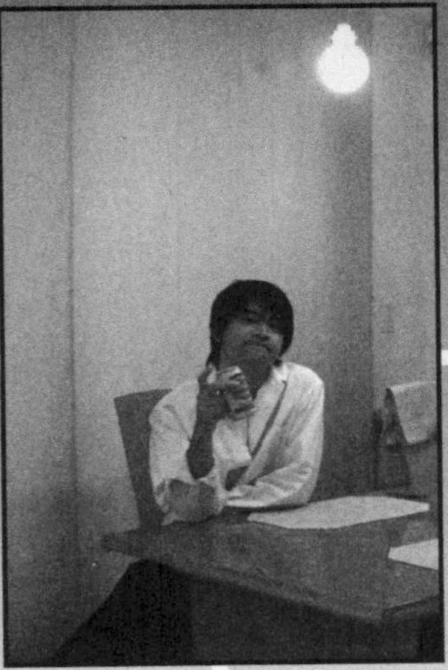

Beer after work rules!! It's the best.♥

But a few minutes later I'm all red... Coming to you from Konomi, who has no tolerance.

- Takeshi Konomi, 2005

About Takeshi Konomi

Takeshi Konomi exploded onto the manga scene with the incredible **THE PRINCE OF TENNIS**. His refined art style and sleek character designs proved popular with **Weekly Shonen Jump** readers, and **THE PRINCE OF TENNIS** became the number one sports manga in Japan almost overnight. Its cast of fascinating male tennis players attracted legions of female readers even though it was originally intended to be a boys' comic. The manga continues to be a success in Japan and has inspired a hit anime series, as well as several video games and mountains of merchandise.

THE PRINCE OF TENNIS
VOL. 29
The SHONEN JUMP Manga Edition

STORY AND ART BY
TAKESHI KONOMI

Translation/Joe Yamazaki
Touch-up Art & Lettering/Vanessa Satone
Design/Sam Elzway
Editor/Leyla Aker

Editor in Chief, Books/Alvin Lu
Editor in Chief, Magazines/Marc Weidenbaum
VP, Publishing Licensing/Rika Inouye
VP, Sales & Product Marketing/Gonzalo Ferreyra
VP, Creative/Linda Espinosa
Publisher/Hyoe Narita

Printed in the U.S.A.

Published by VIZ Media, LLC
P.O. Box 77010
San Francisco, CA 94107

SHONEN JUMP Manga Edition
10 9 8 7 6 5 4 3 2 1
First printing, January 2009

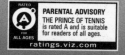

PARENTAL ADVISORY
THE PRINCE OF TENNIS is rated A and is suitable for readers of all ages.
ratings.viz.com

THE WORLD'S MOST POPULAR MANGA

www.viz.com

www.shonenjump.com

SHONEN JUMP Manga

テニスの王子様

THE PRINCE OF TENNIS

VOL. 29
The Nationals Begin!

Story & Art by
Takeshi Konomi

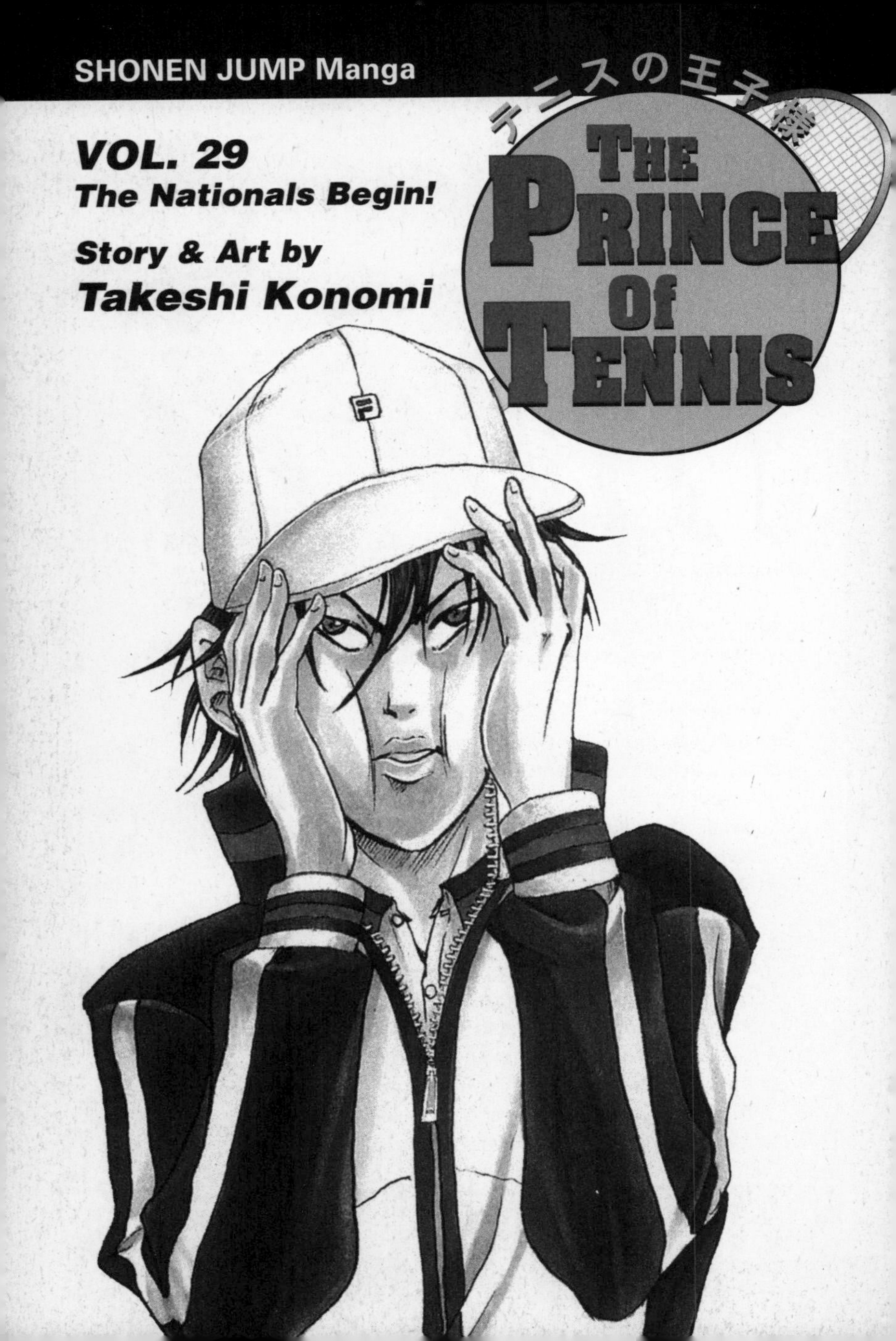

ENNIS CLUB

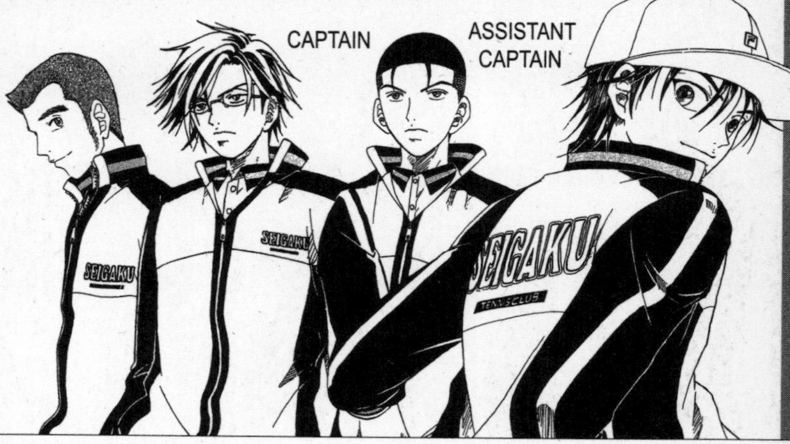
CAPTAIN
ASSISTANT CAPTAIN

• TAKASHI KAWAMURA • KUNIMITSU TEZUKA • SHUICHIRO OISHI • RYOMA ECHIZEN •

Seishun Academy student Ryoma Echizen is a tennis prodigy, with wins in four consecutive U.S. Junior Tennis Tournaments under his belt. He became a starter as a 7th grader and led his team to the District Preliminaries! Despite a few mishaps, Seishun won the District Prelims and the City Tournament, and earned a ticket to the Kanto Tournament. The team came away victorious from its first-round matches, but captain Kunimitsu injured his shoulder and went to Kyushu for treatment. Despite losing Kunimitsu and assistant captain Shuichiro to injury, Seishun pulled together as a team, winning the Kanto Tournament and earning a slot at the Nationals!

The Hyotei Academy team, who were eliminated in the first round of the Kanto Tournament, receives some good news: with the Nationals set to take place in Tokyo, they're given a special bracket to represent the region. With the support of the entire student body, Keigo vows revenge. Meanwhile, Kintaro Toyama from Shitenhoji Junior High School is headed toward Tokyo...

STORY & CHARACTERS

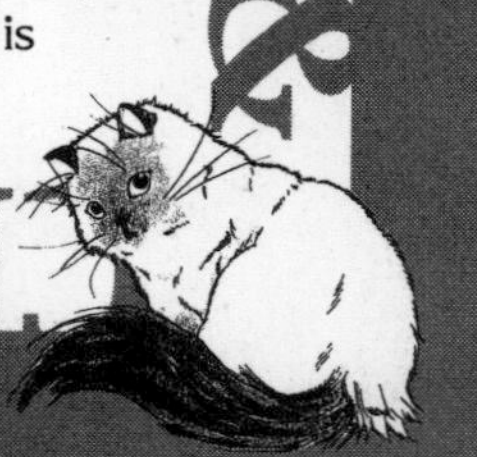

SEIGAKU TE

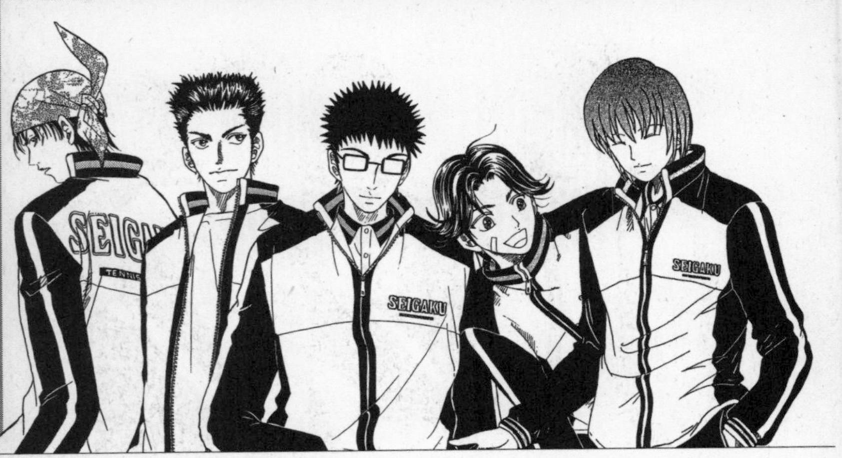

SEIGAKU
SEIGAKU

• KAORU KAIDO • TAKESHI MOMOSHIRO • SADAHARU INUI • EIJI KIKUMARU • SHUSUKE FUJI •

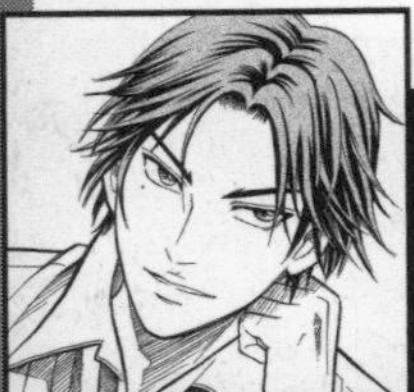

HYOTEI

KEIGO ATOBE

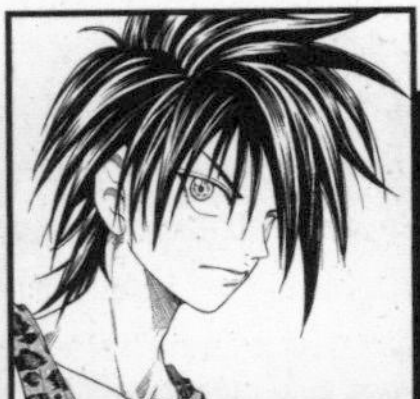

SHITENHOJI

KINTARO TOYAMA

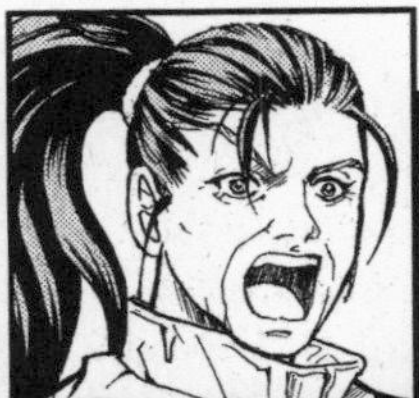

SEISHUN ACADEMY TENNIS COACH

SUMIRE RYUZAKI

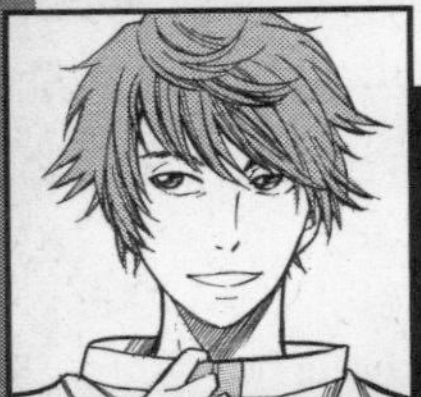

YAMABUKI

KIYOSUMI SENGOKU

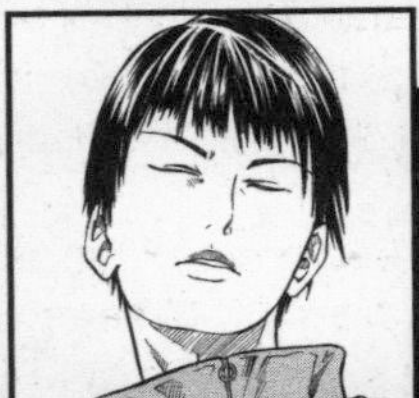

RIKKAI

RENJI YANAGI

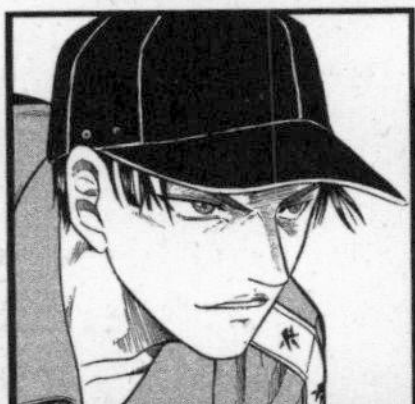

RIKKAI

GENICHIRO SANADA

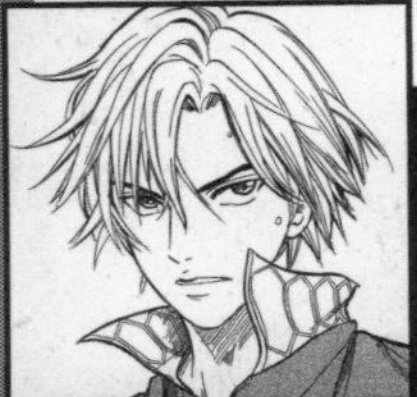

ROKKAKU

KOJIRO SAEKI

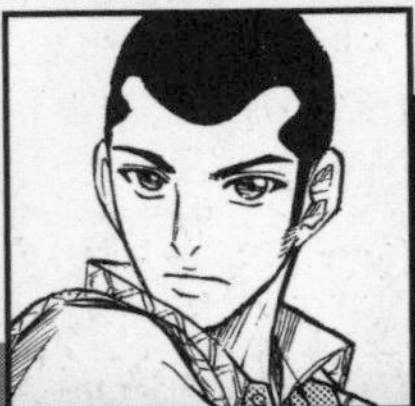

ROKKAKU

KENTARO AOI

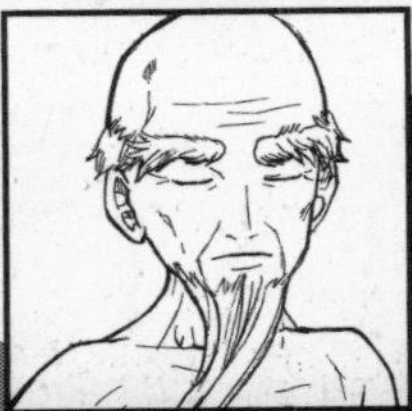

ROKKAKU TENNIS COACH

OJI

CONTENTS Vol. 29
The Nationals Begin!

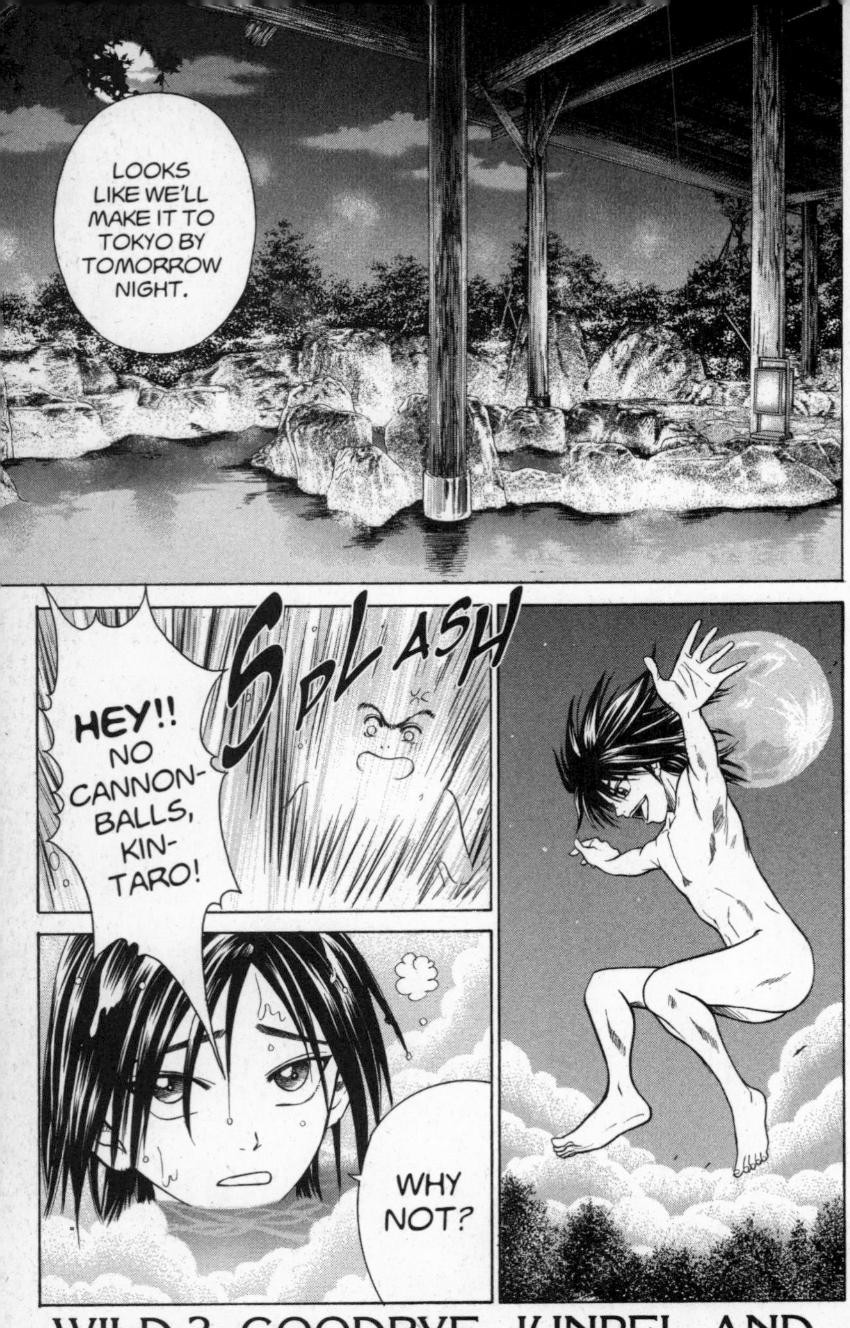
LOOKS LIKE WE'LL MAKE IT TO TOKYO BY TOMORROW NIGHT.
SPLASH
HEY!! NO CANNON-BALLS, KIN-TARO!
WHY NOT?

WILD 3: GOODBYE, JUNPEI... AND...

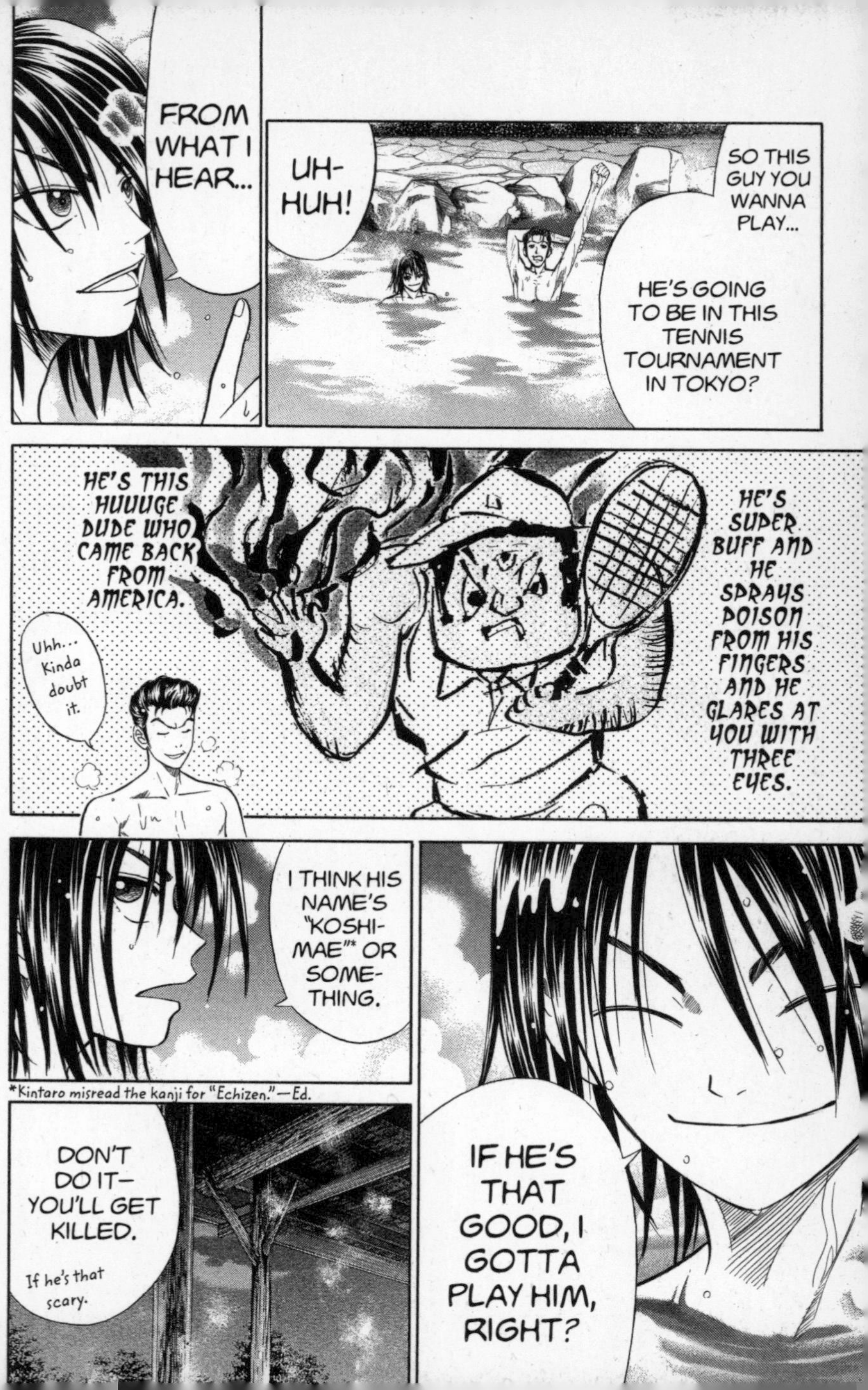
SO THIS GUY YOU WANNA PLAY...
HE'S GOING TO BE IN THIS TENNIS TOURNAMENT IN TOKYO?
UH-HUH!
FROM WHAT I HEAR...
HE'S THIS HUUUGE DUDE WHO CAME BACK FROM AMERICA.
HE'S SUPER BUFF AND HE SPRAYS POISON FROM HIS FINGERS AND HE GLARES AT YOU WITH THREE EYES.
Uhh... Kinda doubt it.
I THINK HIS NAME'S "KOSHIMAE"* OR SOMETHING.
DON'T DO IT—YOU'LL GET KILLED.
If he's that scary.
IF HE'S THAT GOOD, I GOTTA PLAY HIM, RIGHT?

*Kintaro misread the kanji for "Echizen."—Ed.

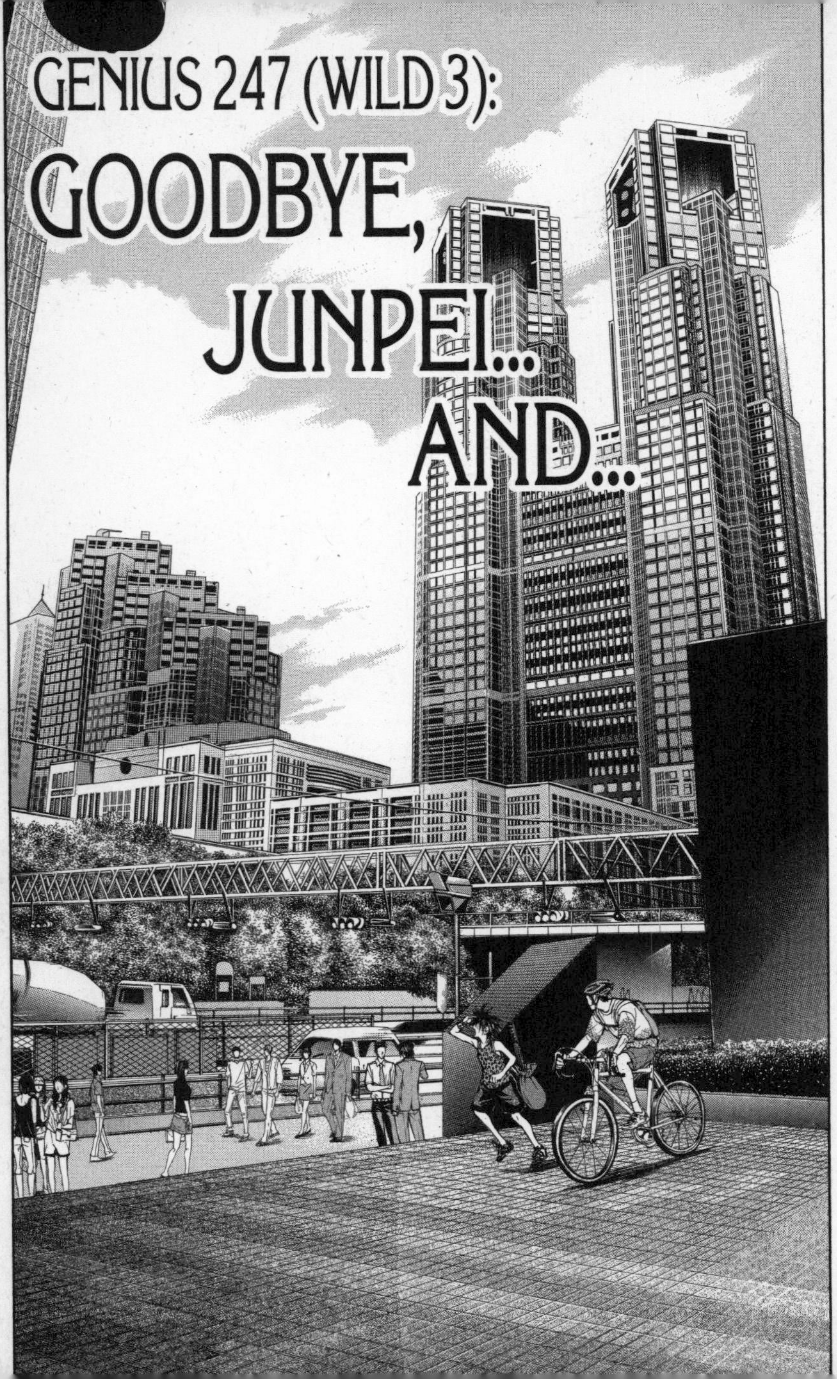
GENIUS 247 (WILD 3):
GOODBYE, JUNPEI... AND...

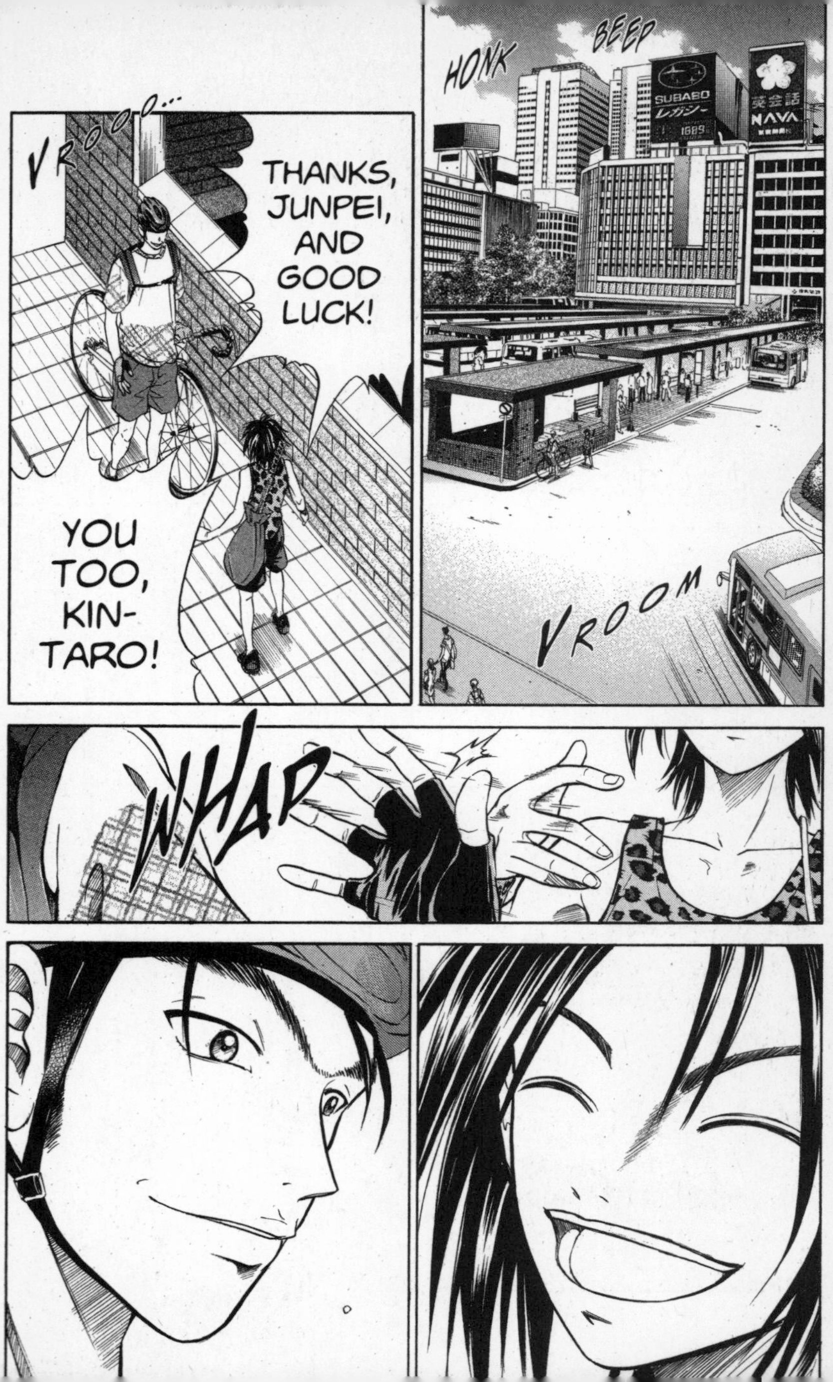
HONK
BEEP
SUBABO
レガシー
英会話
NAVA
VROOM
VROOOO...
THANKS, JUNPEI, AND GOOD LUCK!
YOU TOO, KIN-TARO!
WHAP

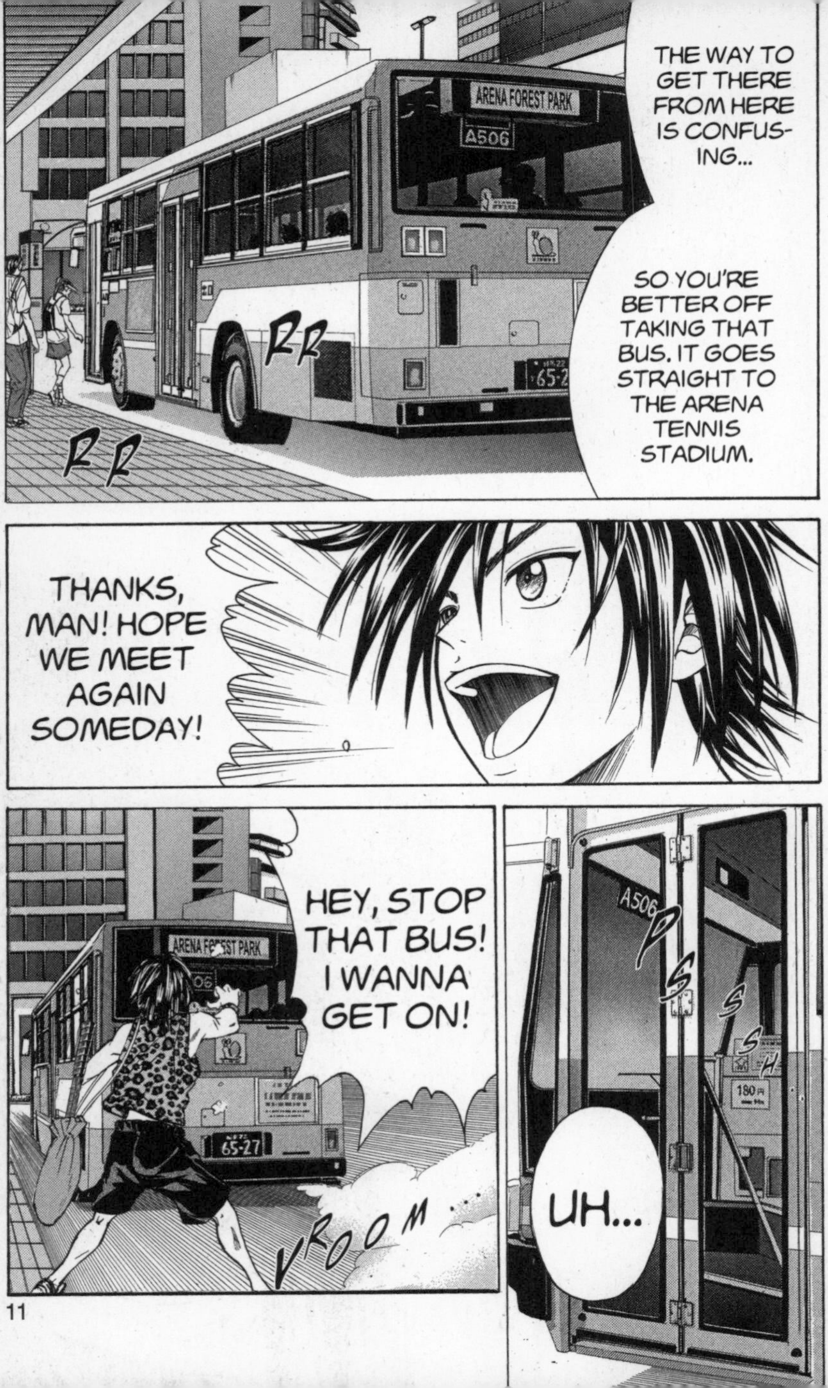
ARENA FOREST PARK
A506
THE WAY TO GET THERE FROM HERE IS CONFUSING...
SO YOU'RE BETTER OFF TAKING THAT BUS. IT GOES STRAIGHT TO THE ARENA TENNIS STADIUM.
RR
RR
THANKS, MAN! HOPE WE MEET AGAIN SOMEDAY!
A506
PSSSH
180円
UH...
ARENA FOREST PARK
HEY, STOP THAT BUS! I WANNA GET ON!
65-27
VROOOM...

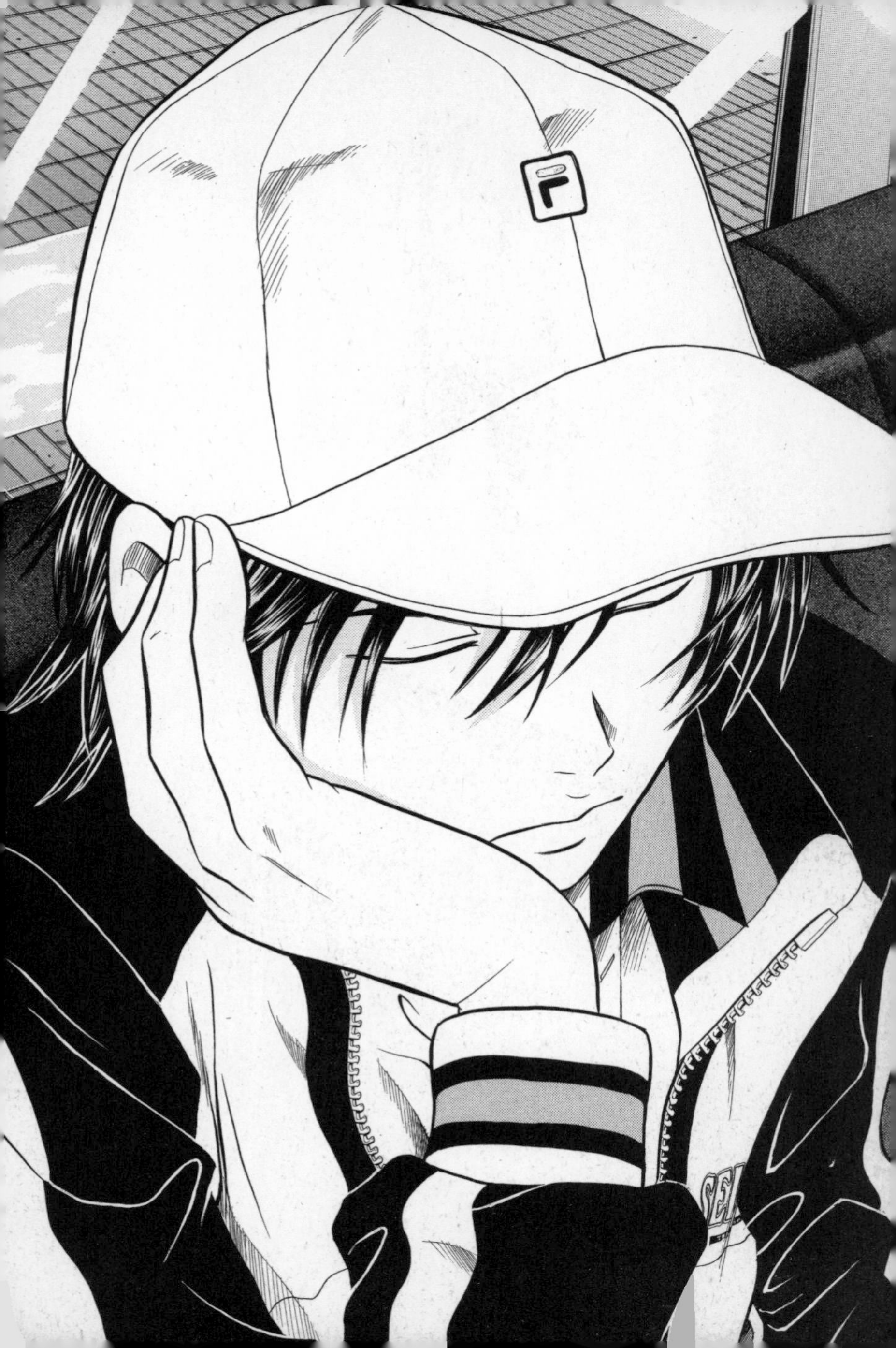

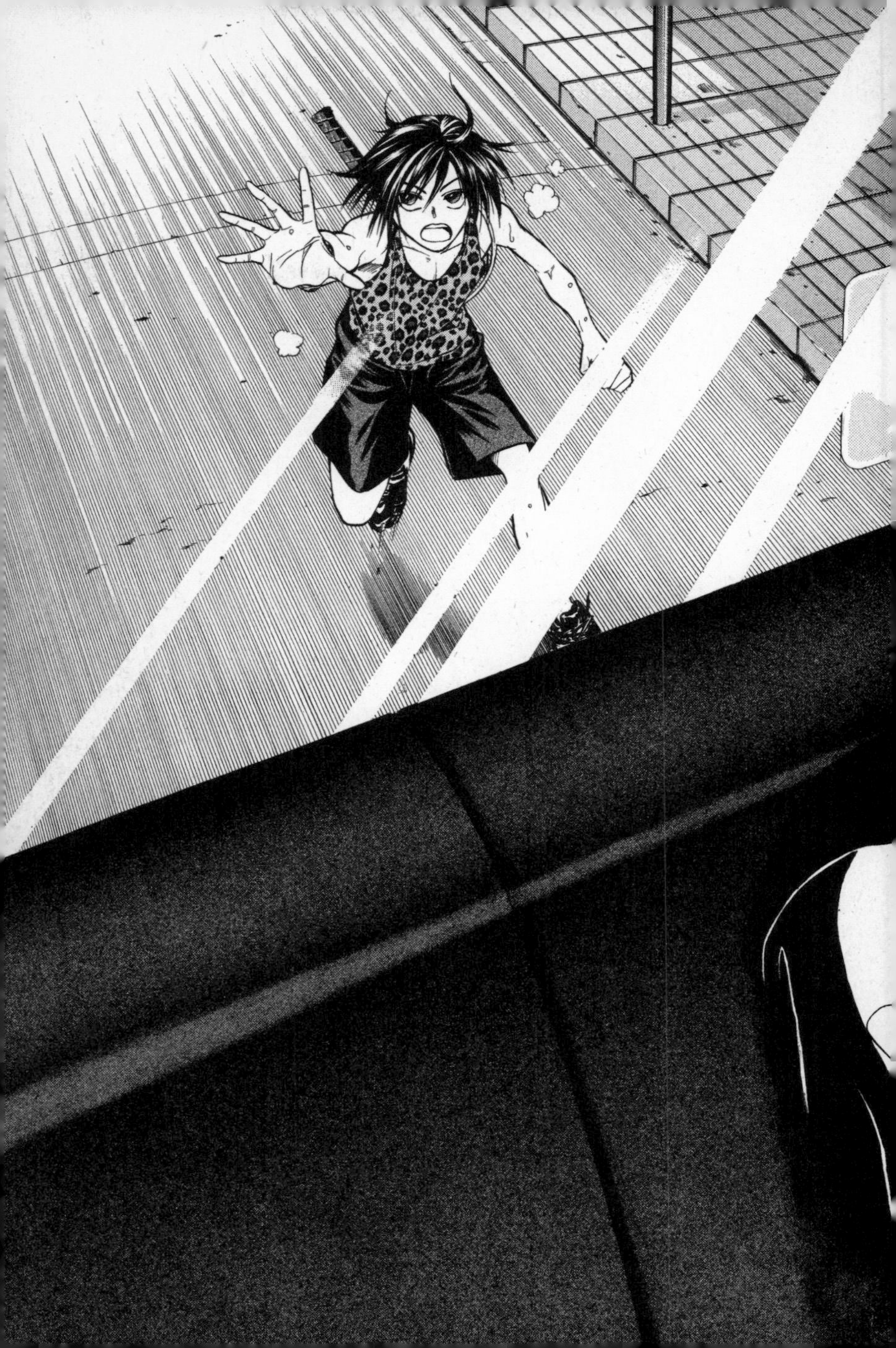

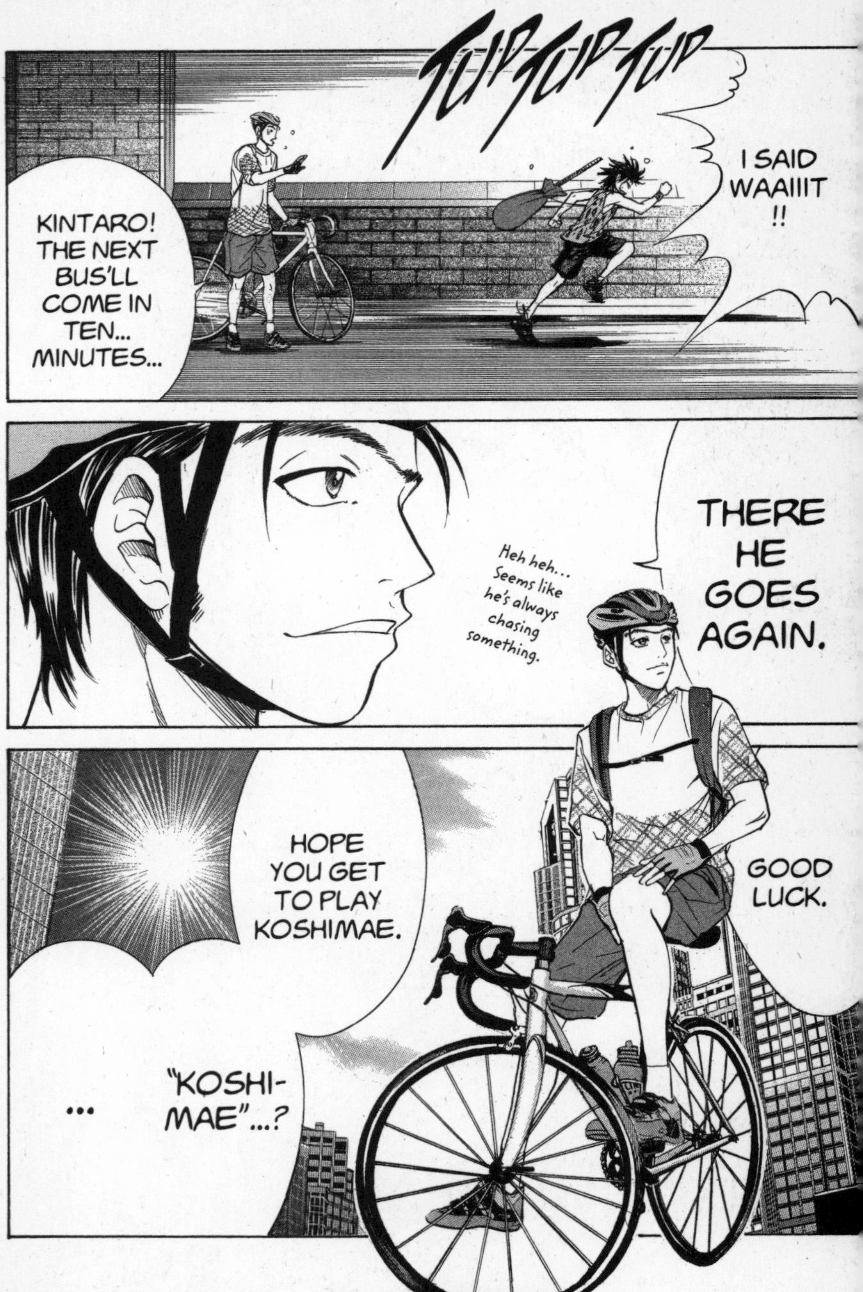
TUP TUP TUP
I SAID WAAIIIT !!
KINTARO! THE NEXT BUS'LL COME IN TEN... MINUTES...
THERE HE GOES AGAIN.
Heh heh... Seems like he's always chasing something.
GOOD LUCK.
HOPE YOU GET TO PLAY KOSHIMAE.
"KOSHI-MAE"...?
...

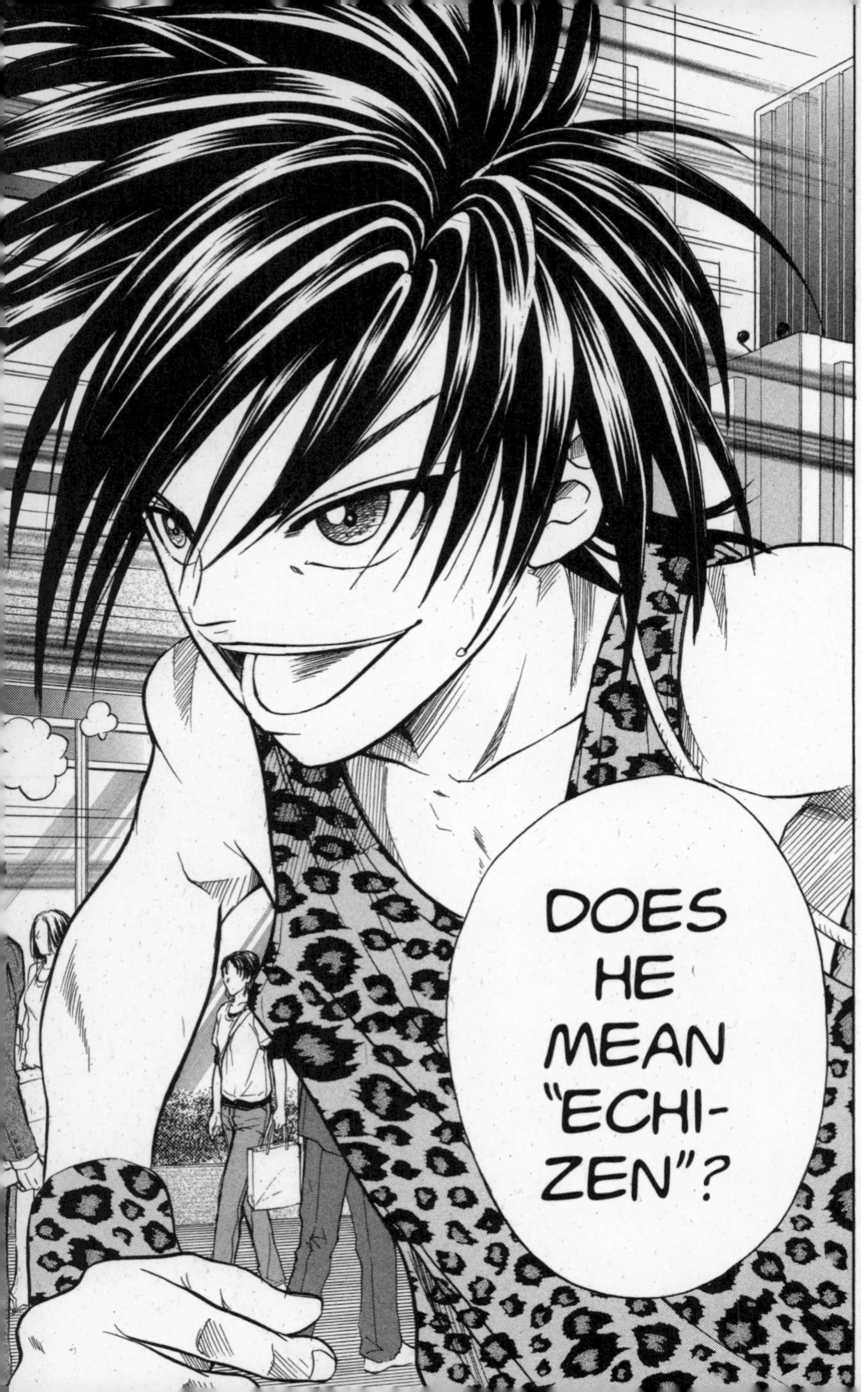
DOES HE MEAN "ECHIZEN"?

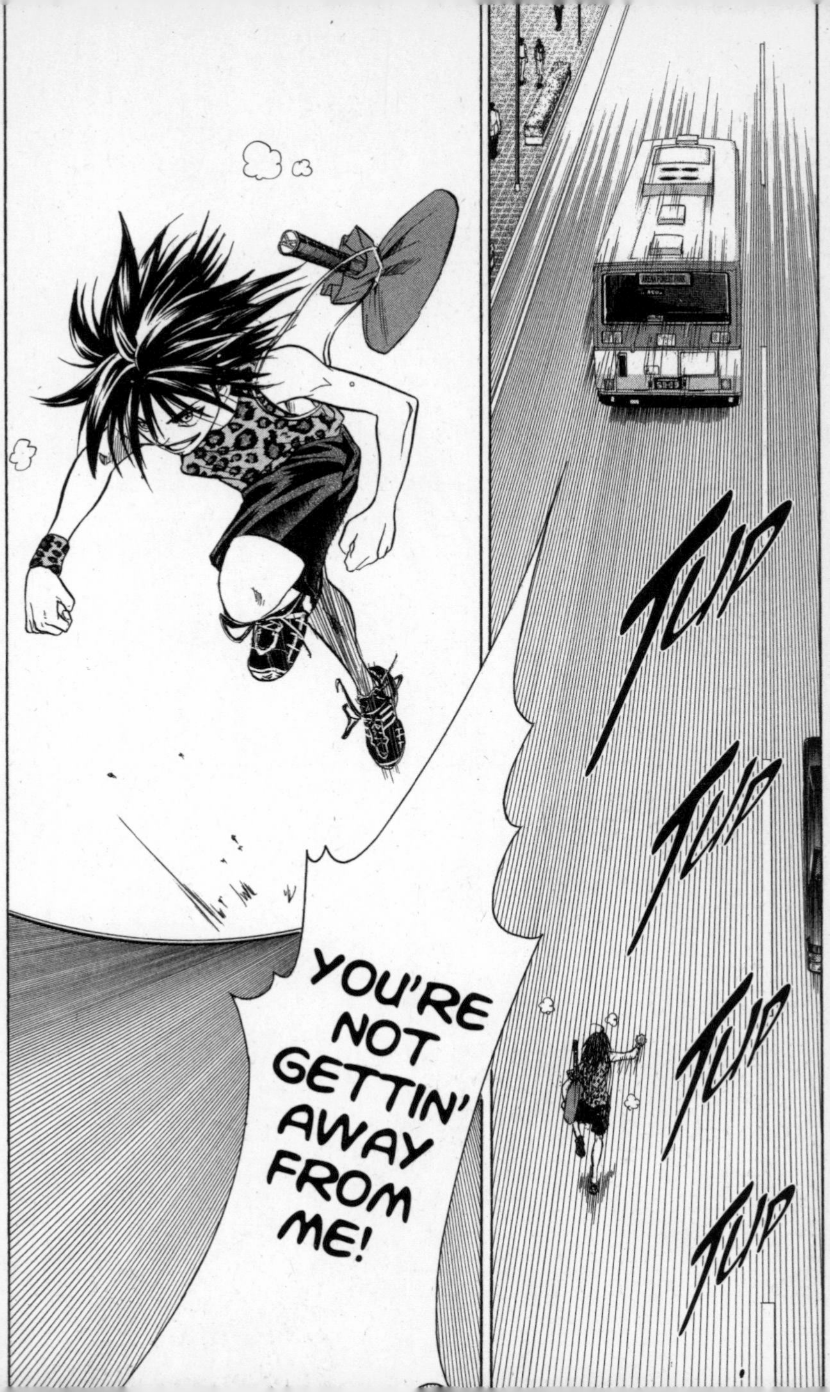
TUD
TUD
TUD
TUD
YOU'RE NOT GETTIN' AWAY FROM ME!

READ THIS WAY

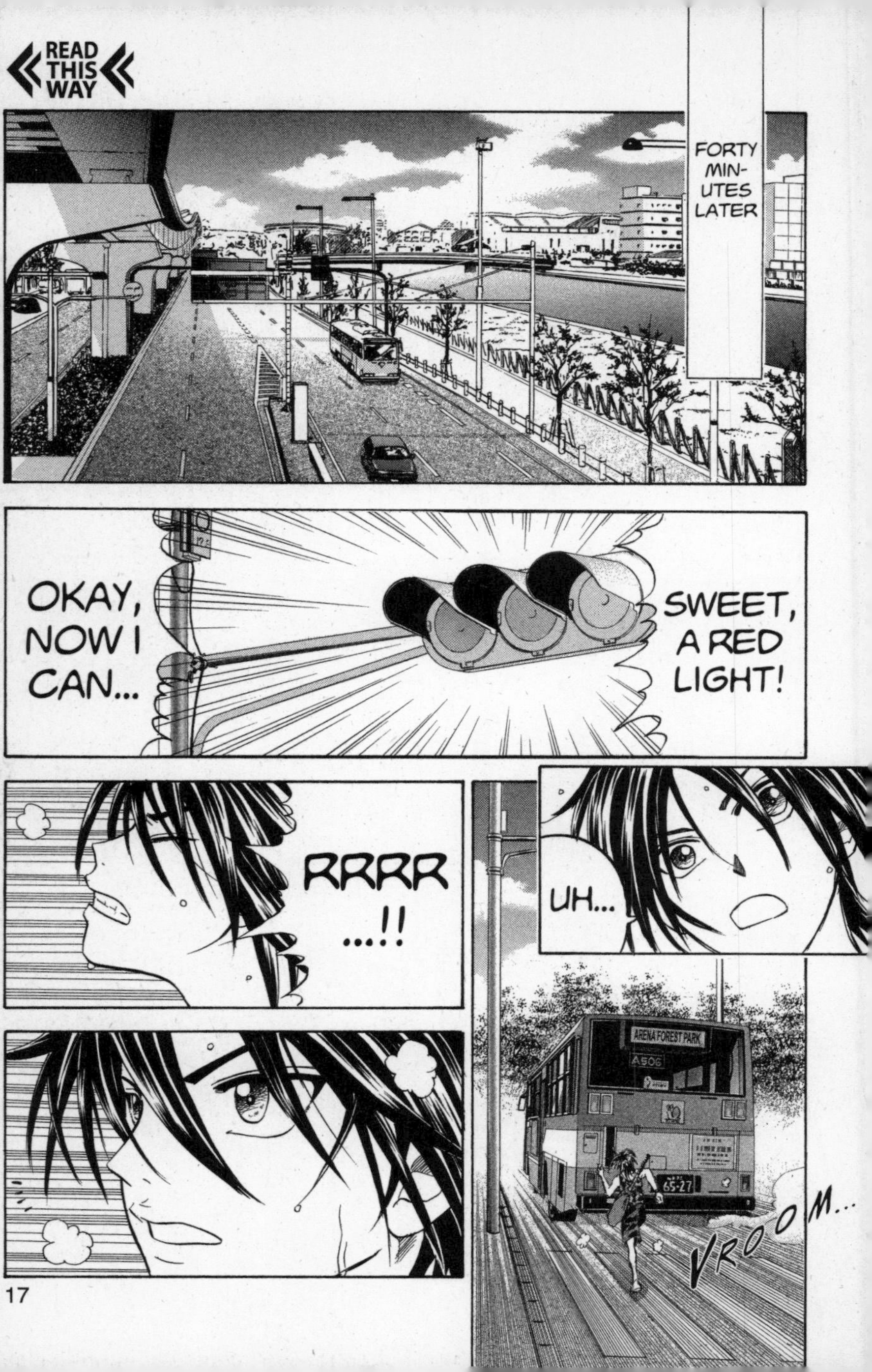
FORTY MIN-UTES LATER
SWEET, A RED LIGHT!
OKAY, NOW I CAN...
UH...
ARENA FOREST PARK
A506
VROOOM...
RRRR ...!!

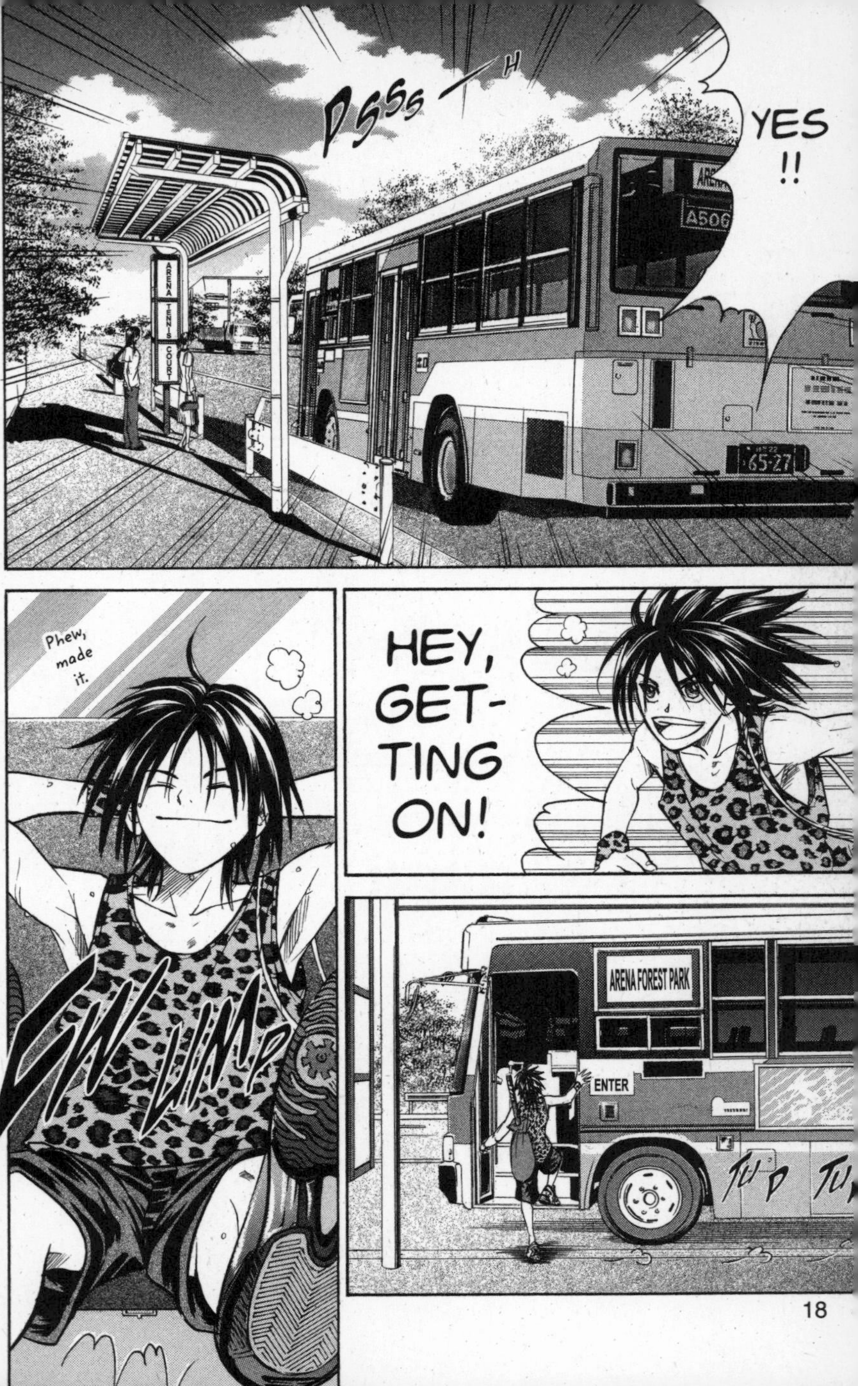
PSSS—H
YES !!
A506
ARENA TENNIS COURT
65-27
HEY, GET-TING ON!
ARENA FOREST PARK
ENTER
Phew, made it.

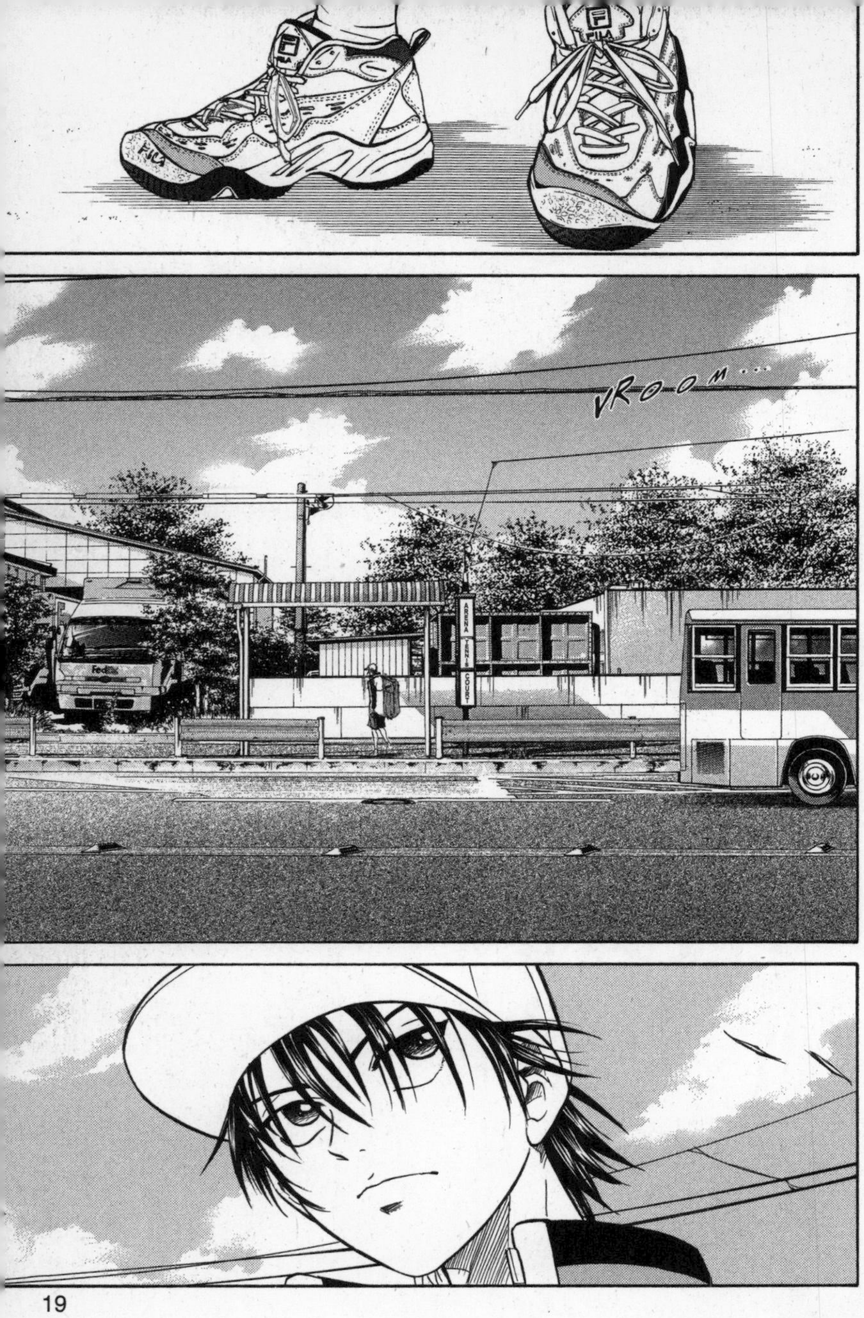
VROOM...
ARENA TENNIS COURT

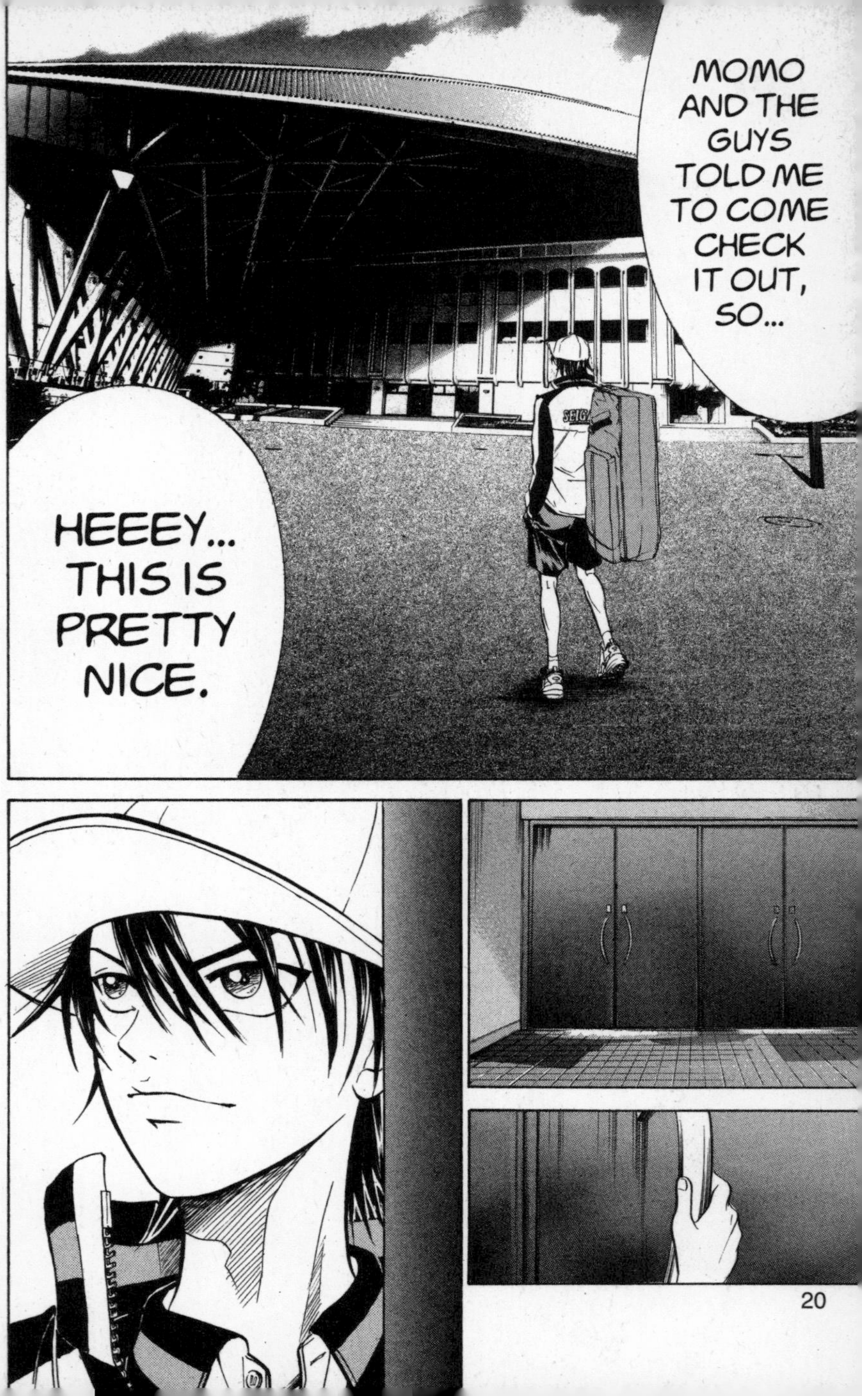
MOMO AND THE GUYS TOLD ME TO COME CHECK IT OUT, SO...
HEEEY... THIS IS PRETTY NICE.

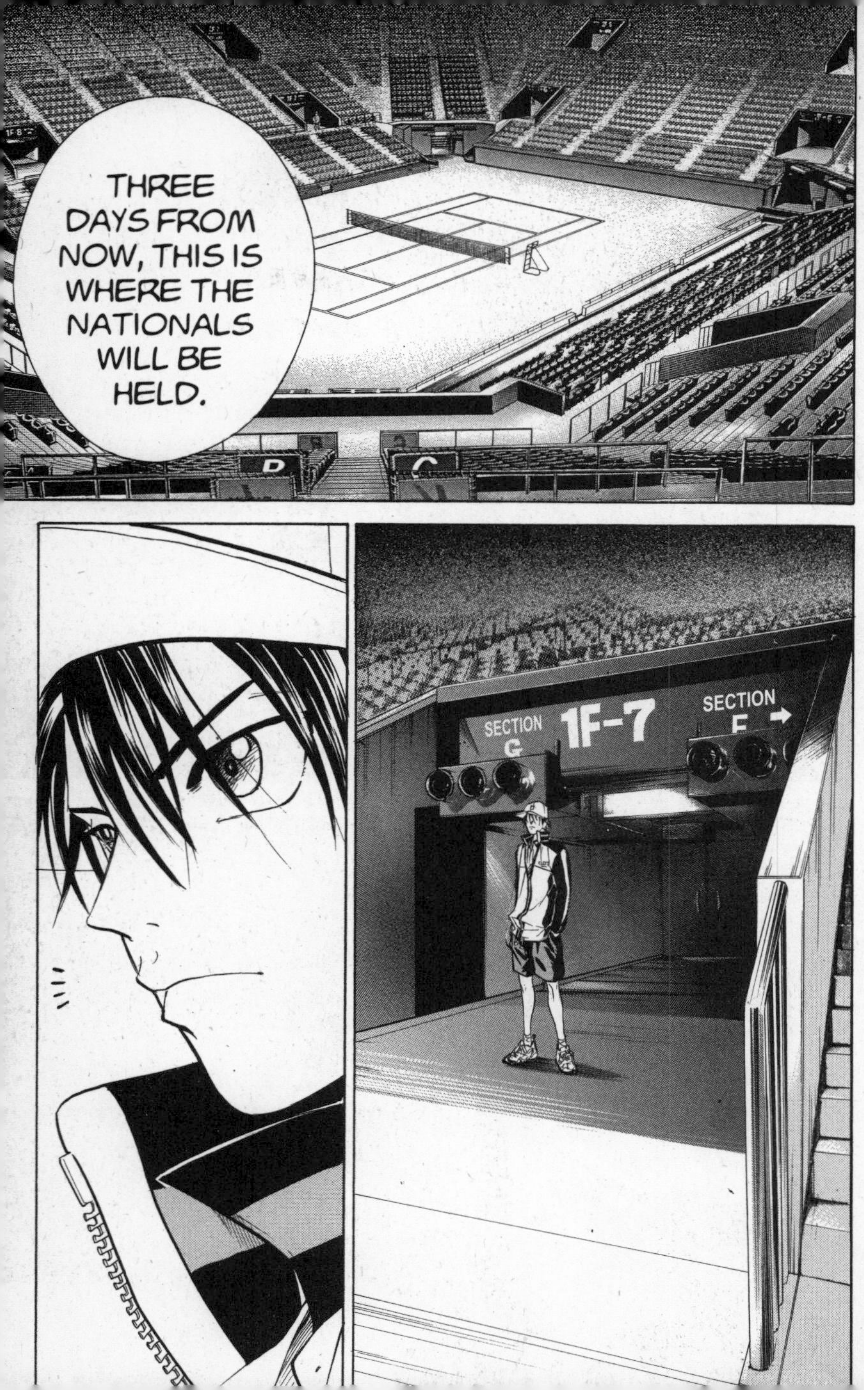
THREE DAYS FROM NOW, THIS IS WHERE THE NATIONALS WILL BE HELD.
SECTION G
1F-7
SECTION

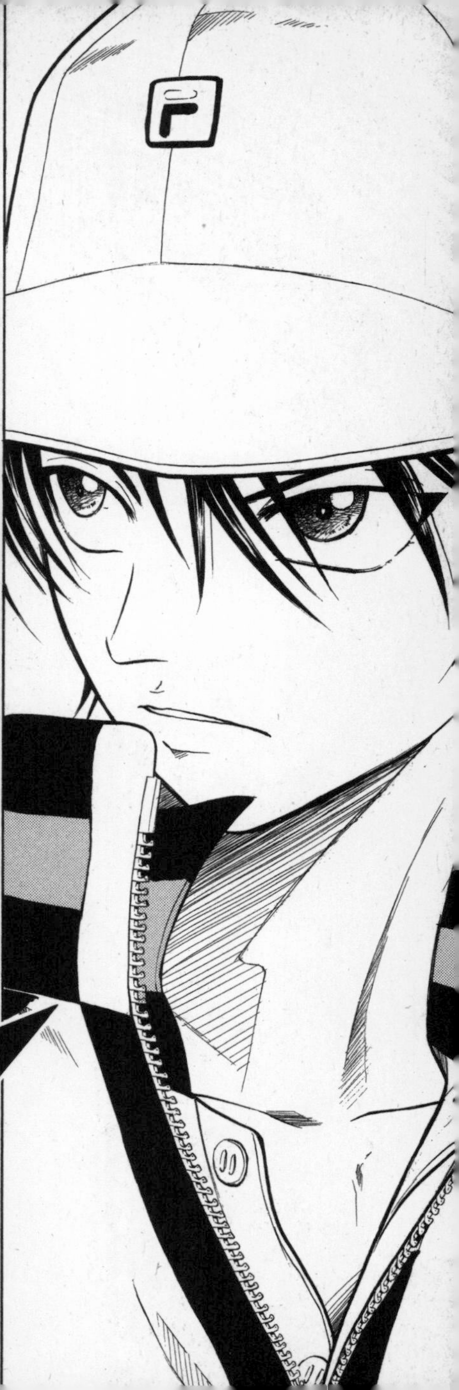

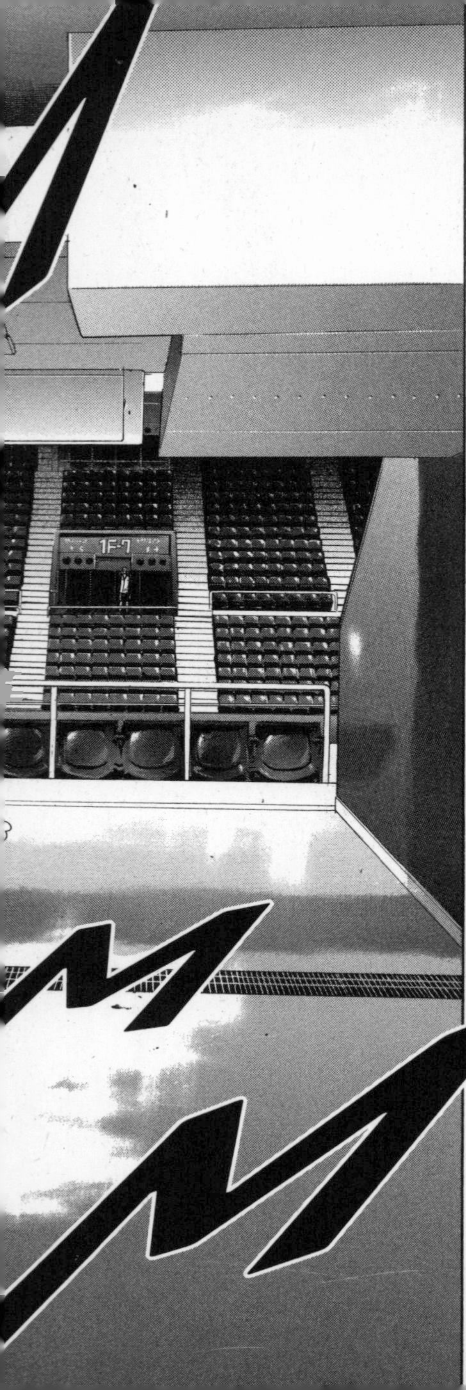
1F-7

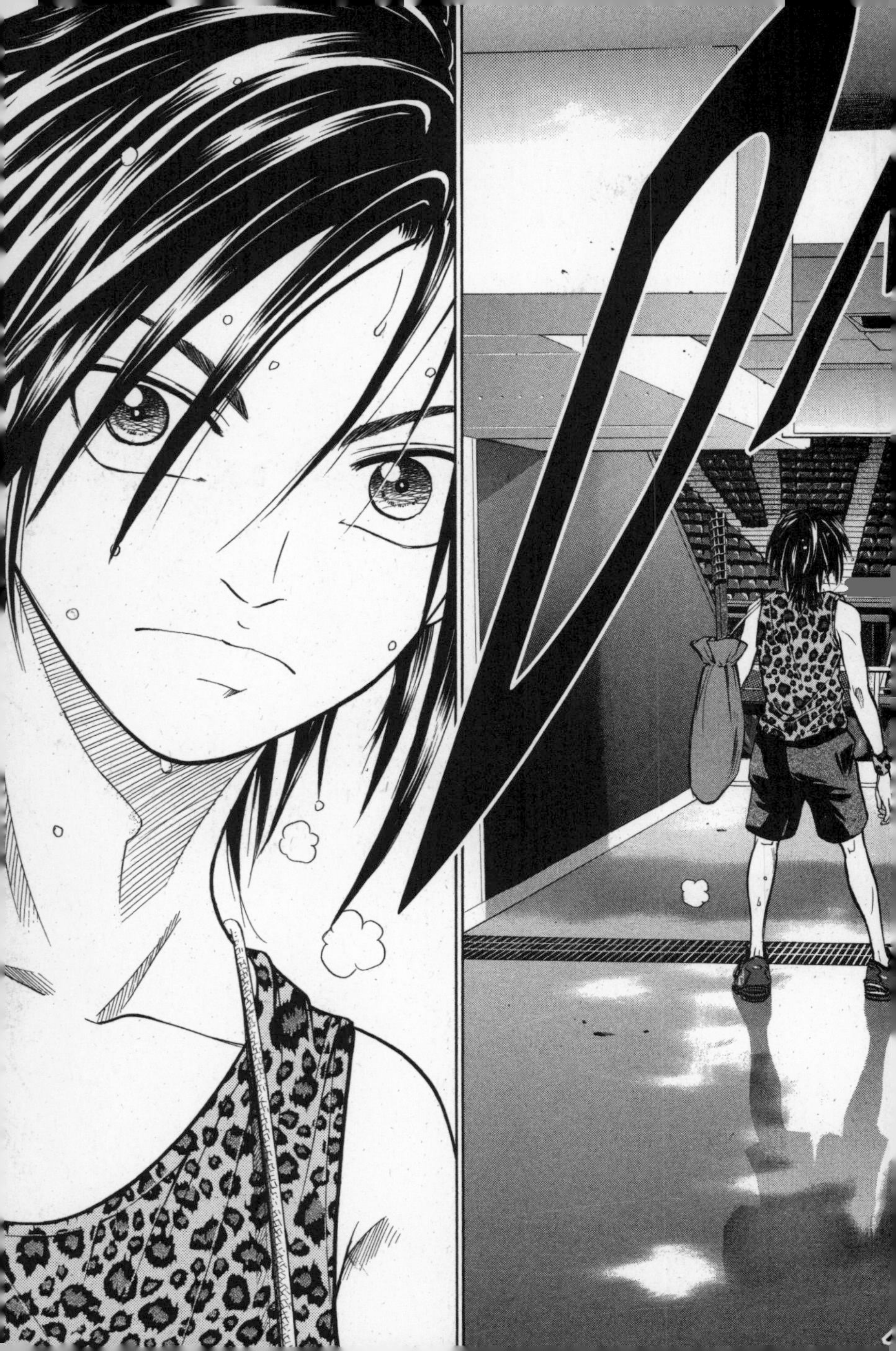

テニスの王子様
THE PRINCE OF TENNIS

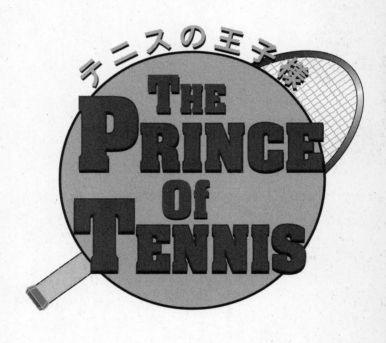

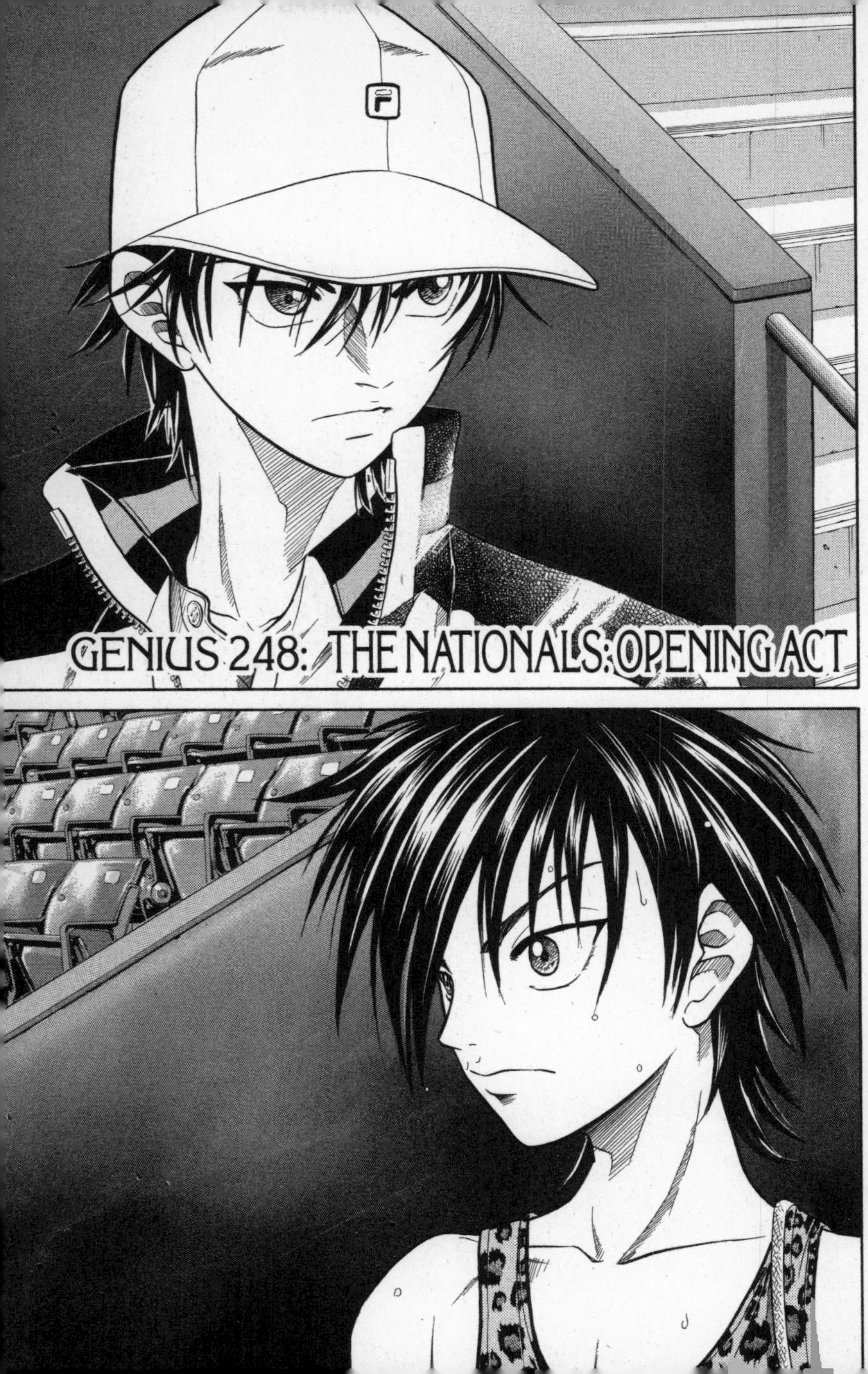
GENIUS 248: THE NATIONALS: OPENING ACT

GENIUS 248:
THE NATIONALS: OPENING ACT

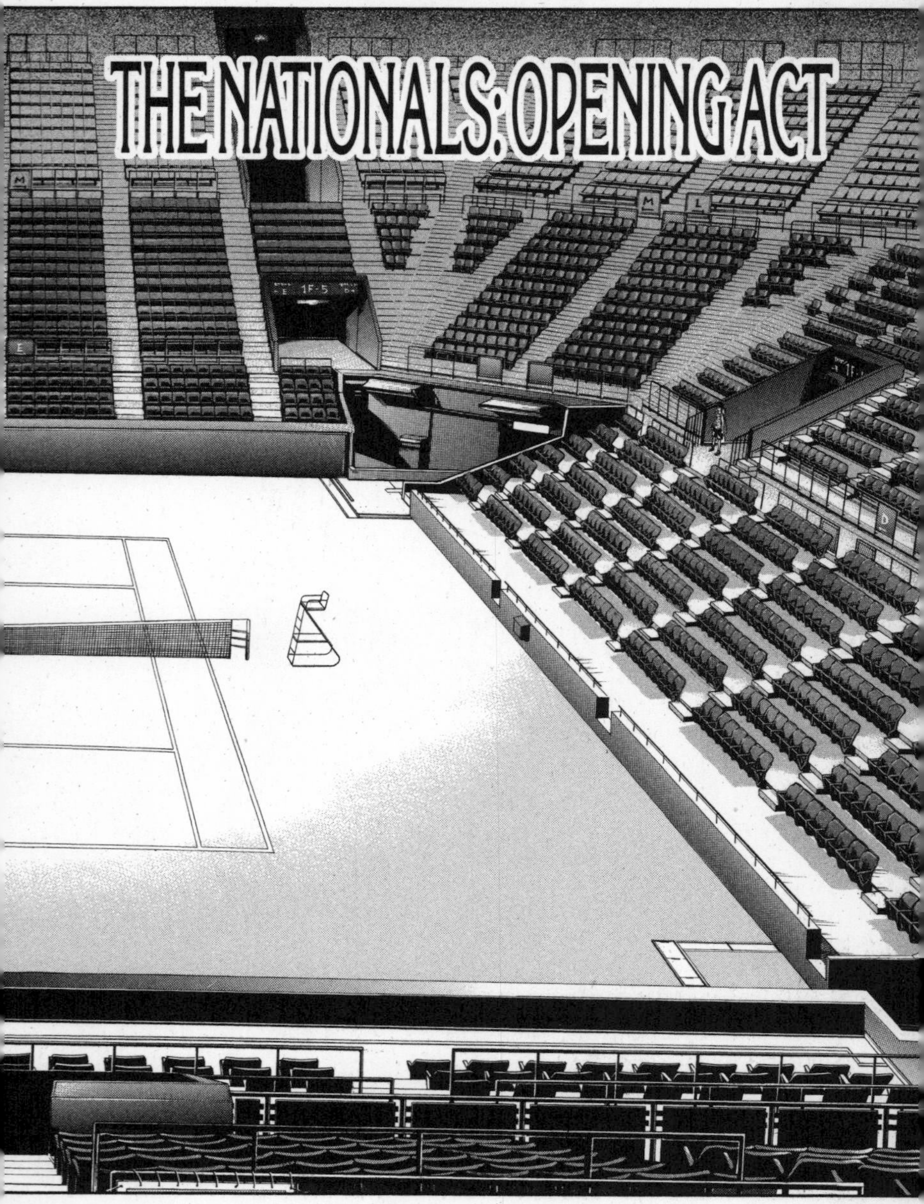

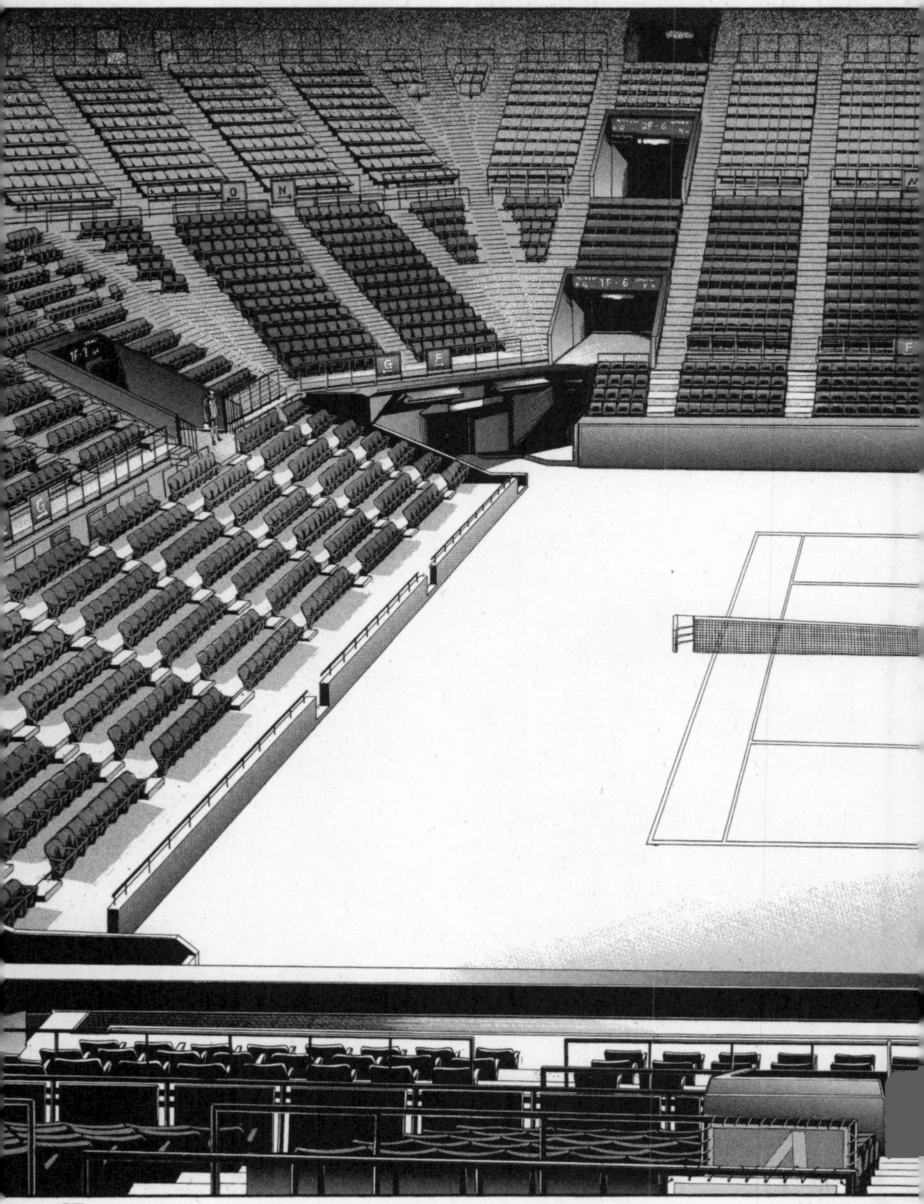
2F·6
1F·6
1F·1
O
N
G
F

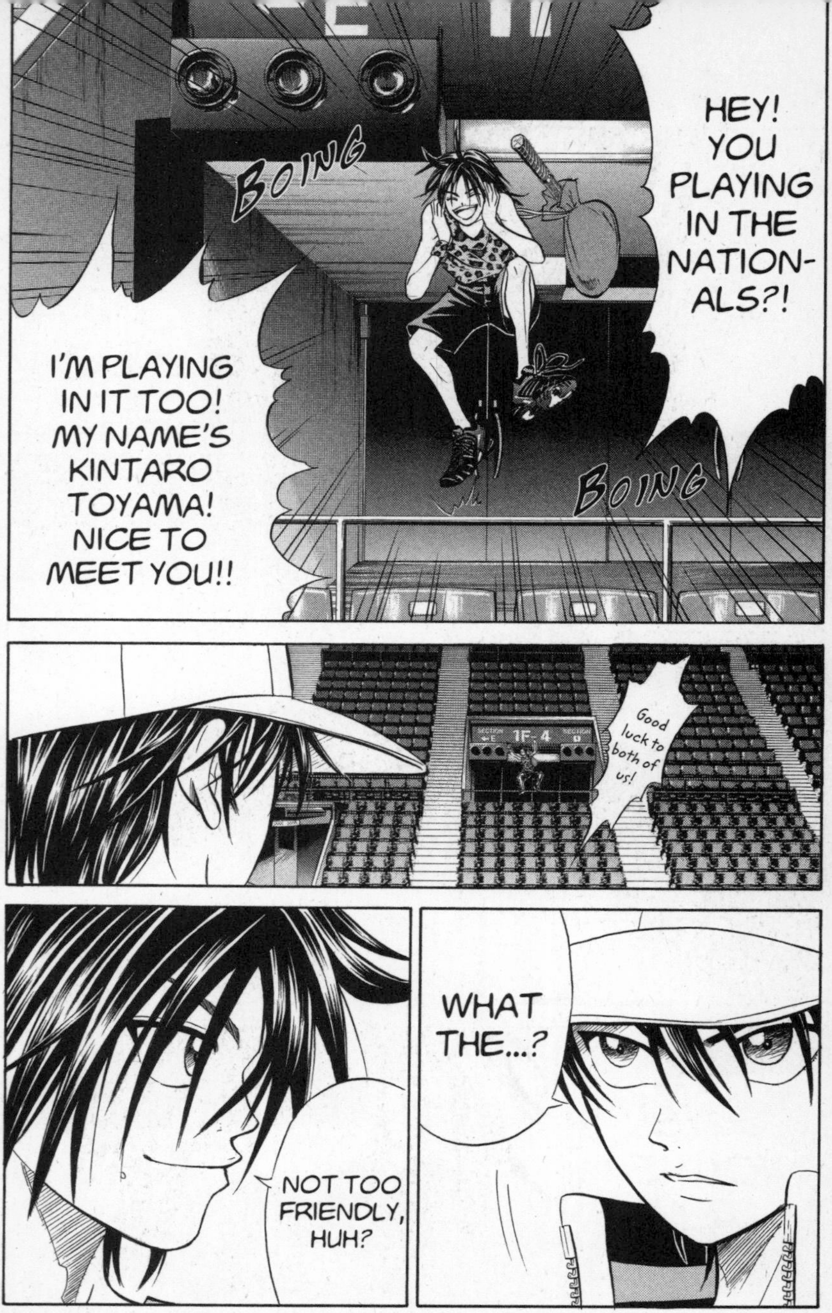
HEY! YOU PLAYING IN THE NATION-ALS?!
BOING
I'M PLAYING IN IT TOO! MY NAME'S KINTARO TOYAMA! NICE TO MEET YOU!!
BOING
1F-4
Good luck to both of us!
WHAT THE...?
NOT TOO FRIENDLY, HUH?

READ THIS WAY

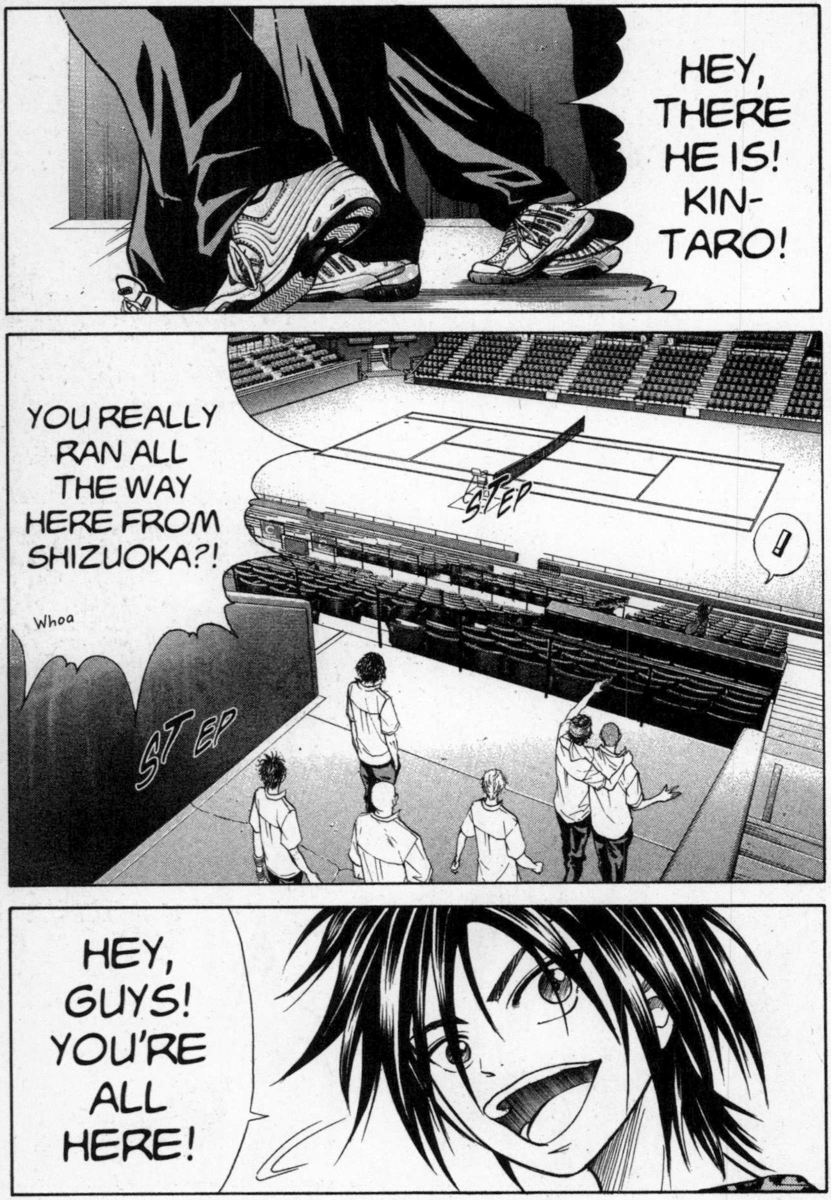
HEY, THERE HE IS! KIN-TARO!
!
STEP
YOU REALLY RAN ALL THE WAY HERE FROM SHIZUOKA?!
Whoa
STEP
HEY, GUYS! YOU'RE ALL HERE!

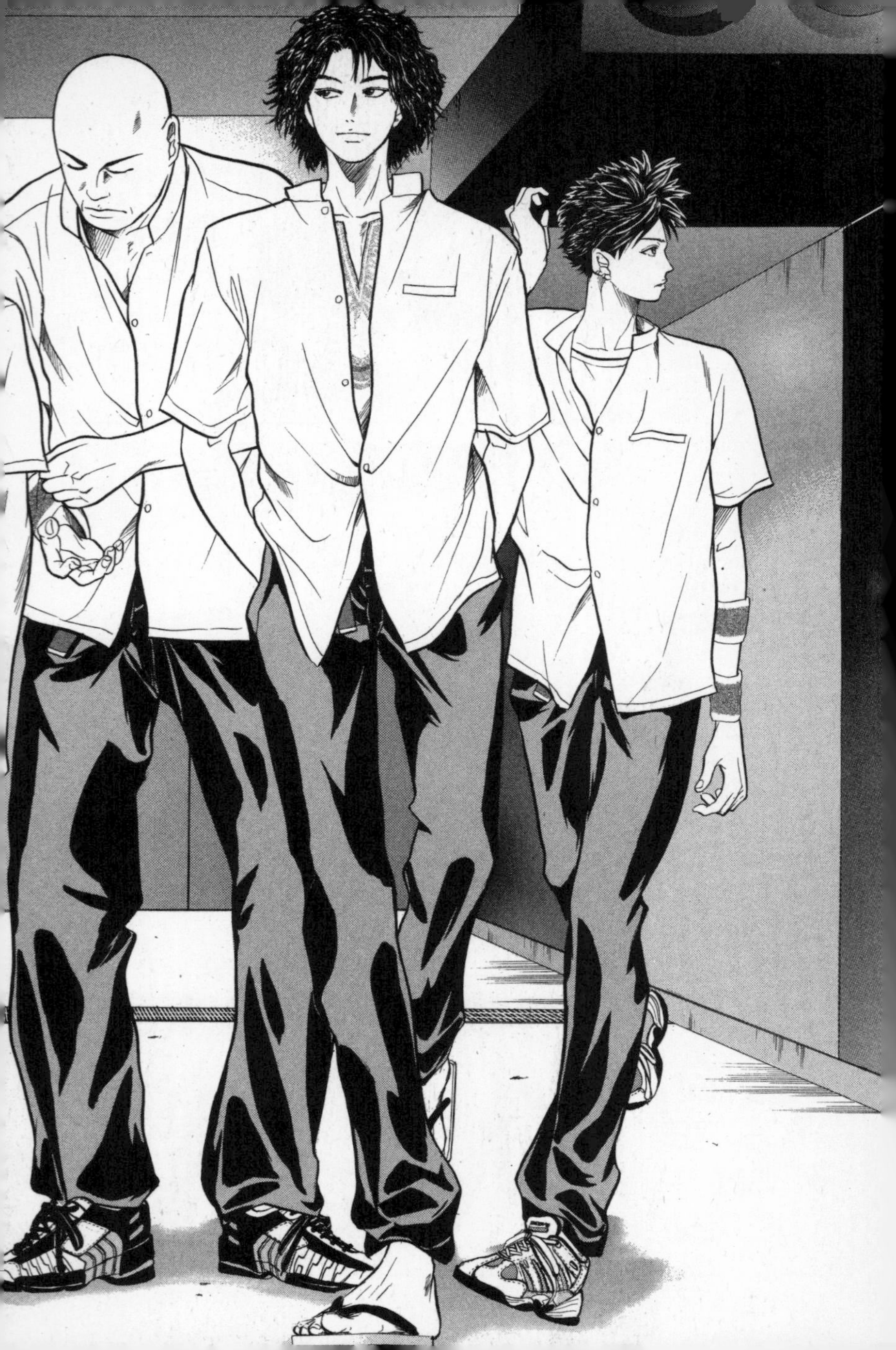

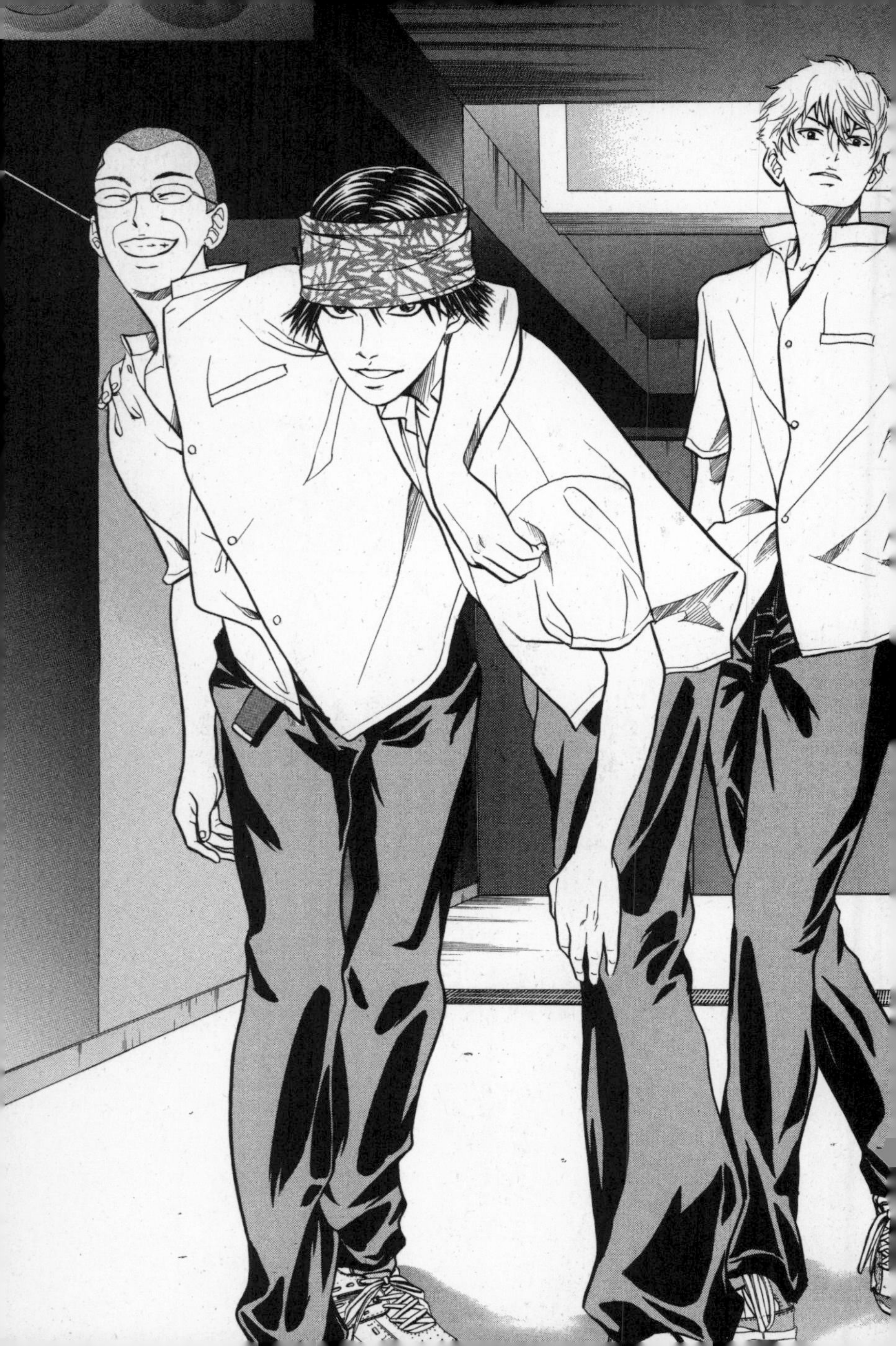

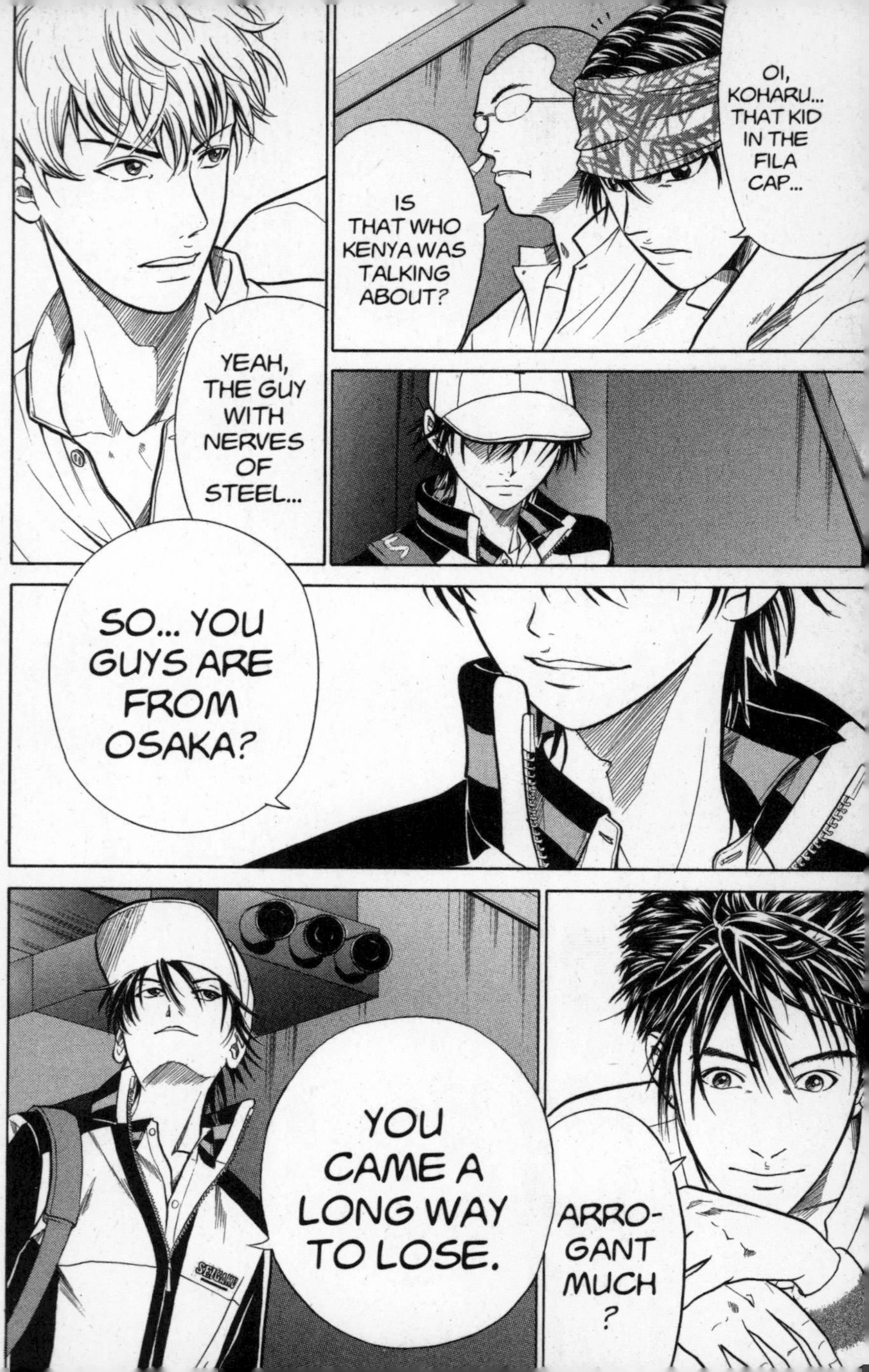
OI, KOHARU... THAT KID IN THE FILA CAP...
IS THAT WHO KENYA WAS TALKING ABOUT?
YEAH, THE GUY WITH NERVES OF STEEL...
SO... YOU GUYS ARE FROM OSAKA?
ARRO-GANT MUCH?
YOU CAME A LONG WAY TO LOSE.

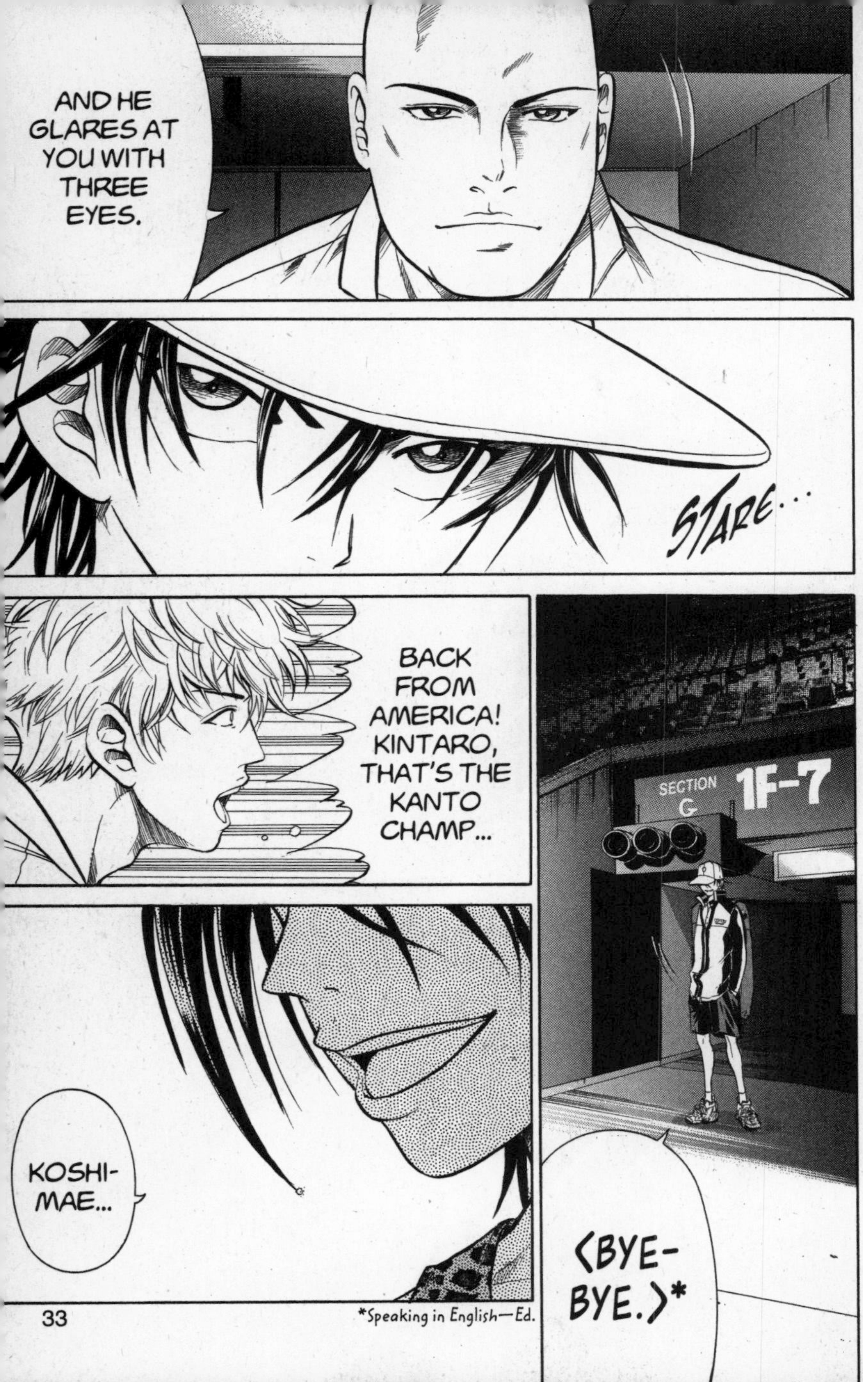
AND HE GLARES AT YOU WITH THREE EYES.
STARE...
SECTION G 1F-7
<BYE-BYE.>*
BACK FROM AMERICA! KINTARO, THAT'S THE KANTO CHAMP...
KOSHI-MAE...

*Speaking in English—Ed.

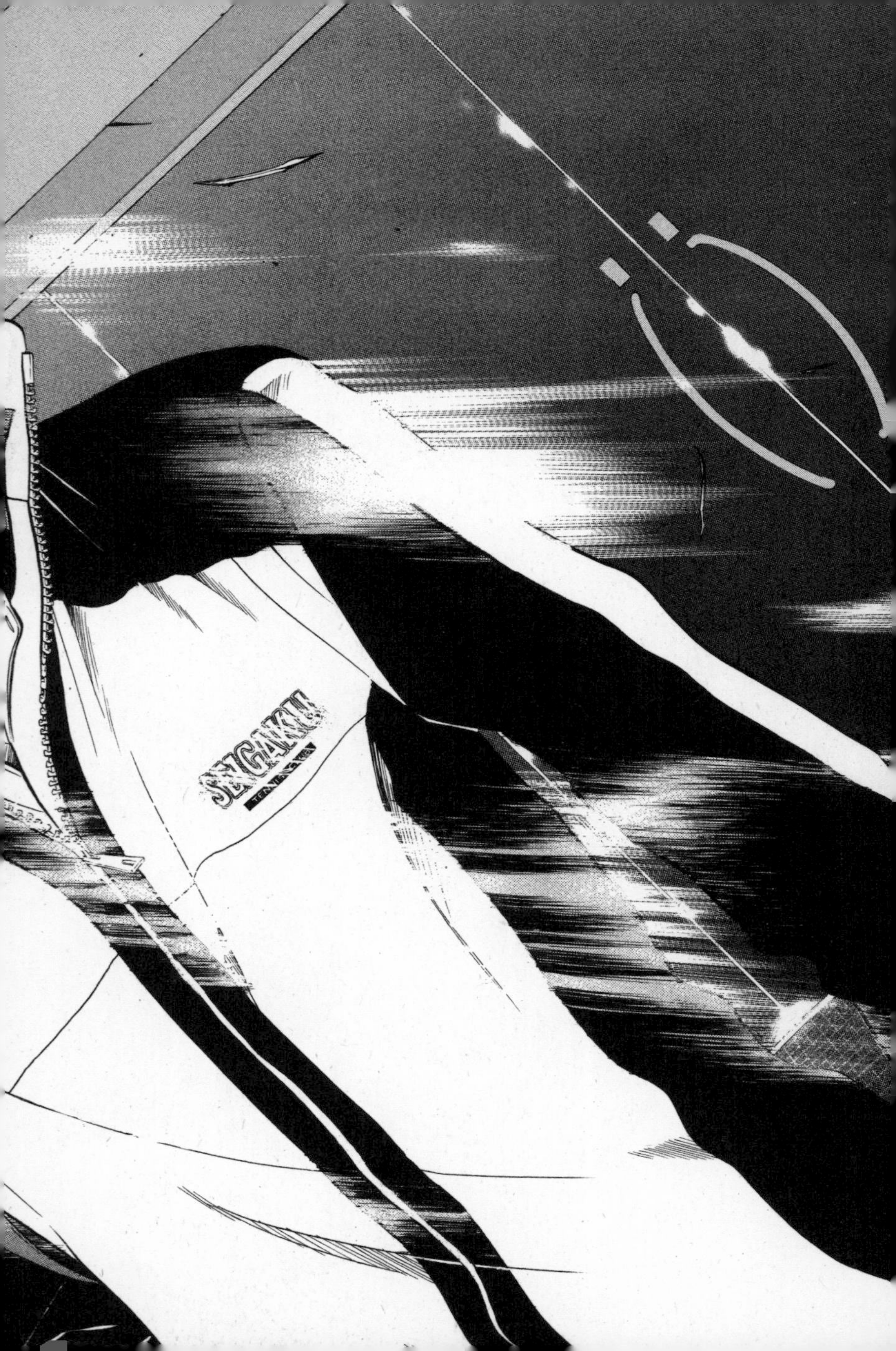
SEIGAKU

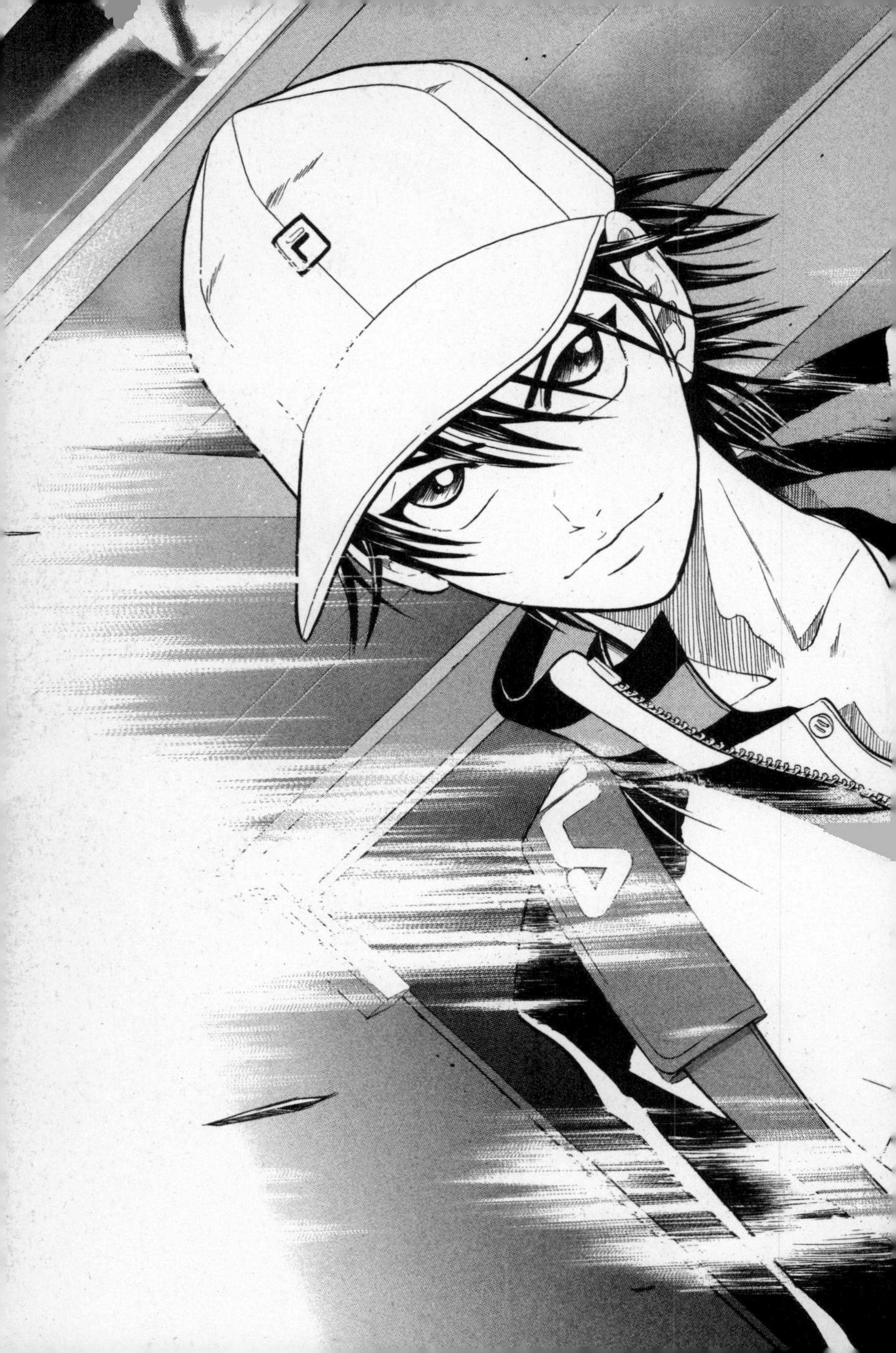

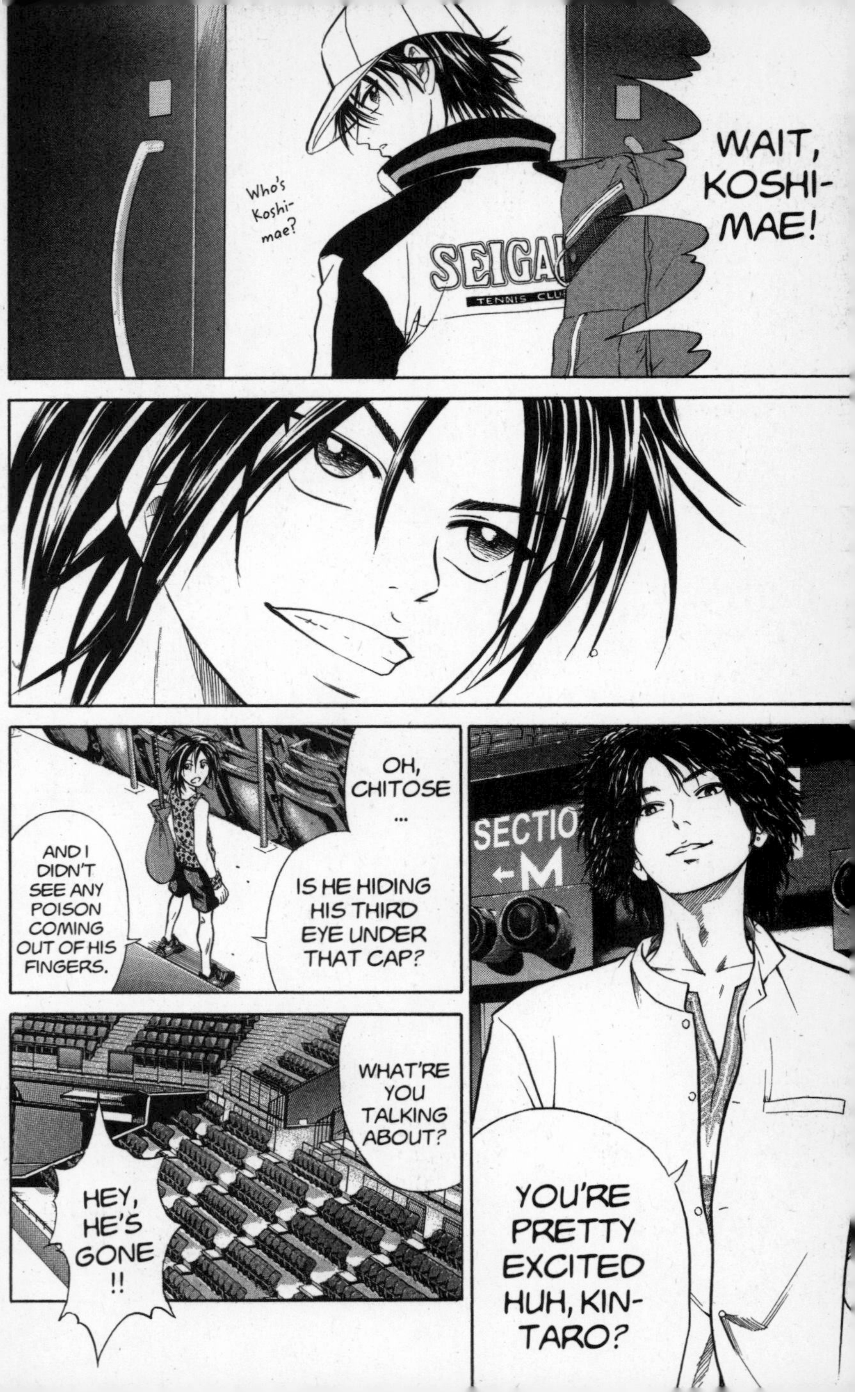
WAIT, KOSHI-MAE!
Who's Koshi-mae?
SEIGAKU
TENNIS CLUB
YOU'RE PRETTY EXCITED HUH, KIN-TARO?
SECTIO
←M
OH, CHITOSE ...
IS HE HIDING HIS THIRD EYE UNDER THAT CAP?
AND I DIDN'T SEE ANY POISON COMING OUT OF HIS FINGERS.
WHAT'RE YOU TALKING ABOUT?
HEY, HE'S GONE !!

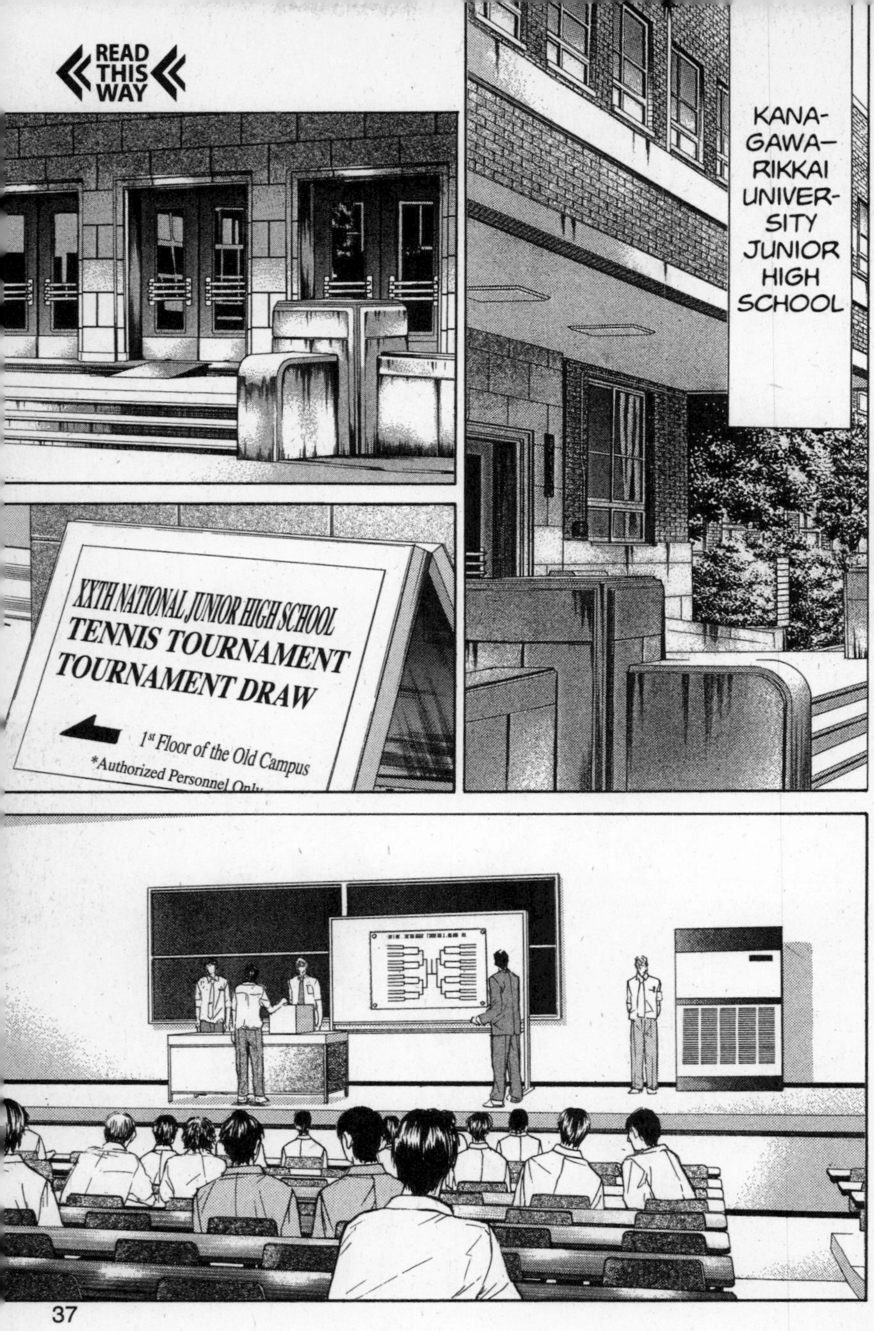

READ THIS WAY
KANA-GAWA-RIKKAI UNIVERSITY JUNIOR HIGH SCHOOL
XXTH NATIONAL JUNIOR HIGH SCHOOL
TENNIS TOURNAMENT
TOURNAMENT DRAW
1st Floor of the Old Campus
*Authorized Personnel Onl

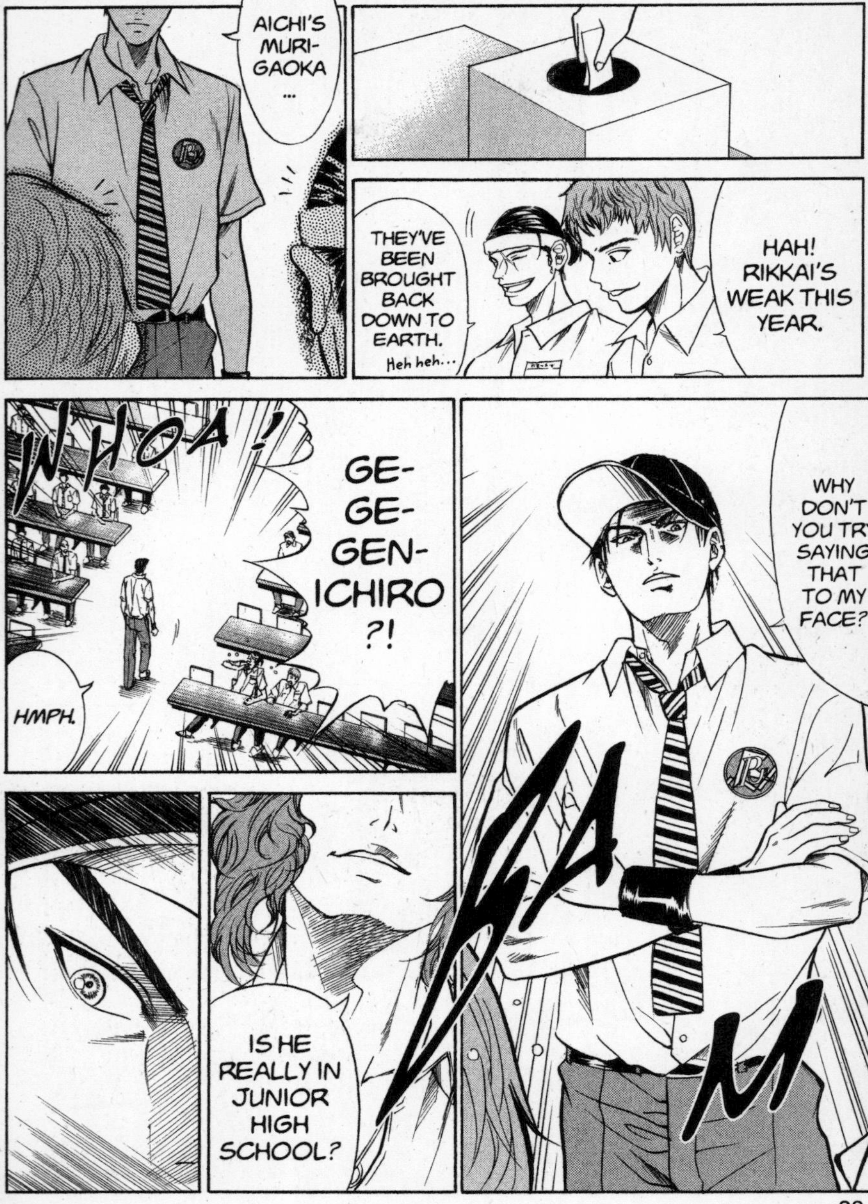

HAH! RIKKAI'S WEAK THIS YEAR.
THEY'VE BEEN BROUGHT BACK DOWN TO EARTH.
Heh heh...
AICHI'S MURI-GAOKA ...
WHY DON'T YOU TRY SAYING THAT TO MY FACE?
WHOA!
GE-GE-GEN-ICHIRO ?!
HMPH.
IS HE REALLY IN JUNIOR HIGH SCHOOL?

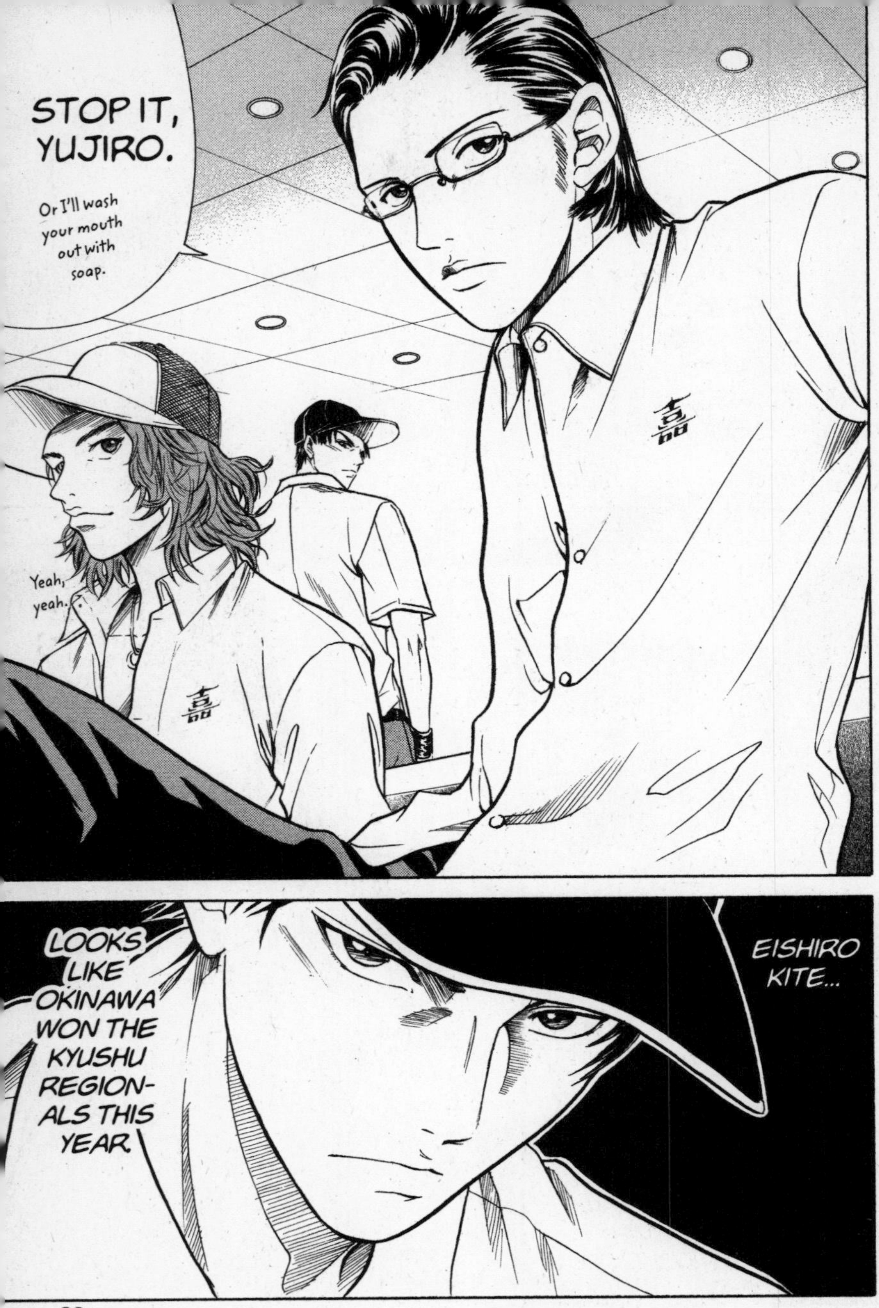
STOP IT, YUJIRO.
Or I'll wash your mouth out with soap.
Yeah, yeah.
EISHIRO KITE...
LOOKS LIKE OKINAWA WON THE KYUSHU REGIONALS THIS YEAR.

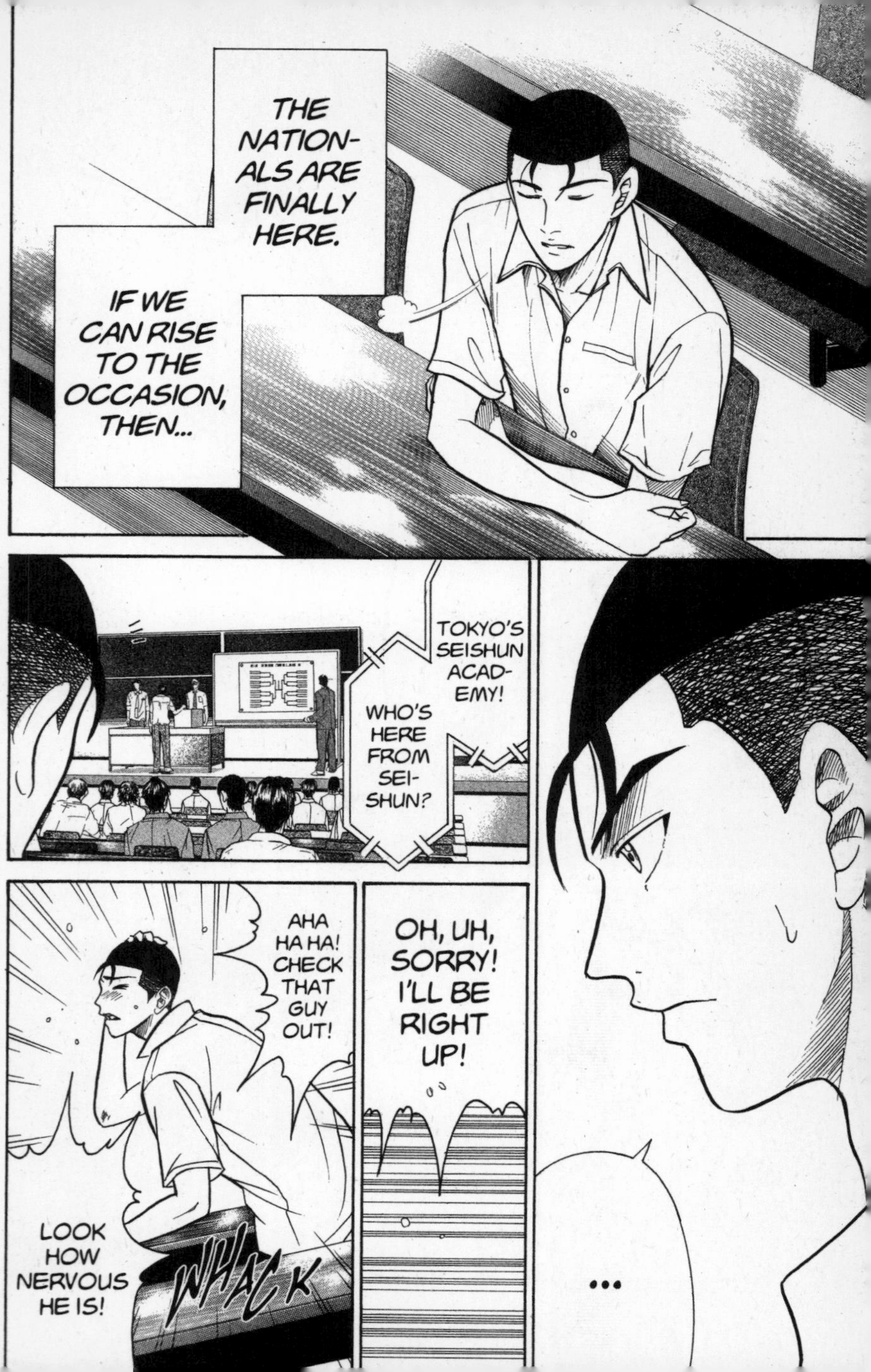
THE NATIONALS ARE FINALLY HERE.
IF WE CAN RISE TO THE OCCASION, THEN...
...
TOKYO'S SEISHUN ACADEMY!
WHO'S HERE FROM SEISHUN?
OH, UH, SORRY! I'LL BE RIGHT UP!
AHA HA HA! CHECK THAT GUY OUT!
LOOK HOW NERVOUS HE IS!
WHACK

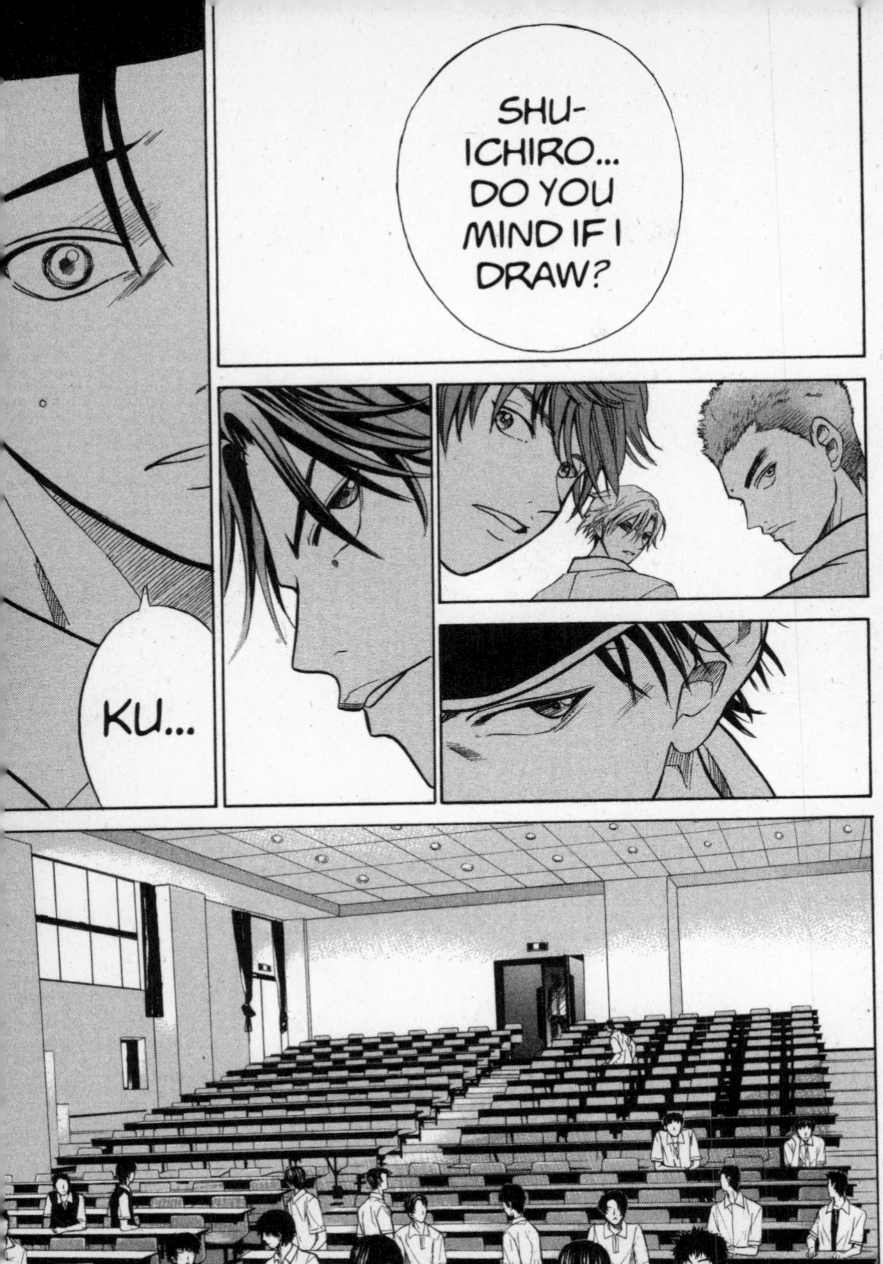
SHU-ICHIRO... DO YOU MIND IF I DRAW?
KU...

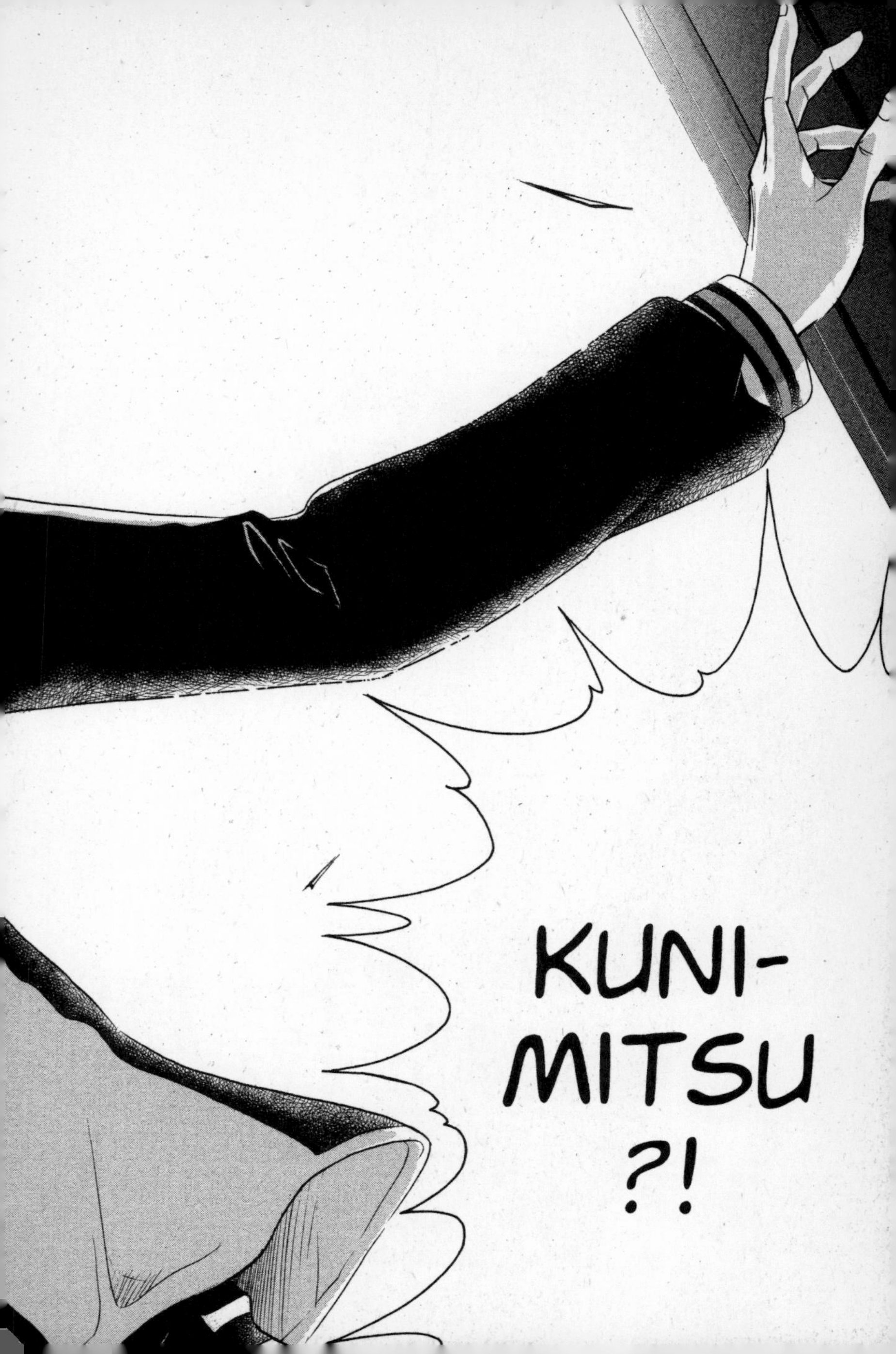

KUNI-
MITSU
?!

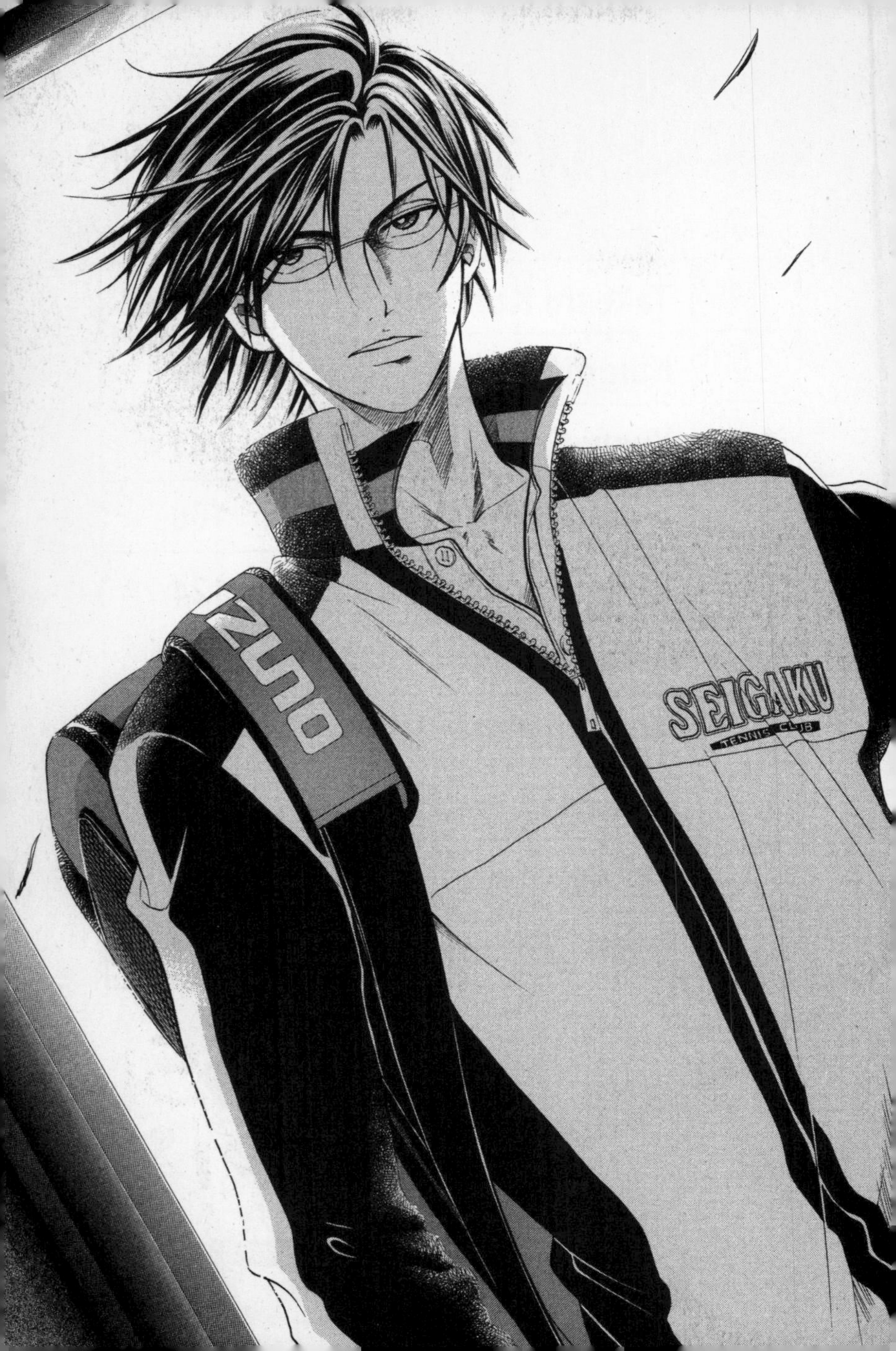
SEIGAKU
TENNIS CLUB

2005

HYOTEI SCORES BIG! SEISHUN IN TROUBLE?!

VALENTINE'S DAY CHOCOLATE TALLY RESULTS (PART 1)

THANKS SO MUCH FOR ALL THE CHOCOLATES! 2273 Total

1st	Takeshi Konomi	264
2nd	Keigo Atobe	226
3rd	Yushi Oshitari	241
4th	Shusuke Fuji	169
5th	Ryoma Echizen	124
	Chotaro Ohtori	
7th	Ryo Shishido	117
8th	Kunimitsu Tezuka	69
9th	Eiji Kikumaru	64
10th	Takeshi Momoshiro	62

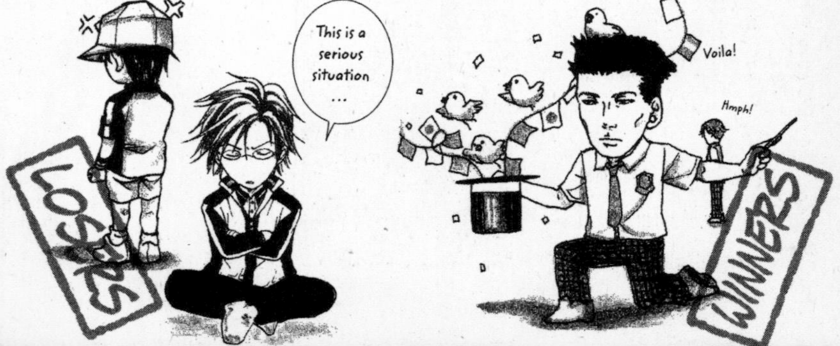

LOSERS
This is a serious situation ...
Voila!
Hmph!
WINNERS

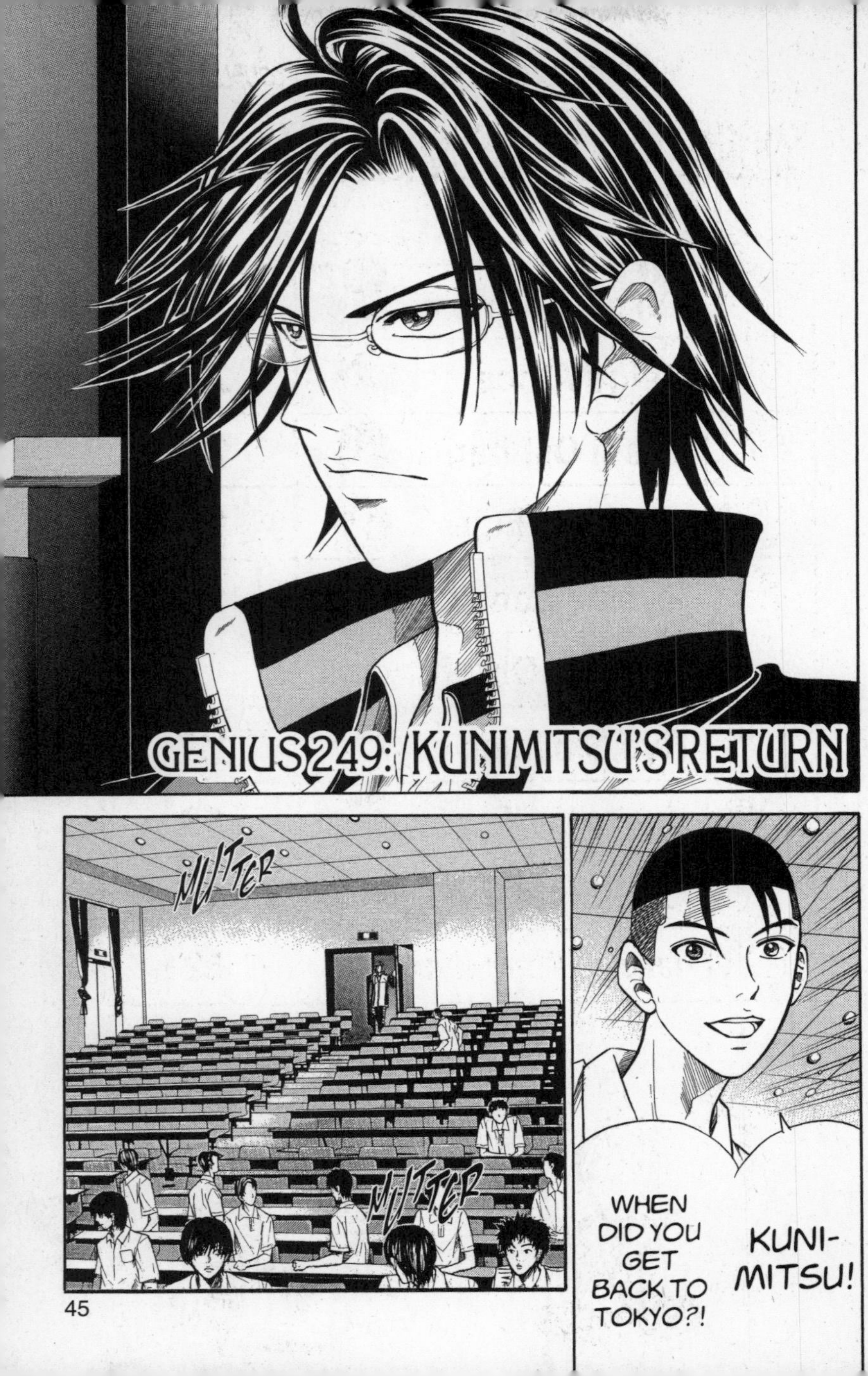
GENIUS 249: KUNIMITSU'S RETURN
KUNI-MITSU!
WHEN DID YOU GET BACK TO TOKYO?!
MUTTER
MUTTER

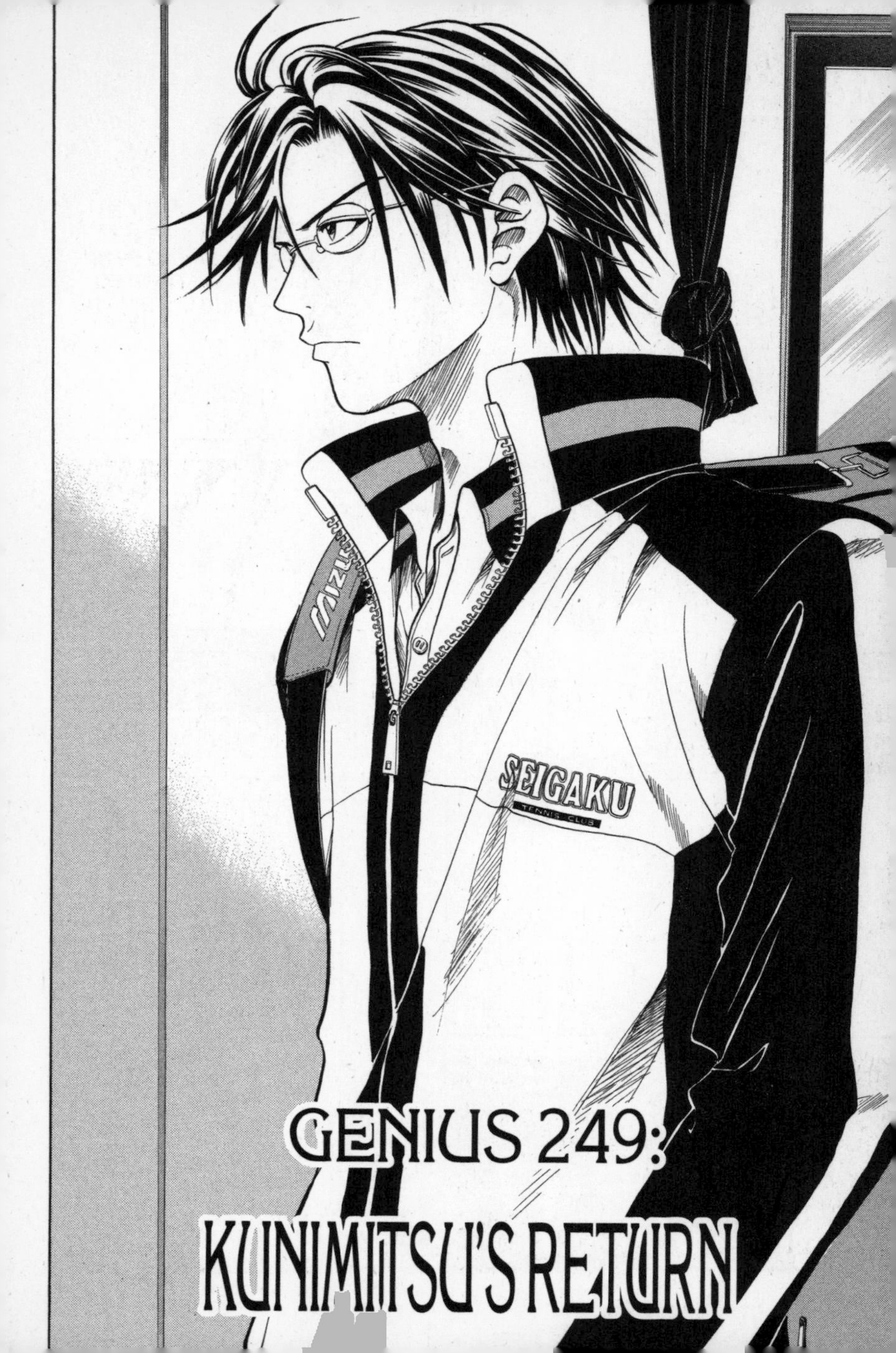
SEIGAKU
TENNIS CLUB
GENIUS 249:
KUNIMITSU'S RETURN

READ THIS WAY

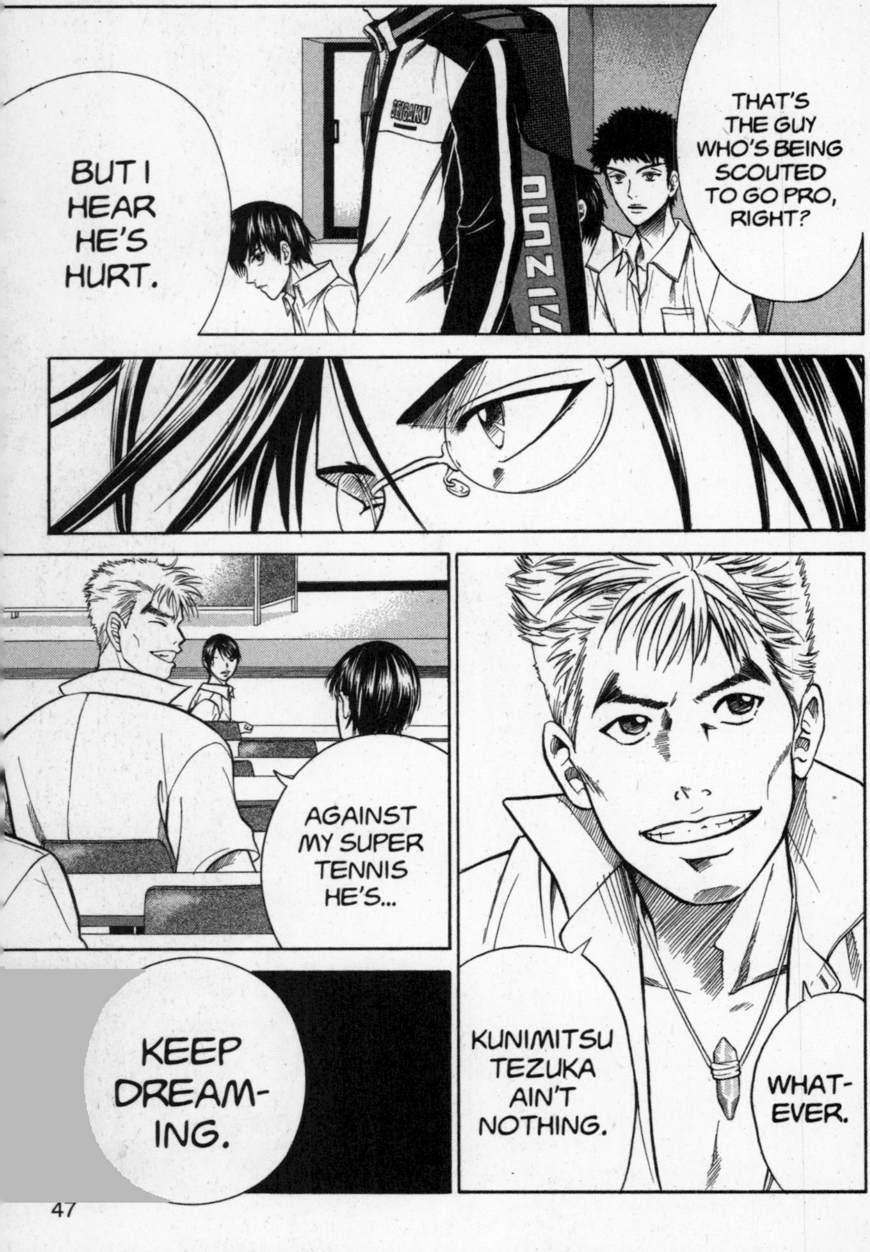
THAT'S THE GUY WHO'S BEING SCOUTED TO GO PRO, RIGHT?
BUT I HEAR HE'S HURT.
WHAT-EVER.
KUNIMITSU TEZUKA AIN'T NOTHING.
AGAINST MY SUPER TENNIS HE'S...
KEEP DREAM-ING.

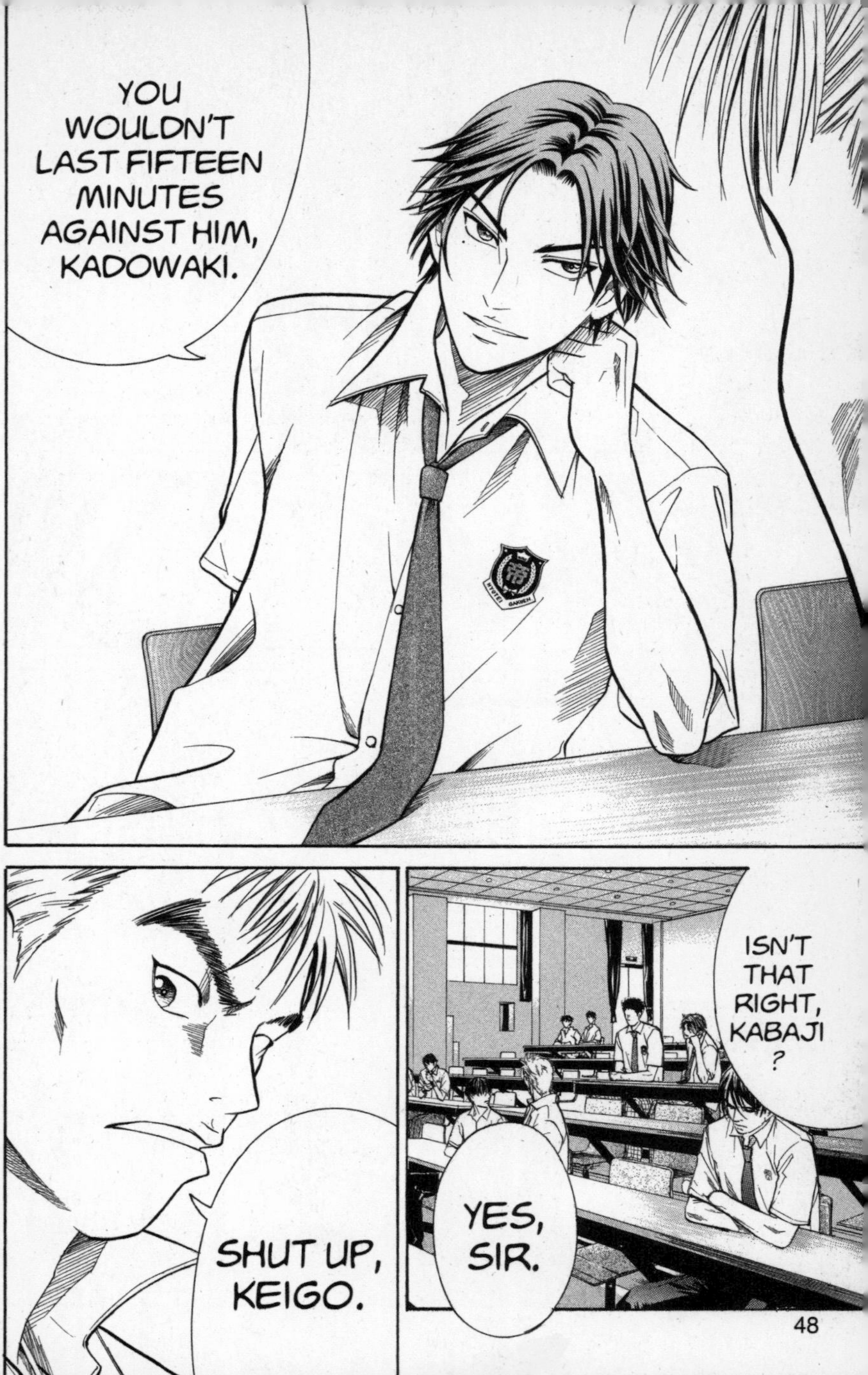
YOU WOULDN'T LAST FIFTEEN MINUTES AGAINST HIM, KADOWAKI.
ISN'T THAT RIGHT, KABAJI?
YES, SIR.
SHUT UP, KEIGO.

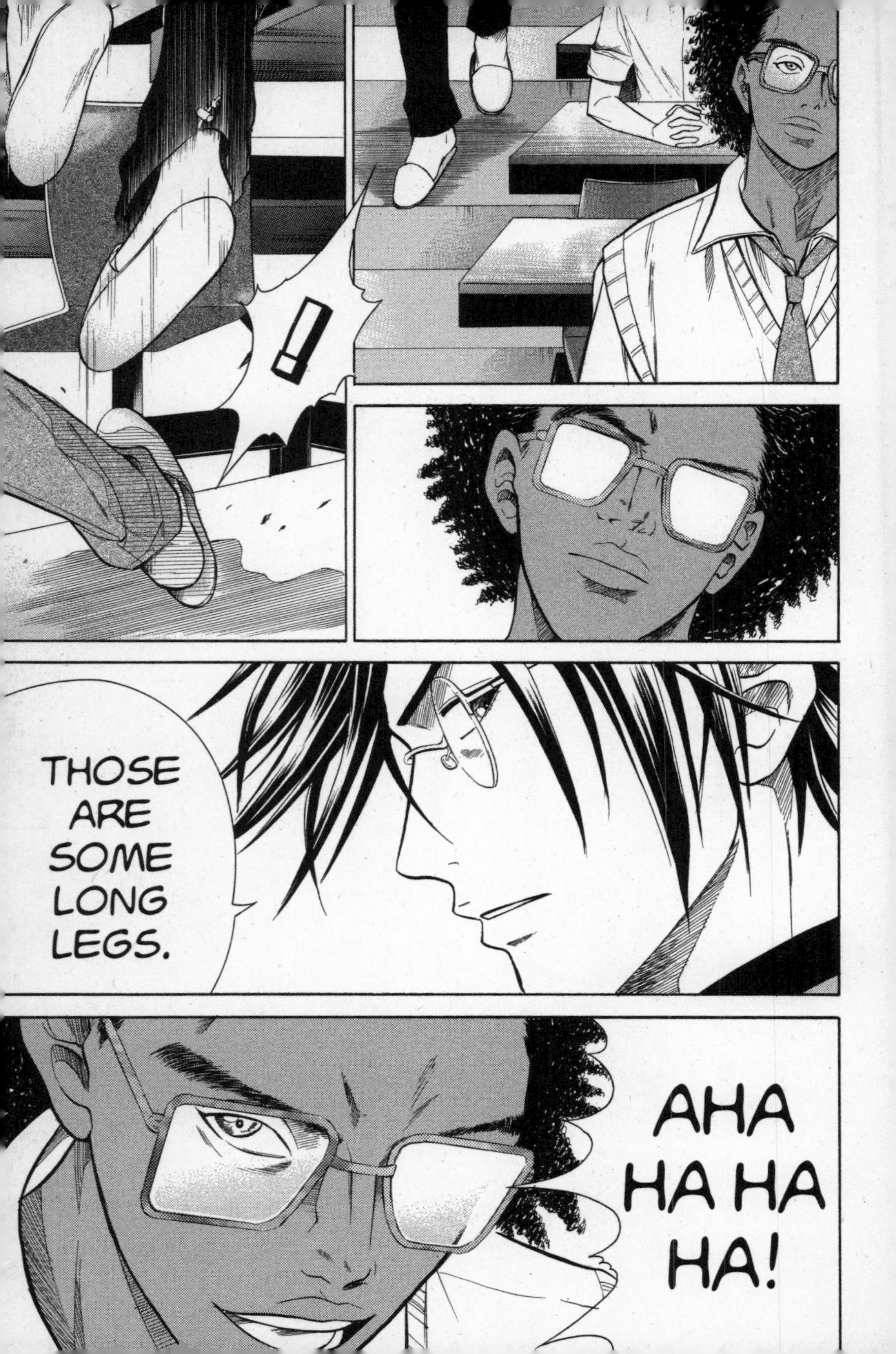
!
THOSE ARE SOME LONG LEGS.
AHA HA HA HA HA!

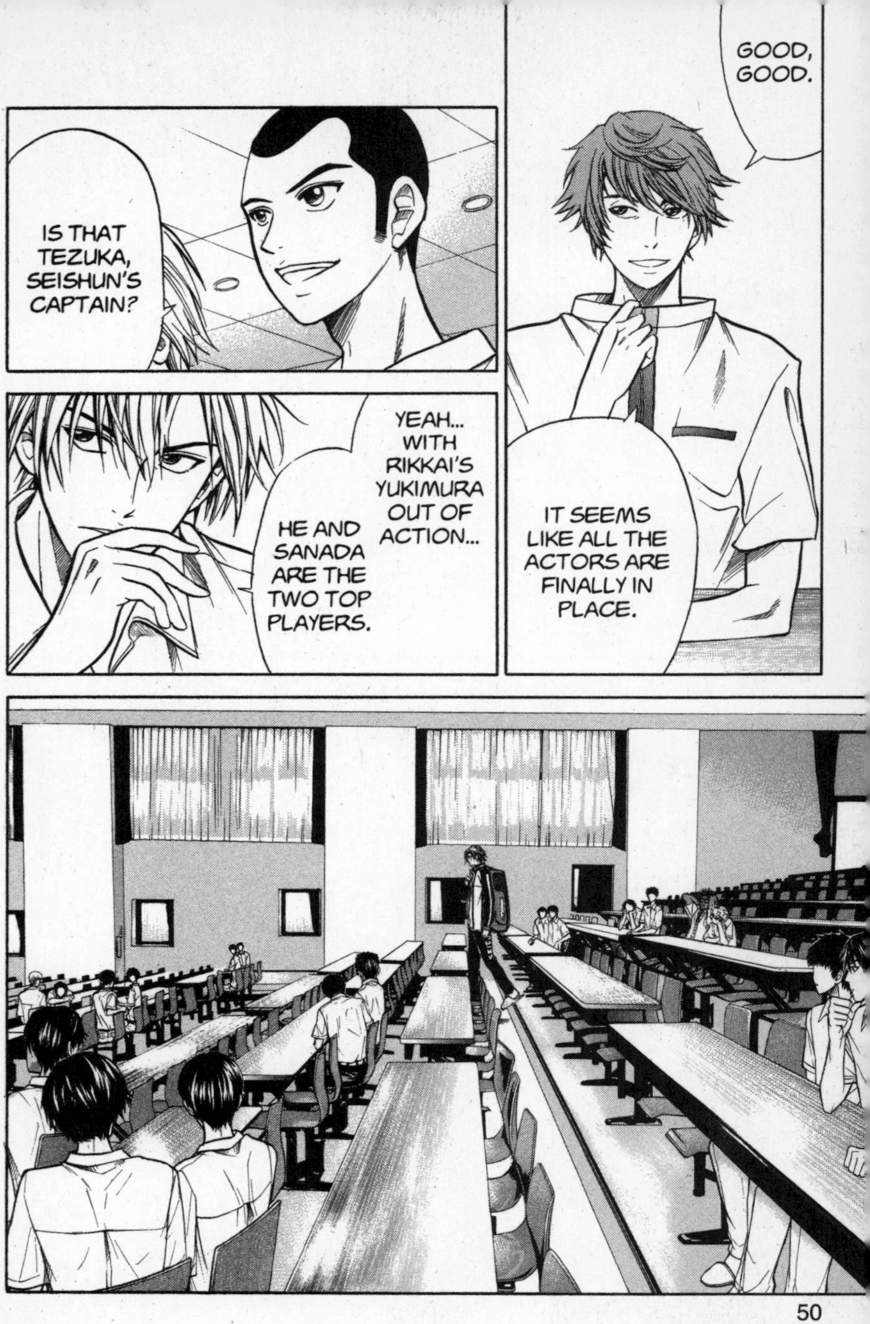
GOOD, GOOD.
IT SEEMS LIKE ALL THE ACTORS ARE FINALLY IN PLACE.
IS THAT TEZUKA, SEISHUN'S CAPTAIN?
YEAH... WITH RIKKAI'S YUKIMURA OUT OF ACTION...
HE AND SANADA ARE THE TWO TOP PLAYERS.

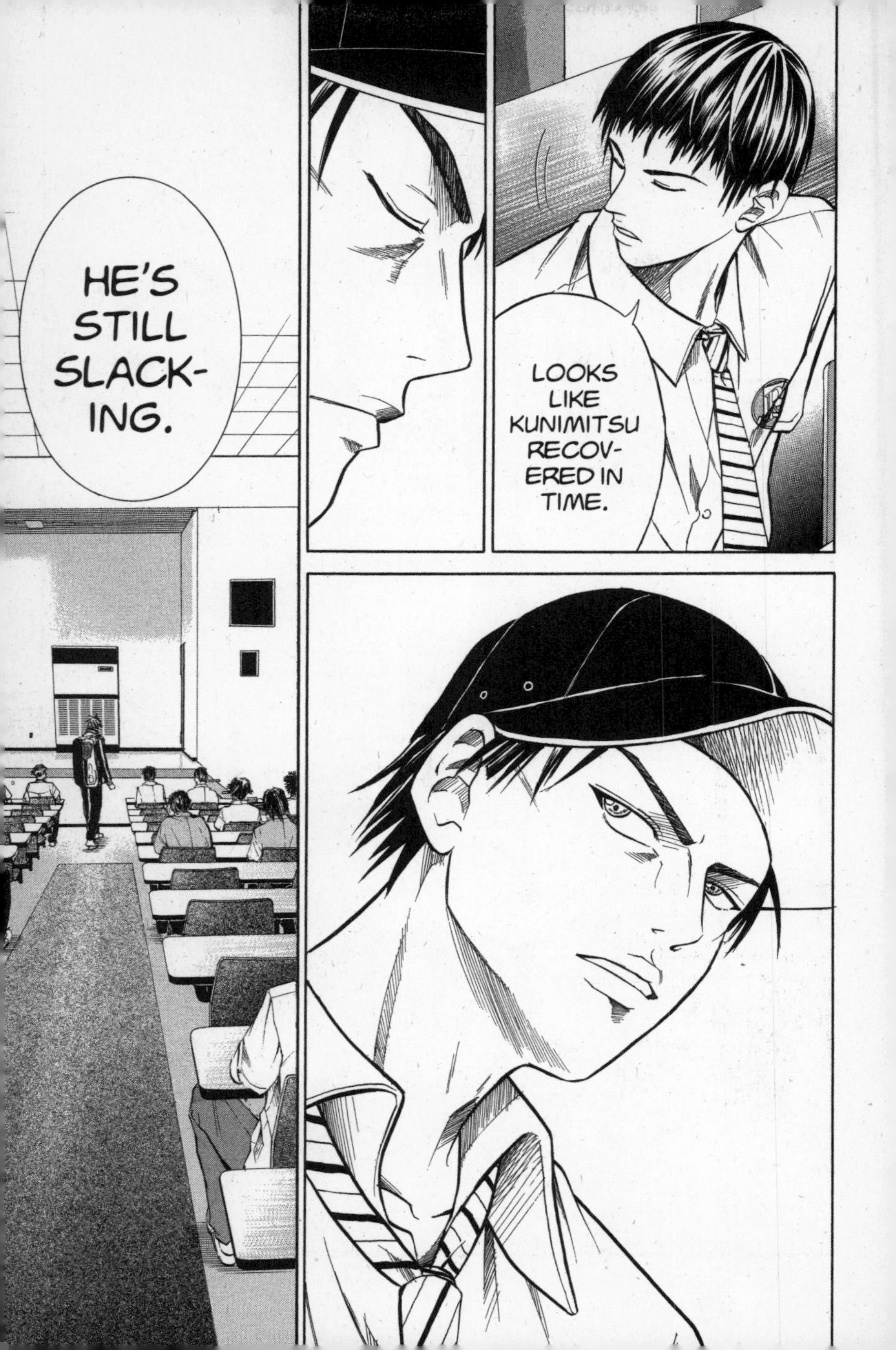
LOOKS LIKE KUNIMITSU RECOVERED IN TIME.
HE'S STILL SLACKING.

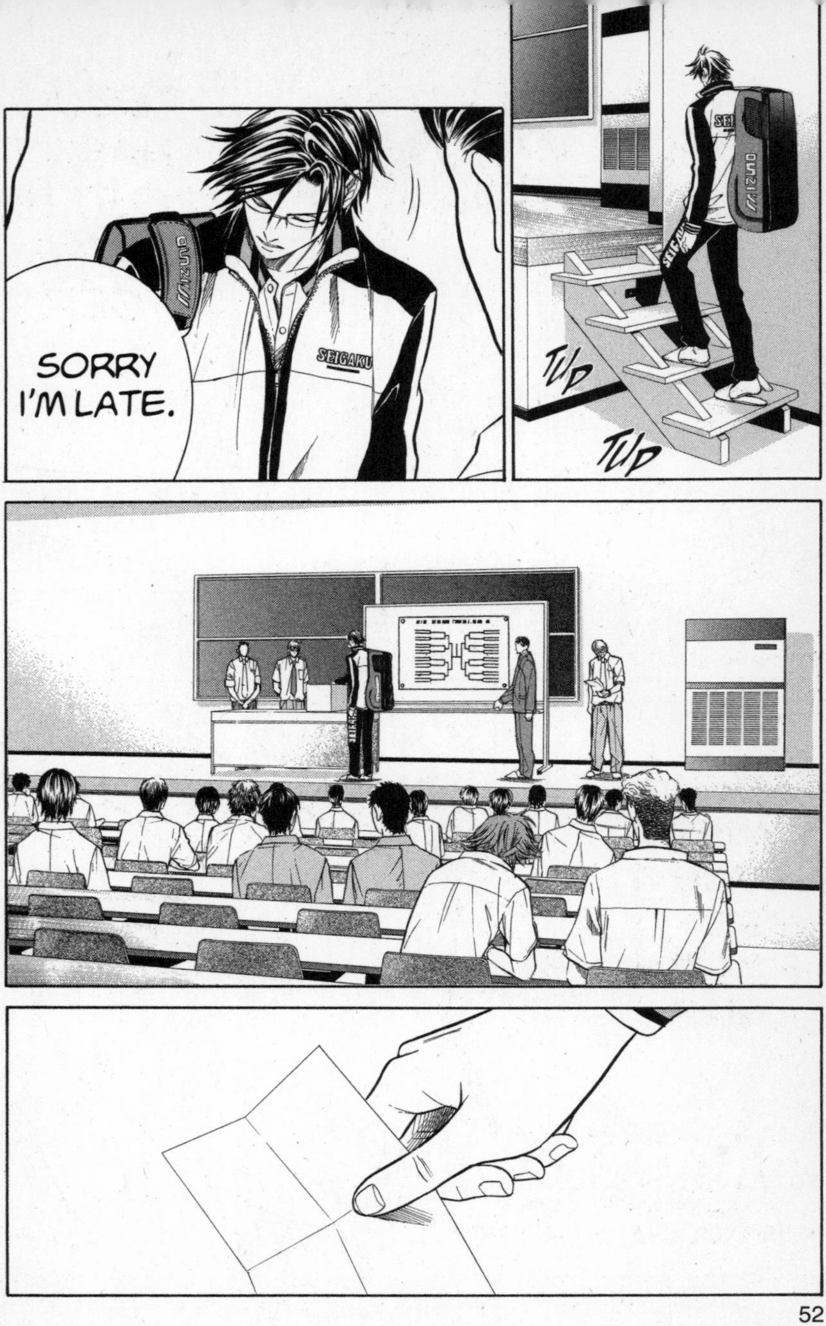
TUD
TUD
SORRY I'M LATE.

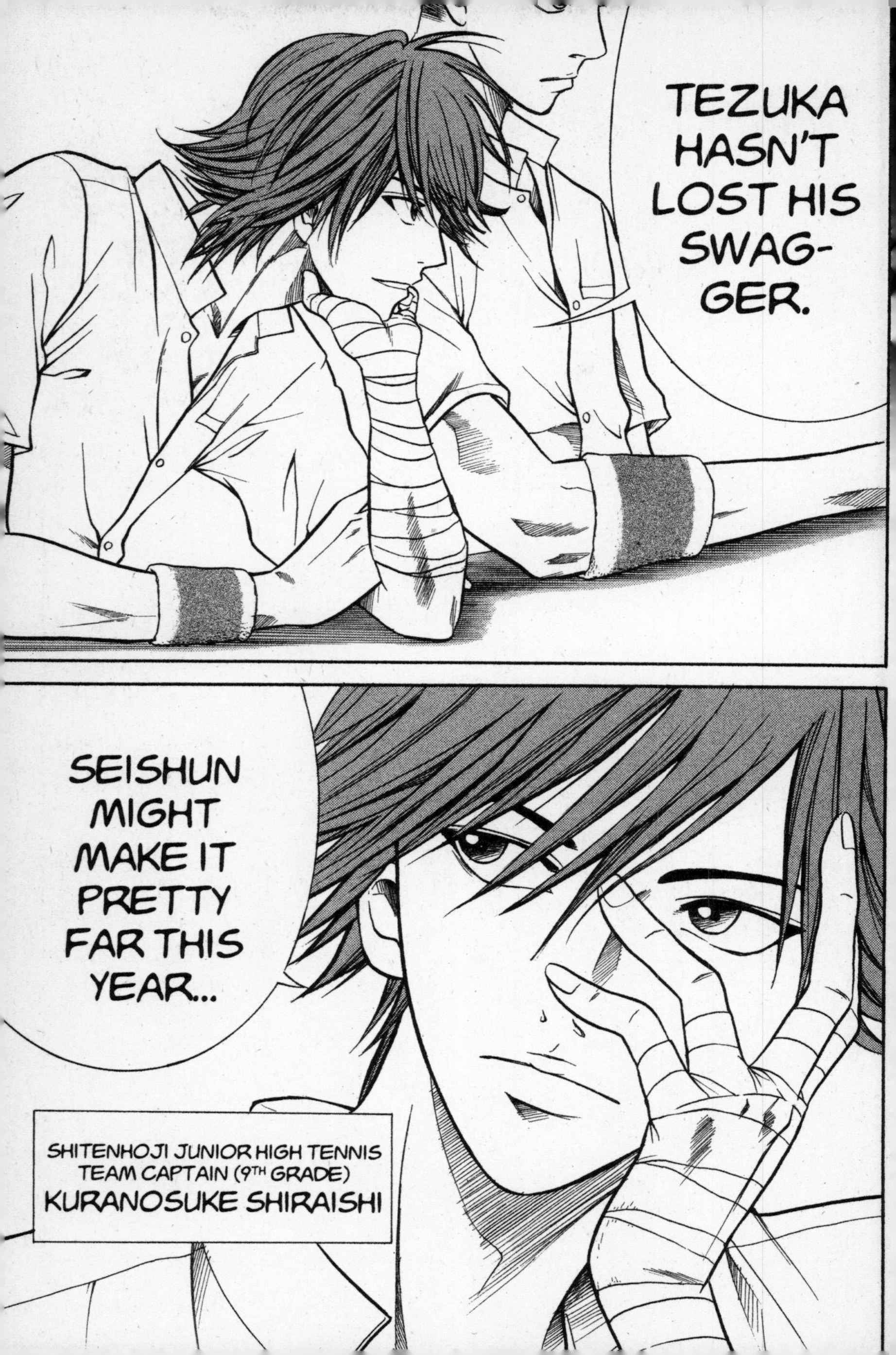
TEZUKA HASN'T LOST HIS SWAG-GER.
SEISHUN MIGHT MAKE IT PRETTY FAR THIS YEAR...
SHITENHOJI JUNIOR HIGH TENNIS TEAM CAPTAIN (9TH GRADE) KURANOSUKE SHIRAISHI

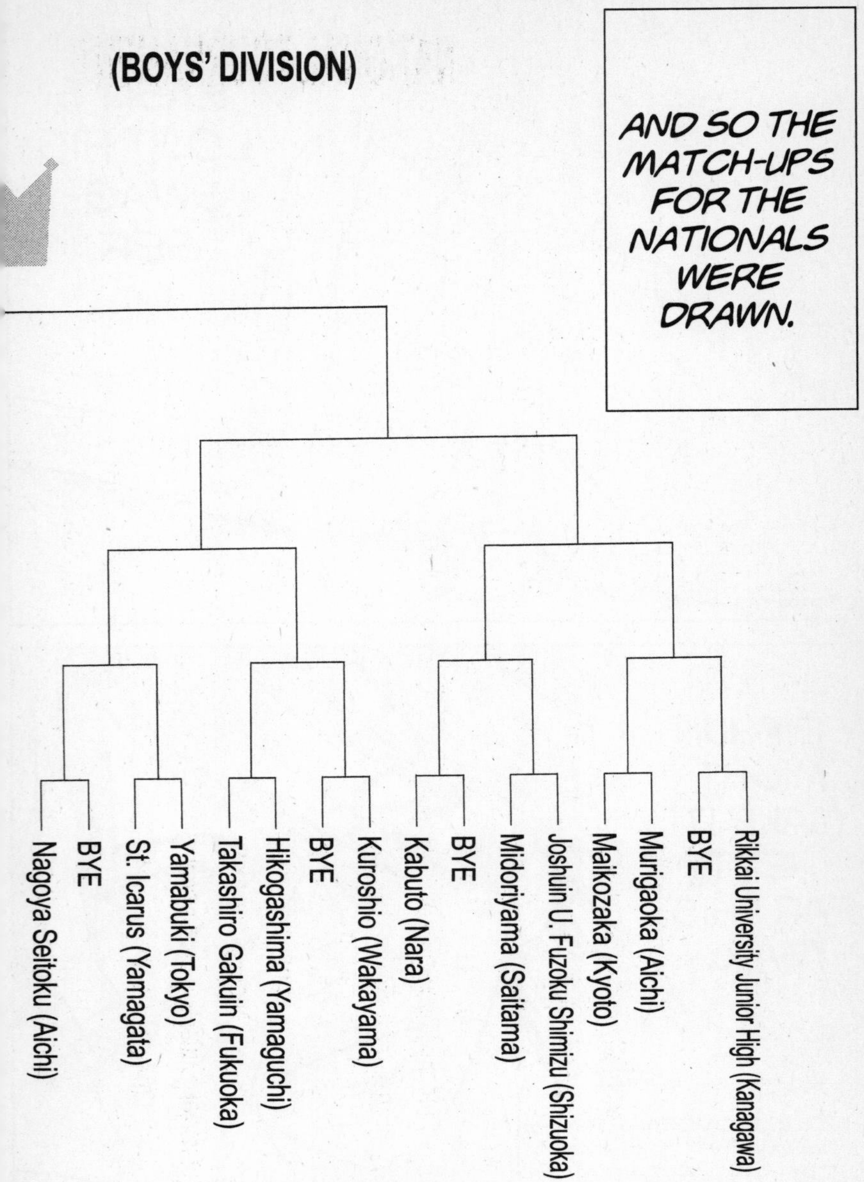
AND SO THE MATCH-UPS FOR THE NATIONALS WERE DRAWN.
(BOYS' DIVISION)
Nagoya Seitoku (Aichi)
BYE
St. Icarus (Yamagata)
Yamabuki (Tokyo)
Takashiro Gakuin (Fukuoka)
Hikogashima (Yamaguchi)
BYE
Kuroshio (Wakayama)
Kabuto (Nara)
BYE
Midoriyama (Saitama)
Joshuin U. Fuzoku Shimizu (Shizuoka)
Maikozaka (Kyoto)
Murigaoka (Aichi)
BYE
Rikkai University Junior High (Kanagawa)

NATIONAL TOURNAMENT

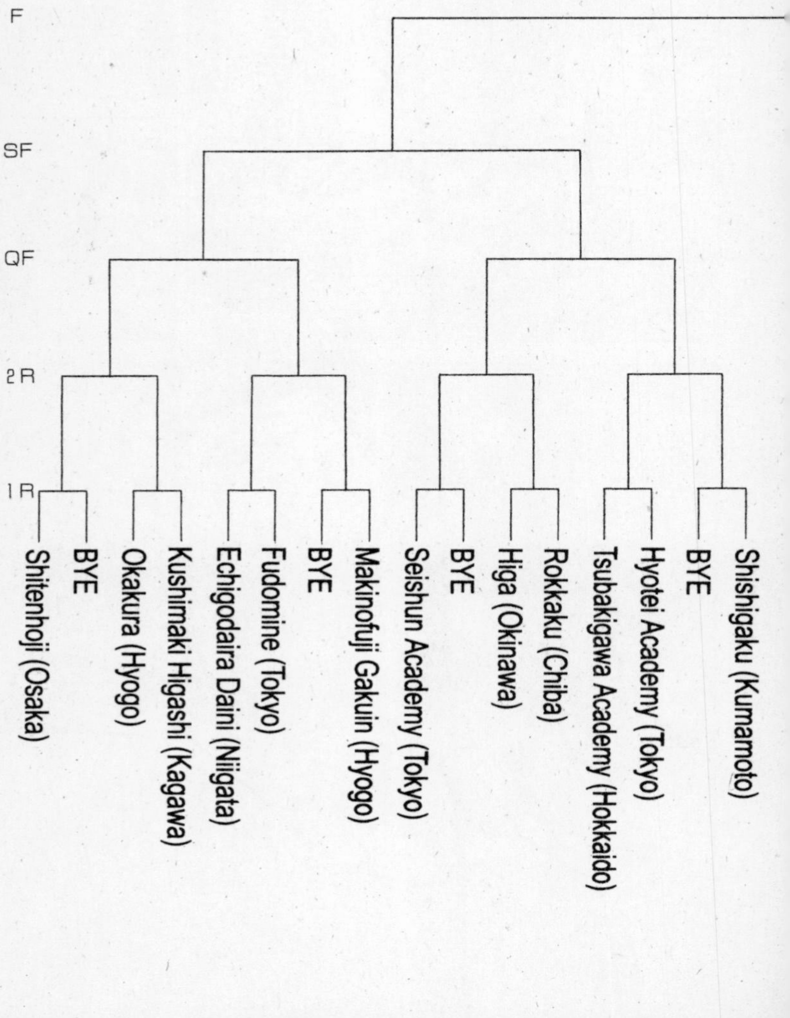
F
SF
QF
2R
1R
Shitenhoji (Osaka)
BYE
Okakura (Hyogo)
Kushimaki Higashi (Kagawa)
Echigodaira Daini (Niigata)
Fudomine (Tokyo)
BYE
Makinofuji Gakuin (Hyogo)
Seishun Academy (Tokyo)
BYE
Higa (Okinawa)
Rokkaku (Chiba)
Tsubakigawa Academy (Hokkaido)
Hyotei Academy (Tokyo)
BYE
Shishigaku (Kumamoto)

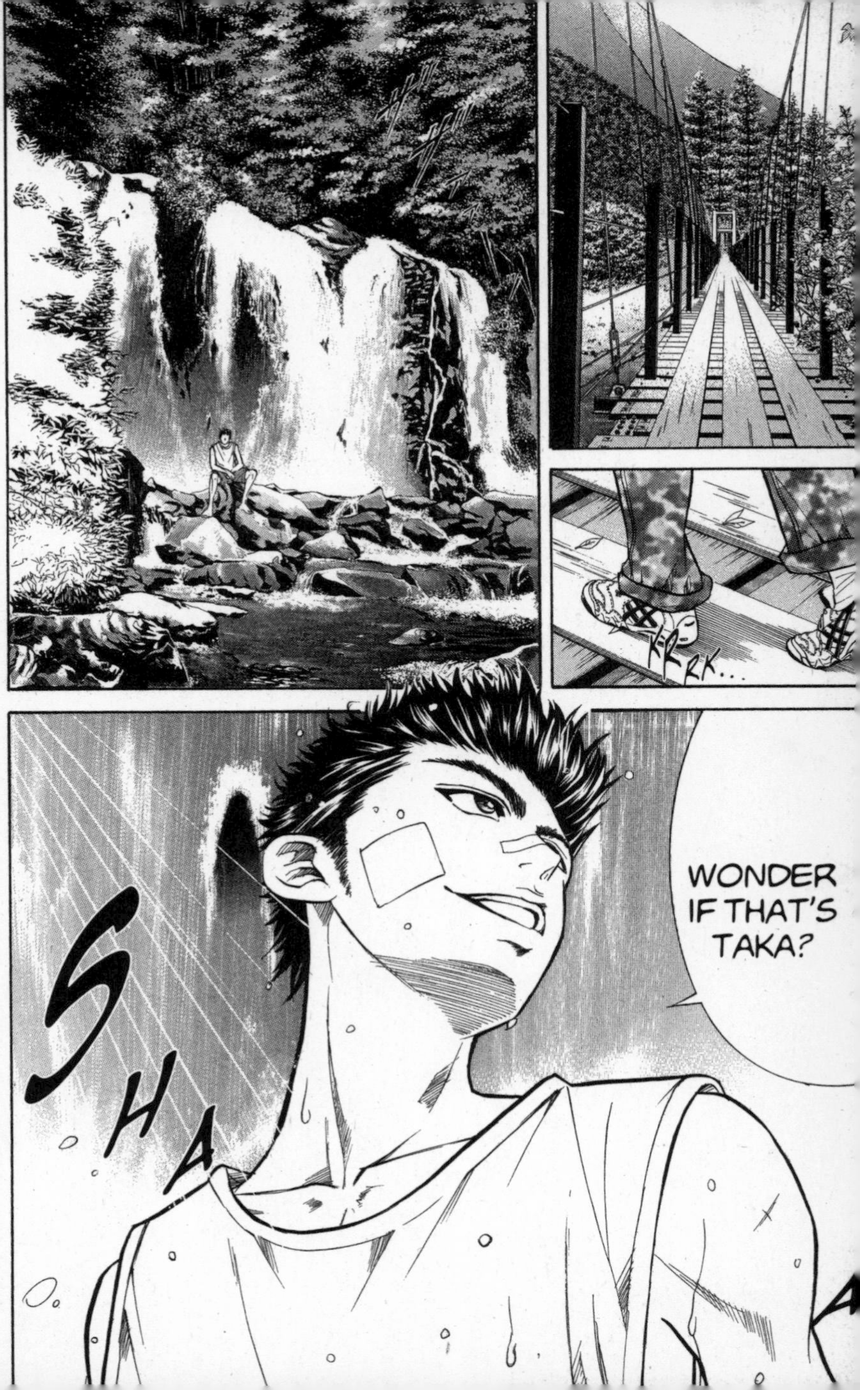
KR RK...
WONDER IF THAT'S TAKA?
SHA

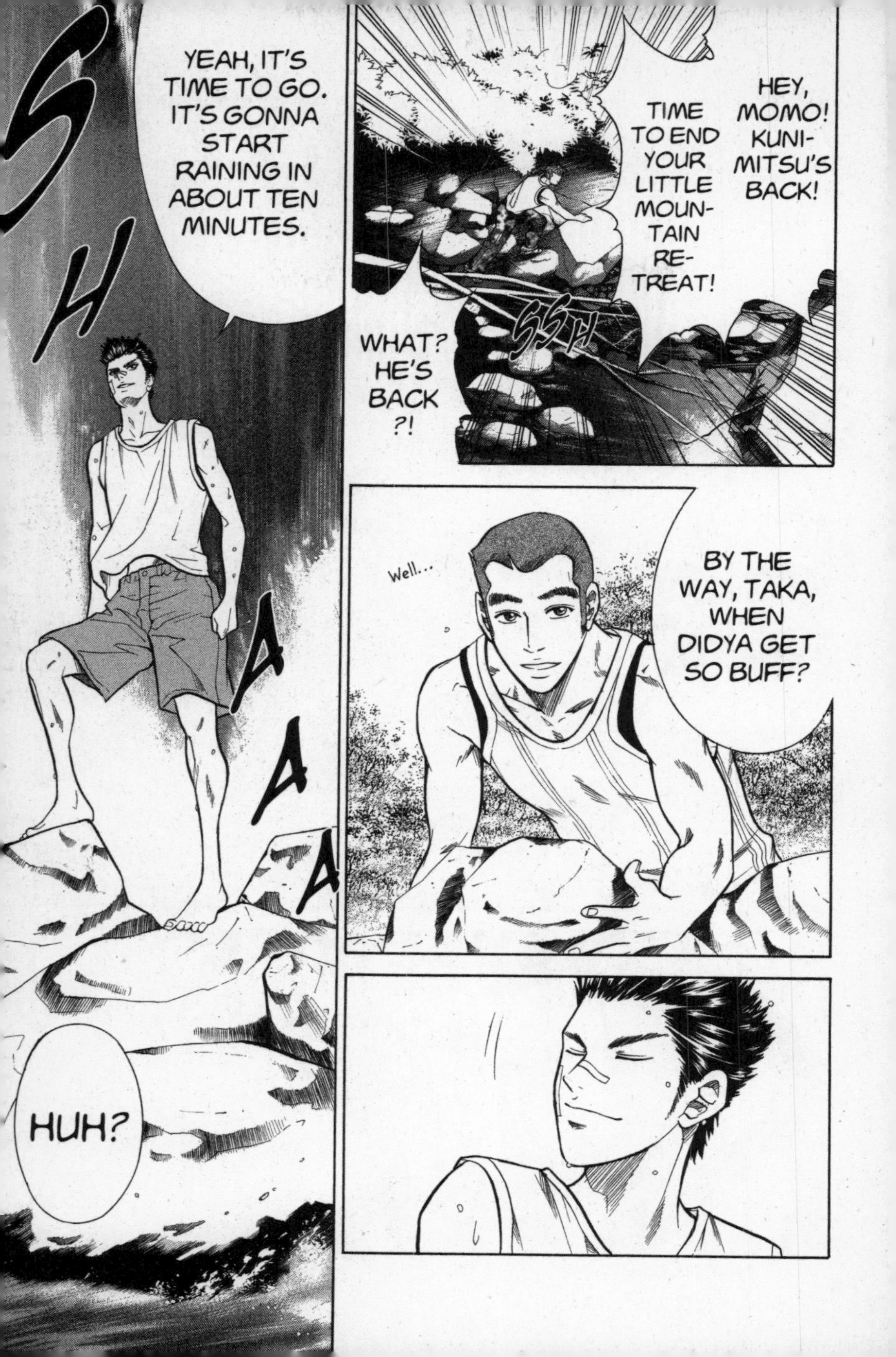
HEY, MOMO! KUNI-MITSU'S BACK!
TIME TO END YOUR LITTLE MOUN-TAIN RE-TREAT!
SSH
WHAT? HE'S BACK ?!
BY THE WAY, TAKA, WHEN DIDYA GET SO BUFF?
Well...
YEAH, IT'S TIME TO GO. IT'S GONNA START RAINING IN ABOUT TEN MINUTES.
SH
AAAA
HUH?

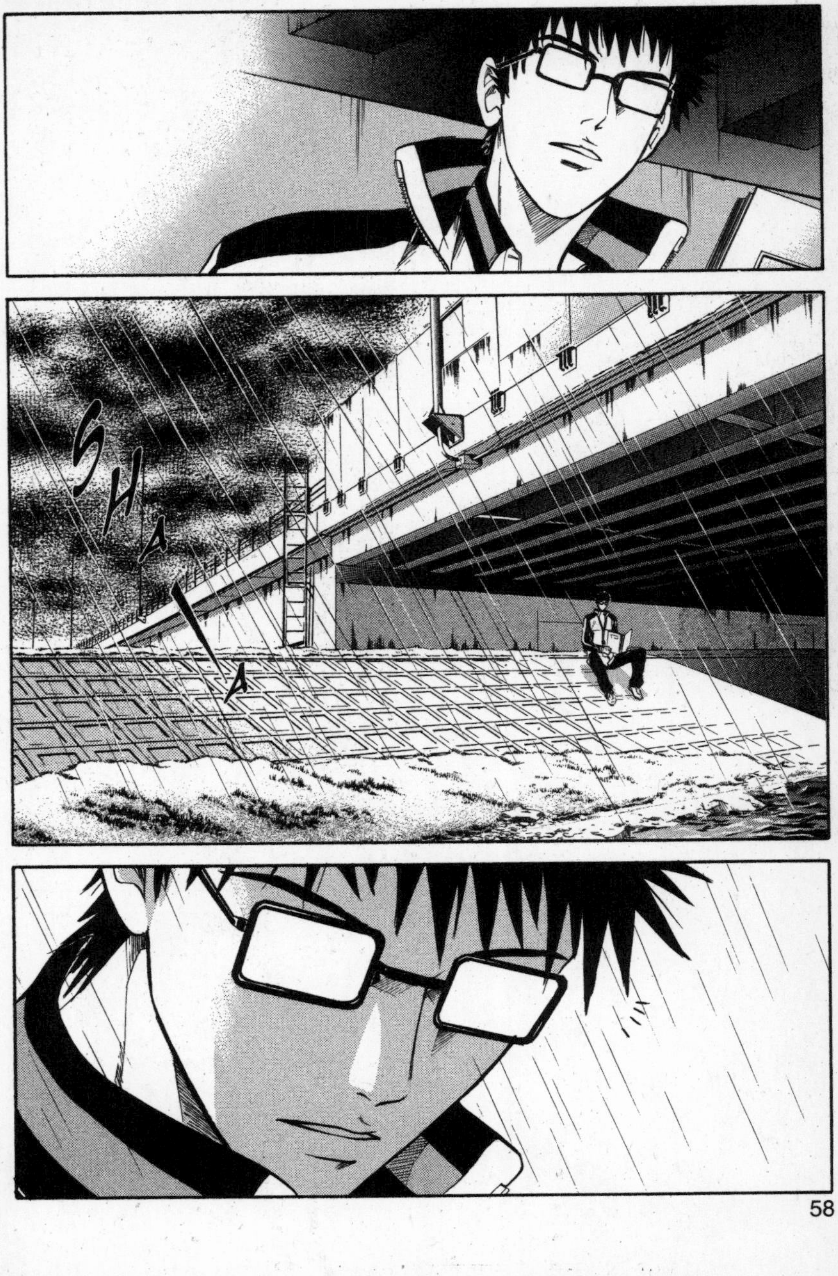
SHA—A

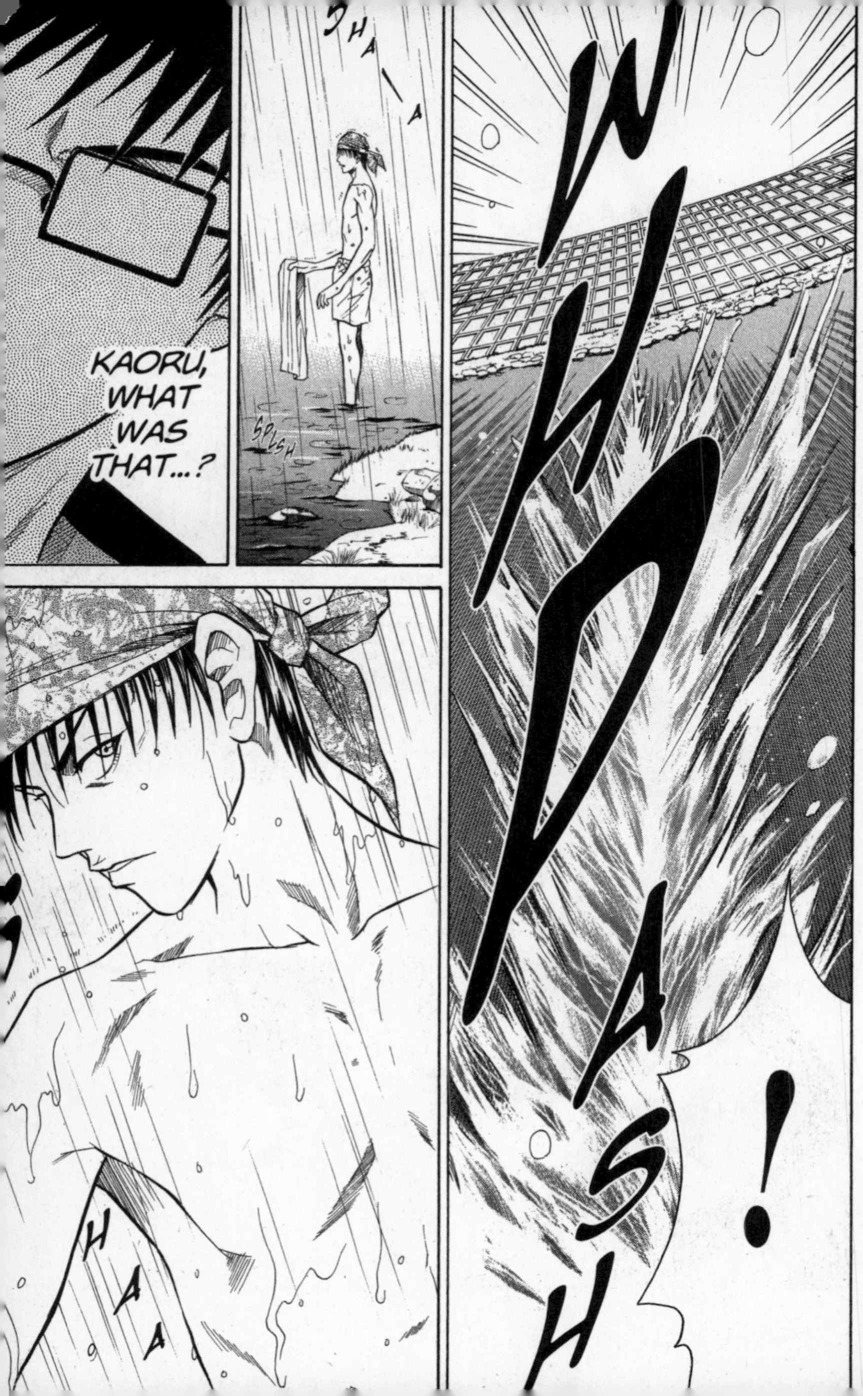
WHAAASH!
HAA
SPLSH
KAORU, WHAT WAS THAT...?
HAA

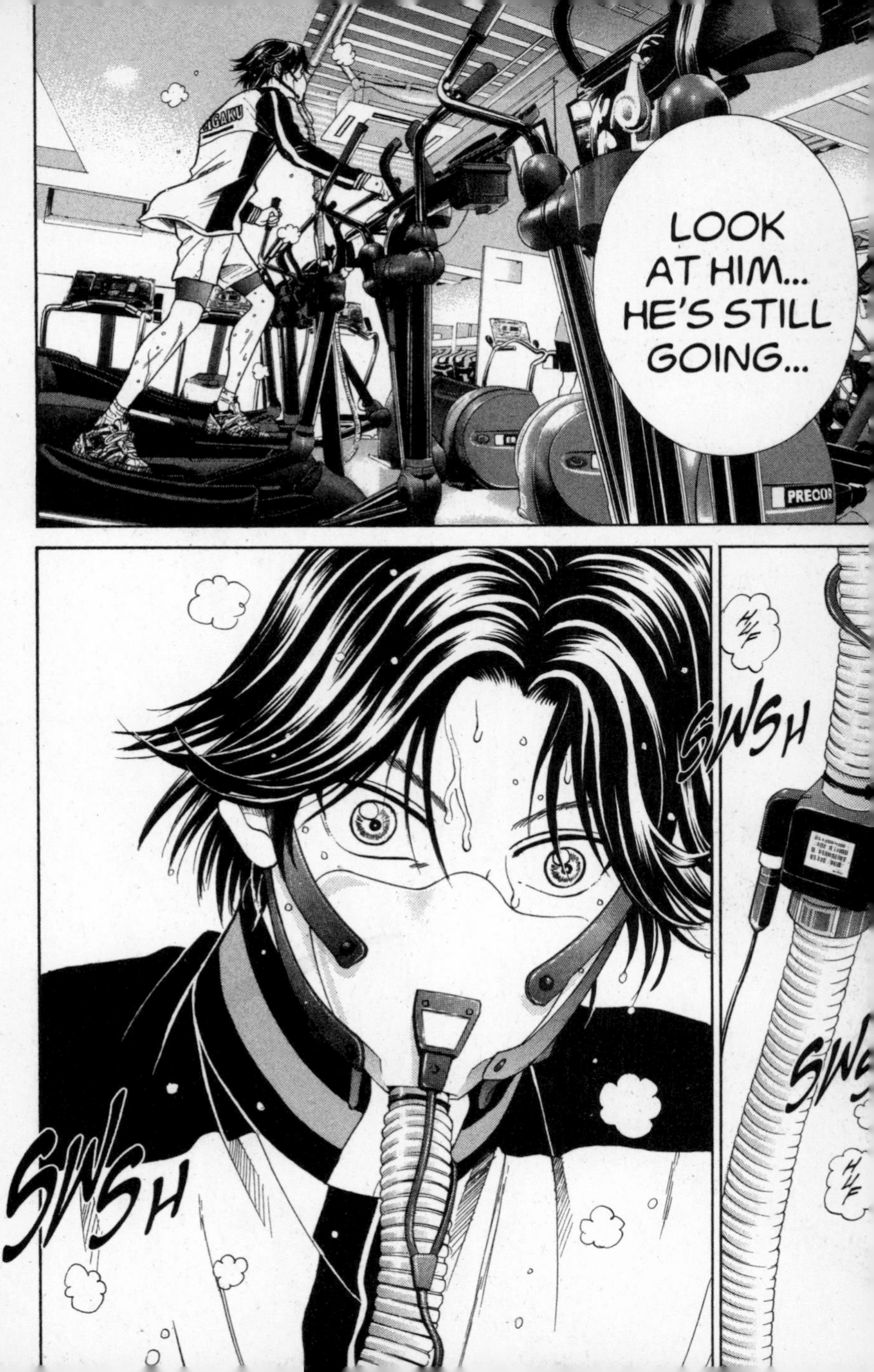
LOOK AT HIM... HE'S STILL GOING...
HUF
HUF
SWSH
SWSH

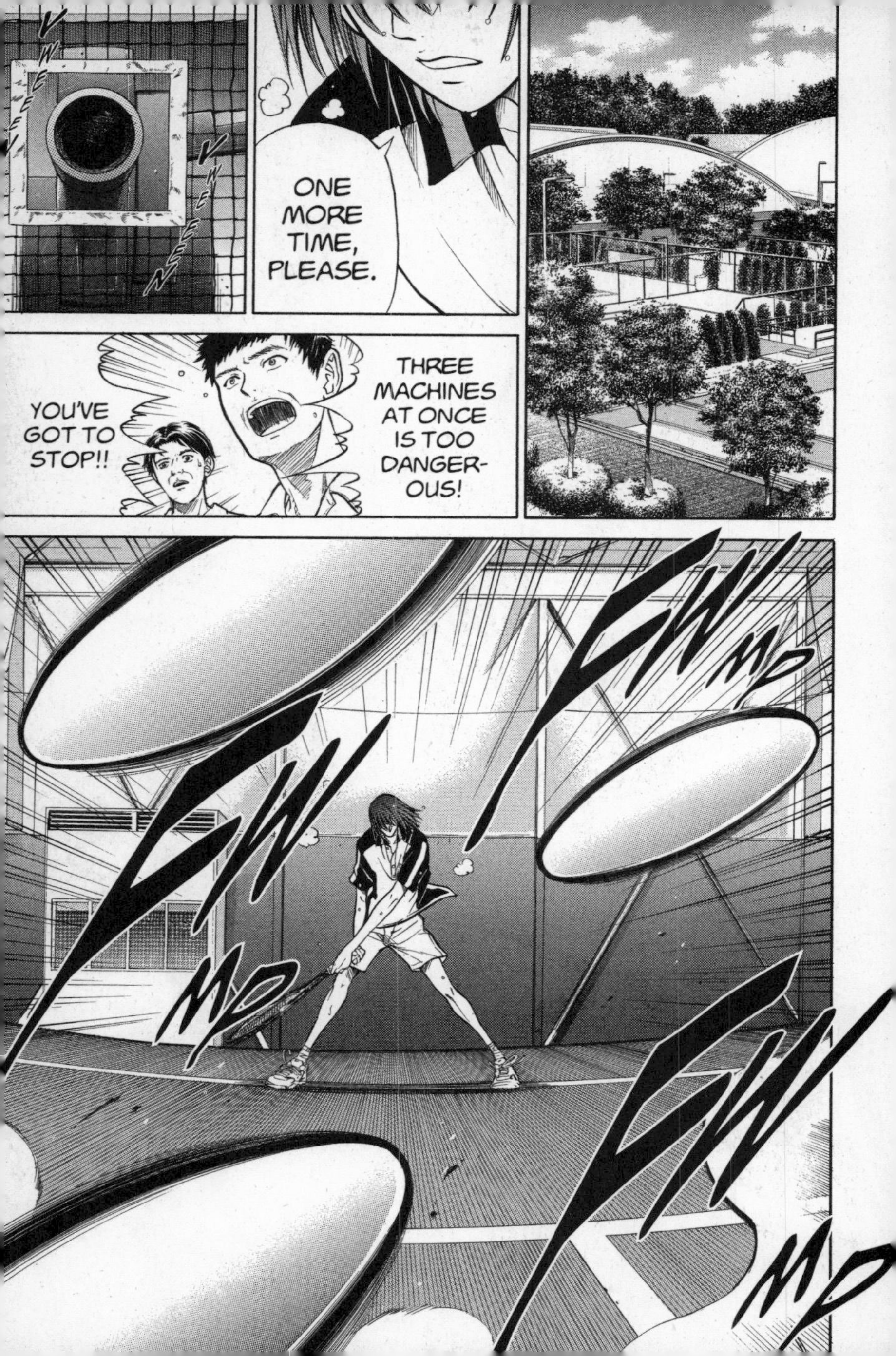
ONE MORE TIME, PLEASE.
VWEEEN
VWEEEEN
THREE MACHINES AT ONCE IS TOO DANGER-OUS!
YOU'VE GOT TO STOP!!
FWMP
FWMP
FWMP

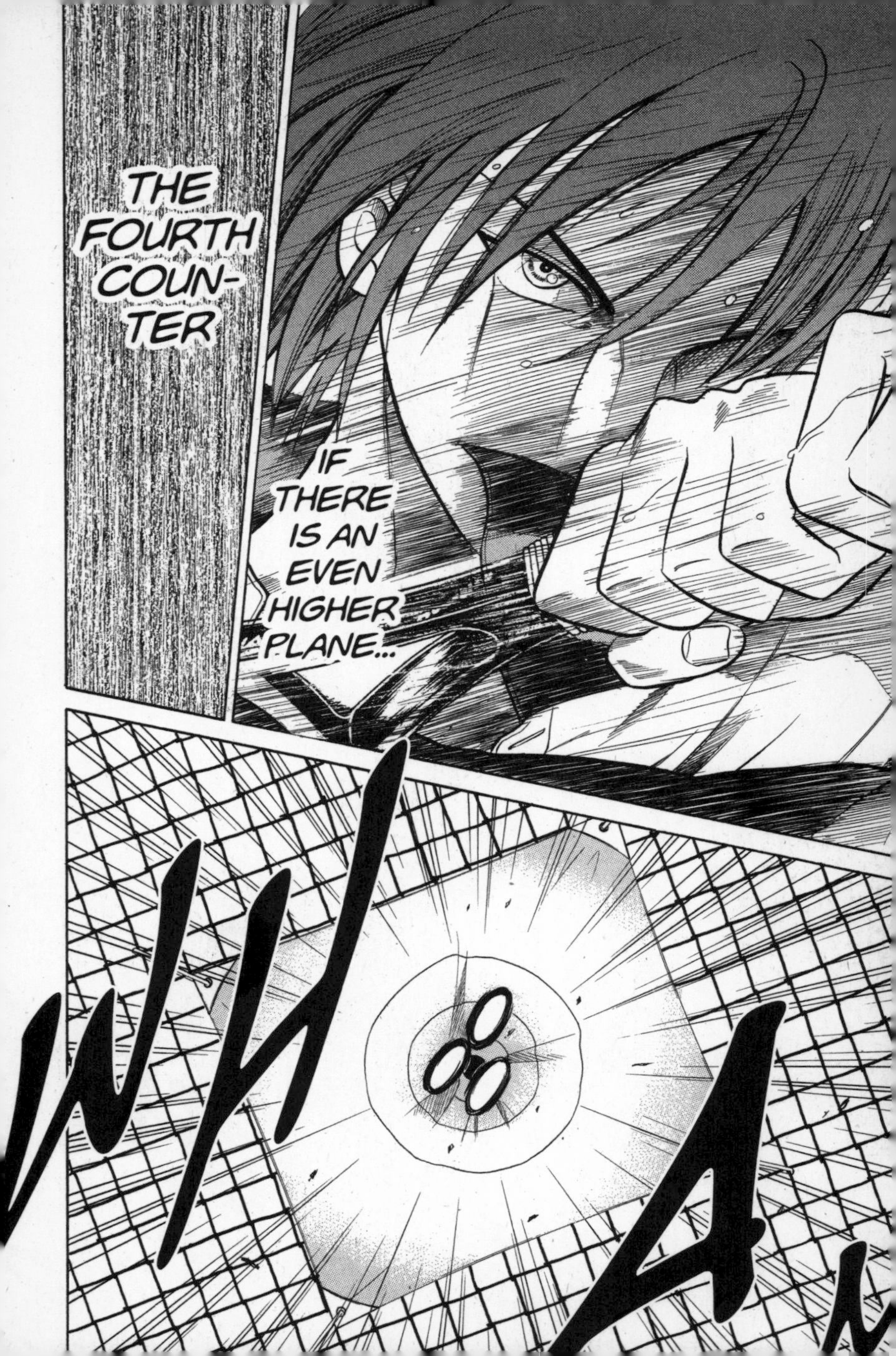
IF THERE IS AN EVEN HIGHER PLANE...
THE FOURTH COUN-TER

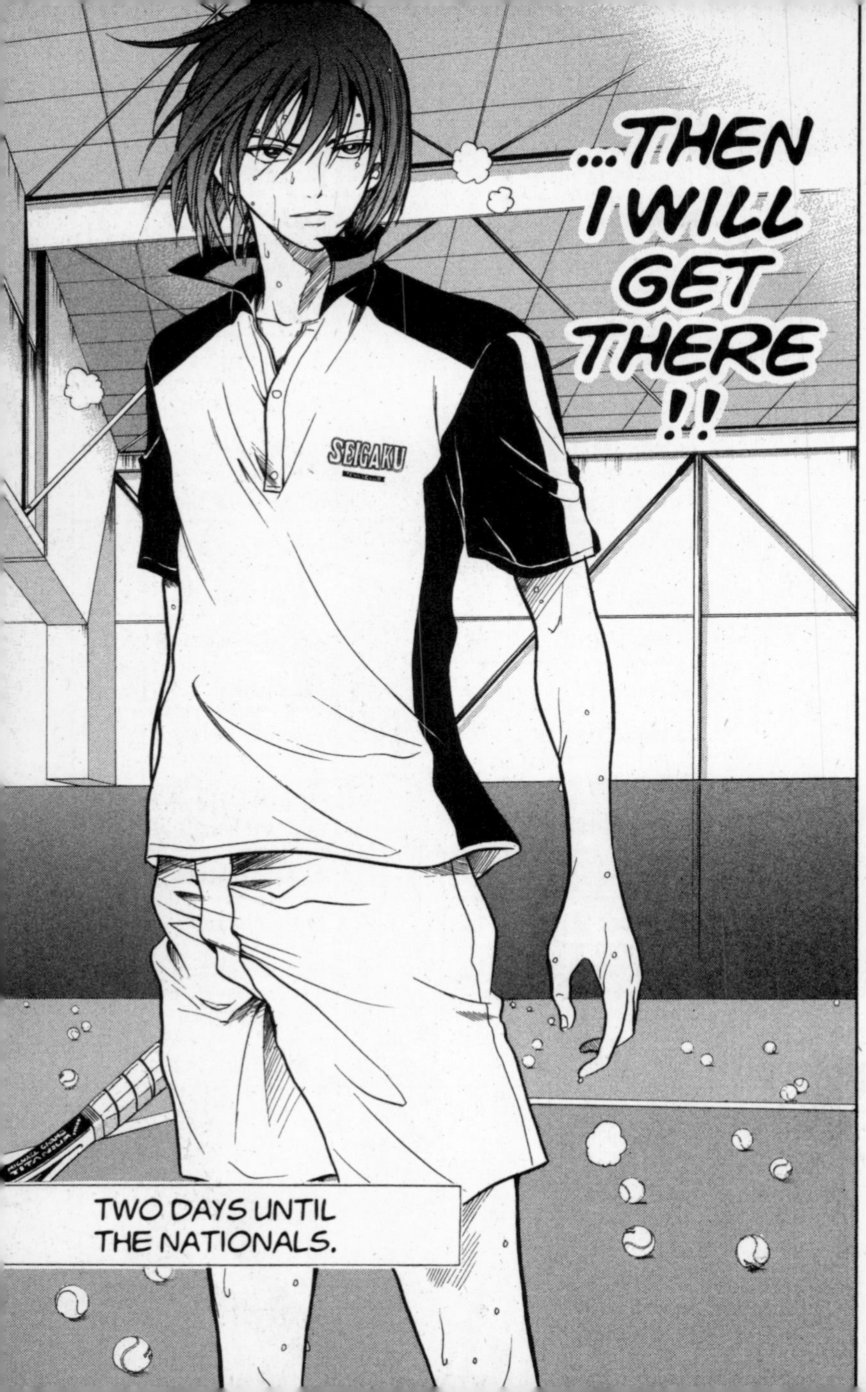
...THEN I WILL GET THERE!!
SEIGAKU
TWO DAYS UNTIL THE NATIONALS.

VALENTINE'S DAY CHOCOLATE TALLY RESULTS (PART 2)

11TH AND BELOW!

11th	Jiro Akutagawa	48	28th	Hiroshi Yagyu	15
12th	Shuichiro Oishi	44	32nd	Ryoga Echizen	13
	Kaoru Kaido			Yuta Fuji	
14th	Akaya Kirihara	41	34th	Atsushi Kisarazu	12
	Genichiro Sanada		35th	Shinji Ibu	10
16th	Sadaharu Inui	38		Munehiro Kabaji	
	Gakuto Mukahi		37th	Jin Akutsu	8
18th	Kiyosumi Sengoku	36		Kippei Tachibana	
19th	Seiichi Yukimura	34	39th	Hikaru Amane	7
20th	Wakashi Hiyoshi	32		Yudai Yamato	
21st	Bunta Marui	28	41st	Yoshiro Akazawa	6
22nd	Kojiro Saeki	26		TK Works	
23rd	Takashi Kawamura	24	43rd	Kyosuke Uchimura	5
	Masaharu Nio			Kuranosuke Shiraishi	
25th	Akira Kamio	22		Michiru Hukushi	
	Renji Yanagi			Shinya Yanagisawa	
27th	Producer Matsui	18	47th	Masashi Arai	3
28th	Haginosuke Taki	15		Ichiro Kaneda	
	Hajime Mizuki			Taro Sakaki	
	Kentaro Minami			The Hyotei Team	

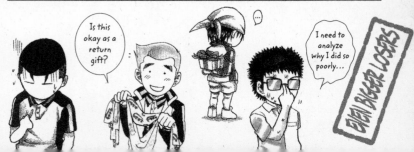

EVEN BIGGER LOSERS
I need to analyze why I did so poorly...
...
Is this okay as a return gift?

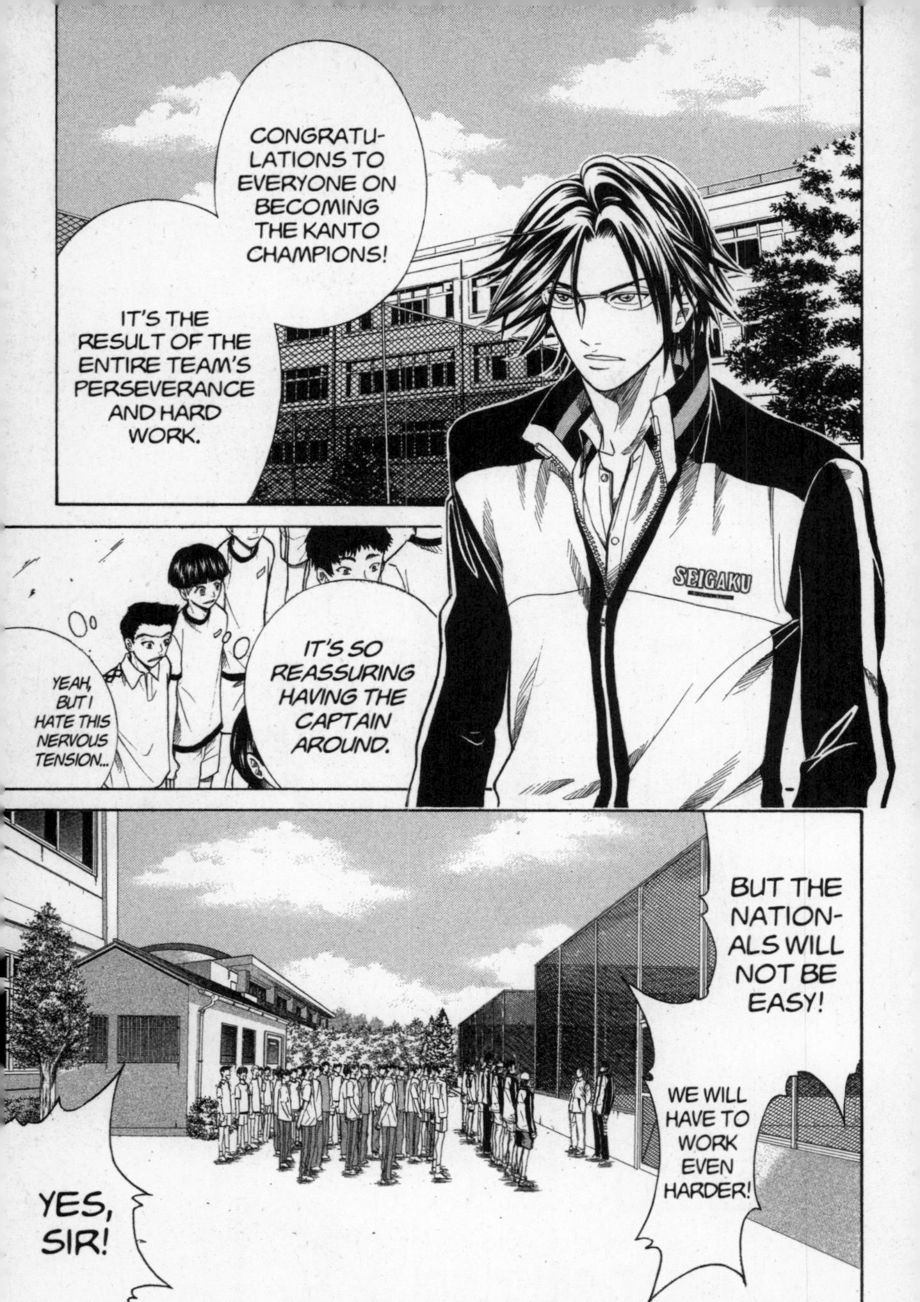
CONGRATULATIONS TO EVERYONE ON BECOMING THE KANTO CHAMPIONS!
IT'S THE RESULT OF THE ENTIRE TEAM'S PERSEVERANCE AND HARD WORK.
IT'S SO REASSURING HAVING THE CAPTAIN AROUND.
YEAH, BUT I HATE THIS NERVOUS TENSION...
SEIGAKU
BUT THE NATIONALS WILL NOT BE EASY!
WE WILL HAVE TO WORK EVEN HARDER!
YES, SIR!

GENIUS 250: SHUICHIRO'S DECISION

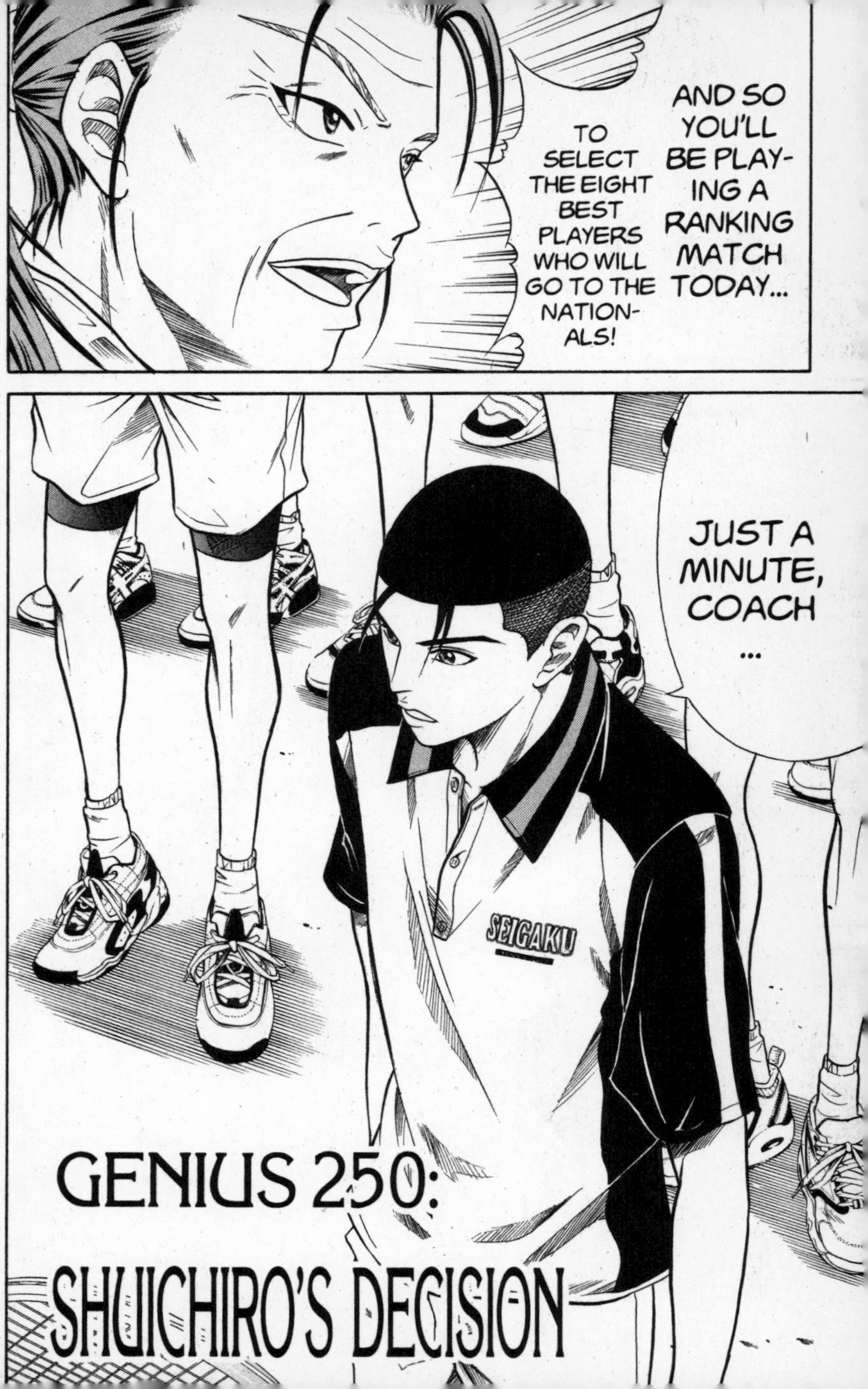
AND SO YOU'LL BE PLAY-ING A RANKING MATCH TODAY...
TO SELECT THE EIGHT BEST PLAYERS WHO WILL GO TO THE NATION-ALS!
JUST A MINUTE, COACH ...
GENIUS 250:
SHUICHIRO'S DECISION

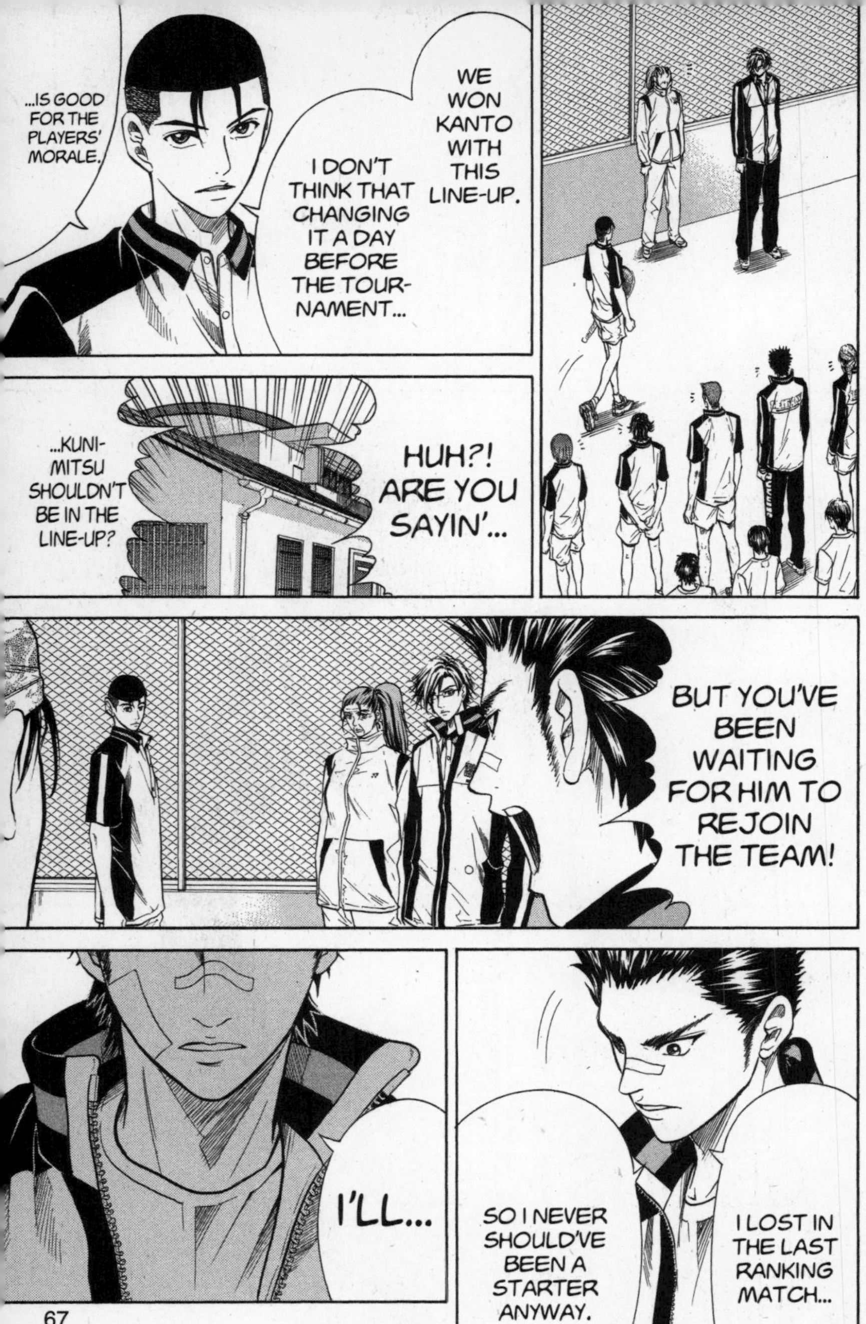
WE WON KANTO WITH THIS LINE-UP.
I DON'T THINK THAT CHANGING IT A DAY BEFORE THE TOURNAMENT...
...IS GOOD FOR THE PLAYERS' MORALE.
HUH?! ARE YOU SAYIN'...
...KUNIMITSU SHOULDN'T BE IN THE LINE-UP?
BUT YOU'VE BEEN WAITING FOR HIM TO REJOIN THE TEAM!
I LOST IN THE LAST RANKING MATCH...
SO I NEVER SHOULD'VE BEEN A STARTER ANYWAY.
I'LL...

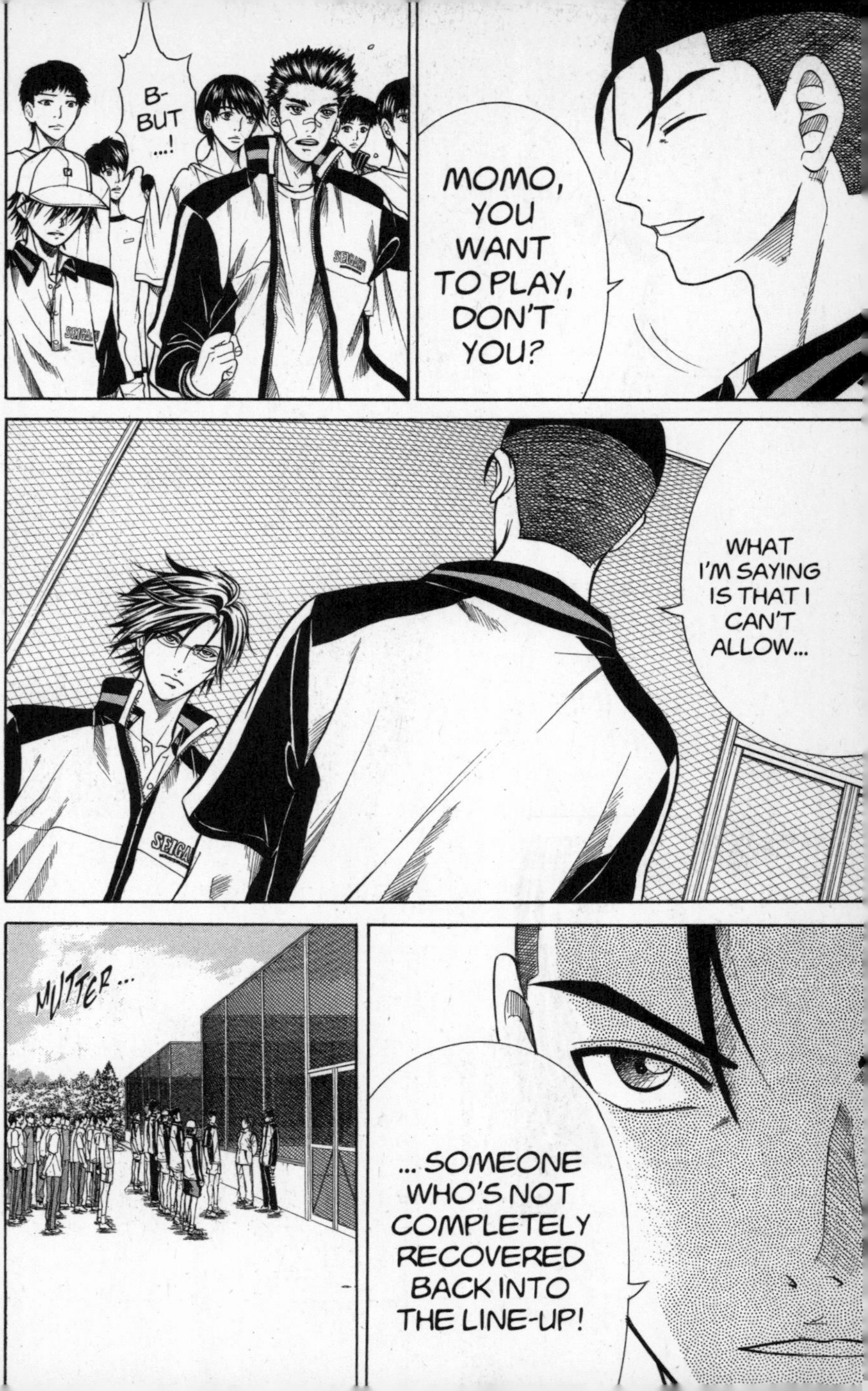
MOMO, YOU WANT TO PLAY, DON'T YOU?
B-BUT ...!
WHAT I'M SAYING IS THAT I CAN'T ALLOW...
... SOMEONE WHO'S NOT COMPLETELY RECOVERED BACK INTO THE LINE-UP!
MUTTER...

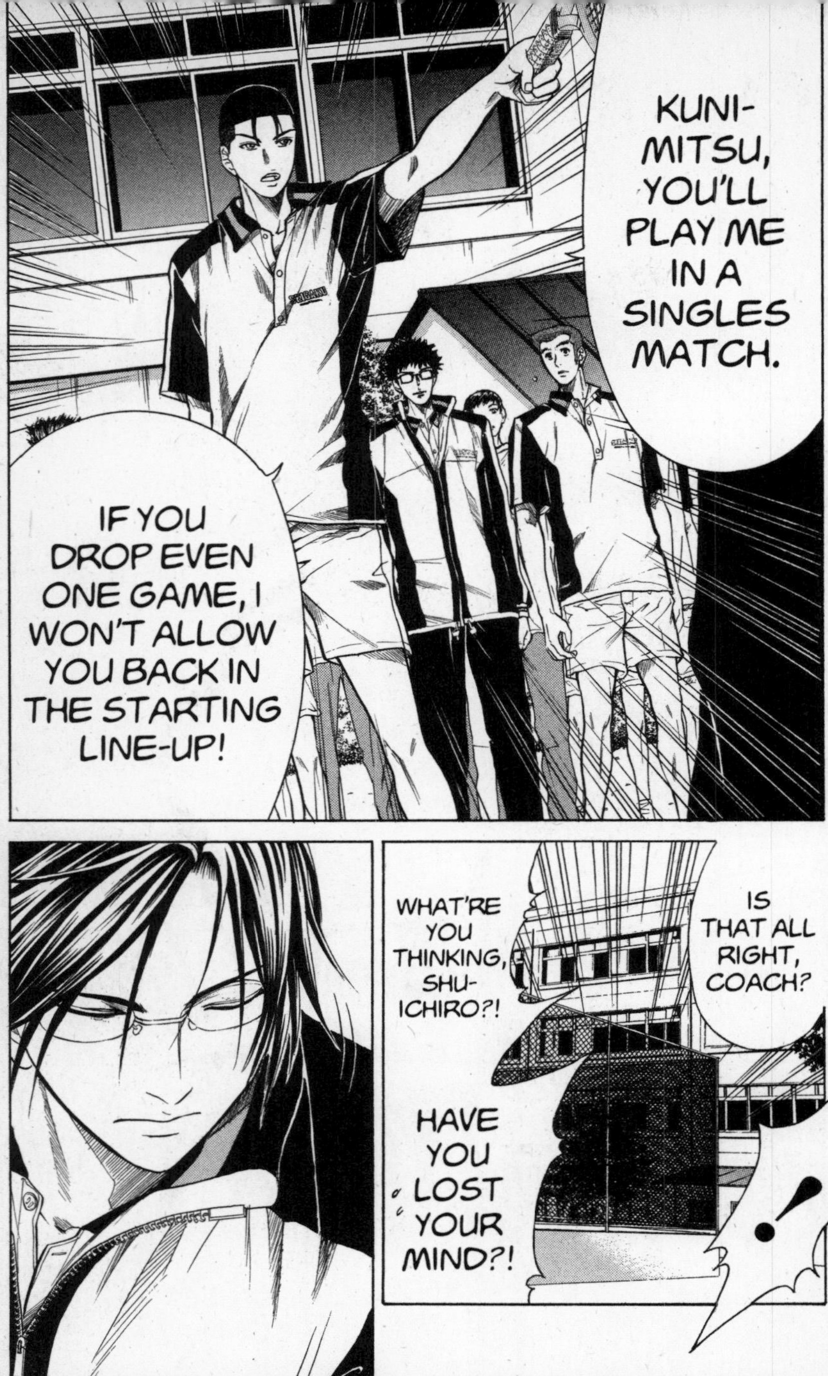
KUNI-MITSU, YOU'LL PLAY ME IN A SINGLES MATCH.
IF YOU DROP EVEN ONE GAME, I WON'T ALLOW YOU BACK IN THE STARTING LINE-UP!
IS THAT ALL RIGHT, COACH?
WHAT'RE YOU THINKING, SHU-ICHIRO?!
HAVE YOU LOST YOUR MIND?!
!

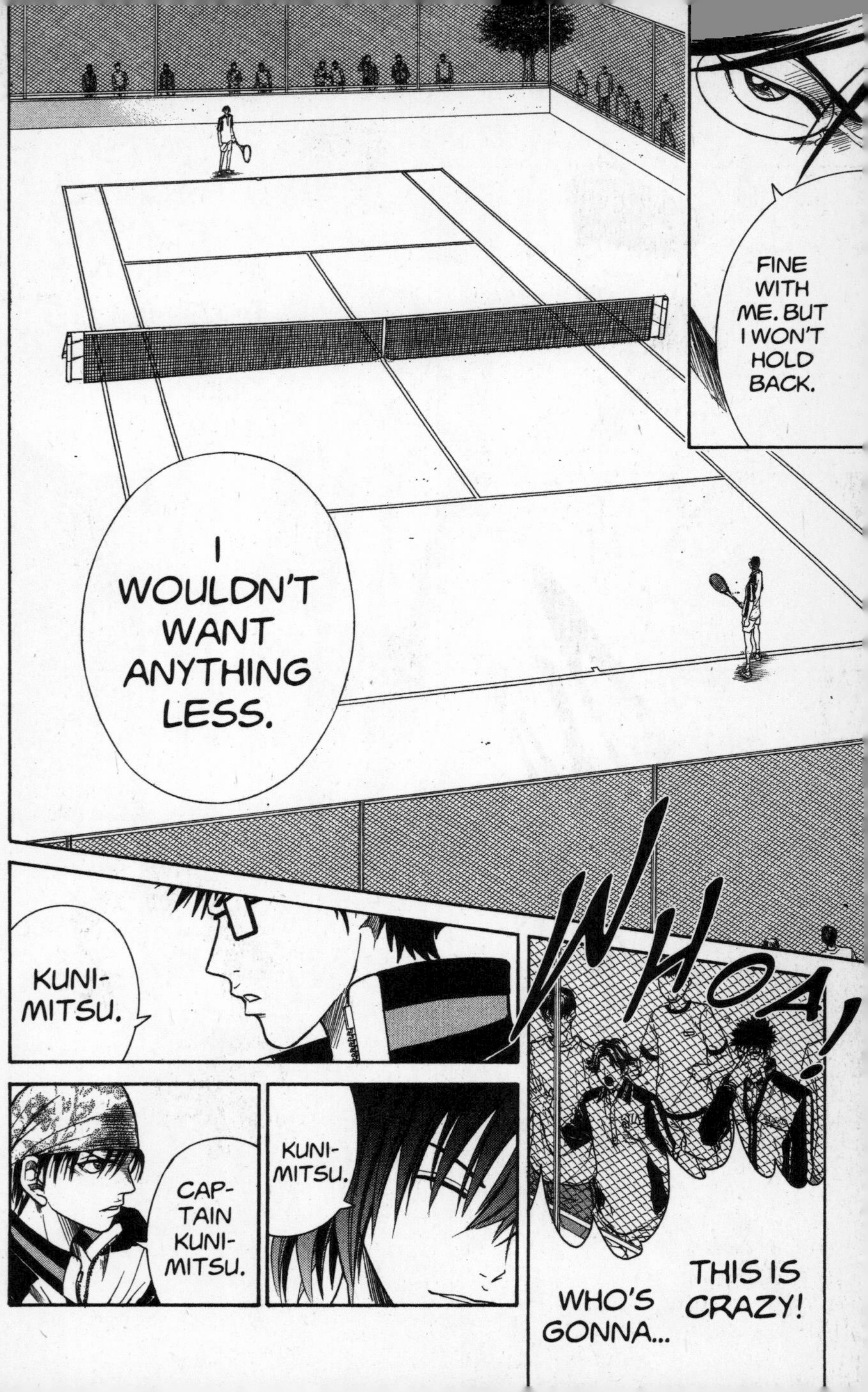
FINE WITH ME. BUT I WON'T HOLD BACK.
I WOULDN'T WANT ANYTHING LESS.
WHOA!
THIS IS CRAZY!
WHO'S GONNA...
KUNI-MITSU.
KUNI-MITSU.
CAP-TAIN KUNI-MITSU.

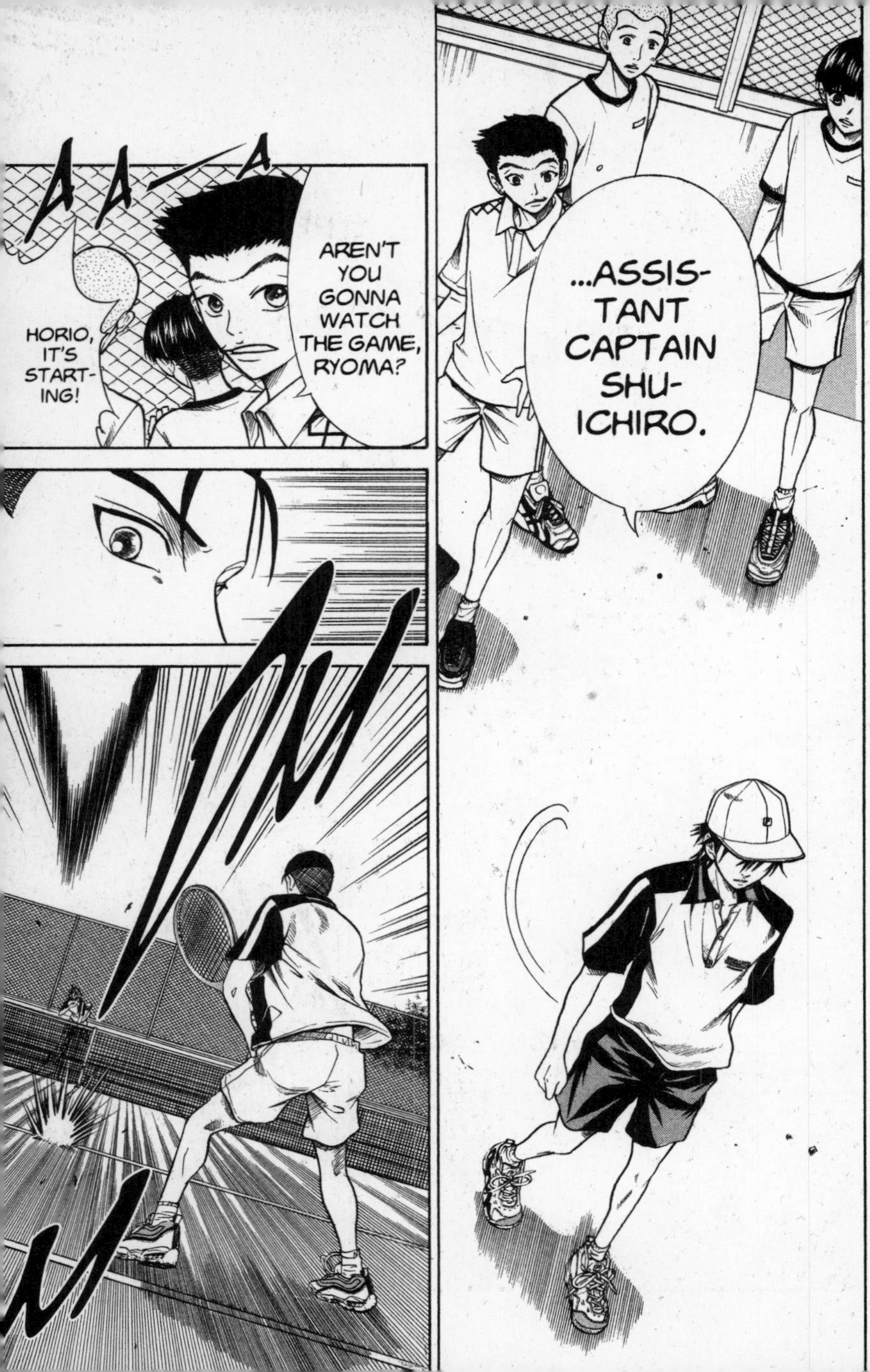
...ASSIS-TANT CAPTAIN SHU-ICHIRO.
AREN'T YOU GONNA WATCH THE GAME, RYOMA?
HORIO, IT'S START-ING!

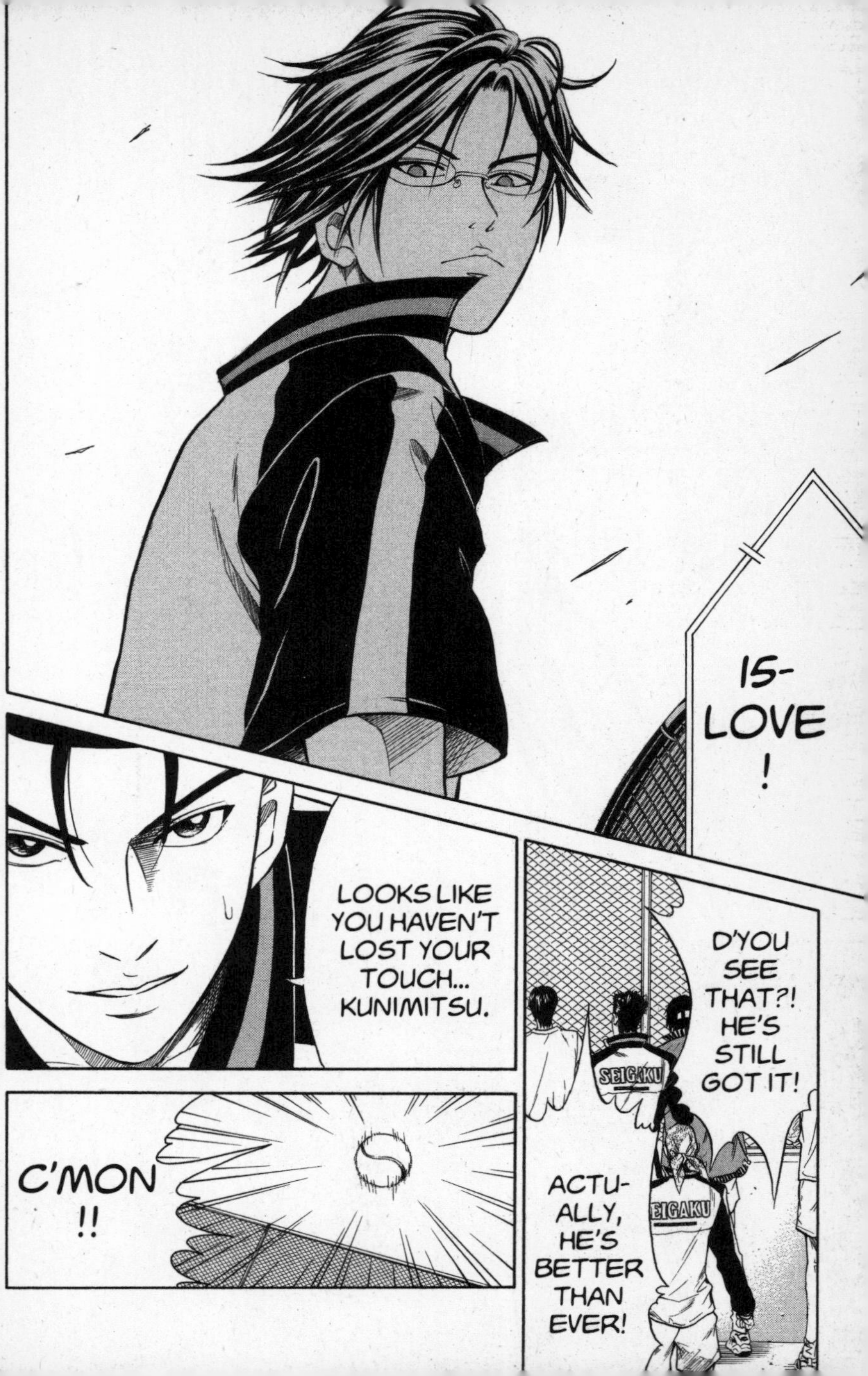
15-LOVE!
D'YOU SEE THAT?! HE'S STILL GOT IT!
ACTU-ALLY, HE'S BETTER THAN EVER!
SEIGAKU
SEIGAKU
LOOKS LIKE YOU HAVEN'T LOST YOUR TOUCH... KUNIMITSU.
C'MON!!

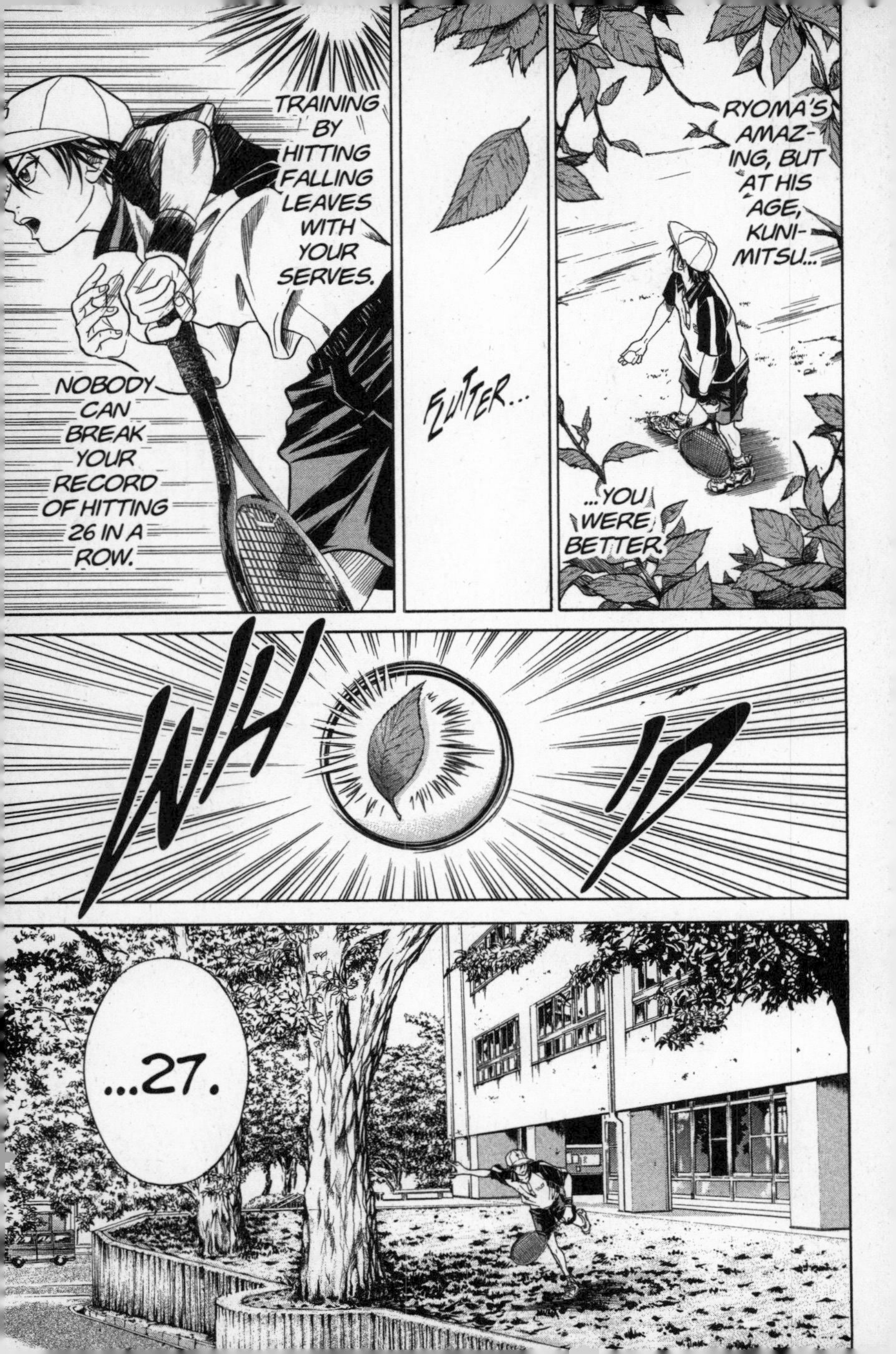
RYOMA'S AMAZING, BUT AT HIS AGE, KUNIMITSU...
...YOU WERE BETTER.
FLUTTER...
TRAINING BY HITTING FALLING LEAVES WITH YOUR SERVES.
NOBODY CAN BREAK YOUR RECORD OF HITTING 26 IN A ROW.
...27.

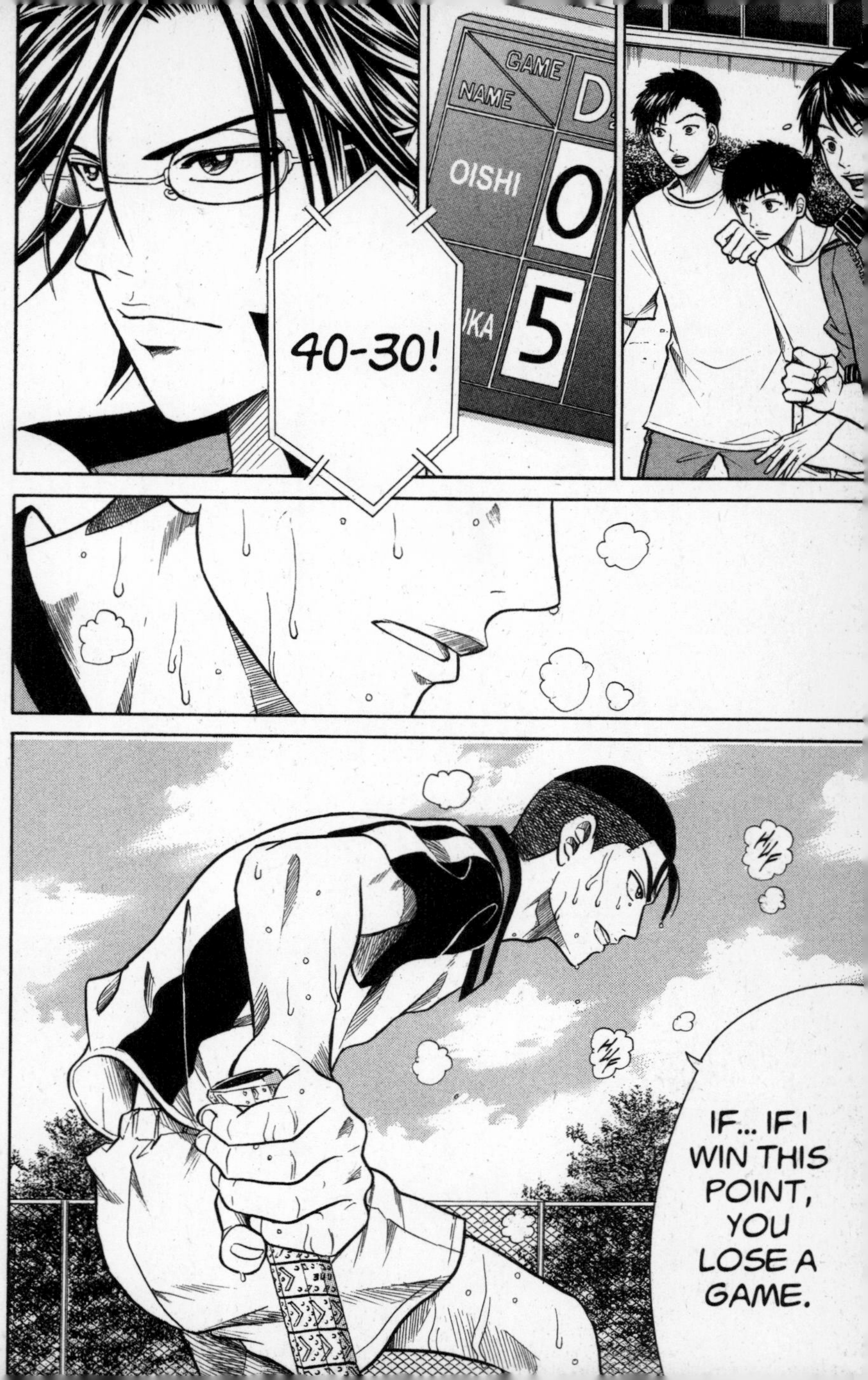
GAME
NAME
OISHI
0
5
40-30!
IF... IF I WIN THIS POINT, YOU LOSE A GAME.

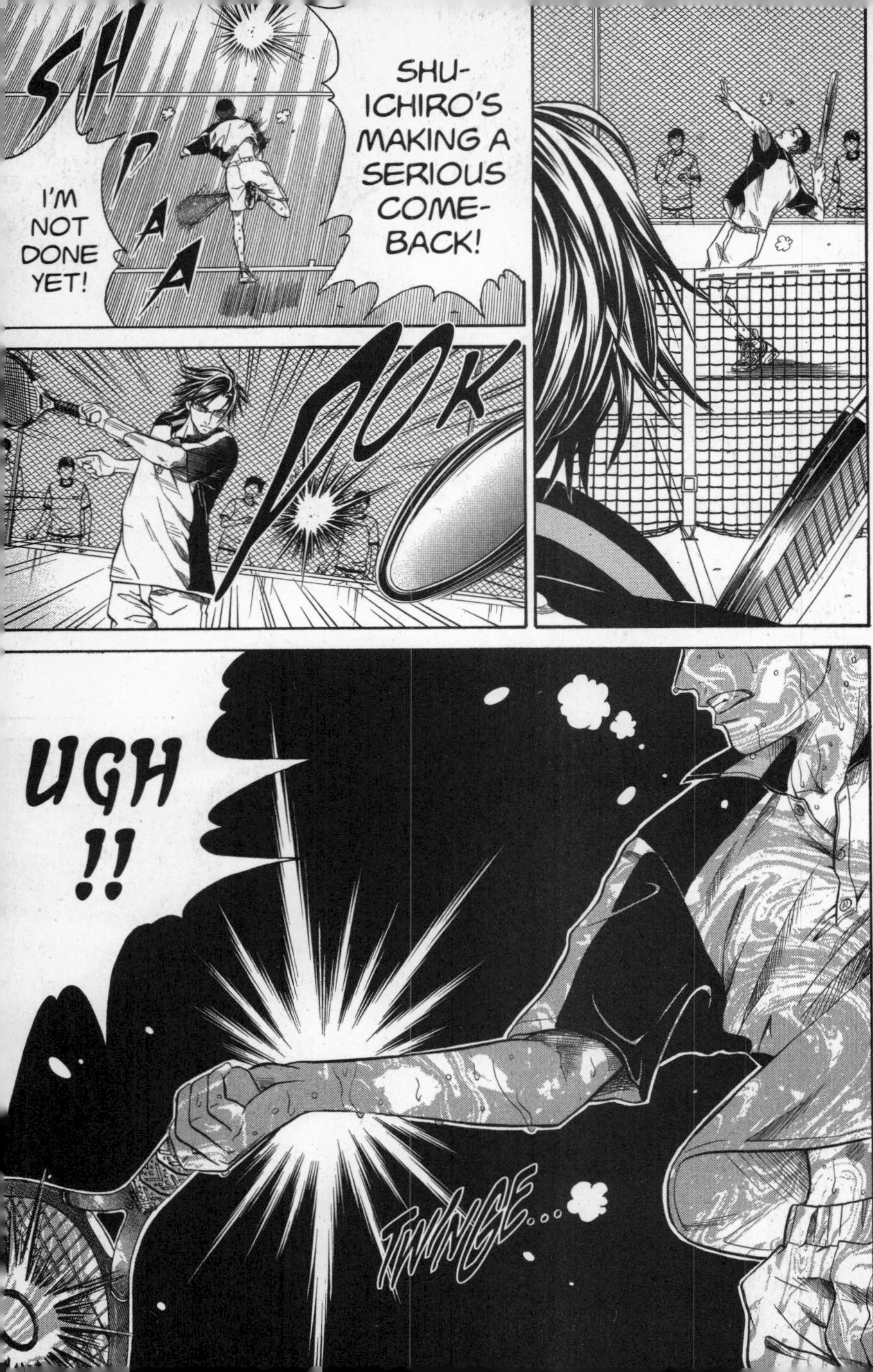

SHU-ICHIRO'S MAKING A SERIOUS COME-BACK!
SHPAAA
I'M NOT DONE YET!
POK
UGH!!
TWINGE...

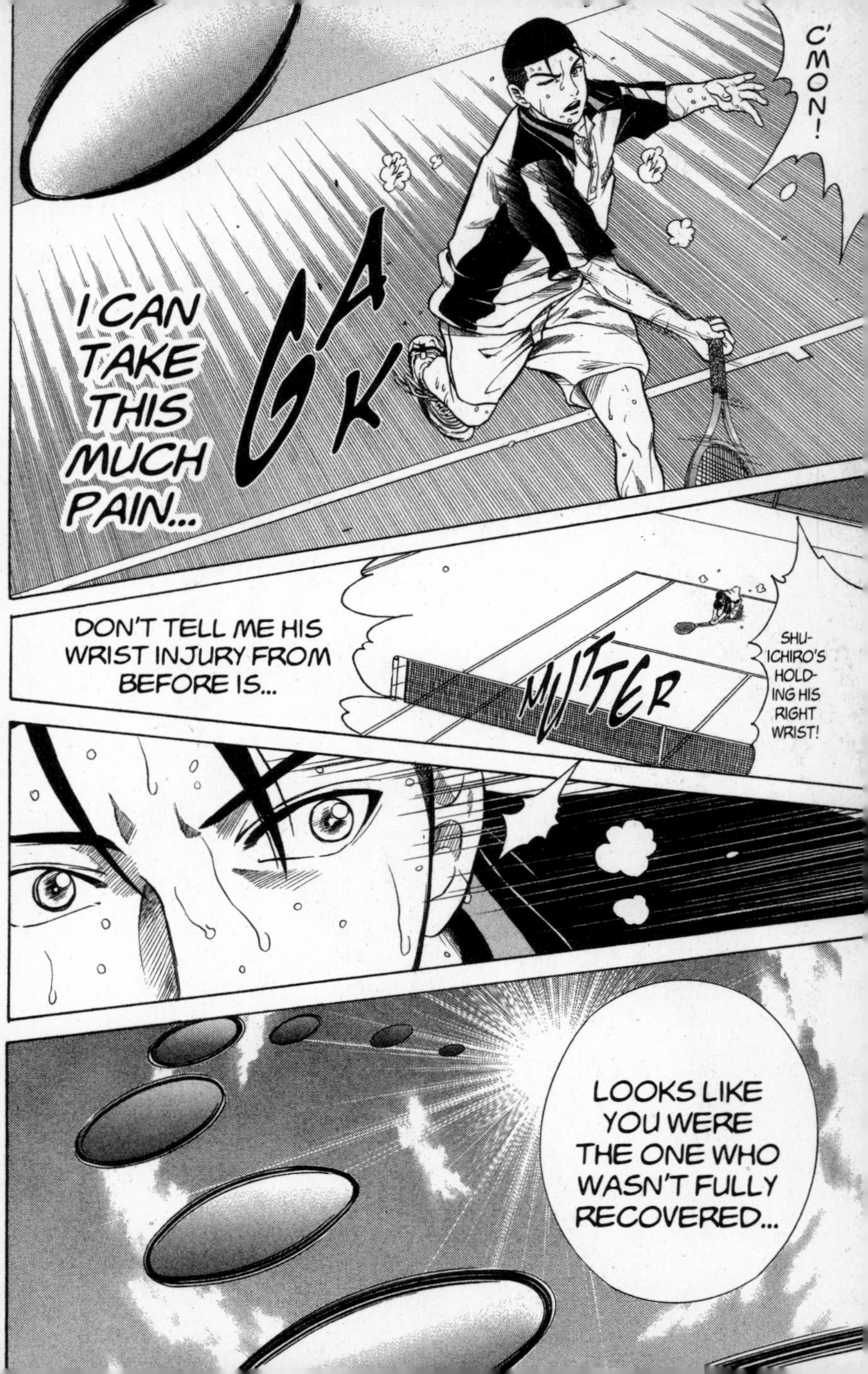
C'MON!
GAK
I CAN TAKE THIS MUCH PAIN...
SHU-ICHIRO'S HOLD-ING HIS RIGHT WRIST!
MUTTER
DON'T TELL ME HIS WRIST INJURY FROM BEFORE IS...
LOOKS LIKE YOU WERE THE ONE WHO WASN'T FULLY RECOVERED...

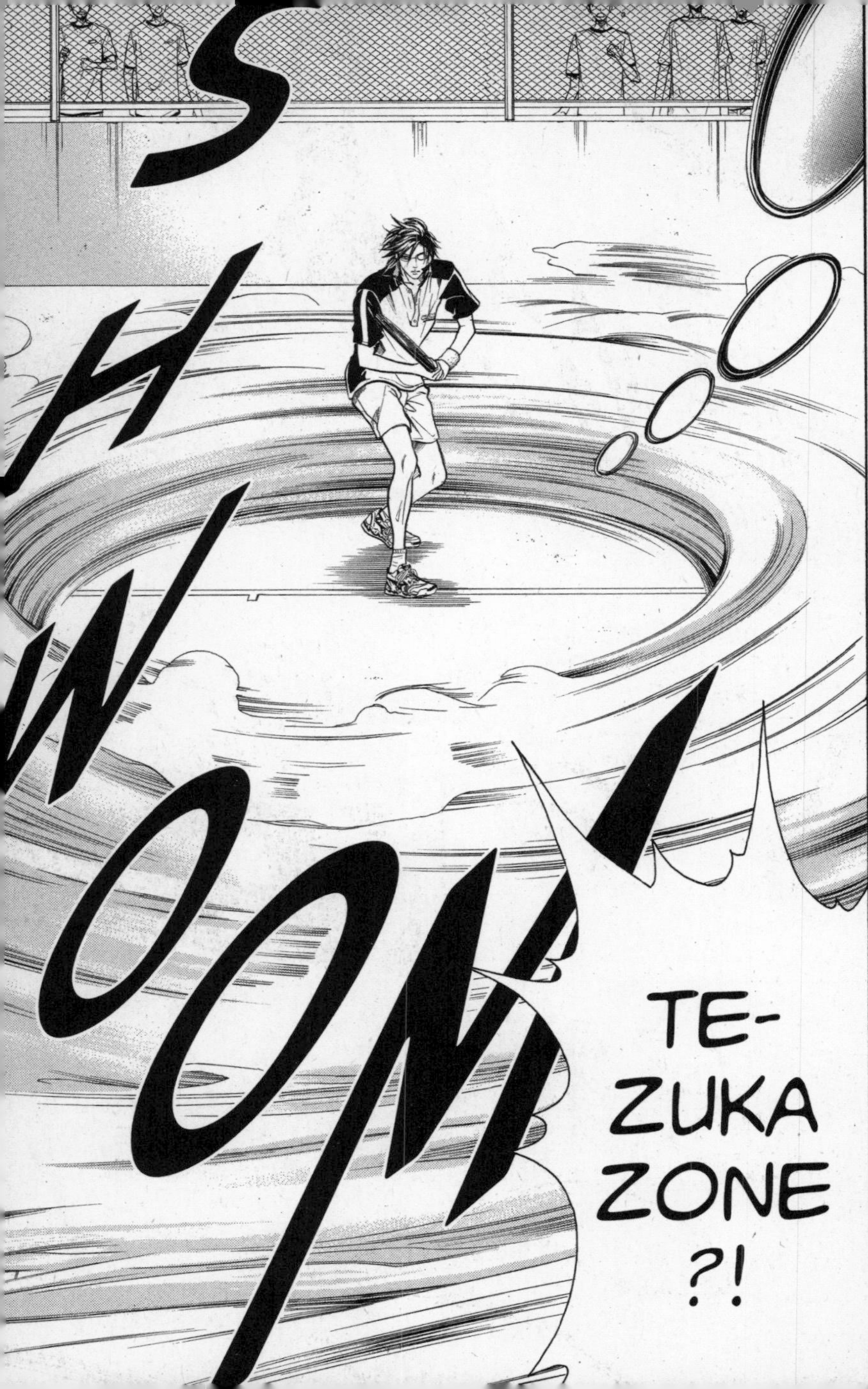
SHWOOM
TE-ZUKA ZONE ?!

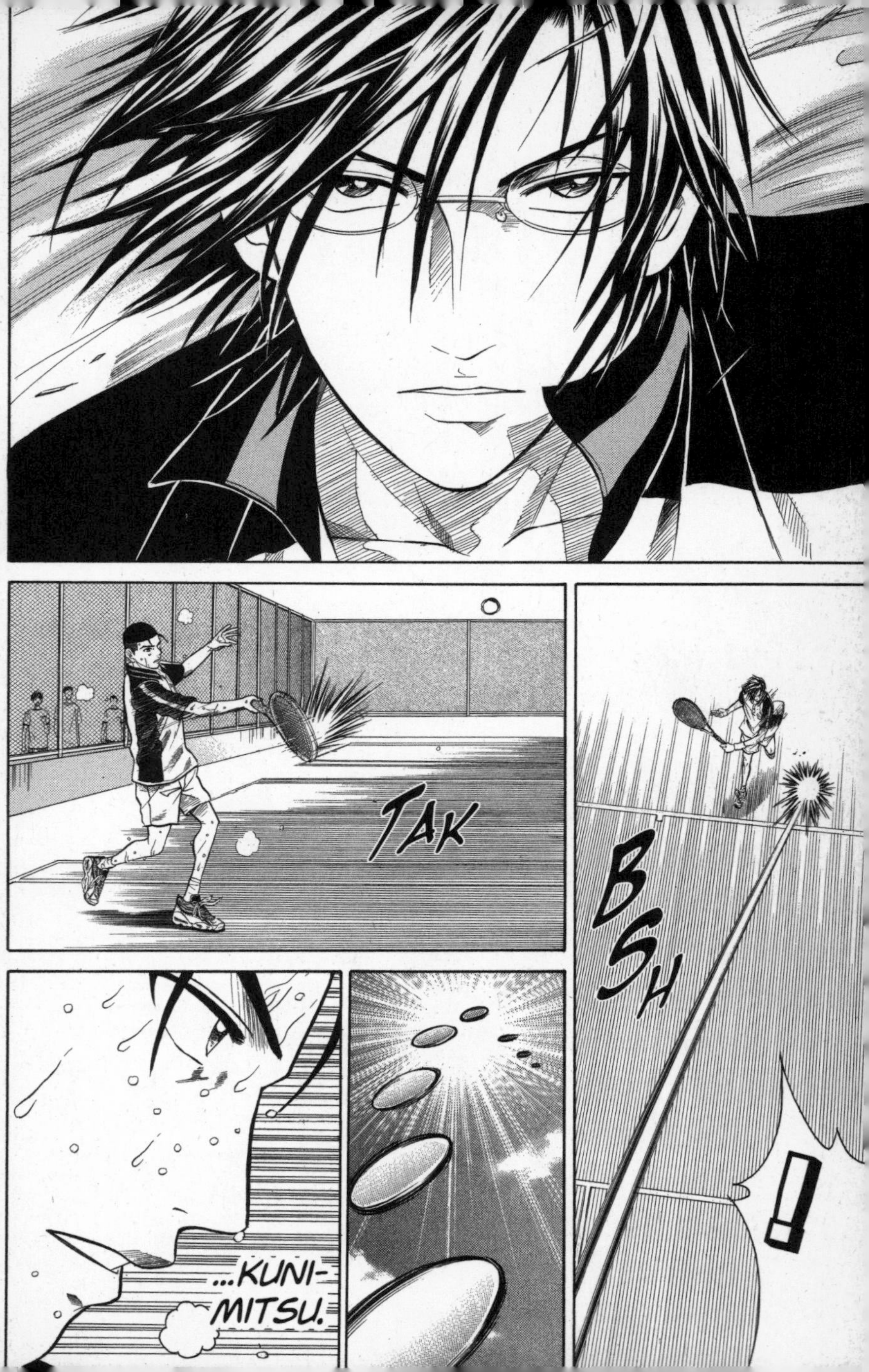
BSH
!
TAK
...KUNI-MITSU.

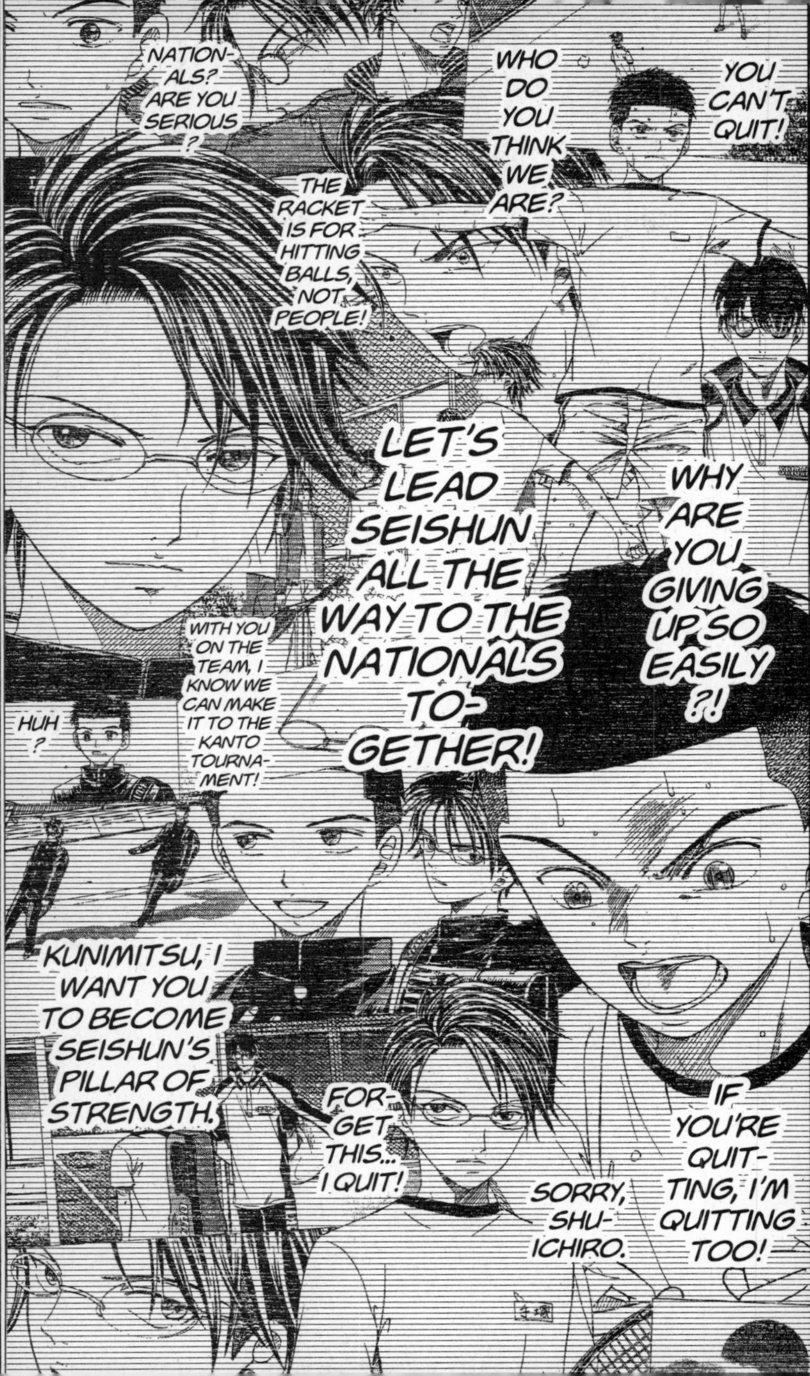
YOU CAN'T QUIT!
WHO DO YOU THINK WE ARE?
THE RACKET IS FOR HITTING BALLS, NOT PEOPLE!
NATIONALS? ARE YOU SERIOUS?
WHY ARE YOU GIVING UP SO EASILY?!
LET'S LEAD SEISHUN ALL THE WAY TO THE NATIONALS TOGETHER!
WITH YOU ON THE TEAM, I KNOW WE CAN MAKE IT TO THE KANTO TOURNAMENT!
HUH?
IF YOU'RE QUITTING, I'M QUITTING TOO!
SORRY, SHUICHIRO.
FORGET THIS... I QUIT!
KUNIMITSU, I WANT YOU TO BECOME SEISHUN'S PILLAR OF STRENGTH.

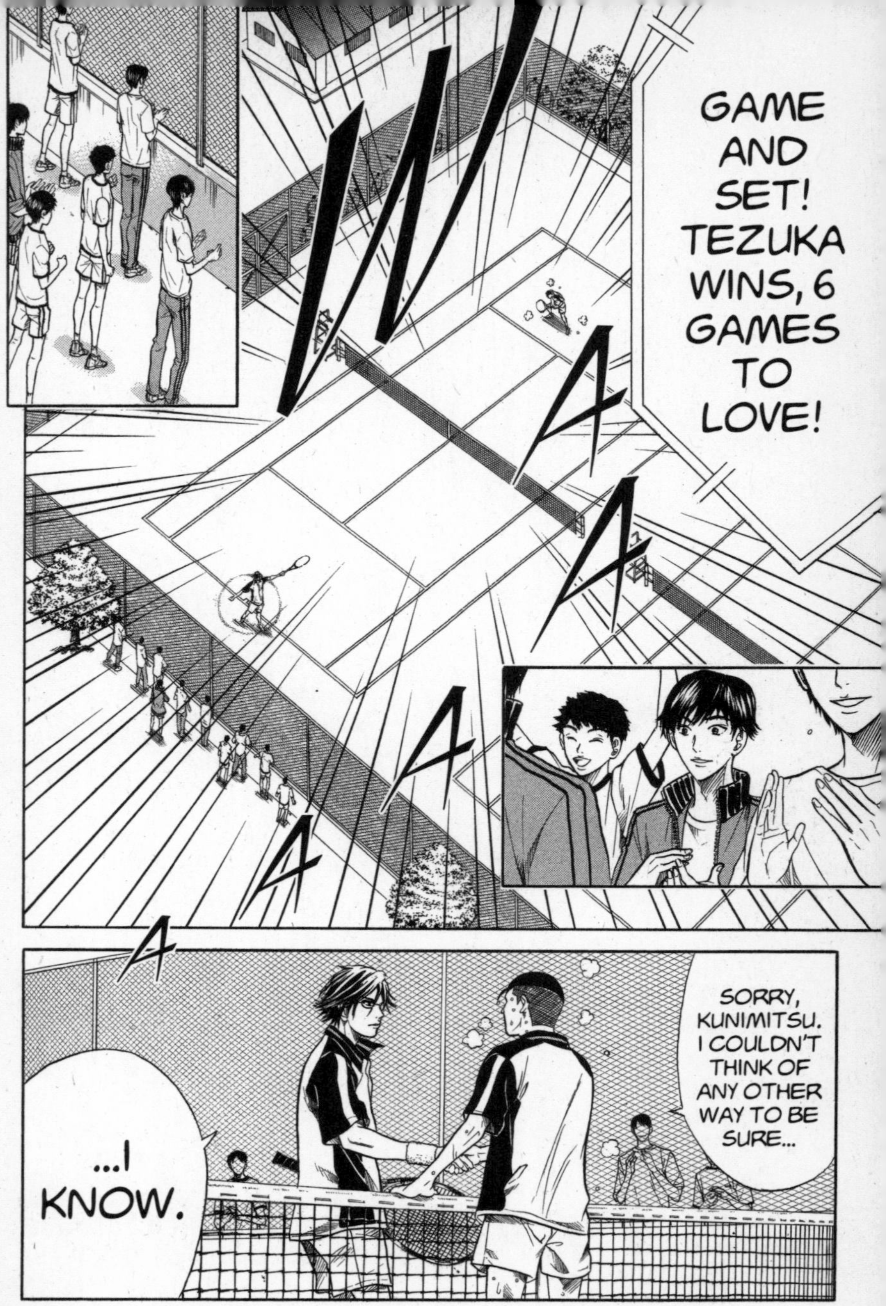
GAME AND SET! TEZUKA WINS, 6 GAMES TO LOVE!
WAAAAA
SORRY, KUNIMITSU. I COULDN'T THINK OF ANY OTHER WAY TO BE SURE...
...I KNOW.

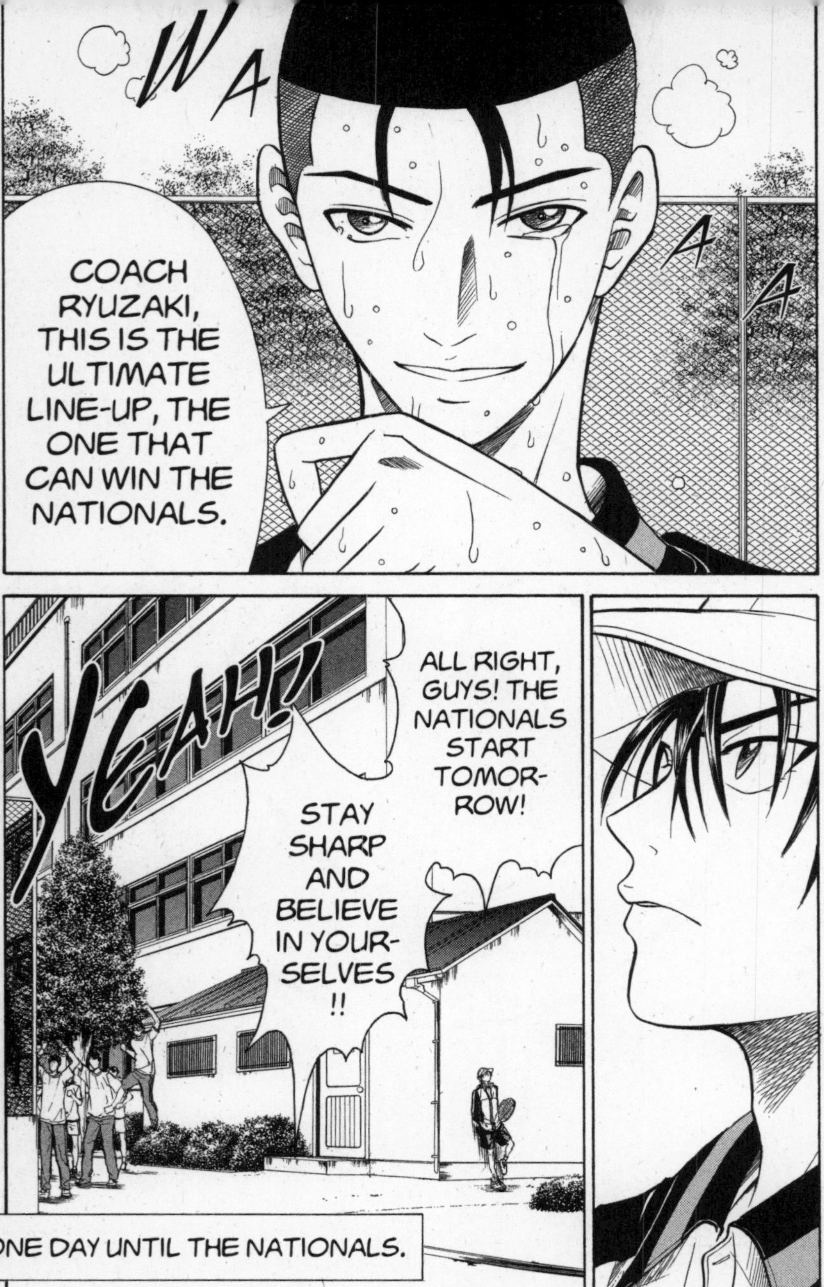
WAAA
COACH RYUZAKI, THIS IS THE ULTIMATE LINE-UP, THE ONE THAT CAN WIN THE NATIONALS.
ALL RIGHT, GUYS! THE NATIONALS START TOMOR-ROW!
STAY SHARP AND BELIEVE IN YOUR-SELVES !!
YEAH!
ONE DAY UNTIL THE NATIONALS.

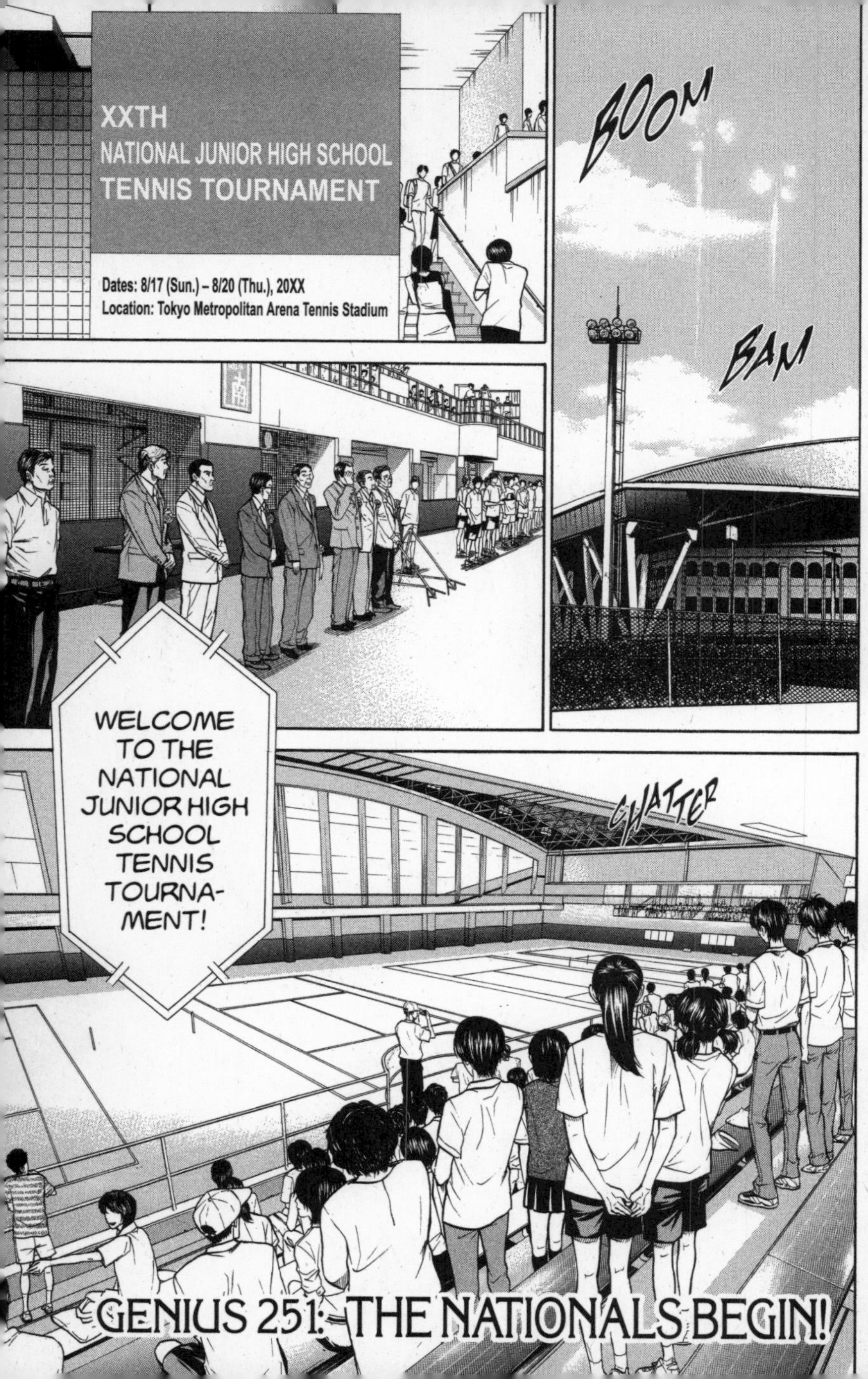
BOOM
BAM
XXTH
NATIONAL JUNIOR HIGH SCHOOL
TENNIS TOURNAMENT
Dates: 8/17 (Sun.) – 8/20 (Thu.), 20XX
Location: Tokyo Metropolitan Arena Tennis Stadium
WELCOME TO THE NATIONAL JUNIOR HIGH SCHOOL TENNIS TOURNAMENT!
CHATTER
GENIUS 251: THE NATIONALS BEGIN!

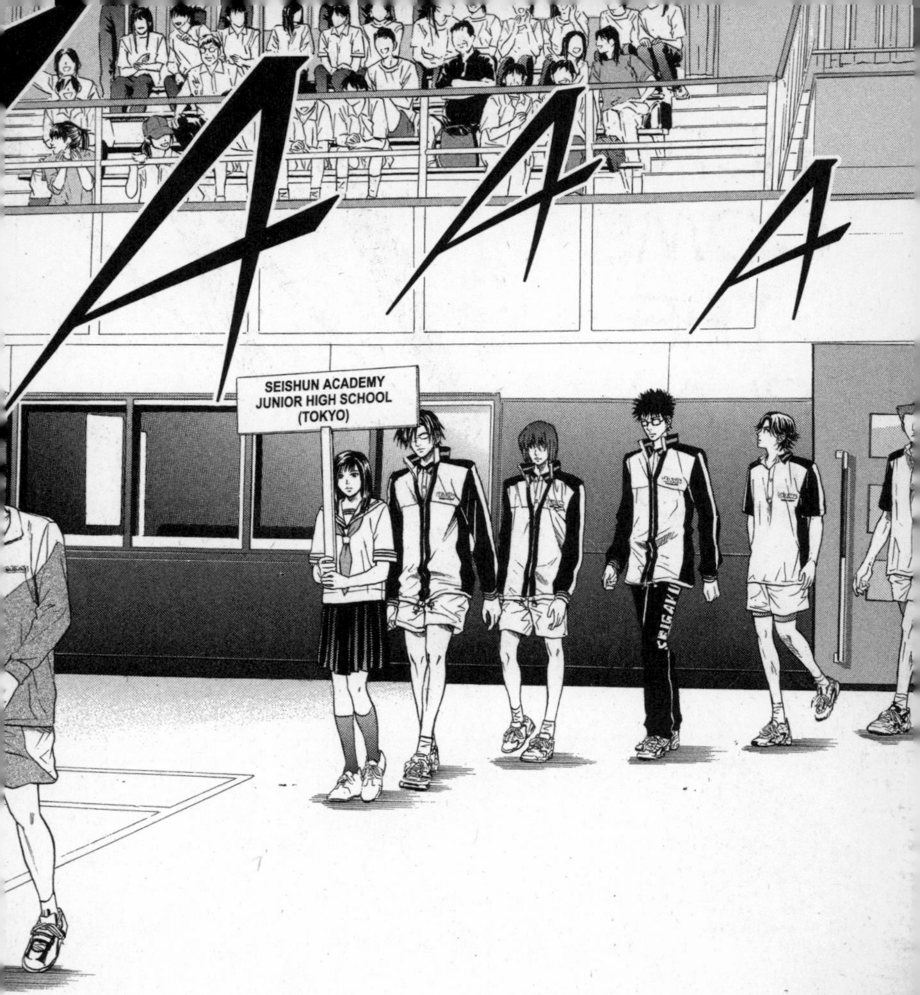
SEISHUN ACADEMY
JUNIOR HIGH SCHOOL
(TOKYO)

GENIUS 251: THE NATIONALS BEGIN!

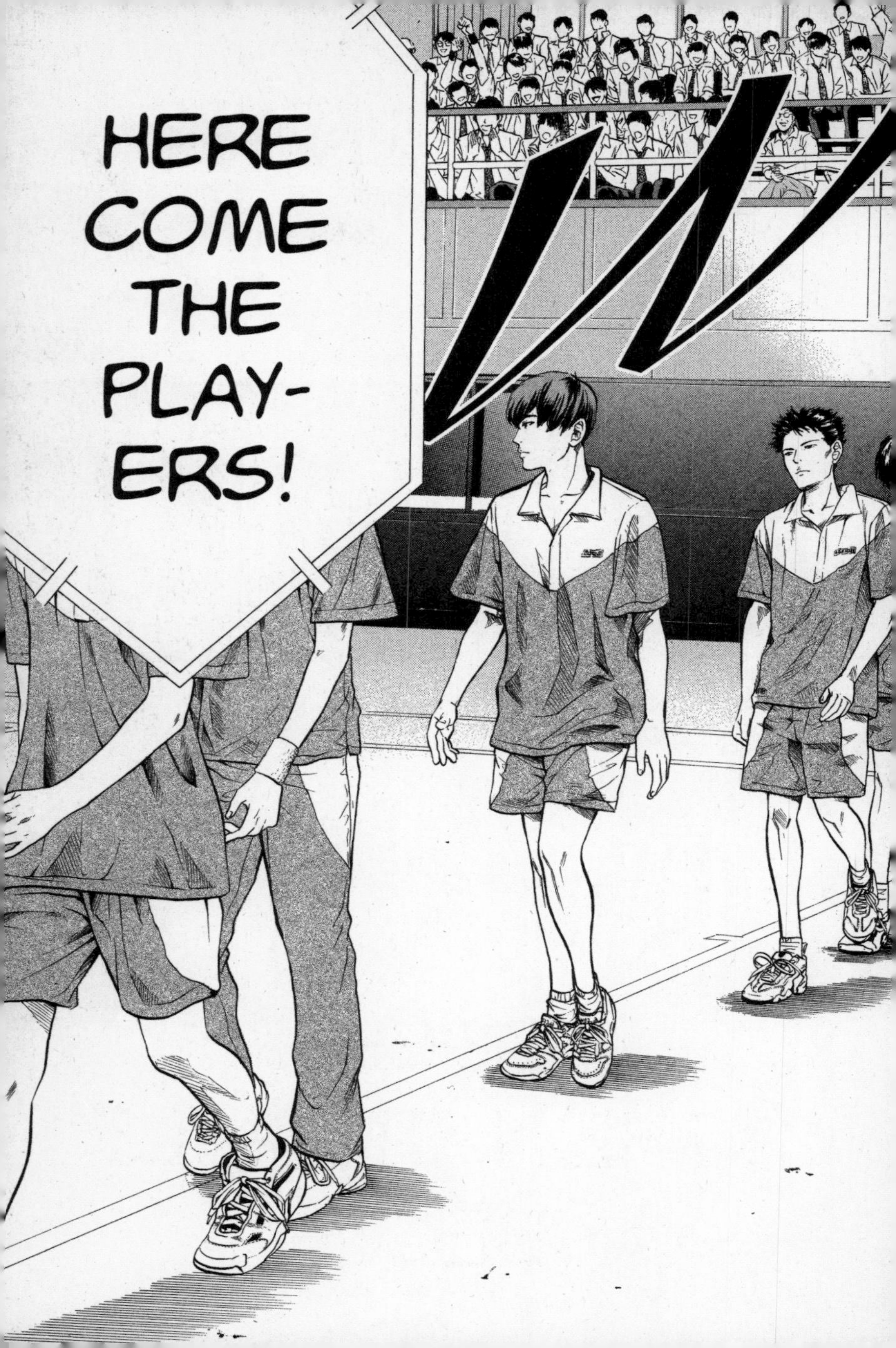
HERE COME THE PLAY- ERS!

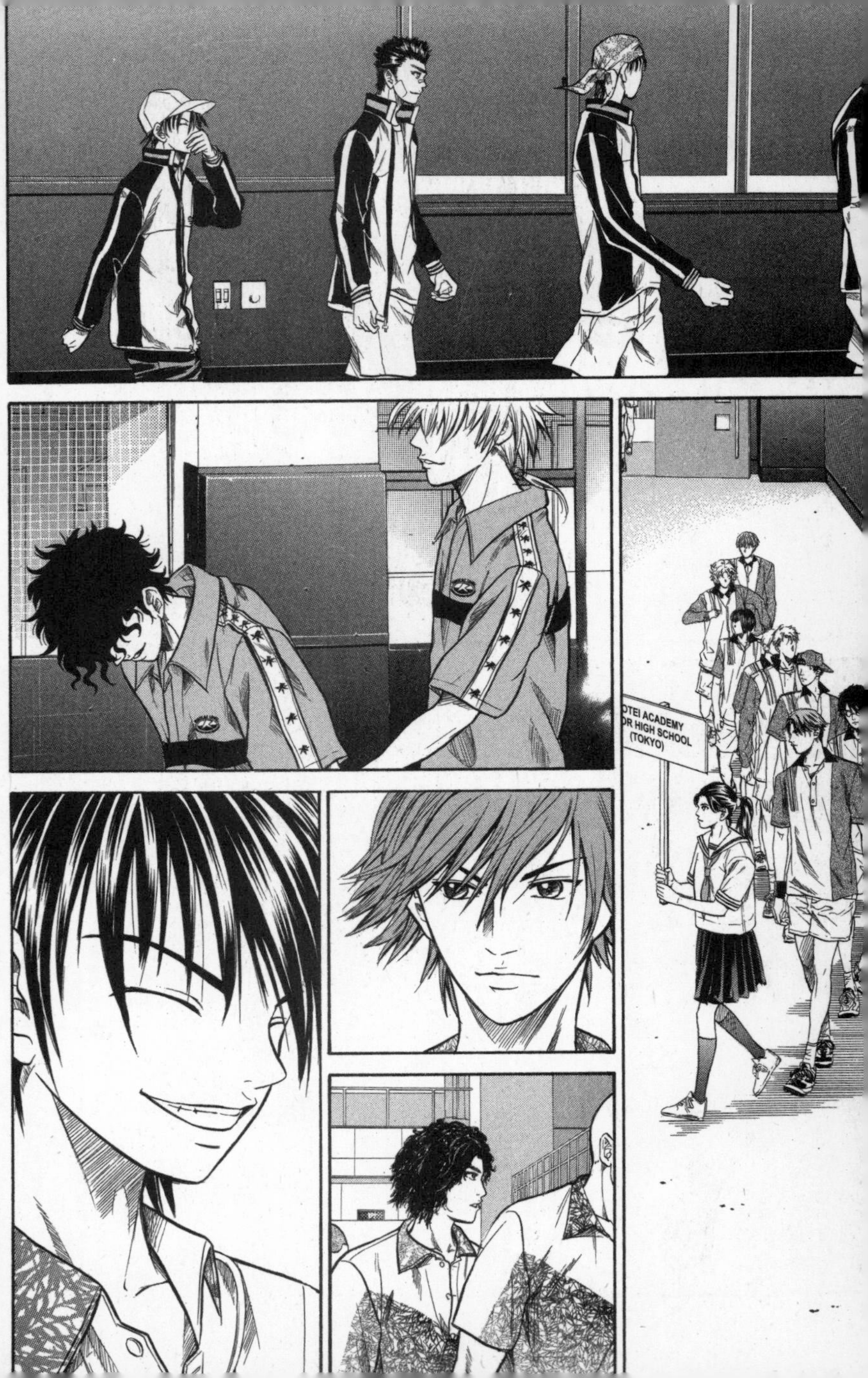
OTEI ACADEMY
OR HIGH SCHOOL
(TOKYO)

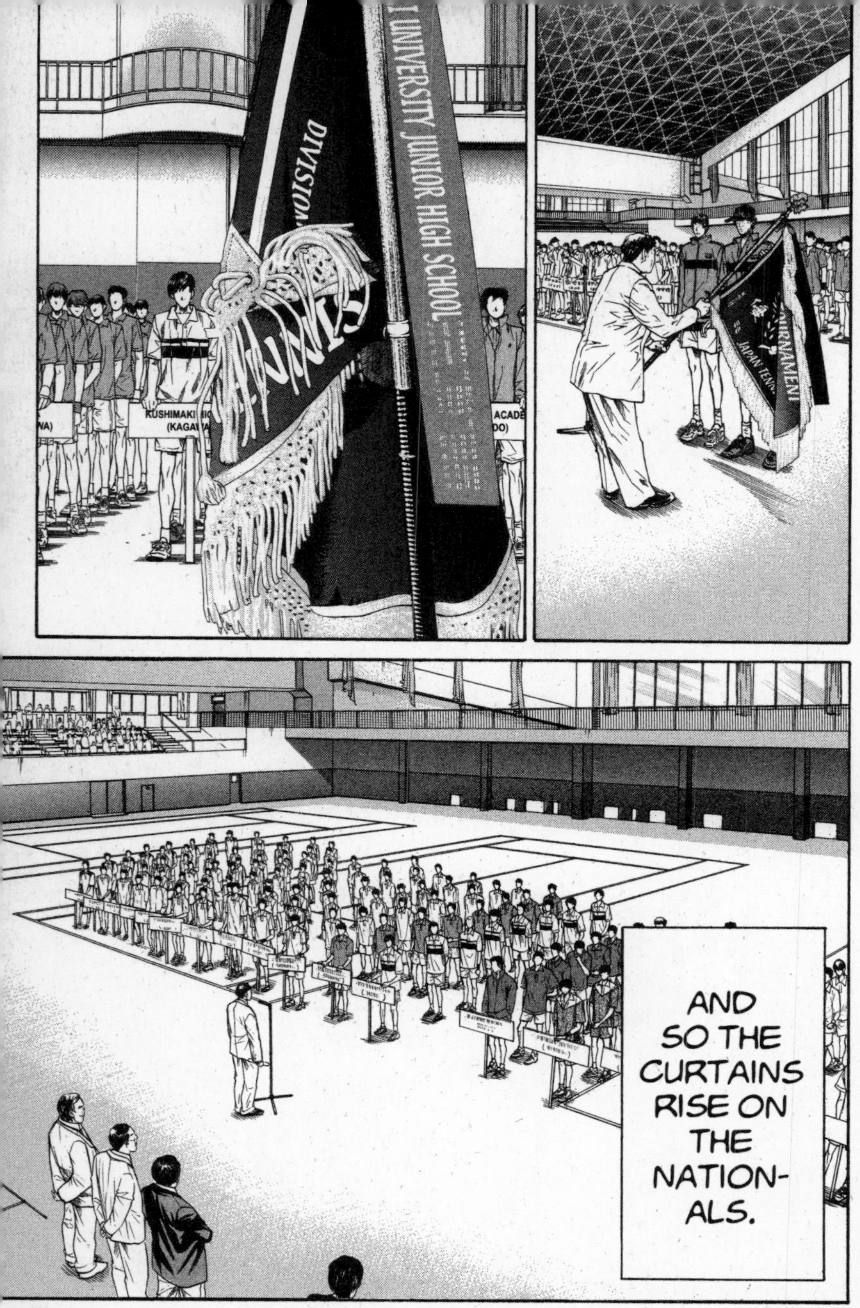
UNIVERSITY JUNIOR HIGH SCHOOL
AND SO THE CURTAINS RISE ON THE NATION-ALS.

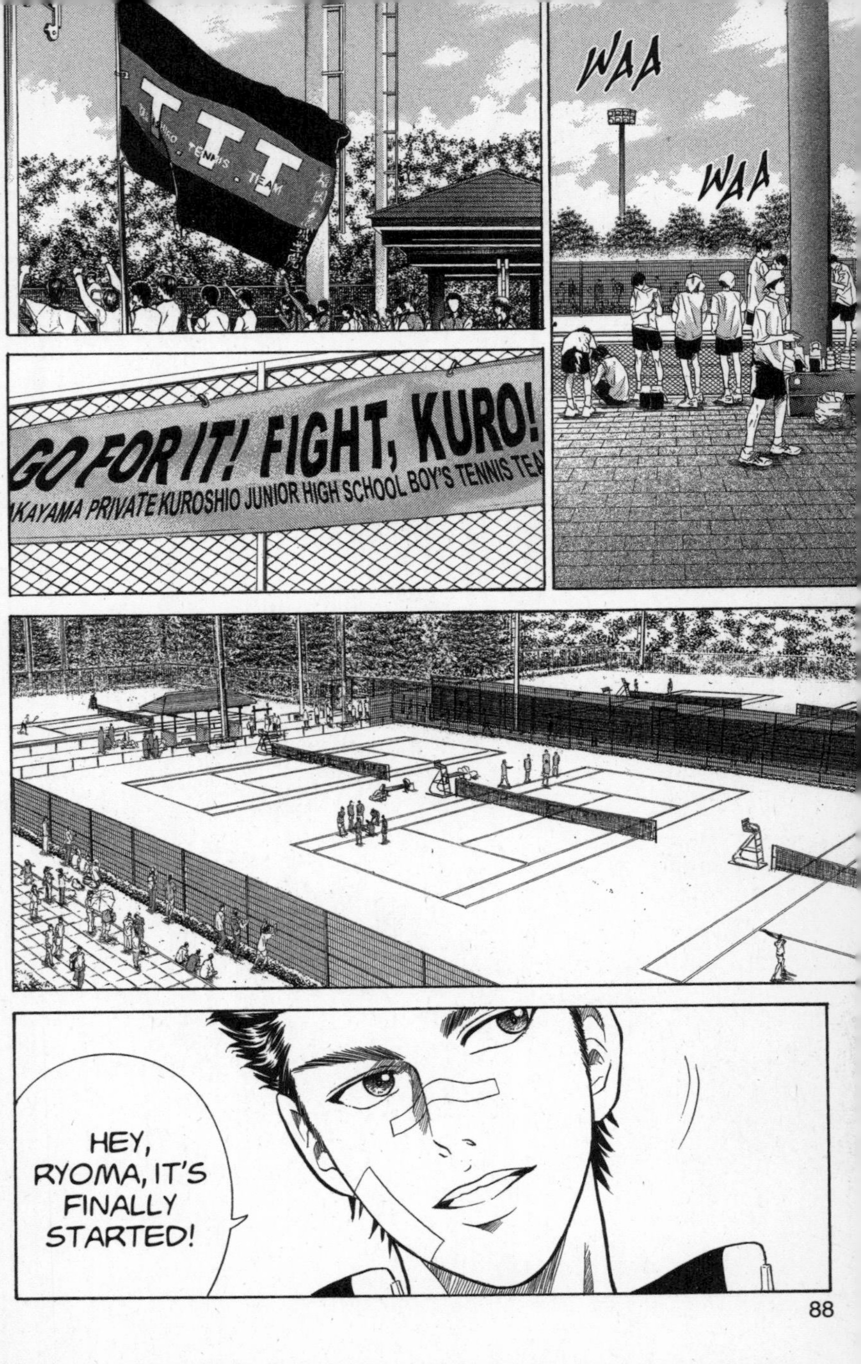
WAA
WAA
T.T.T.
GO FOR IT! FIGHT, KURO!
KAYAMA PRIVATE KUROSHIO JUNIOR HIGH SCHOOL BOY'S TENNIS TEA
HEY, RYOMA, IT'S FINALLY STARTED!

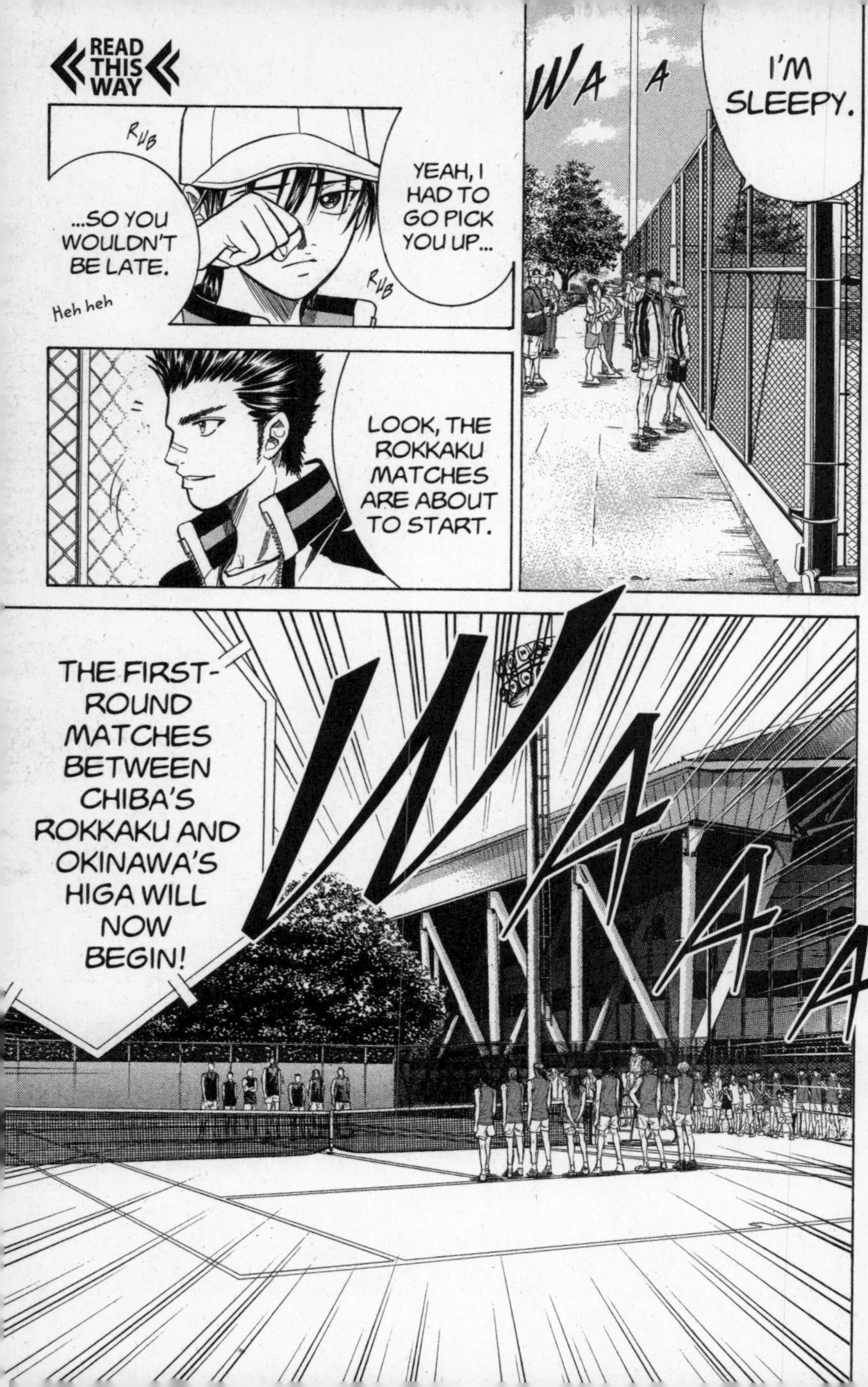
READ THIS WAY
WA A
I'M SLEEPY.
RUB
YEAH, I HAD TO GO PICK YOU UP...
...SO YOU WOULDN'T BE LATE.
RUB
Heh heh
LOOK, THE ROKKAKU MATCHES ARE ABOUT TO START.
THE FIRST-ROUND MATCHES BETWEEN CHIBA'S ROKKAKU AND OKINAWA'S HIGA WILL NOW BEGIN!
WAAAA

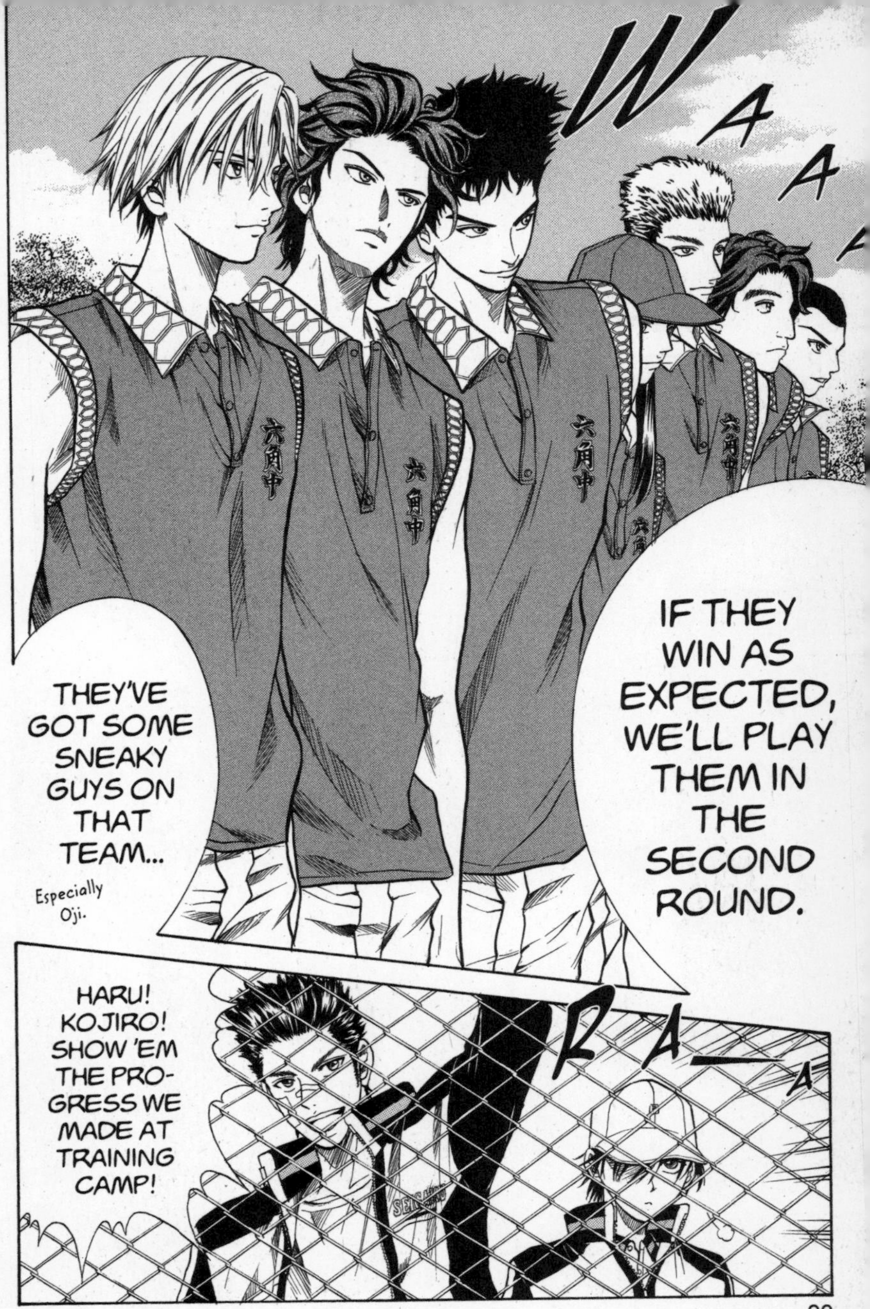
WAAA
六角中
IF THEY WIN AS EXPECTED, WE'LL PLAY THEM IN THE SECOND ROUND.
THEY'VE GOT SOME SNEAKY GUYS ON THAT TEAM...
Especially Oji.
RA—A
HARU! KOJIRO! SHOW 'EM THE PRO-GRESS WE MADE AT TRAINING CAMP!

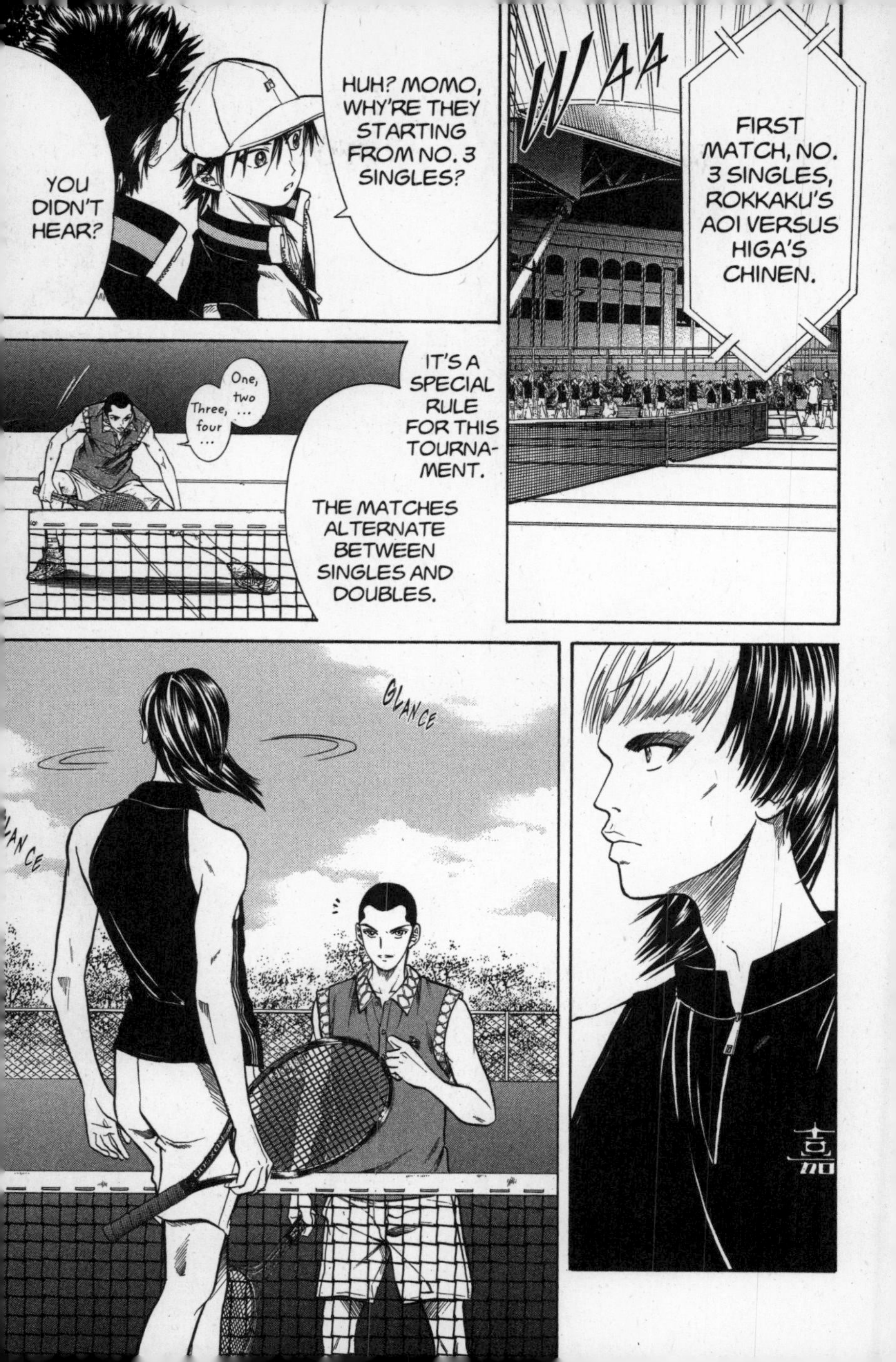

WAA
FIRST MATCH, NO. 3 SINGLES, ROKKAKU'S AOI VERSUS HIGA'S CHINEN.
HUH? MOMO, WHY'RE THEY STARTING FROM NO. 3 SINGLES?
YOU DIDN'T HEAR?
IT'S A SPECIAL RULE FOR THIS TOURNAMENT.
THE MATCHES ALTERNATE BETWEEN SINGLES AND DOUBLES.
One, two ...
Three, four ...
嘉
GLANCE
GLANCE

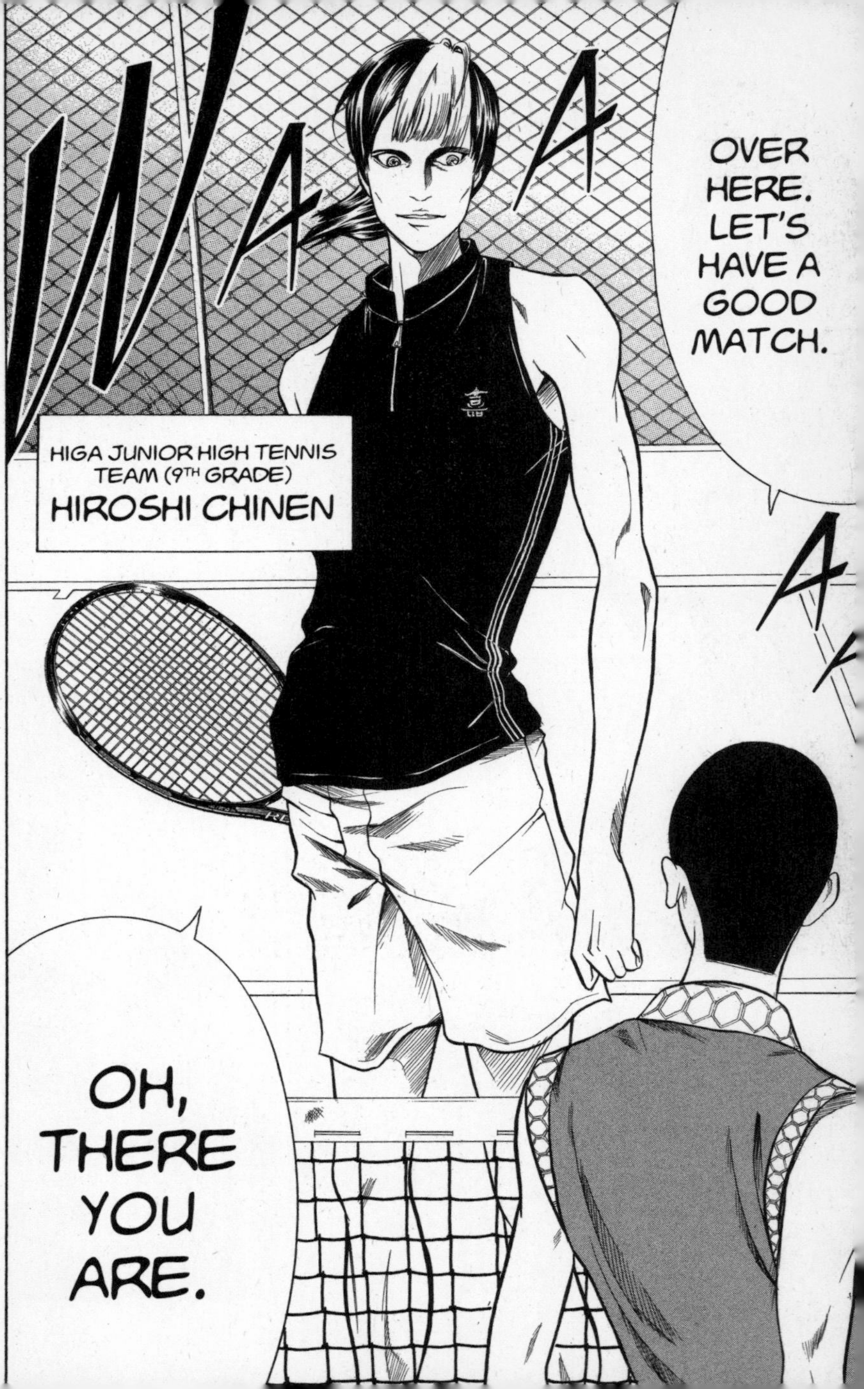
OVER HERE. LET'S HAVE A GOOD MATCH.
WAA
AA
HIGA JUNIOR HIGH TENNIS TEAM (9TH GRADE)
HIROSHI CHINEN
OH, THERE YOU ARE.

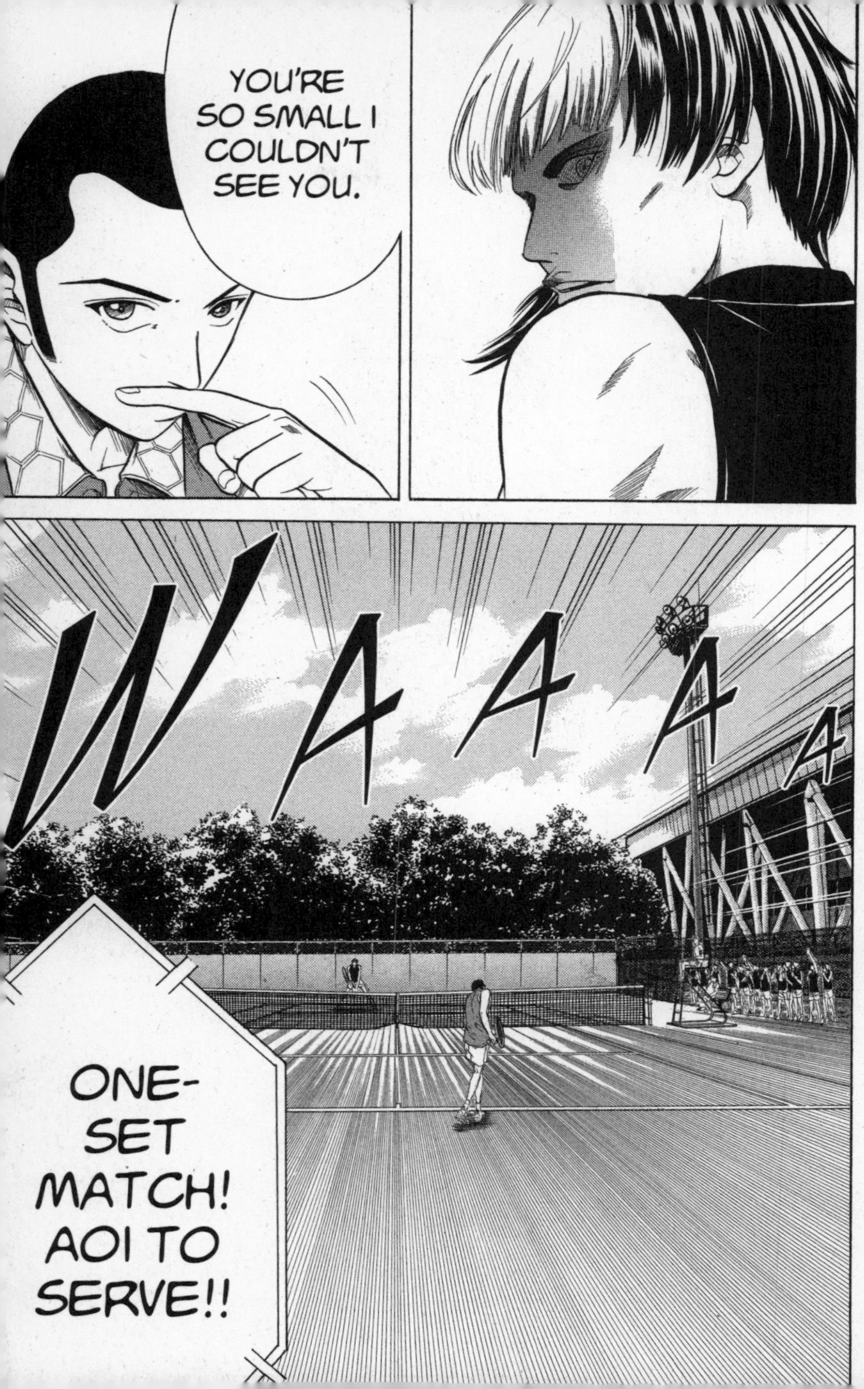
YOU'RE SO SMALL I COULDN'T SEE YOU.
WAAAA
ONE-SET MATCH! AOI TO SERVE!!

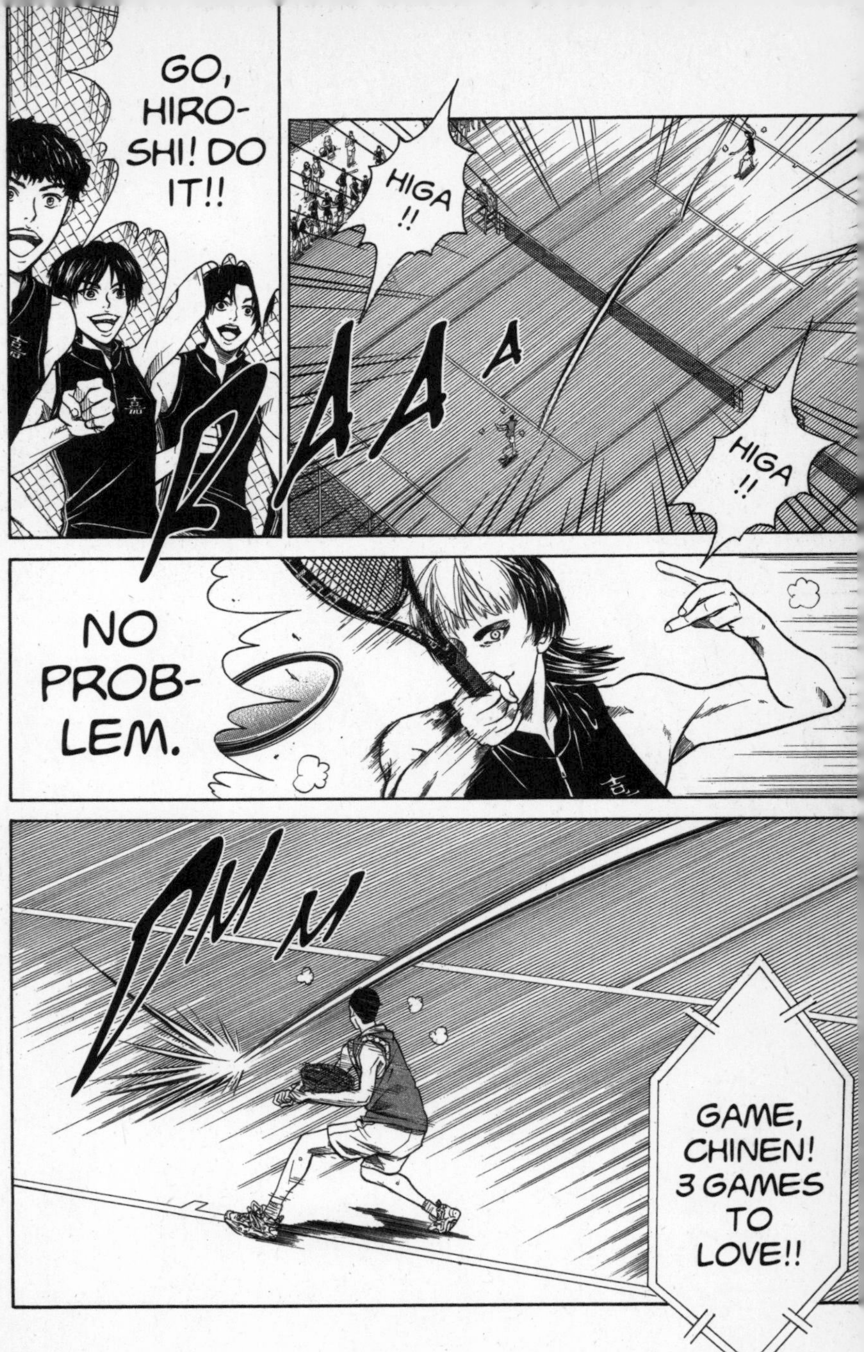
HIGA!!
HIGA!!
WAAA
GO, HIROSHI! DO IT!!
NO PROBLEM.
GAME, CHINEN! 3 GAMES TO LOVE!!

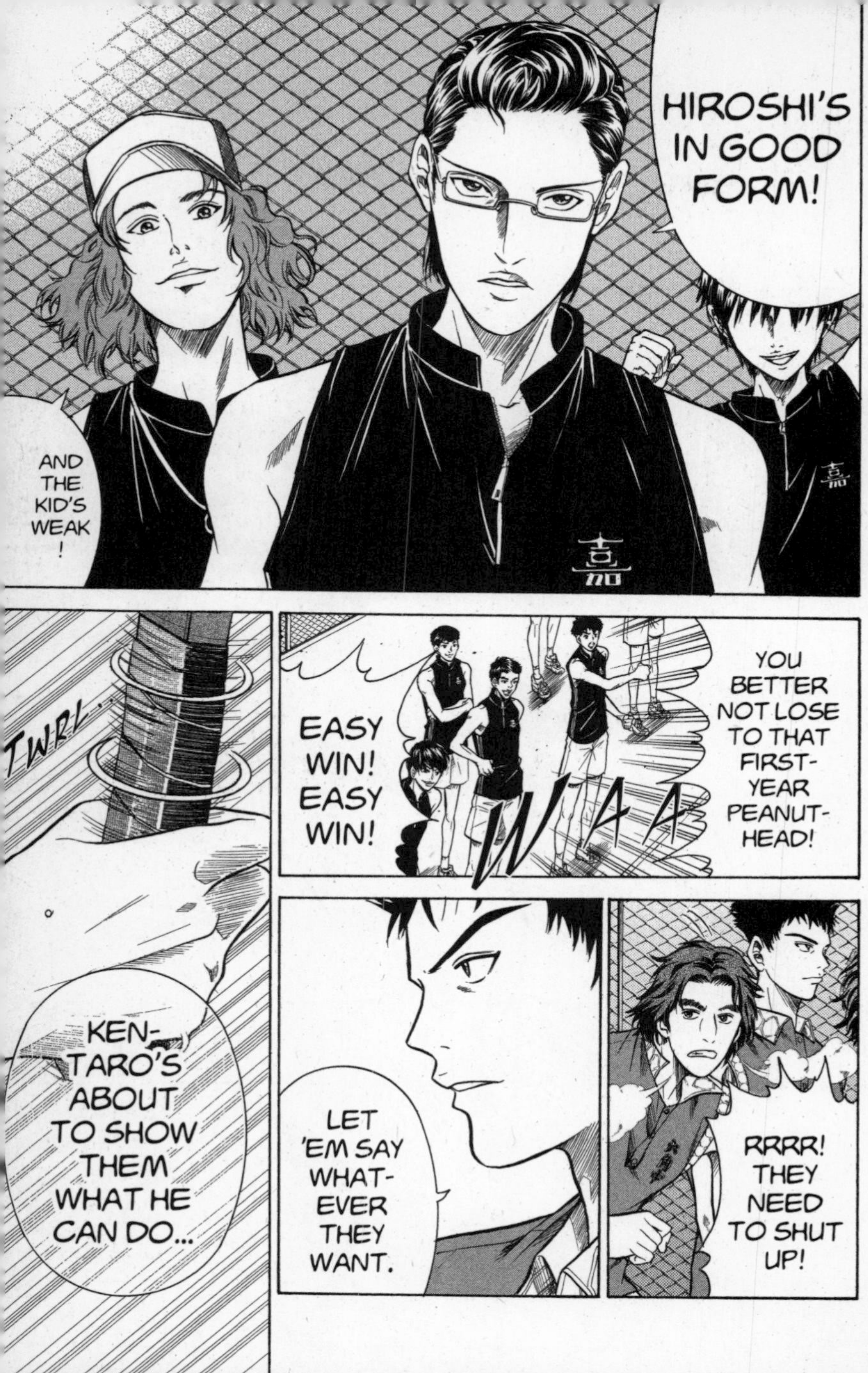
HIROSHI'S IN GOOD FORM!
AND THE KID'S WEAK!
YOU BETTER NOT LOSE TO THAT FIRST-YEAR PEANUT-HEAD!
EASY WIN! EASY WIN!
WAA
RRRR! THEY NEED TO SHUT UP!
LET 'EM SAY WHATEVER THEY WANT.
TWRL...
KENTARO'S ABOUT TO SHOW THEM WHAT HE CAN DO...

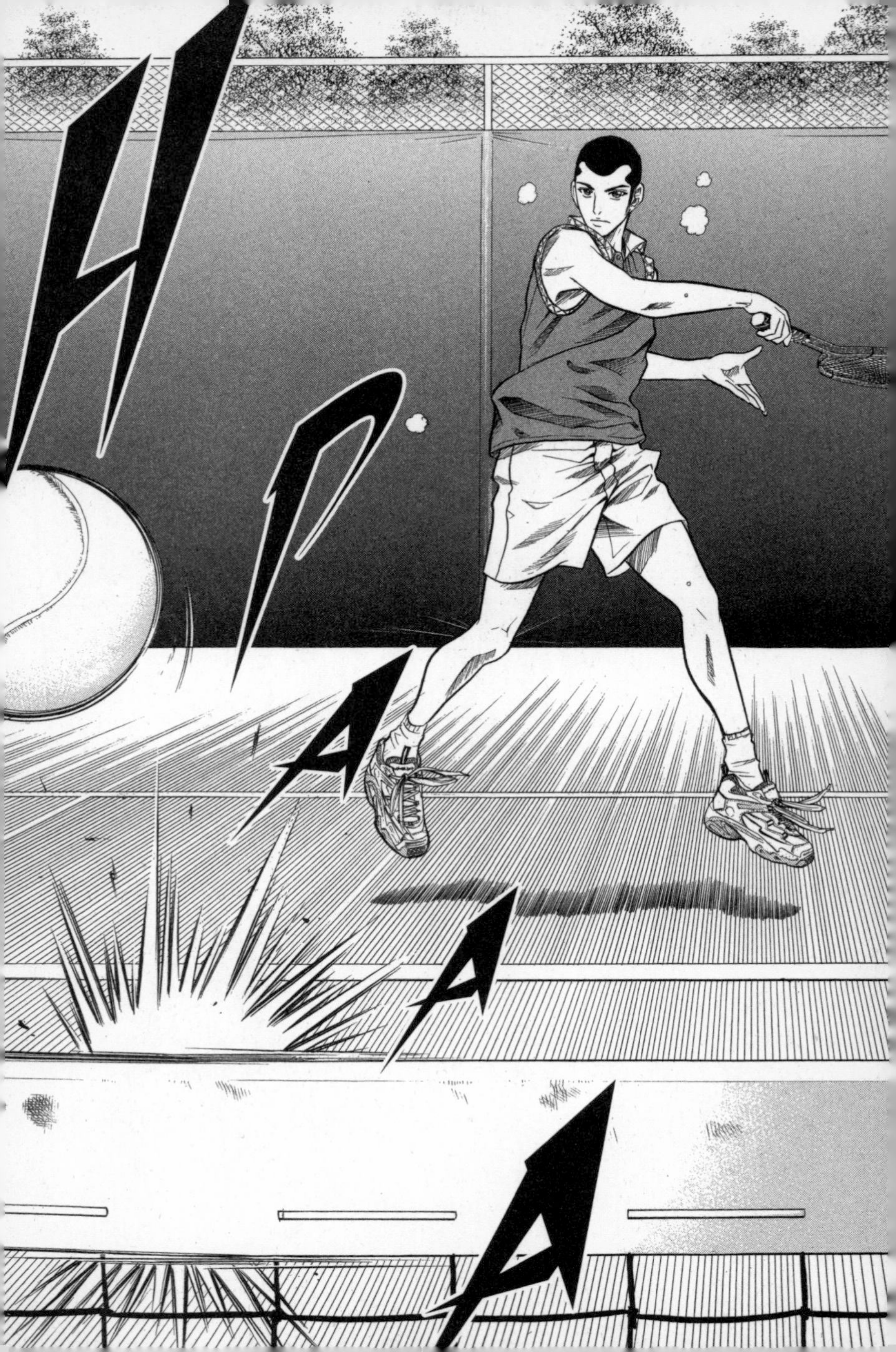

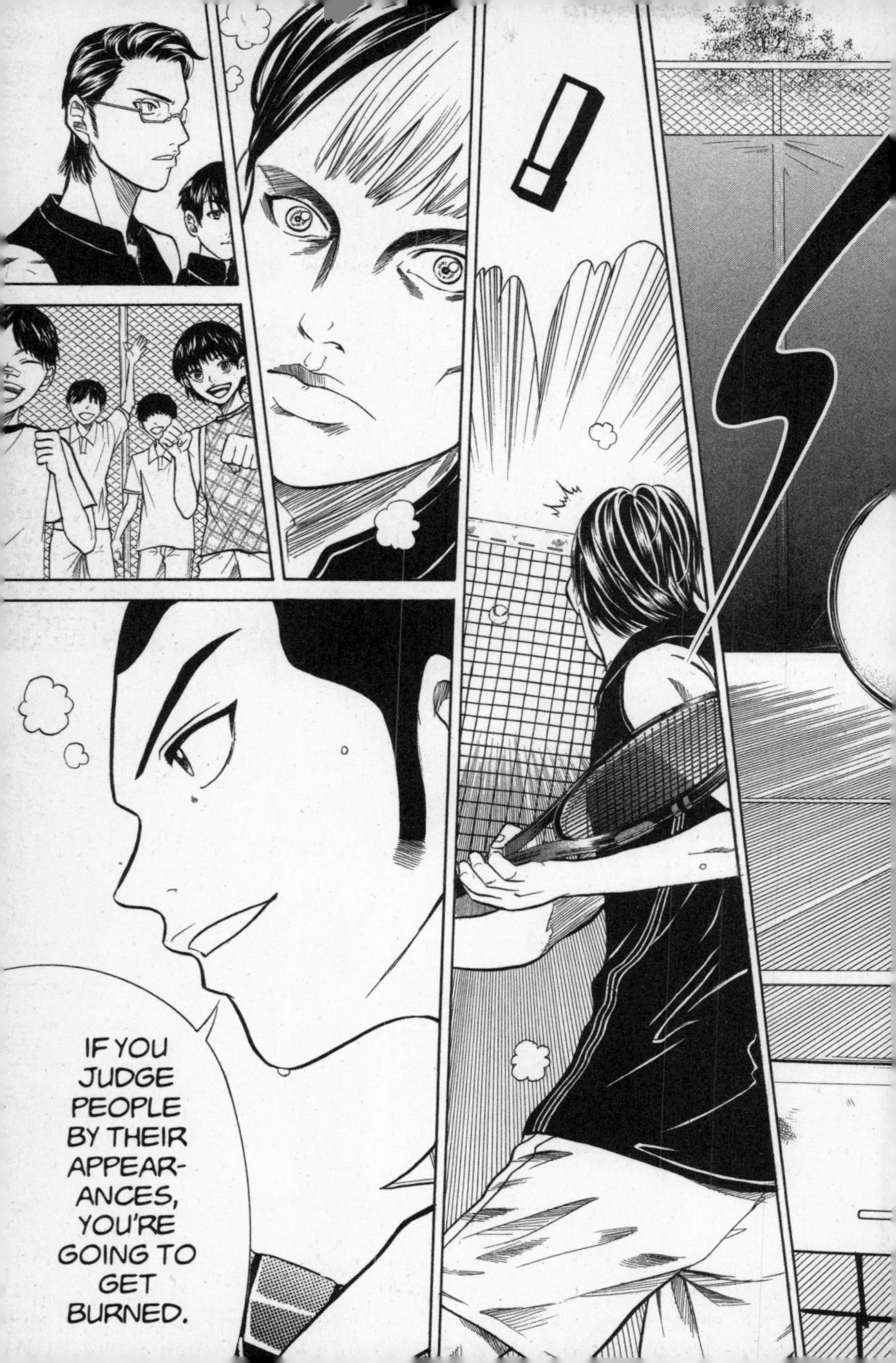
!
IF YOU JUDGE PEOPLE BY THEIR APPEARANCES, YOU'RE GOING TO GET BURNED.

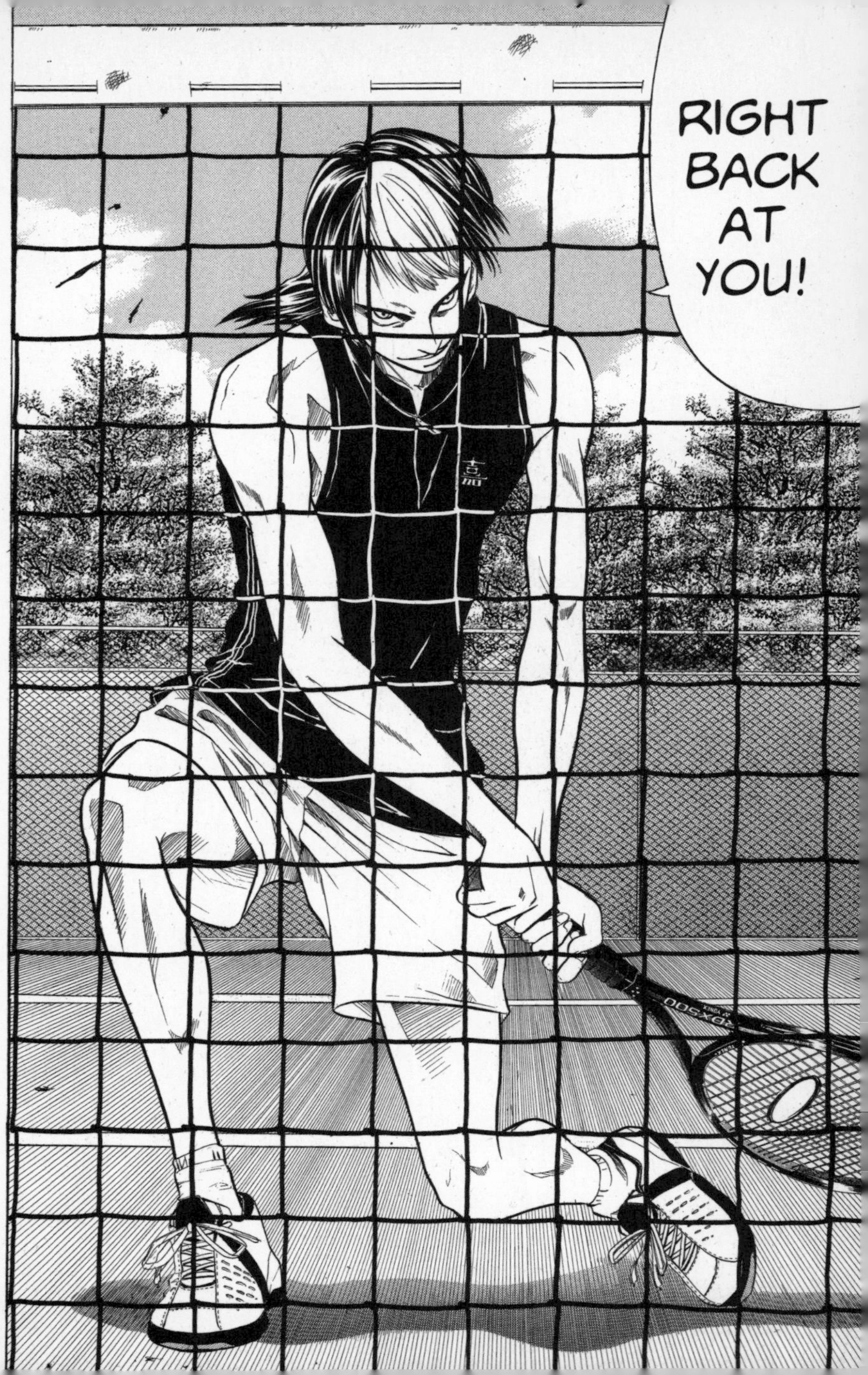
RIGHT BACK AT YOU!

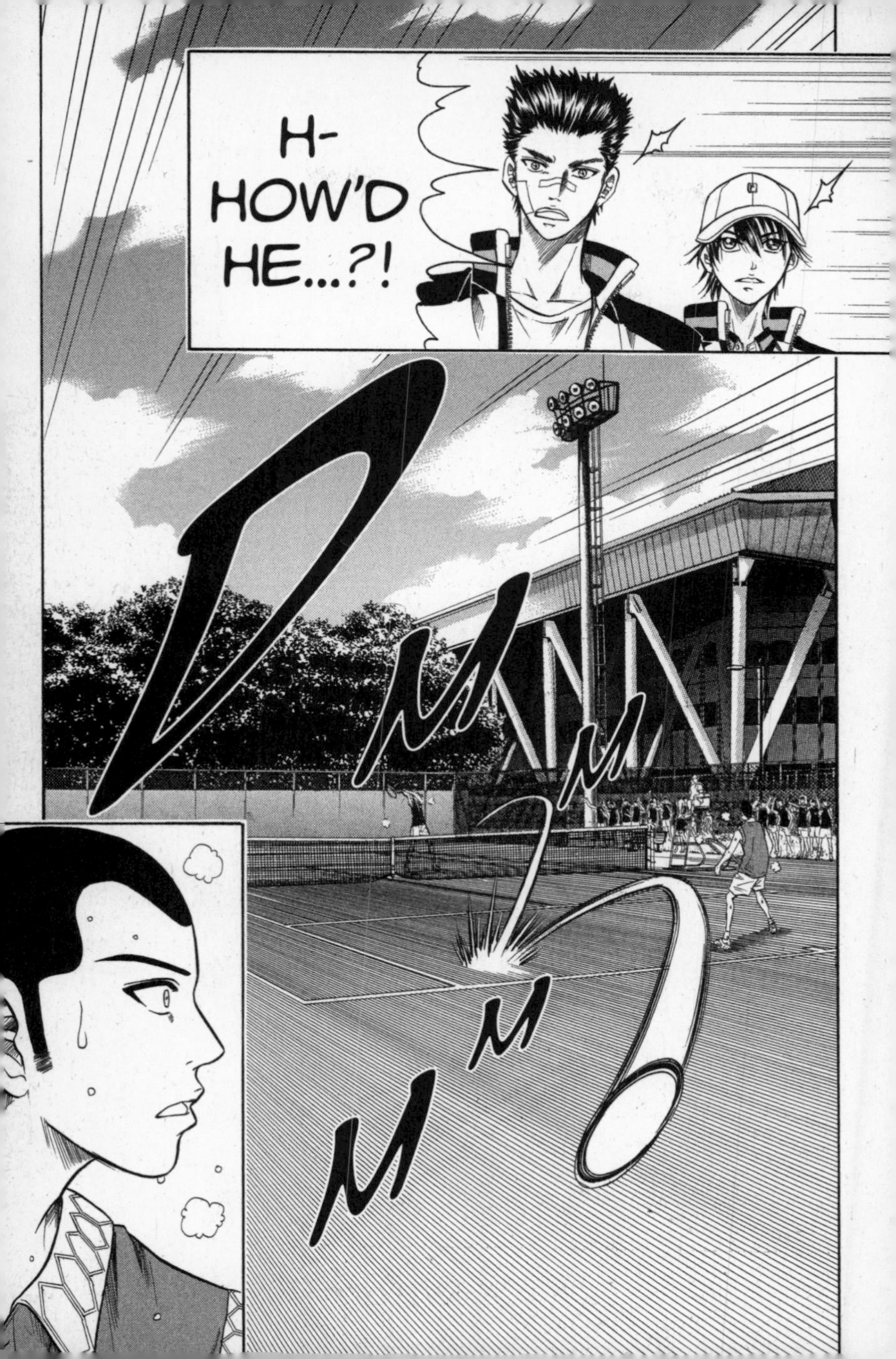
H-HOW'D HE...?!

テニスの王子様
THE PRINCE OF TENNIS

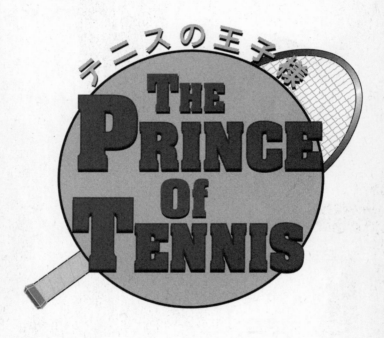

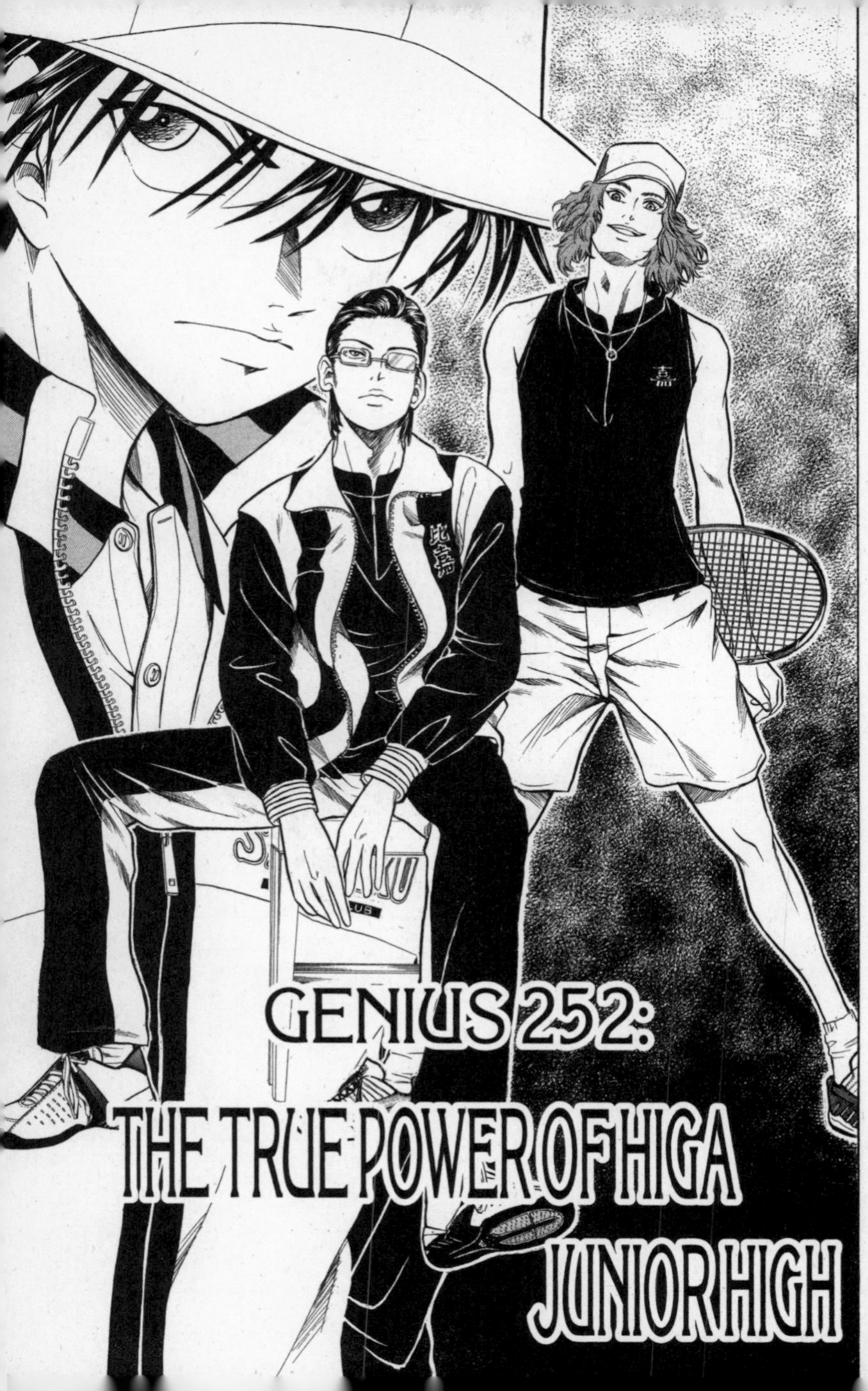
GENIUS 252:
THE TRUE POWER OF HIGA JUNIOR HIGH

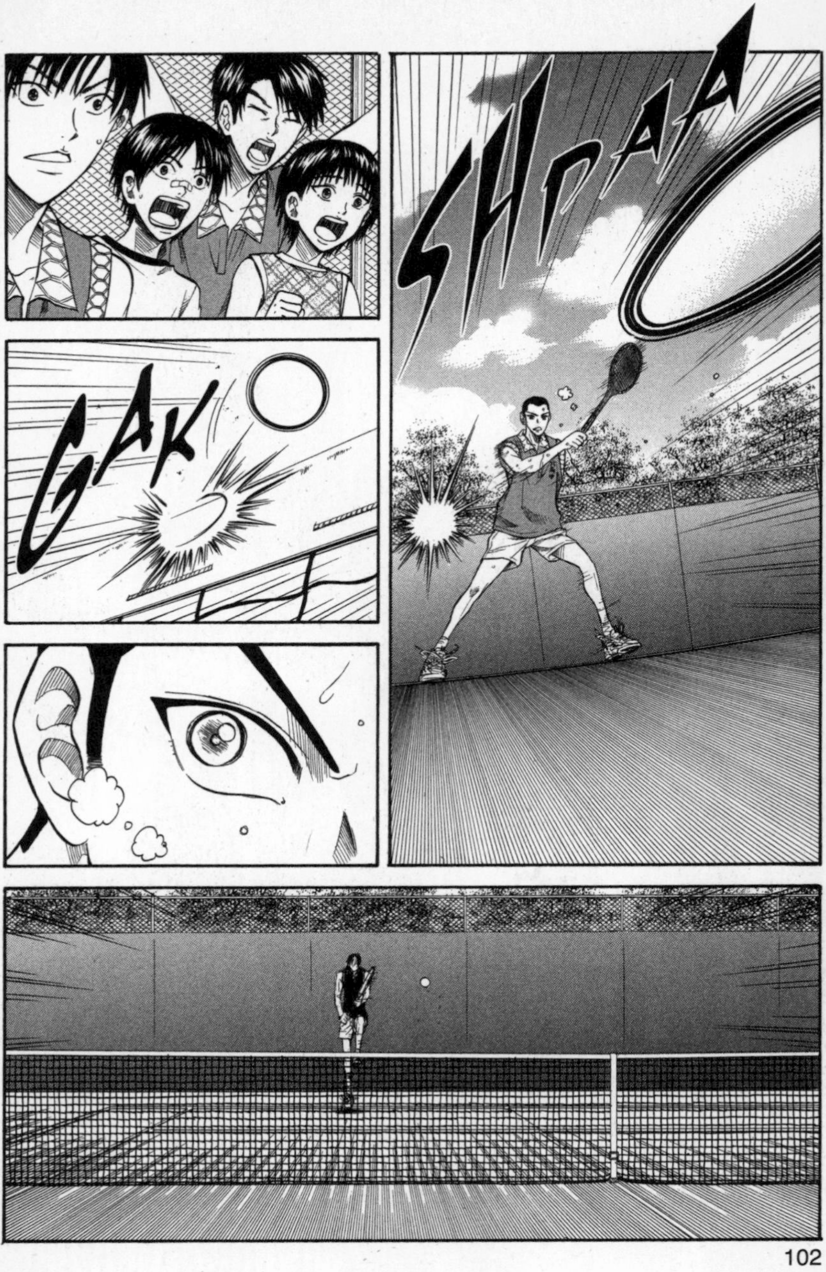
SHDAA
GAK

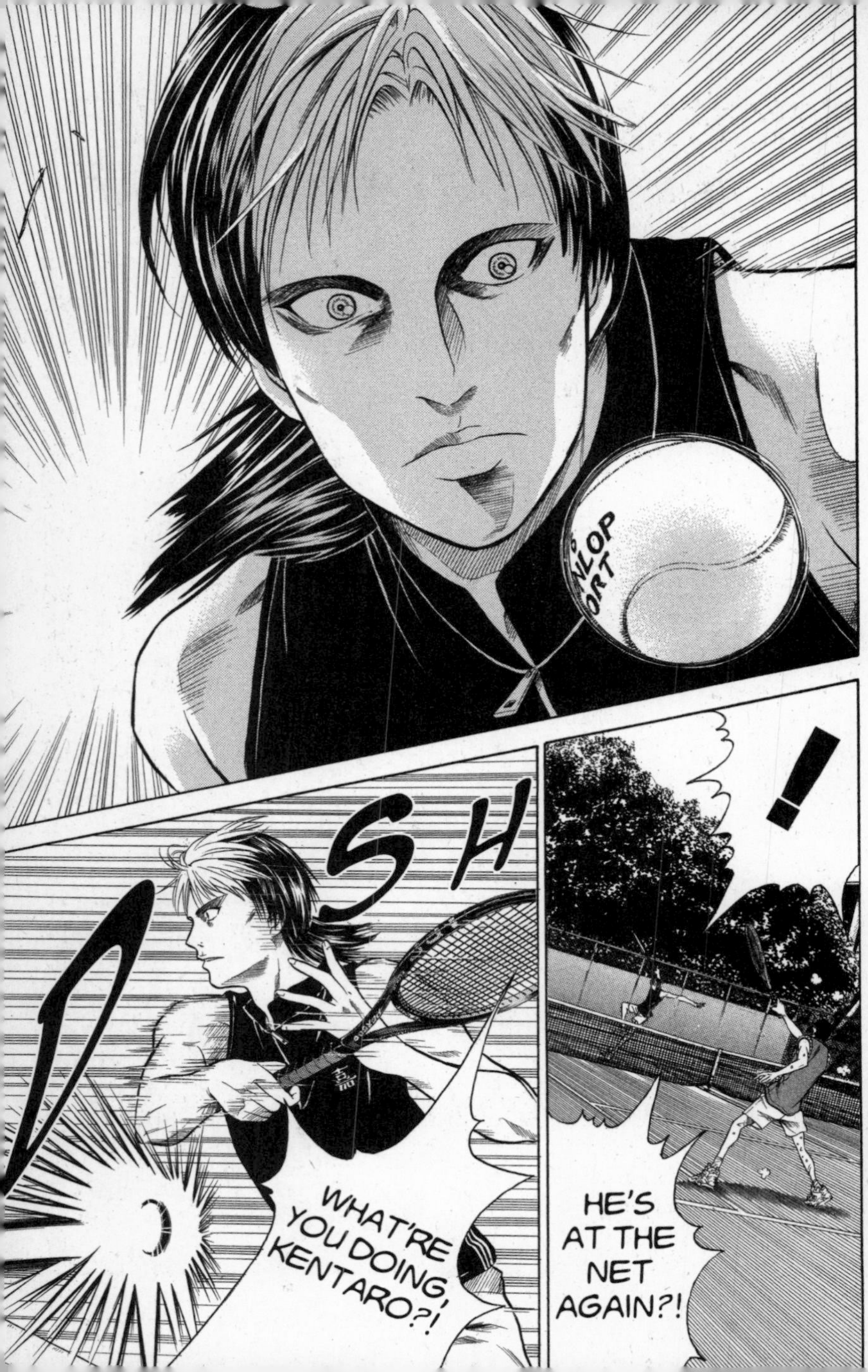
!
HE'S AT THE NET AGAIN?!
SH
WHAT'RE YOU DOING, KENTARO?!

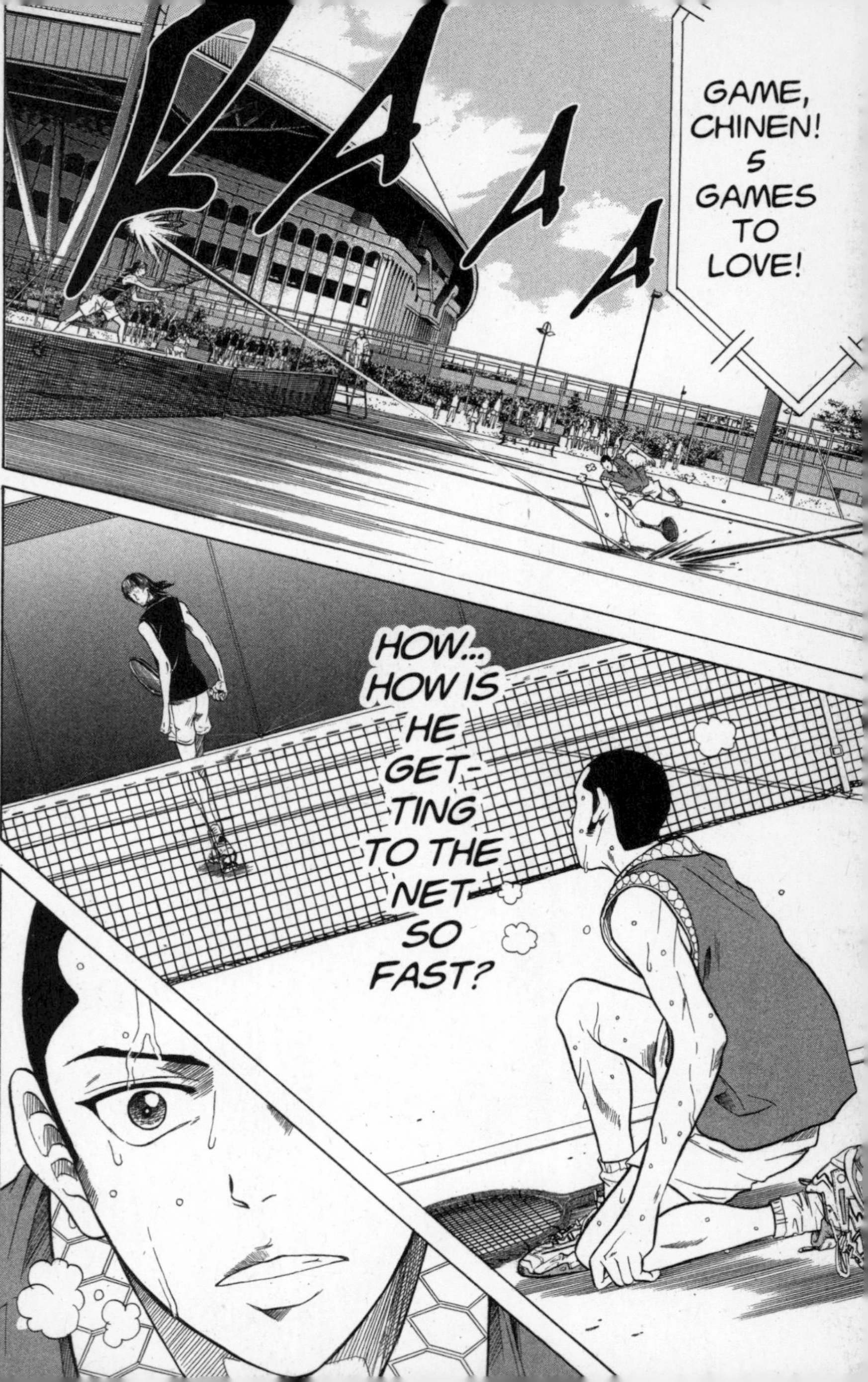
GAME, CHINEN! 5 GAMES TO LOVE!
KAAAA
HOW... HOW IS HE GET-TING TO THE NET SO FAST?

READ THIS WAY

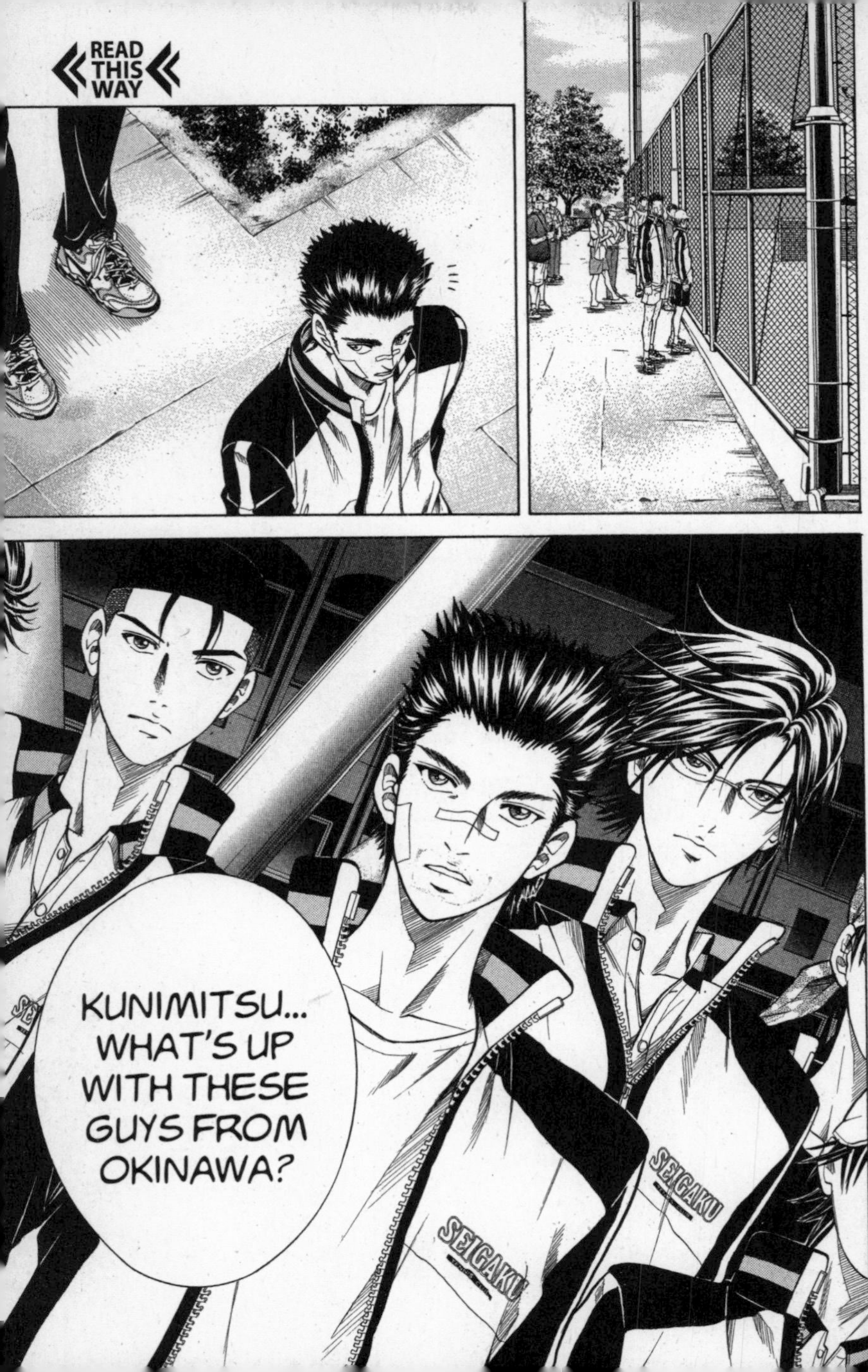
KUNIMITSU... WHAT'S UP WITH THESE GUYS FROM OKINAWA?

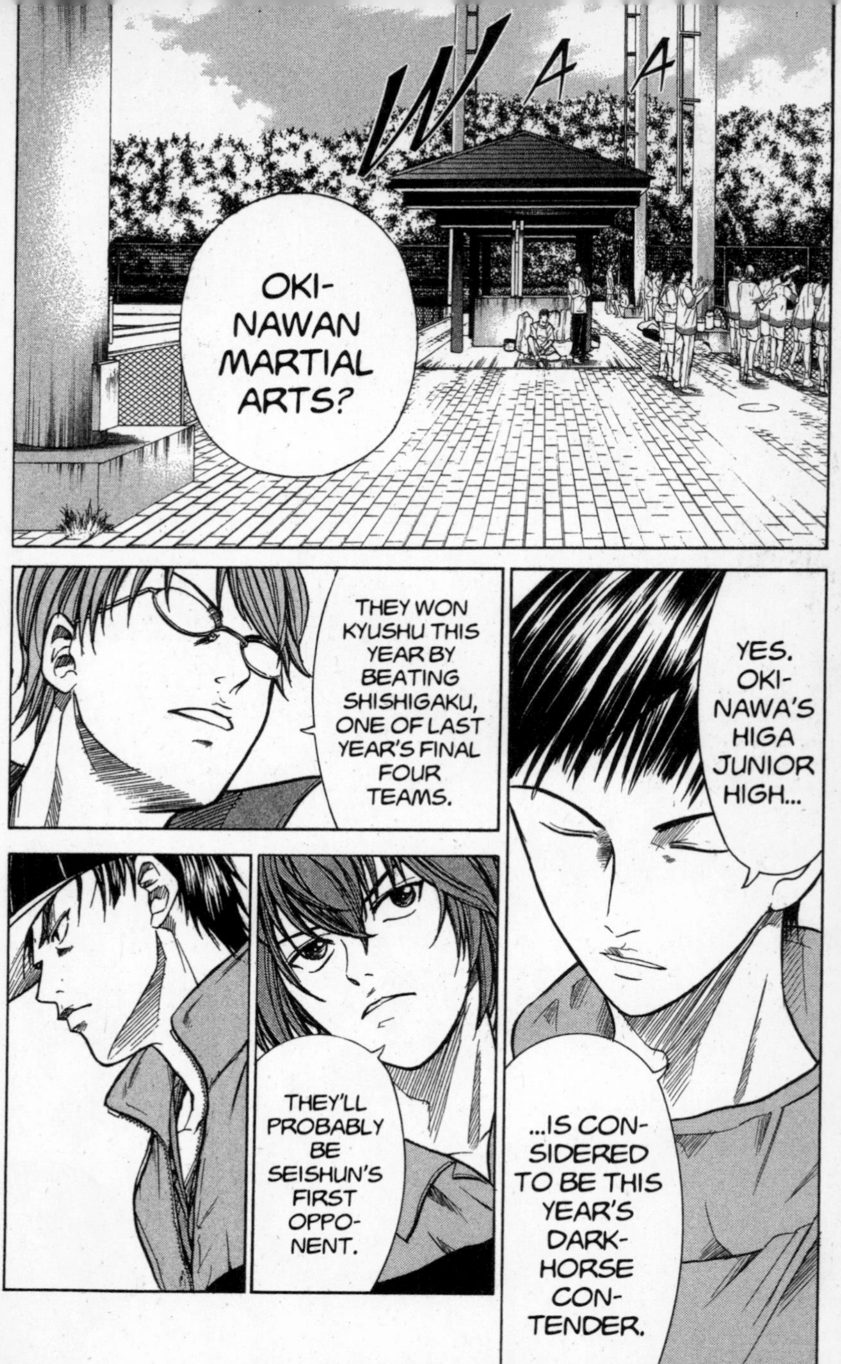
WAA
OKI-NAWAN MARTIAL ARTS?
YES. OKI-NAWA'S HIGA JUNIOR HIGH...
...IS CON-SIDERED TO BE THIS YEAR'S DARK-HORSE CON-TENDER.
THEY WON KYUSHU THIS YEAR BY BEATING SHISHIGAKU, ONE OF LAST YEAR'S FINAL FOUR TEAMS.
THEY'LL PROBABLY BE SEISHUN'S FIRST OPPO-NENT.

READ THIS WAY

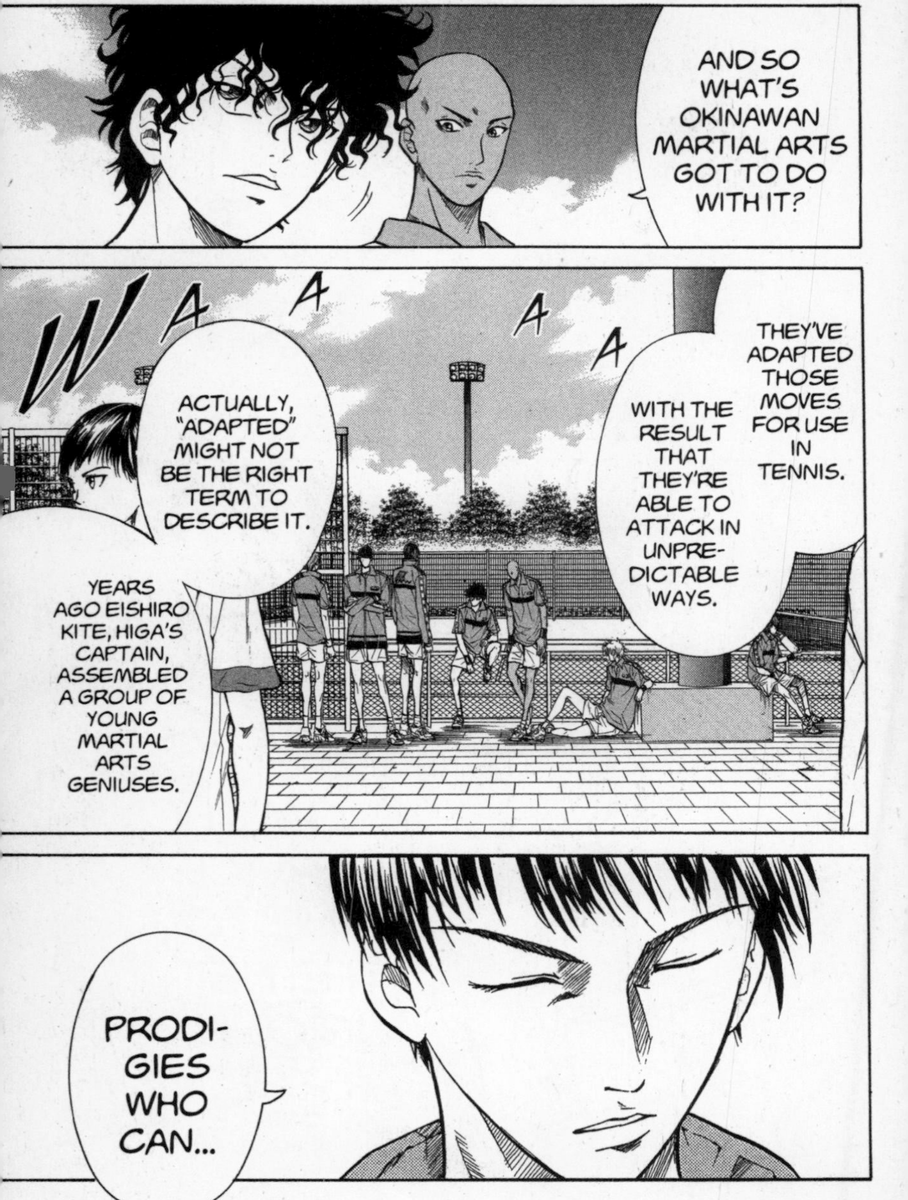
AND SO WHAT'S OKINAWAN MARTIAL ARTS GOT TO DO WITH IT?
THEY'VE ADAPTED THOSE MOVES FOR USE IN TENNIS.
WITH THE RESULT THAT THEY'RE ABLE TO ATTACK IN UNPRE-DICTABLE WAYS.
WAAAA
ACTUALLY, "ADAPTED" MIGHT NOT BE THE RIGHT TERM TO DESCRIBE IT.
YEARS AGO EISHIRO KITE, HIGA'S CAPTAIN, ASSEMBLED A GROUP OF YOUNG MARTIAL ARTS GENIUSES.
PRODI-GIES WHO CAN...

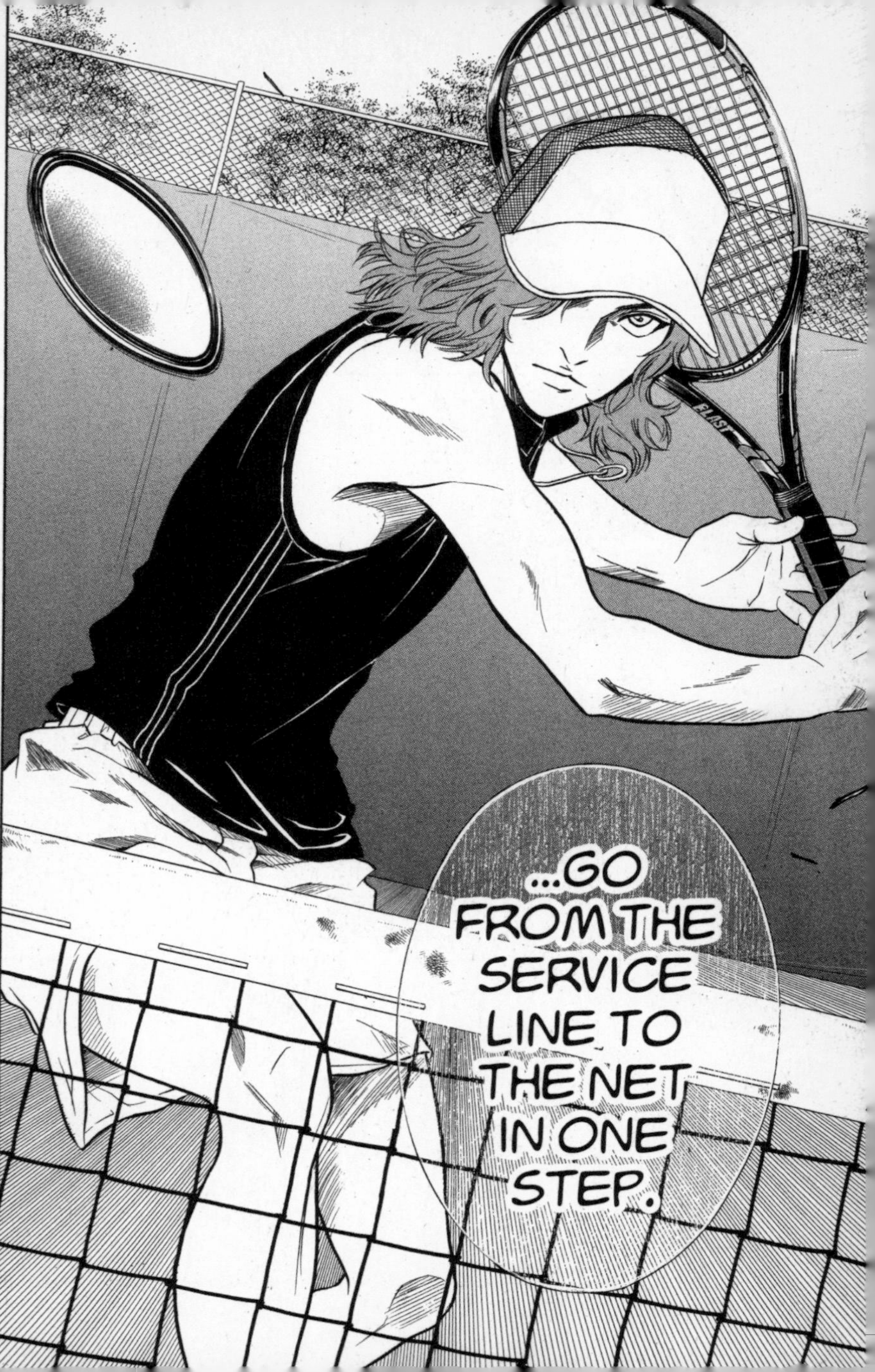
...GO FROM THE SERVICE LINE TO THE NET IN ONE STEP.

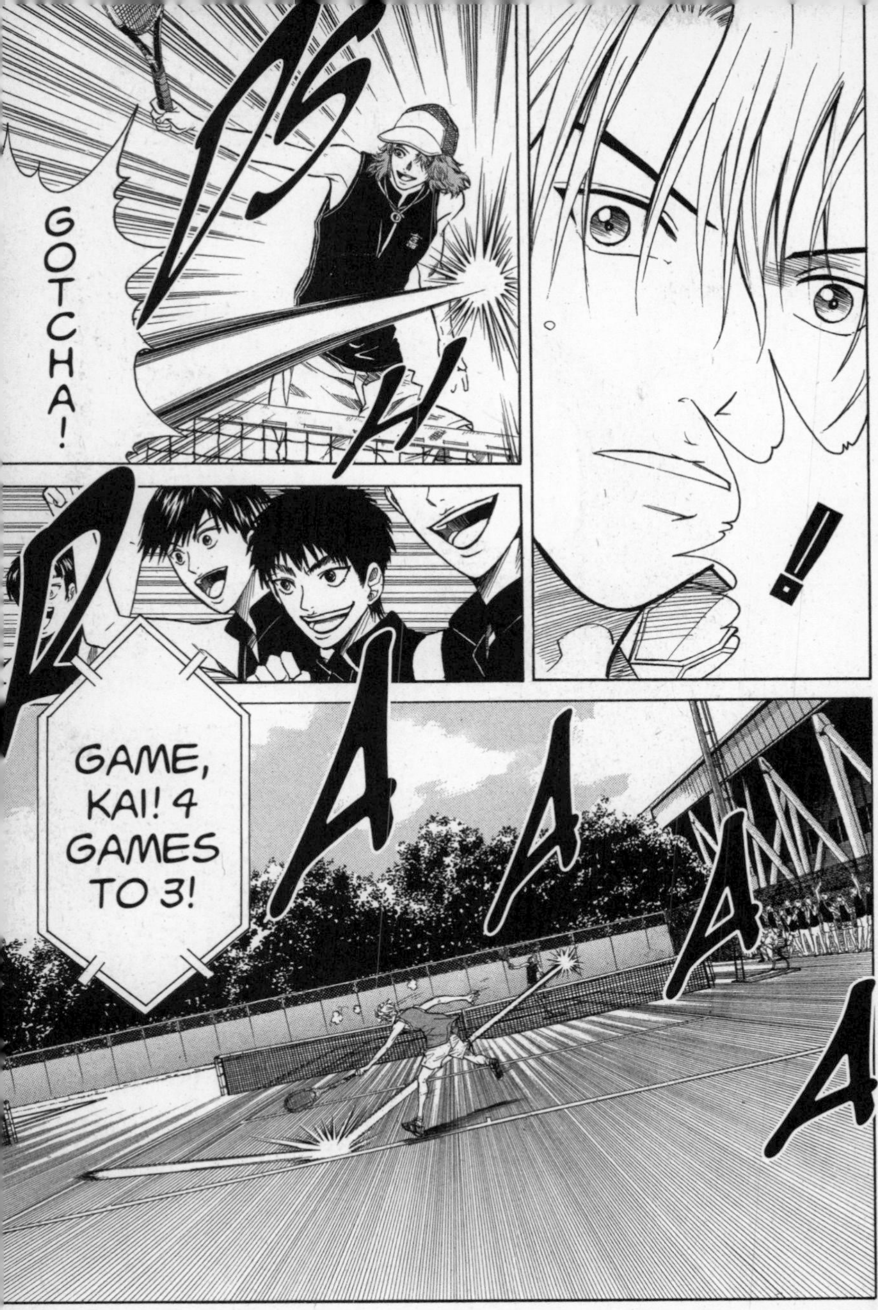
!
GOTCHA!
GAME, KAI! 4 GAMES TO 3!

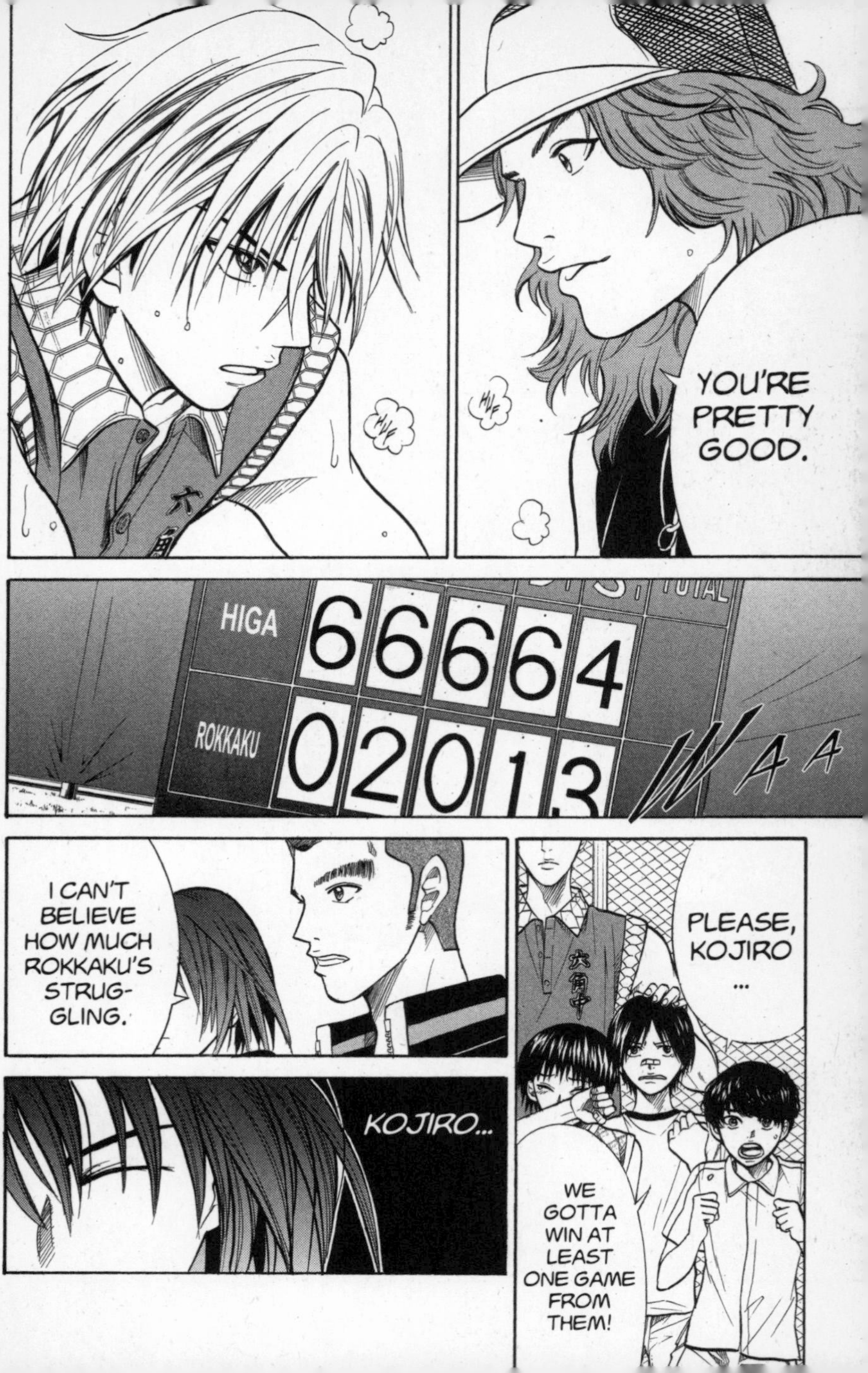
YOU'RE PRETTY GOOD.
TOTAL
HIGA 6 6 6 6 4
ROKKAKU 0 2 0 1 3
WAA
PLEASE, KOJIRO ...
WE GOTTA WIN AT LEAST ONE GAME FROM THEM!
I CAN'T BELIEVE HOW MUCH ROKKAKU'S STRUG-GLING.
KOJIRO...

READ THIS WAY

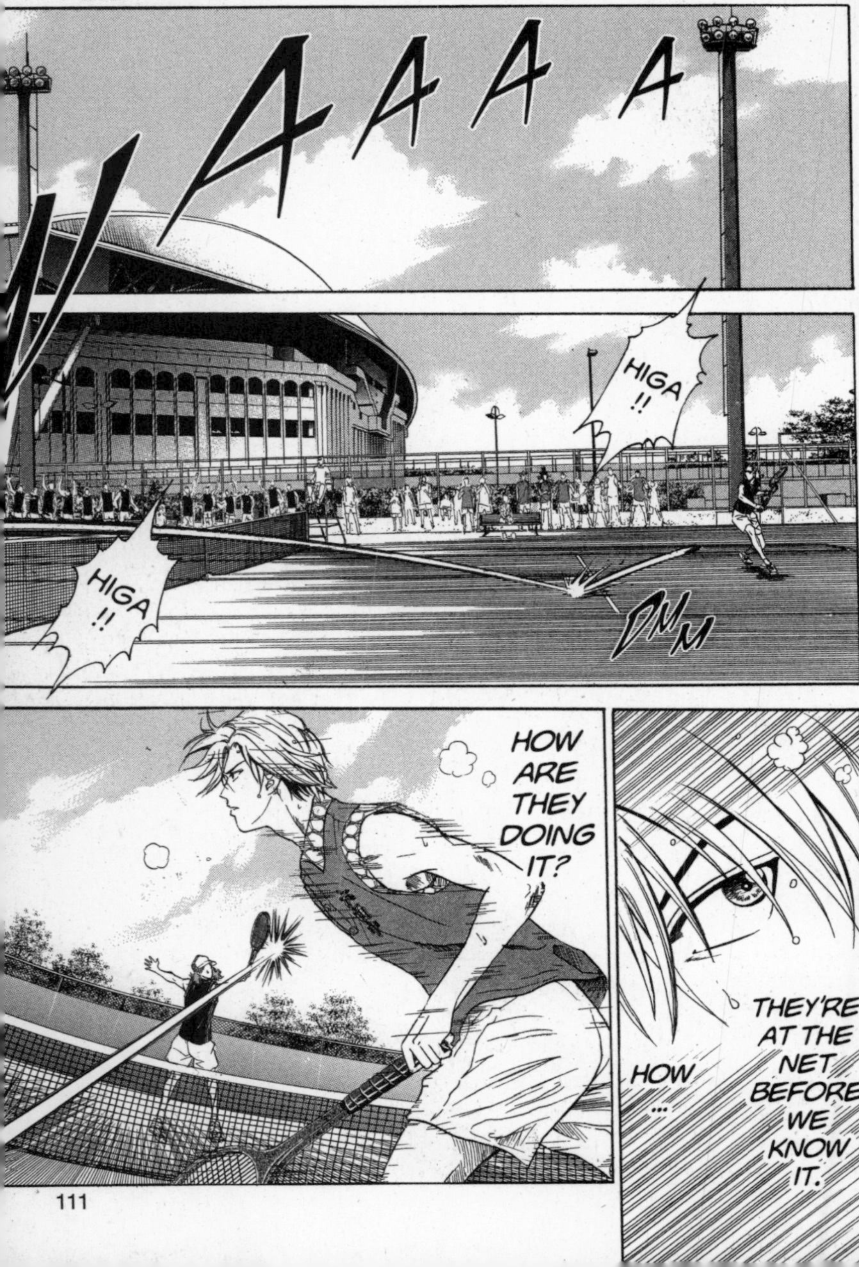

WAAAAA
HIGA!!
HIGA!!
DMM
THEY'RE AT THE NET BEFORE WE KNOW IT.
HOW...
HOW ARE THEY DOING IT?

... SHUKU-CHI-HOU.

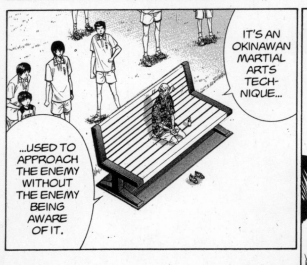

IT'S AN OKINAWAN MARTIAL ARTS TECH-NIQUE...

...USED TO APPROACH THE ENEMY WITHOUT THE ENEMY BEING AWARE OF IT.

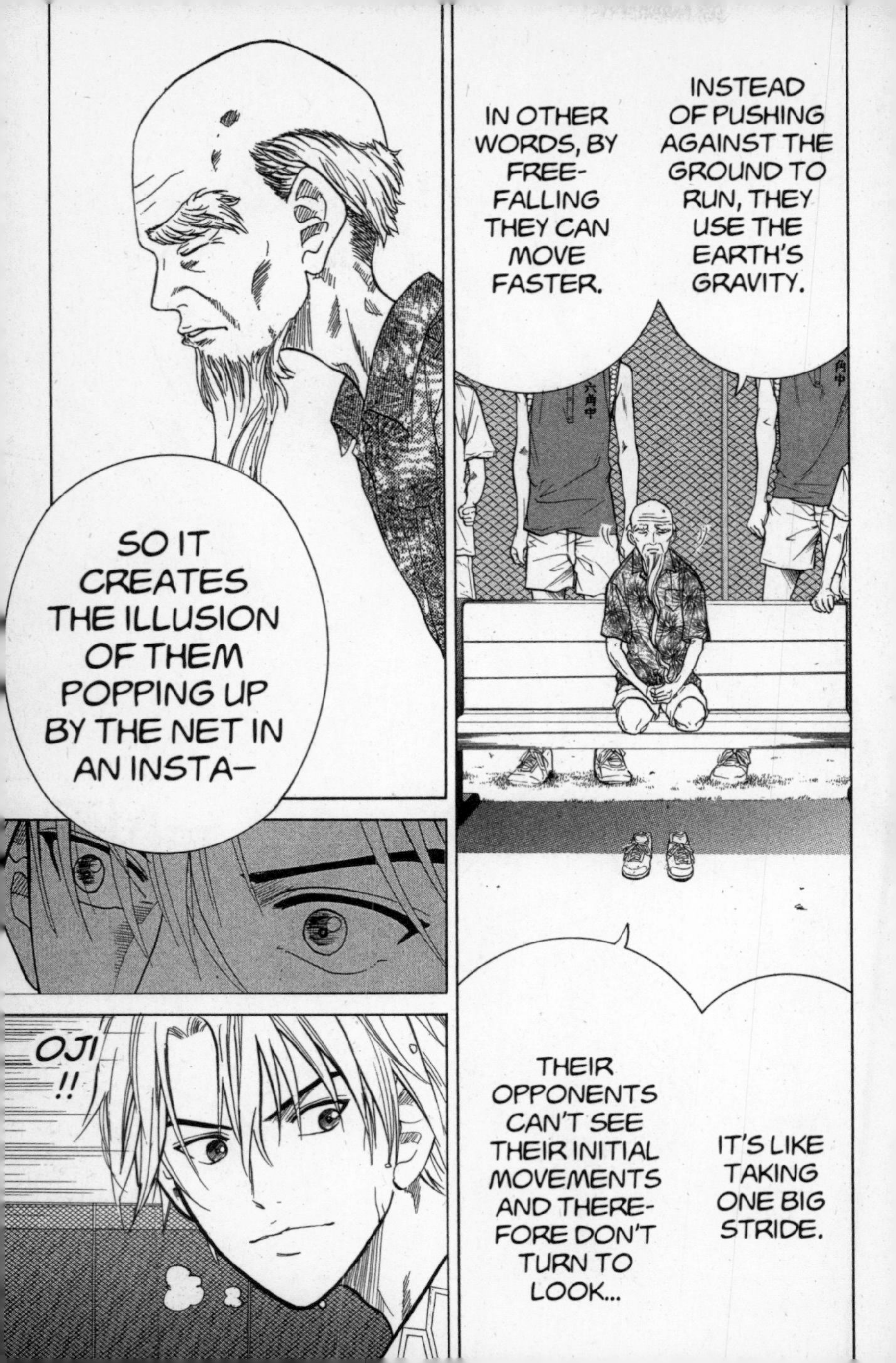
INSTEAD OF PUSHING AGAINST THE GROUND TO RUN, THEY USE THE EARTH'S GRAVITY.
IN OTHER WORDS, BY FREE-FALLING THEY CAN MOVE FASTER.
IT'S LIKE TAKING ONE BIG STRIDE.
THEIR OPPONENTS CAN'T SEE THEIR INITIAL MOVEMENTS AND THERE-FORE DON'T TURN TO LOOK...
SO IT CREATES THE ILLUSION OF THEM POPPING UP BY THE NET IN AN INSTA–
OJI !!

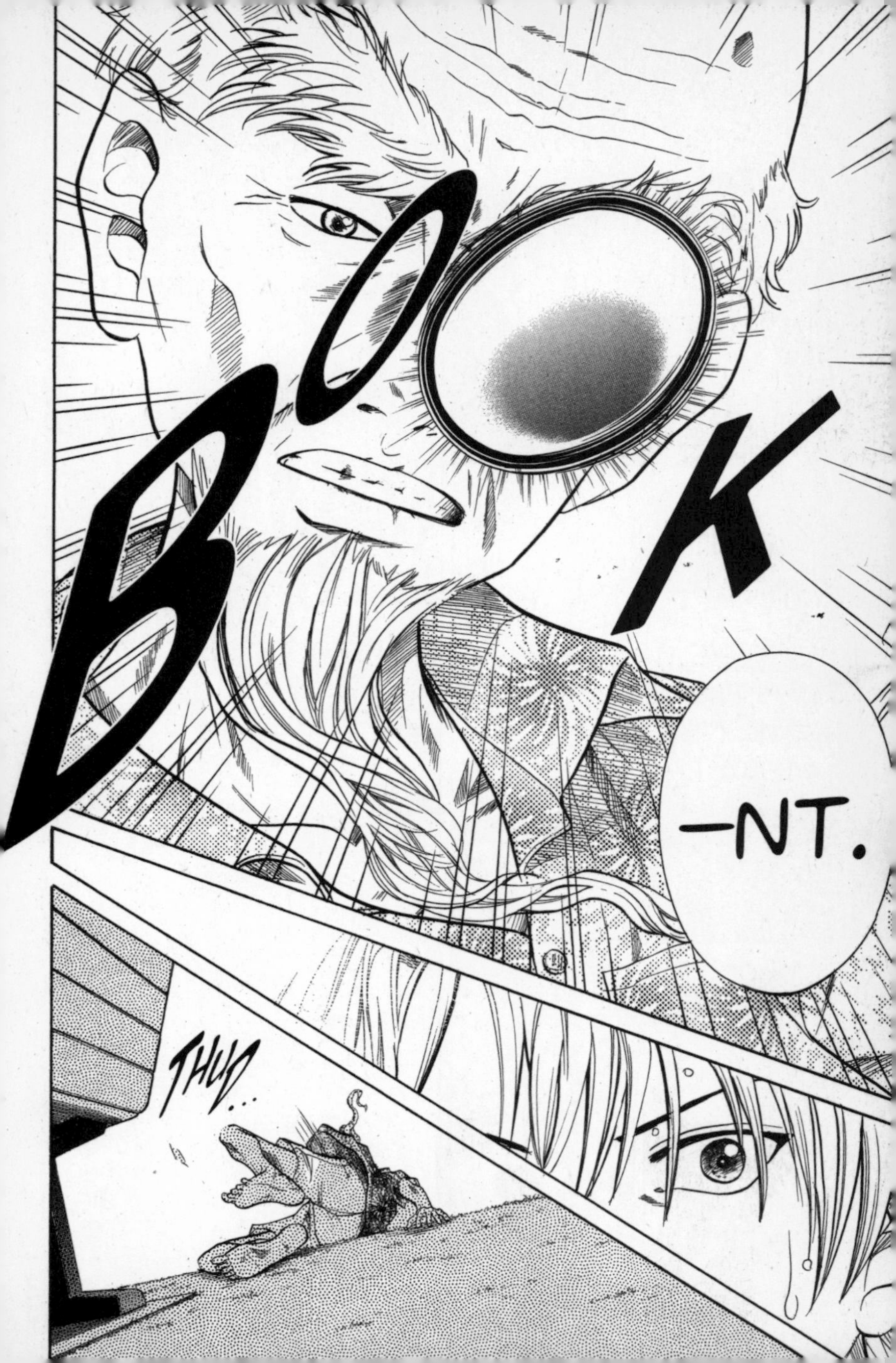
BOOK
—NT.
THUD...

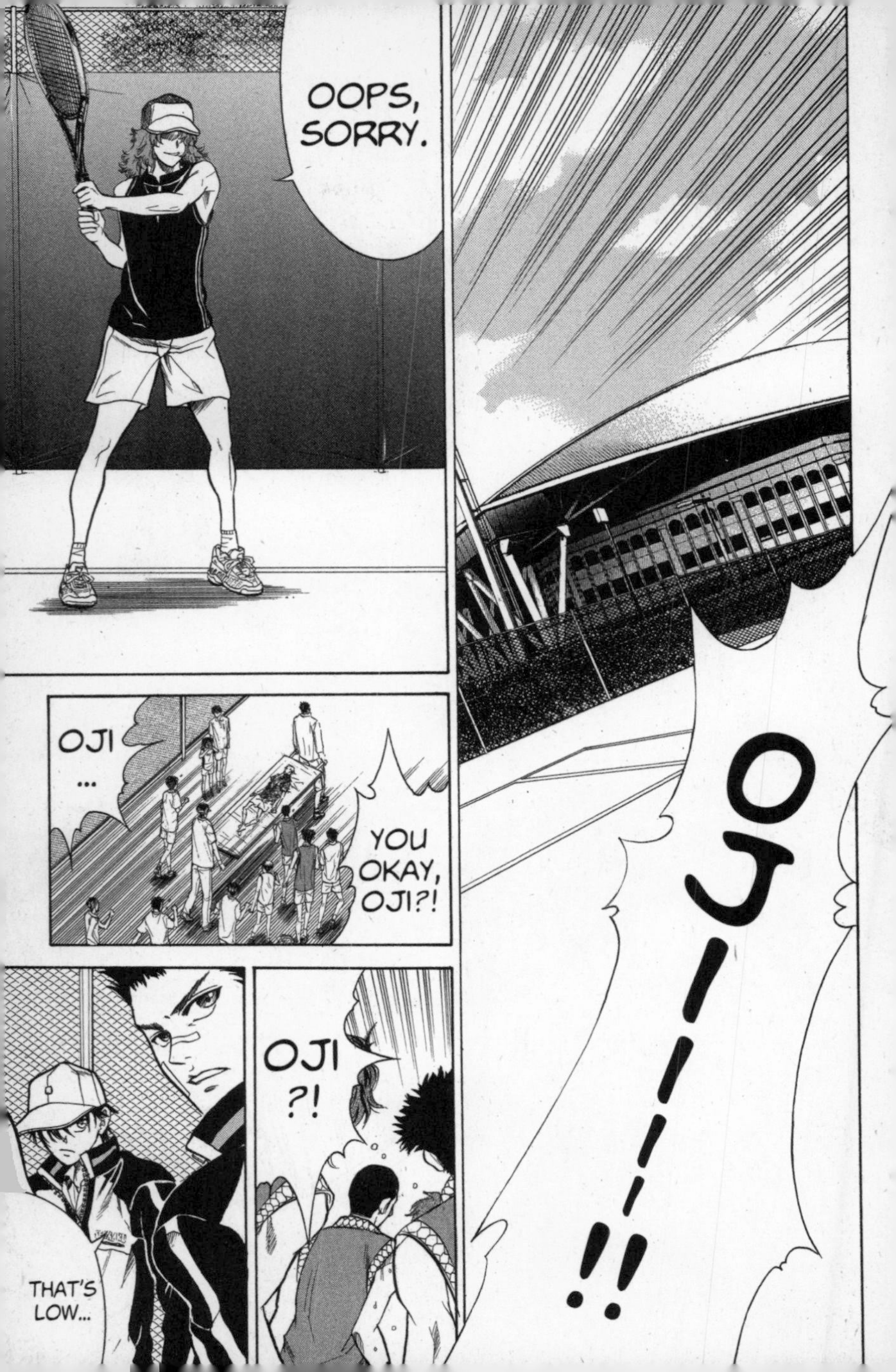
OJI------!!
OOPS, SORRY.
YOU OKAY, OJI?!
OJI ...
OJI ?!
THAT'S LOW...

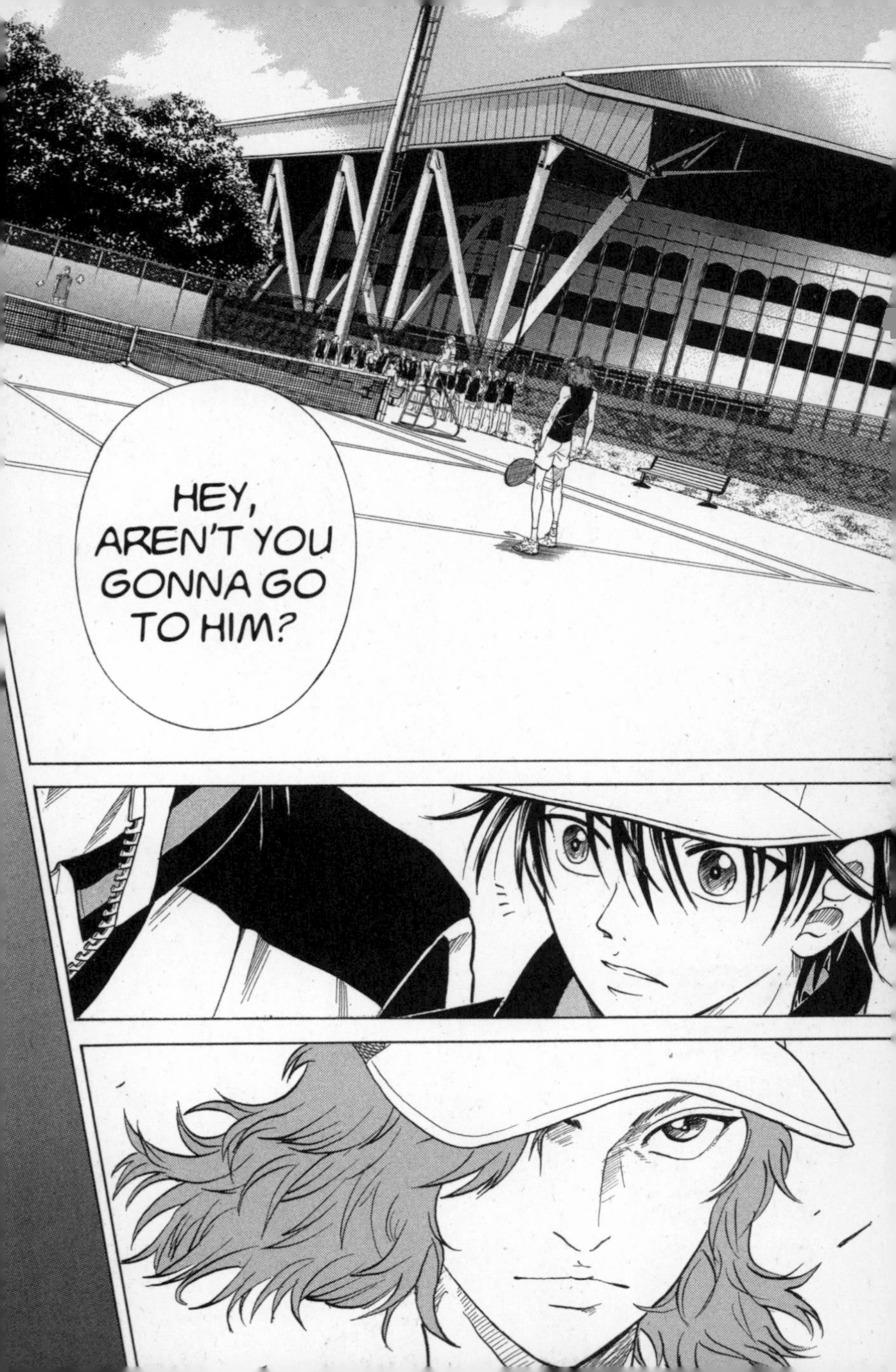
HEY, AREN'T YOU GONNA GO TO HIM?

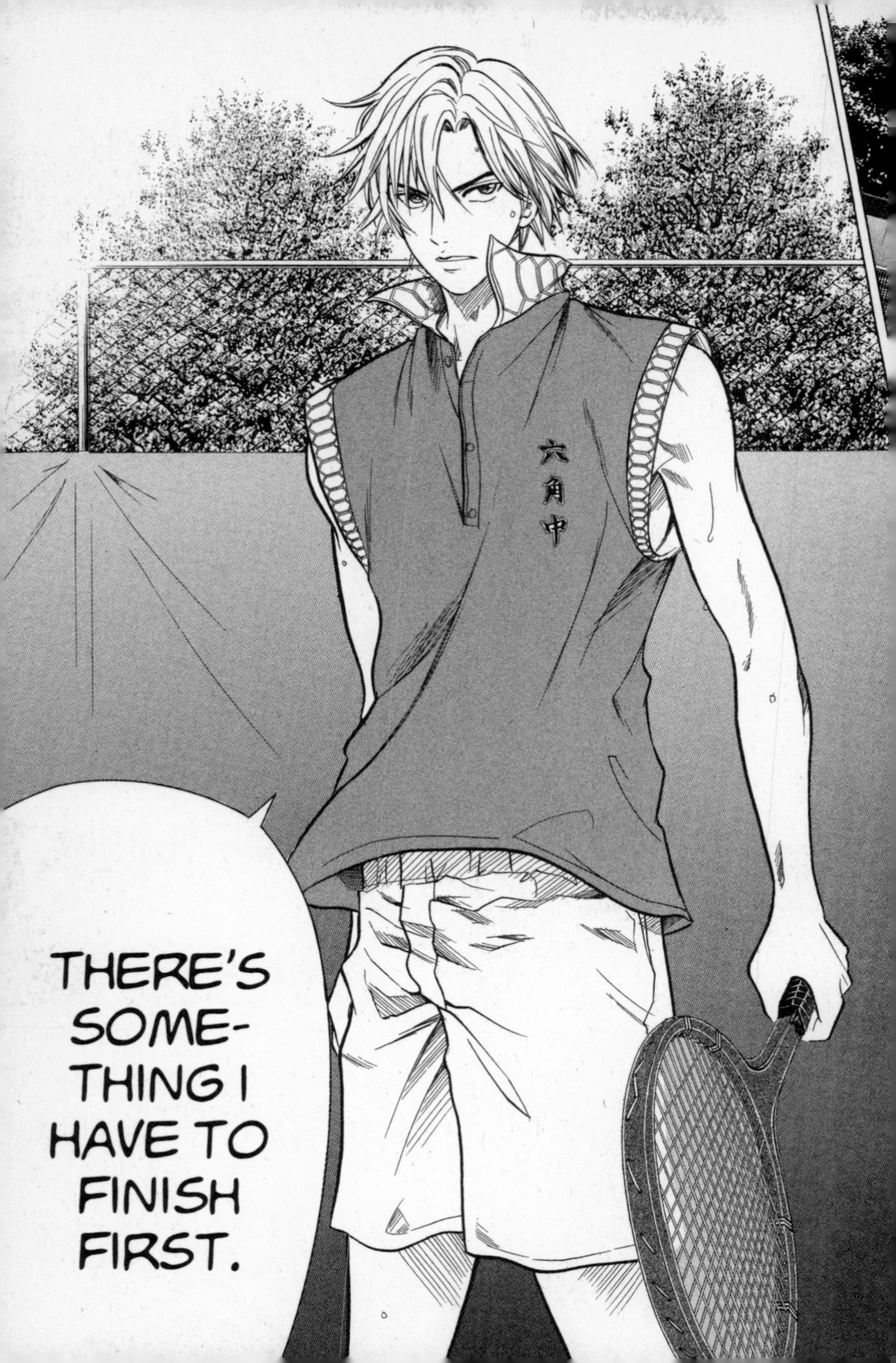
六角中
THERE'S SOMETHING I HAVE TO FINISH FIRST.

テニスの王子様

THE PRINCE OF TENNIS

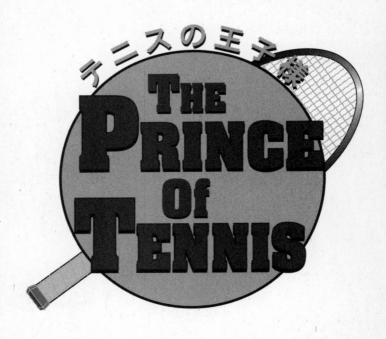

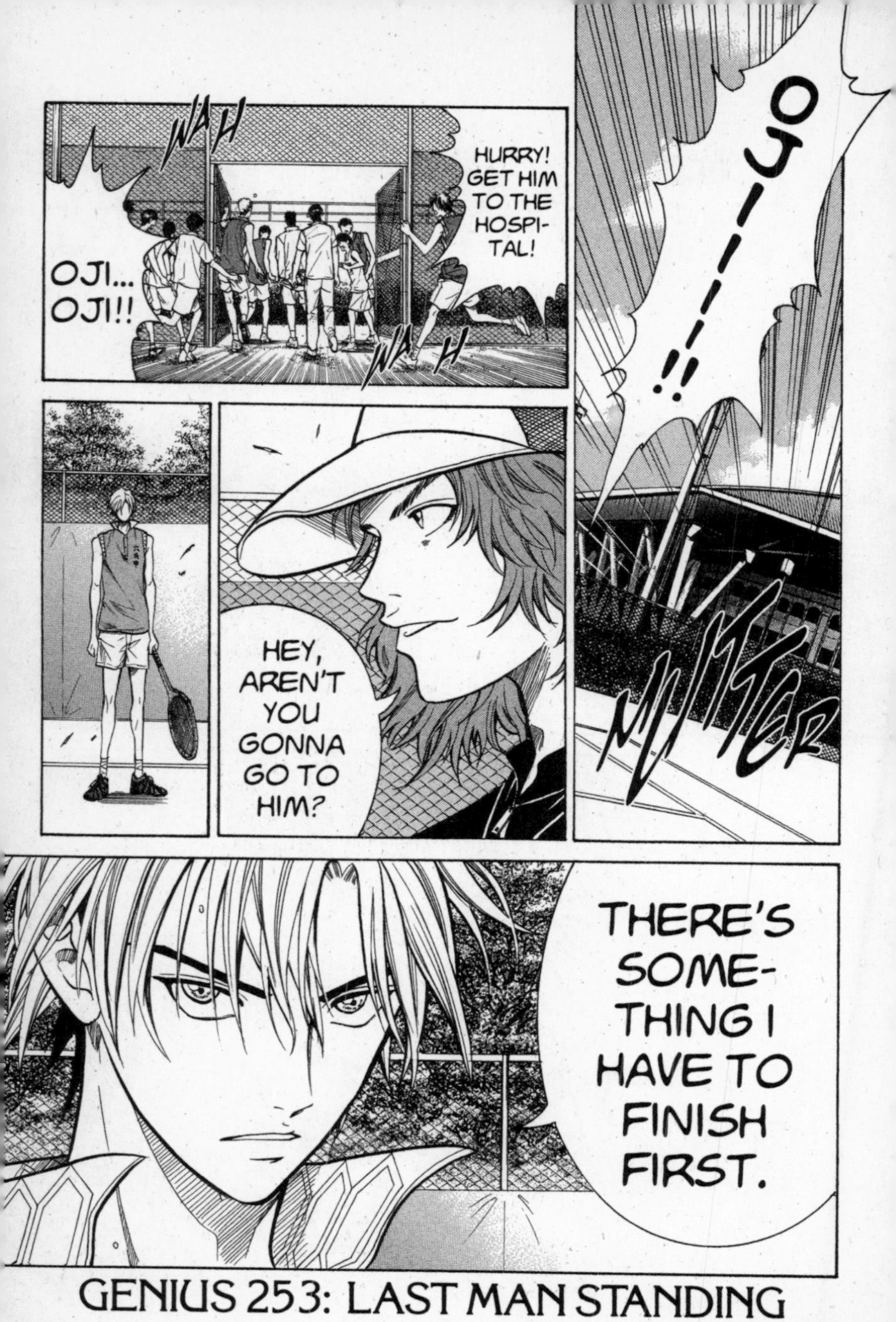
OJI------!!
HURRY! GET HIM TO THE HOSPI-TAL!
WAH
OJI... OJI!!
WAH
HEY, AREN'T YOU GONNA GO TO HIM?
THERE'S SOME-THING I HAVE TO FINISH FIRST.

GENIUS 253: LAST MAN STANDING

GENIUS 253:
LAST MAN STANDING

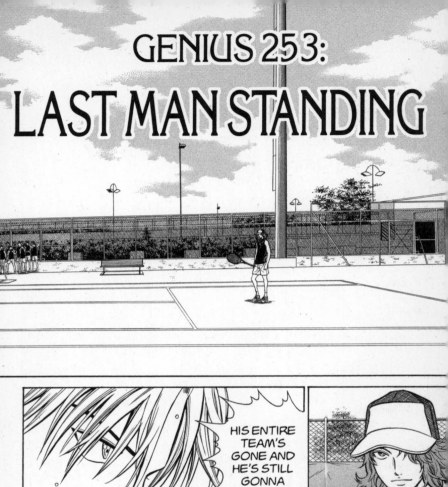

HIS ENTIRE TEAM'S GONE AND HE'S STILL GONNA PLAY?!

HIGA! HIGA!

REALLY?

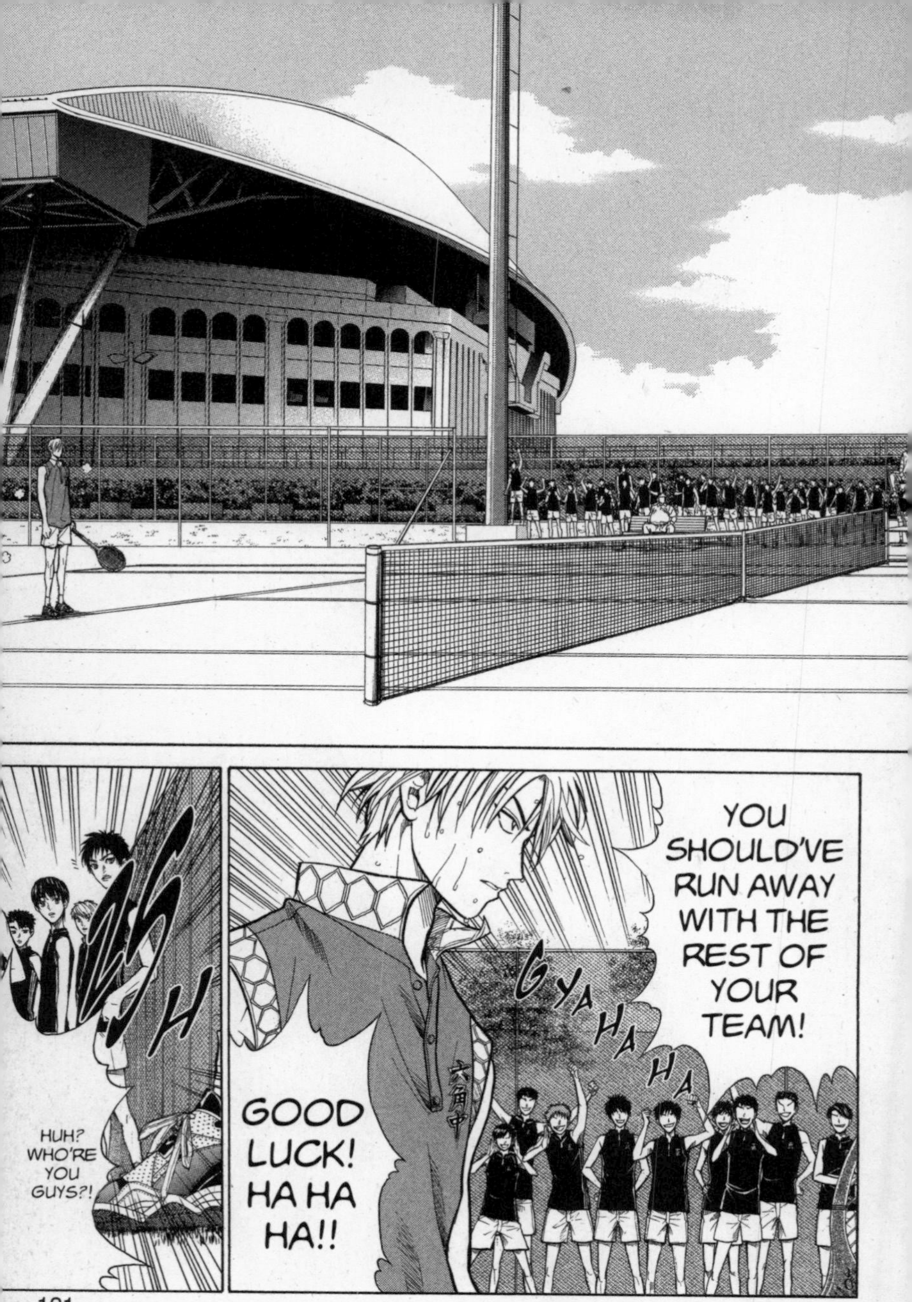
YOU SHOULD'VE RUN AWAY WITH THE REST OF YOUR TEAM!
GYAHAHAHA
GOOD LUCK! HA HA HA!!
HUH? WHO'RE YOU GUYS?!

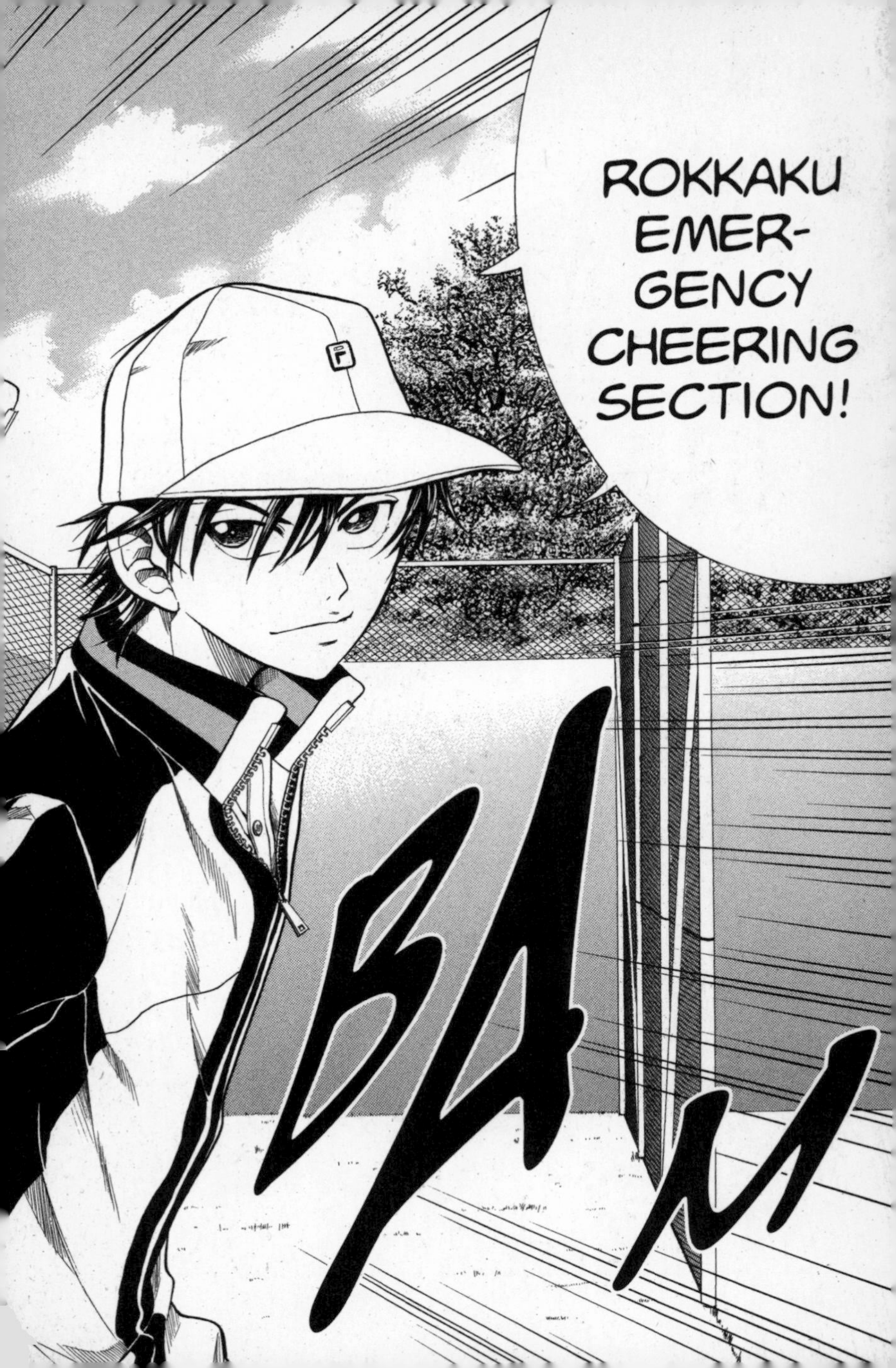
ROKKAKU EMER-GENCY CHEERING SECTION!
BAM

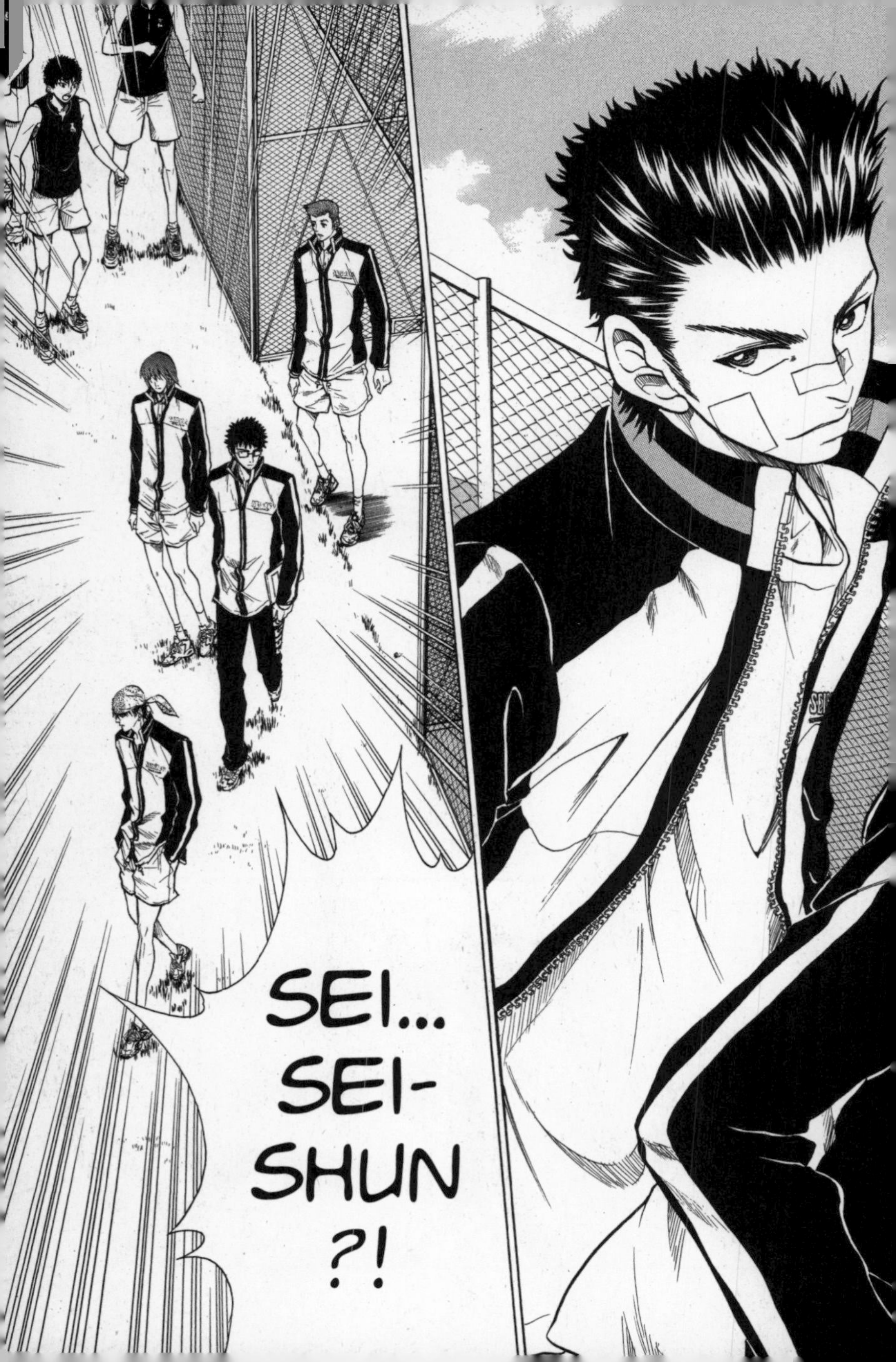
SEI... SEI-SHUN?!

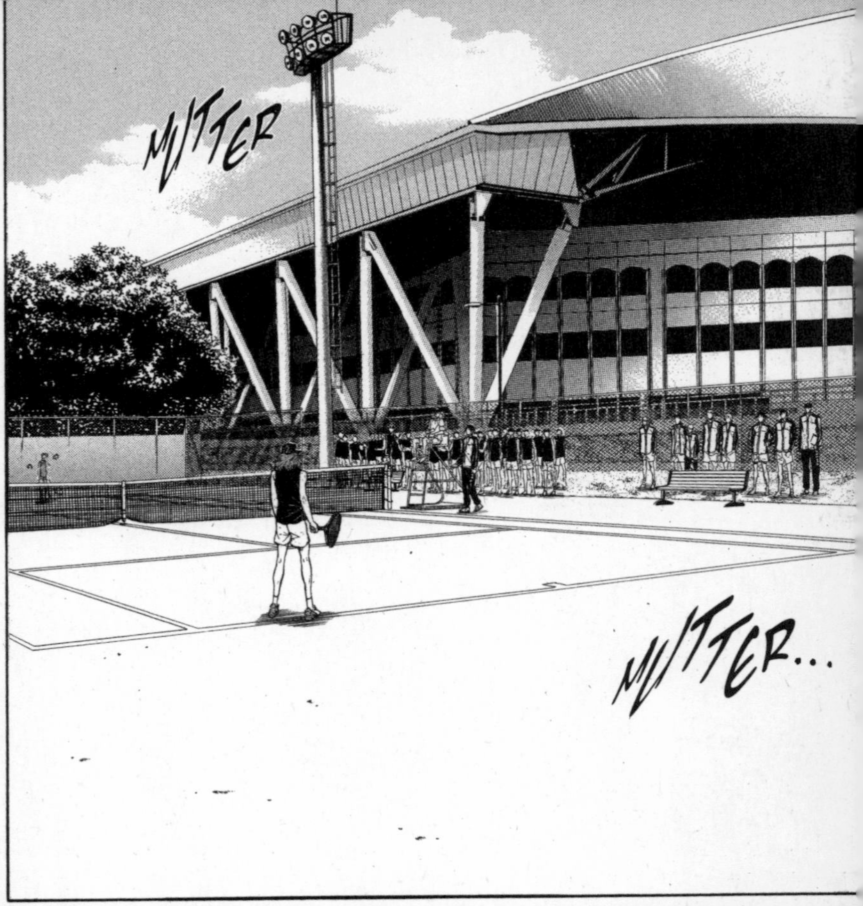
MUTTER
MUTTER...

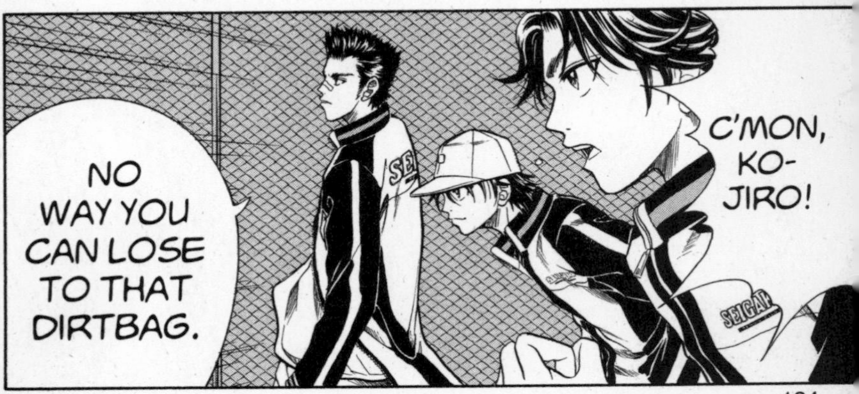
C'MON, KO-JIRO!
NO WAY YOU CAN LOSE TO THAT DIRTBAG.

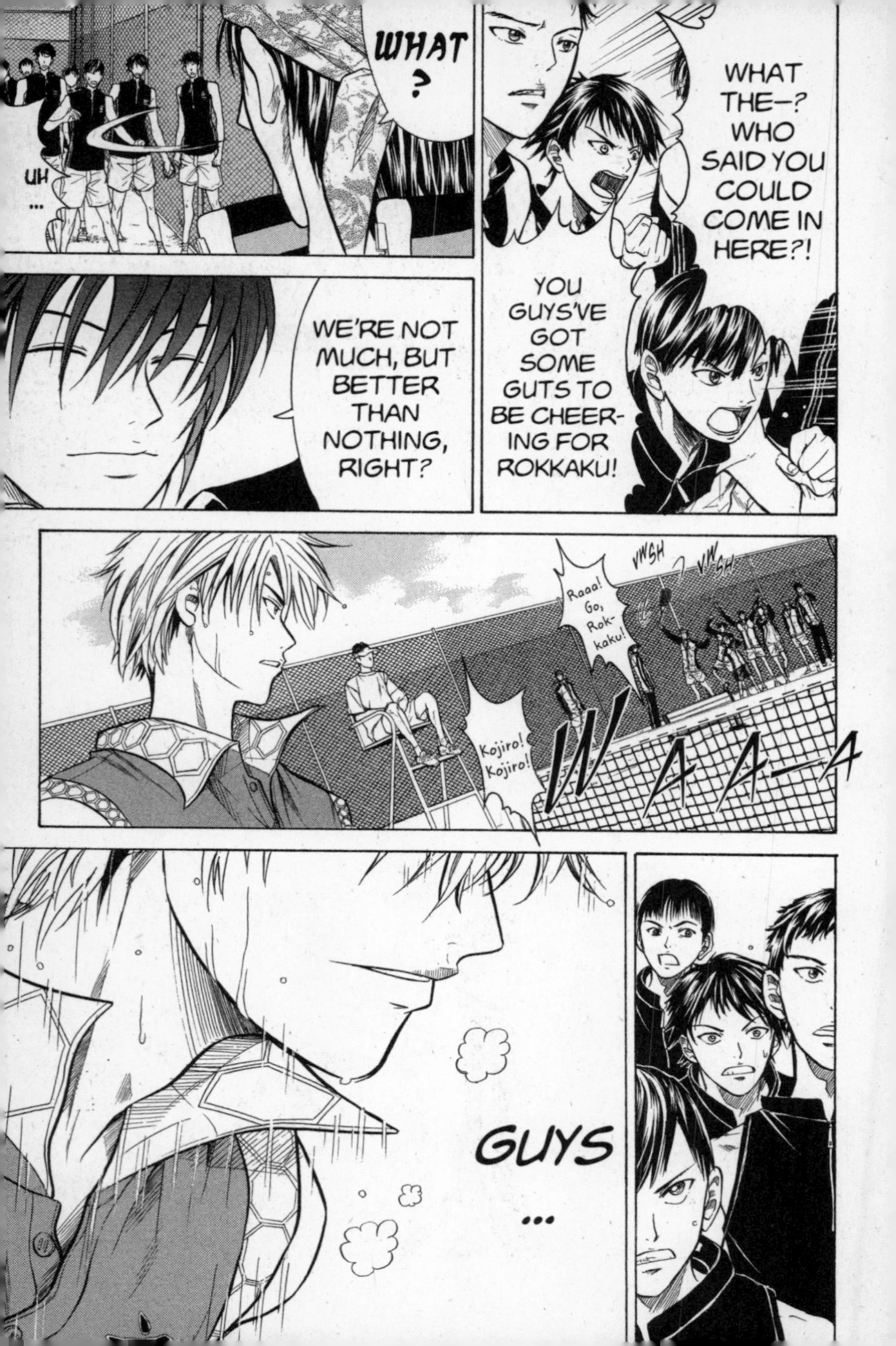
WHAT THE—? WHO SAID YOU COULD COME IN HERE?!
YOU GUYS'VE GOT SOME GUTS TO BE CHEERING FOR ROKKAKU!
WHAT ?
UH ...
WE'RE NOT MUCH, BUT BETTER THAN NOTHING, RIGHT?
VWSH
VWSH
Raaa! Go, Rokkaku!
Kojiro! Kojiro!
WAA-A
GUYS
...

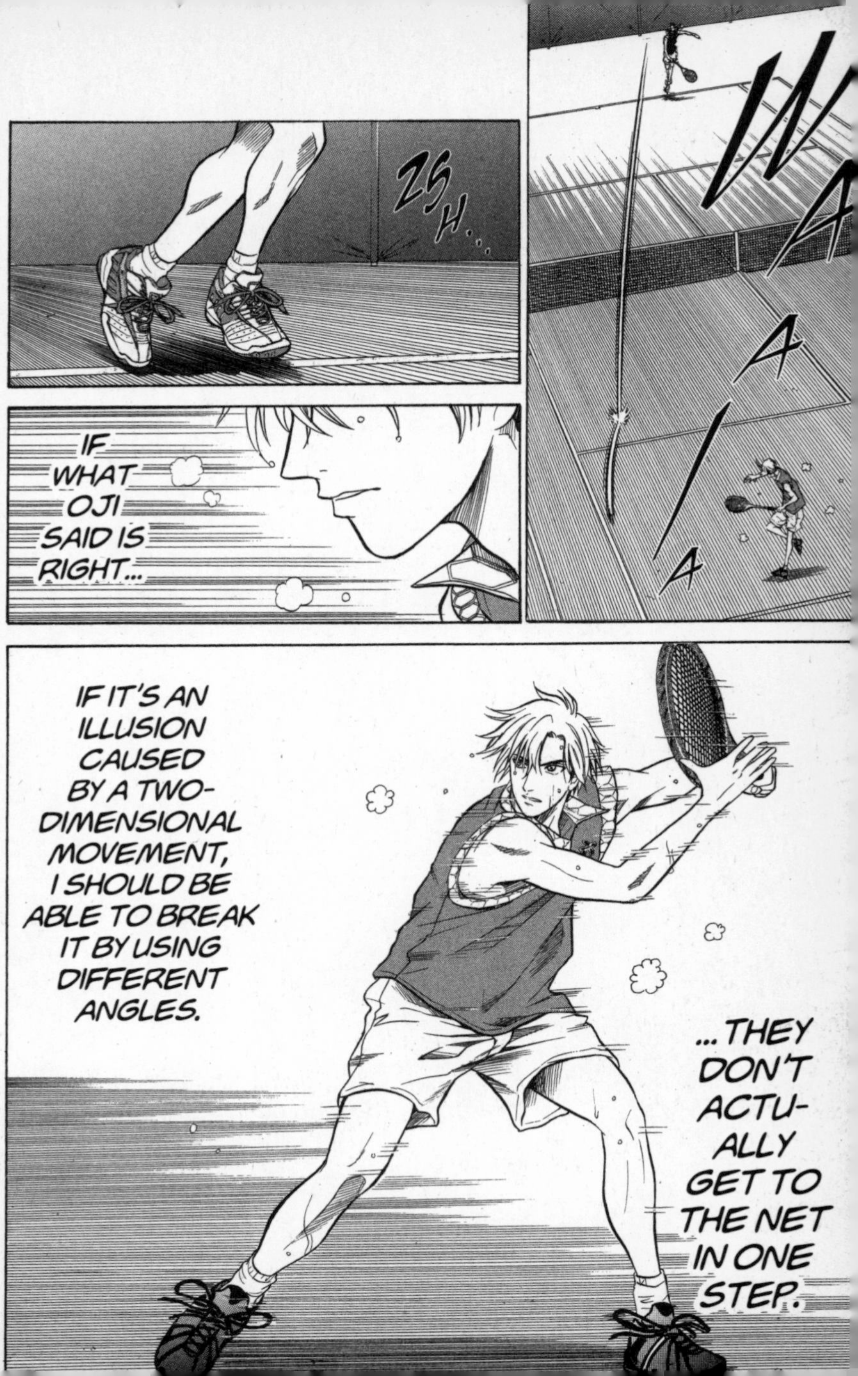
WAAA
ZSH...
IF WHAT OJI SAID IS RIGHT...
...THEY DON'T ACTUALLY GET TO THE NET IN ONE STEP.
IF IT'S AN ILLUSION CAUSED BY A TWO-DIMENSIONAL MOVEMENT, I SHOULD BE ABLE TO BREAK IT BY USING DIFFERENT ANGLES.

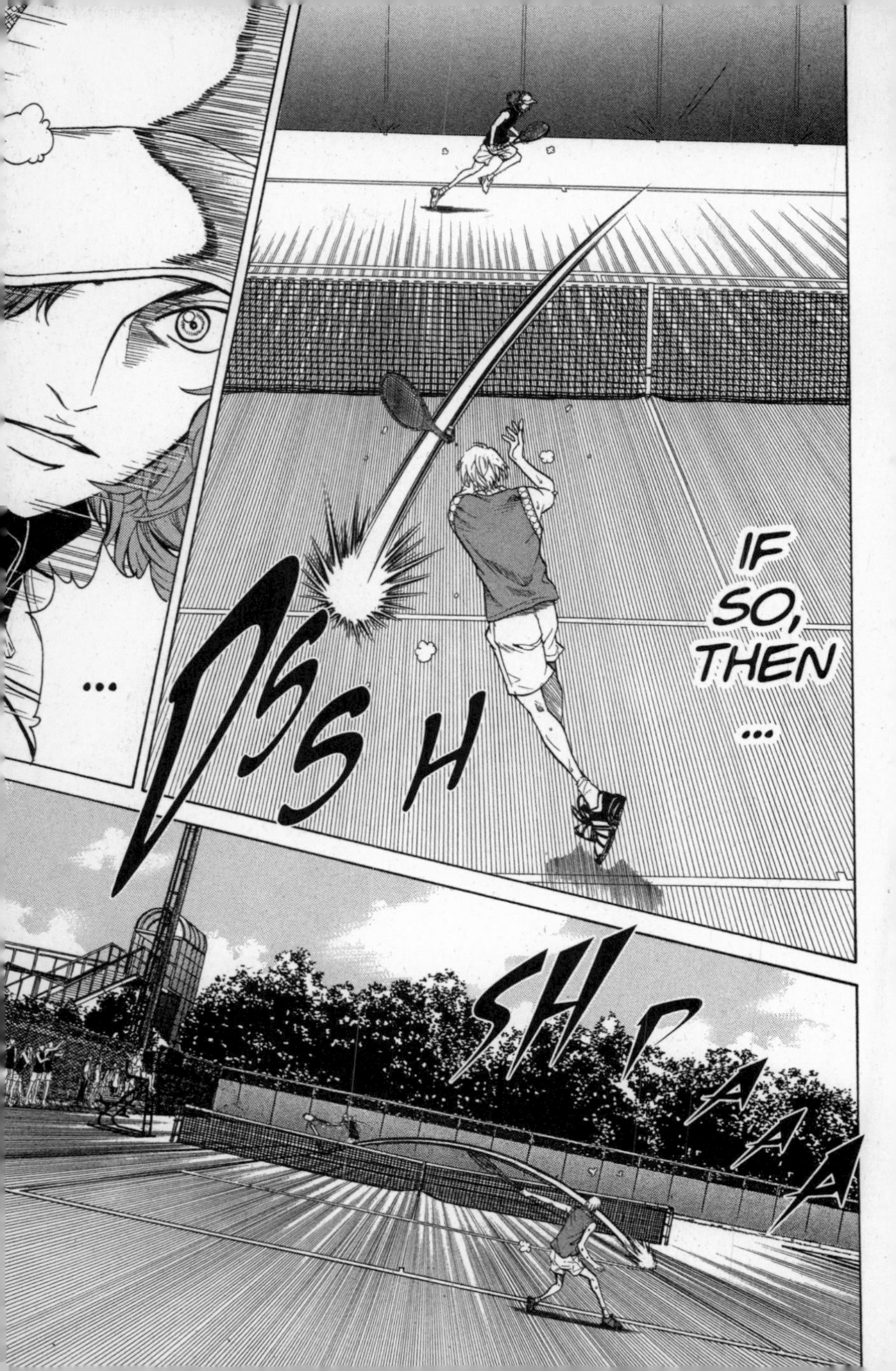
IF SO, THEN ...
DSSH
...
SHPAAAA

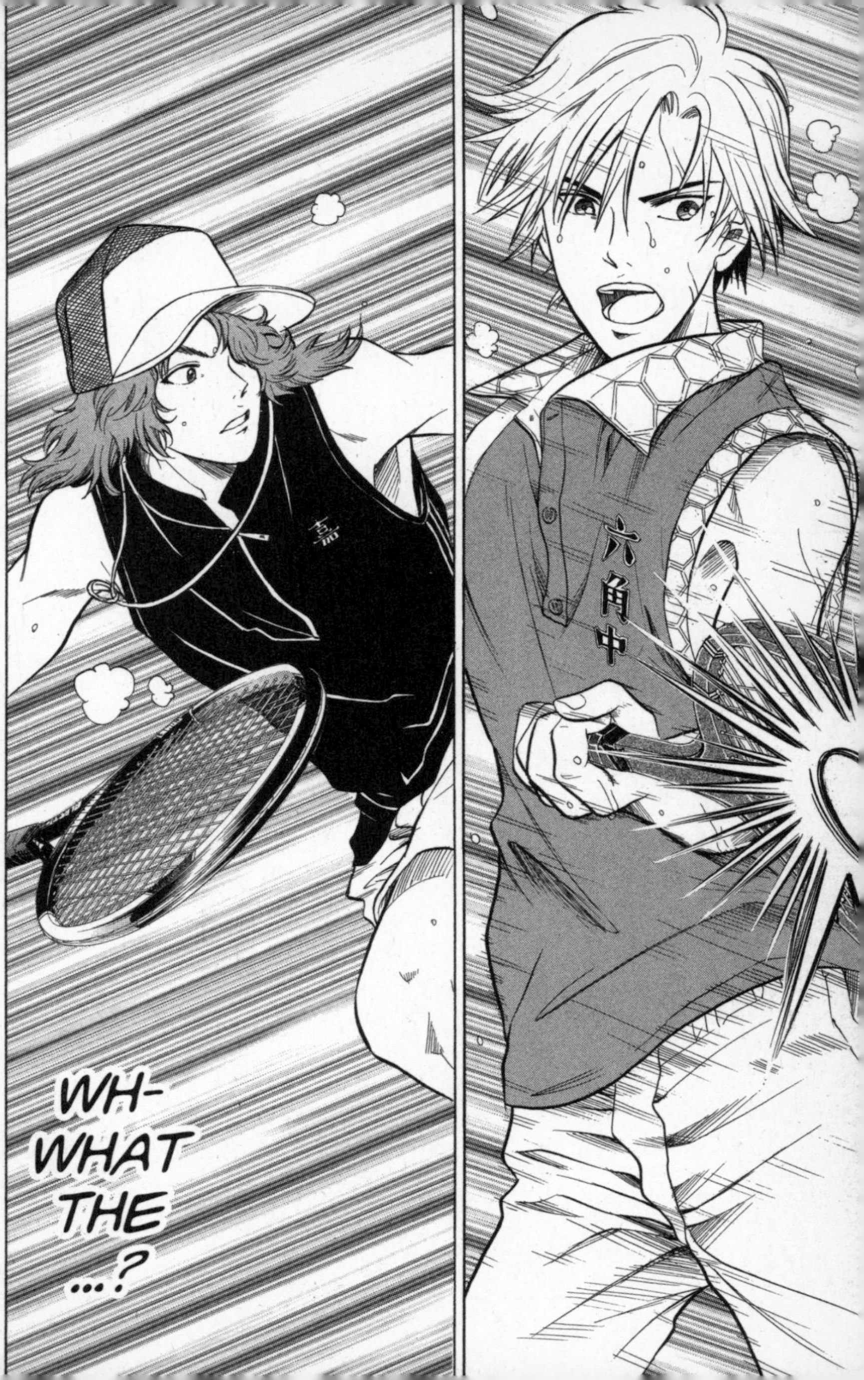
六角中
嘉
WH-
WHAT
THE
...?

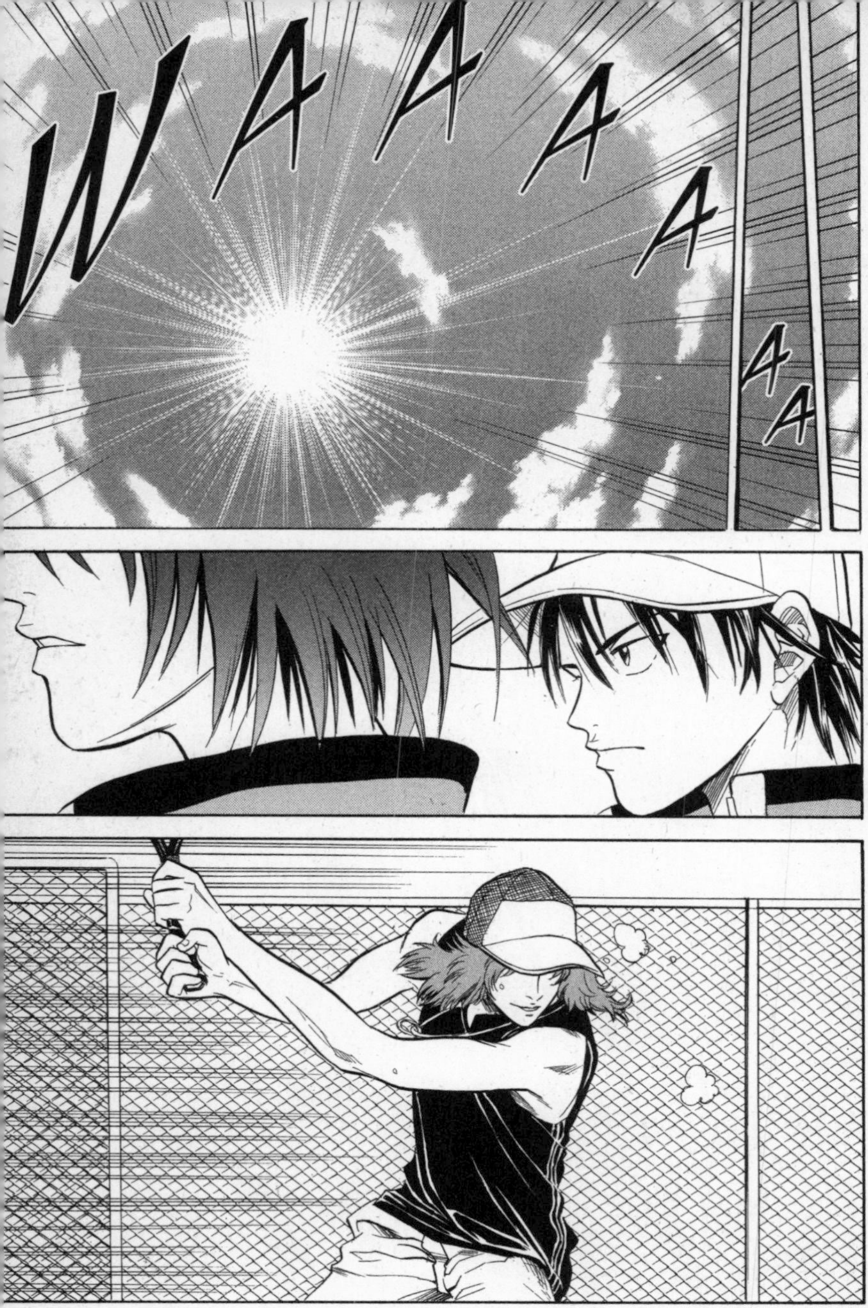

WAAAAAAA

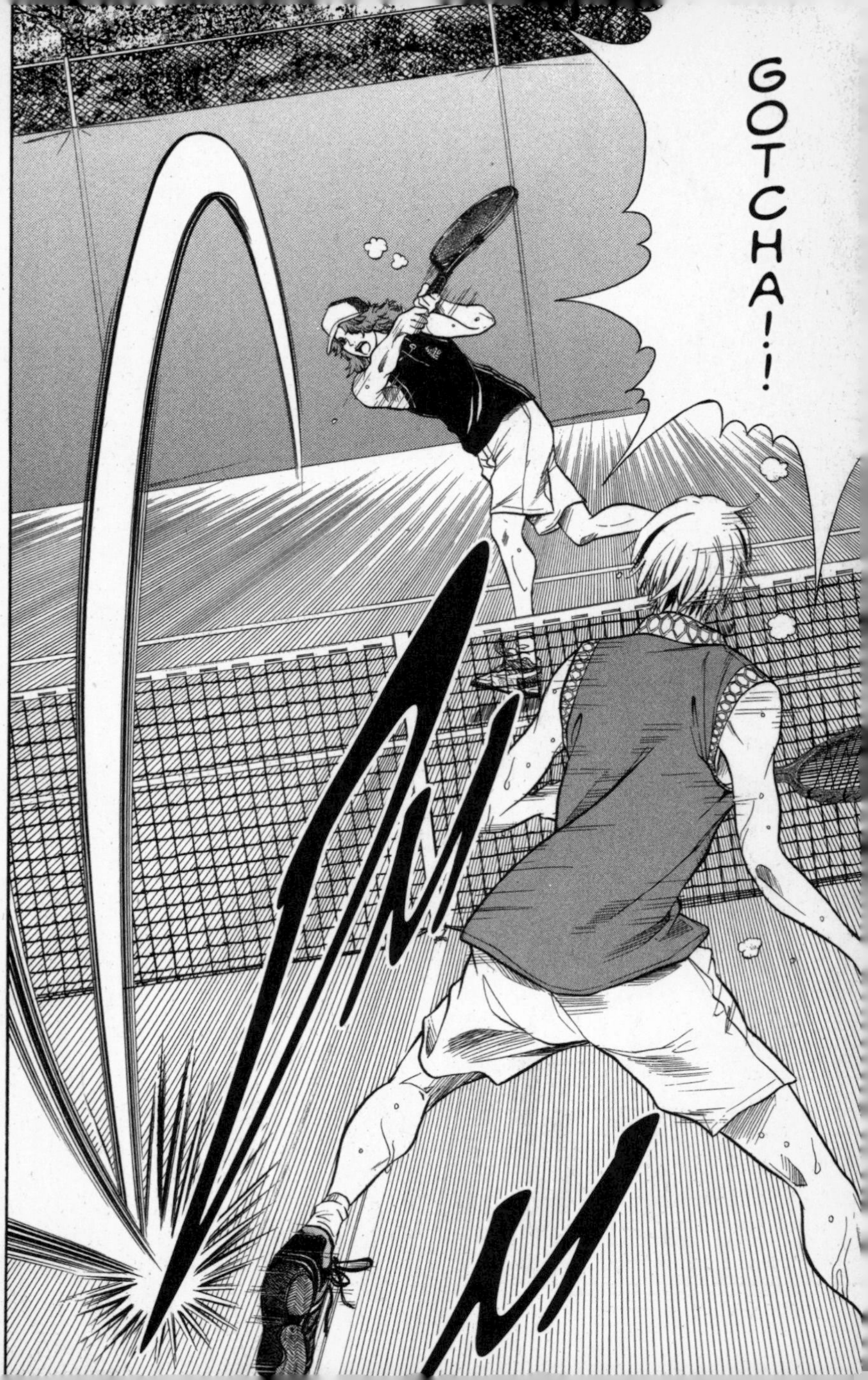
GOTCHA!!

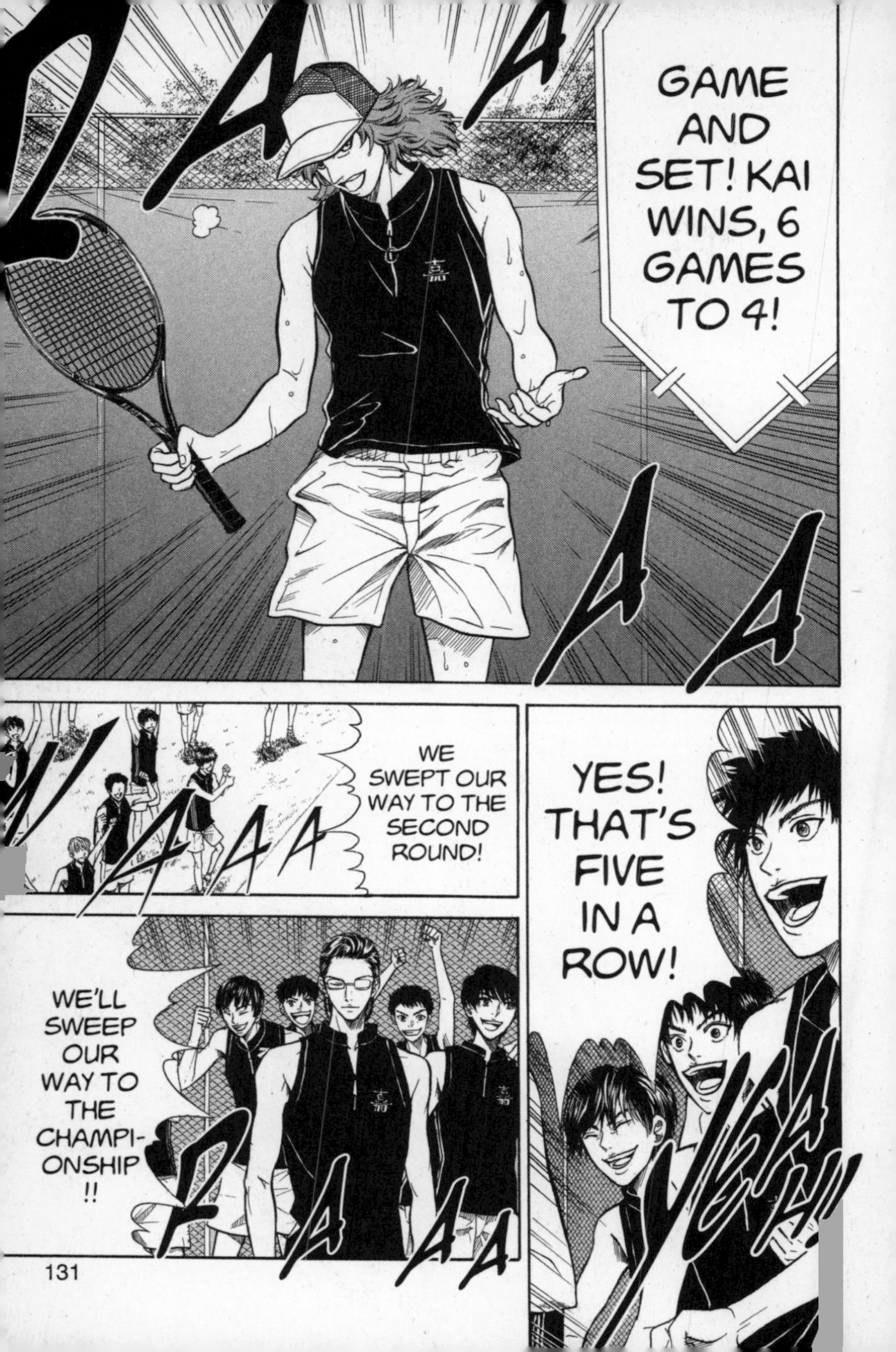
GAME AND SET! KAI WINS, 6 GAMES TO 4!
YES! THAT'S FIVE IN A ROW!
WE SWEPT OUR WAY TO THE SECOND ROUND!
WE'LL SWEEP OUR WAY TO THE CHAMPIONSHIP!!

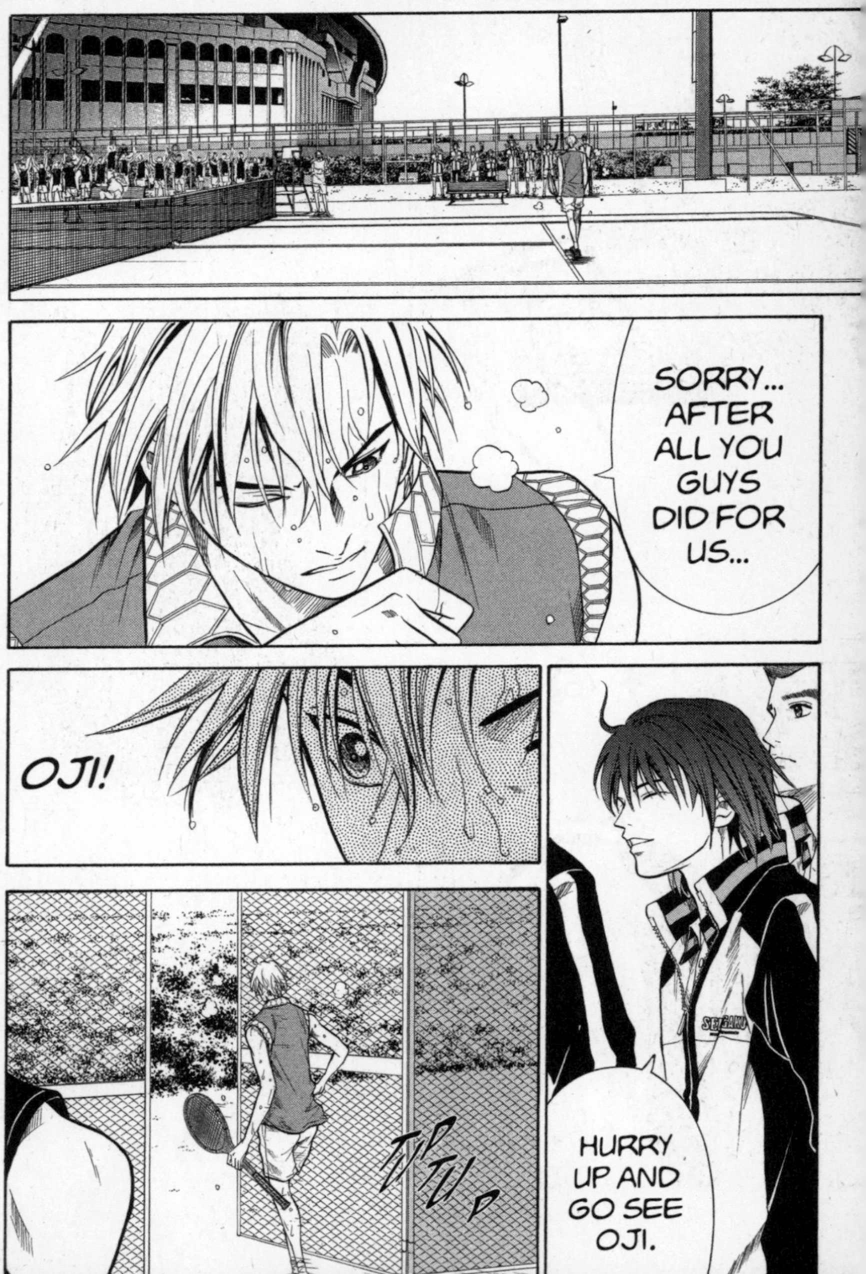
SORRY... AFTER ALL YOU GUYS DID FOR US...
HURRY UP AND GO SEE OJI.
OJI!
TUD TUD

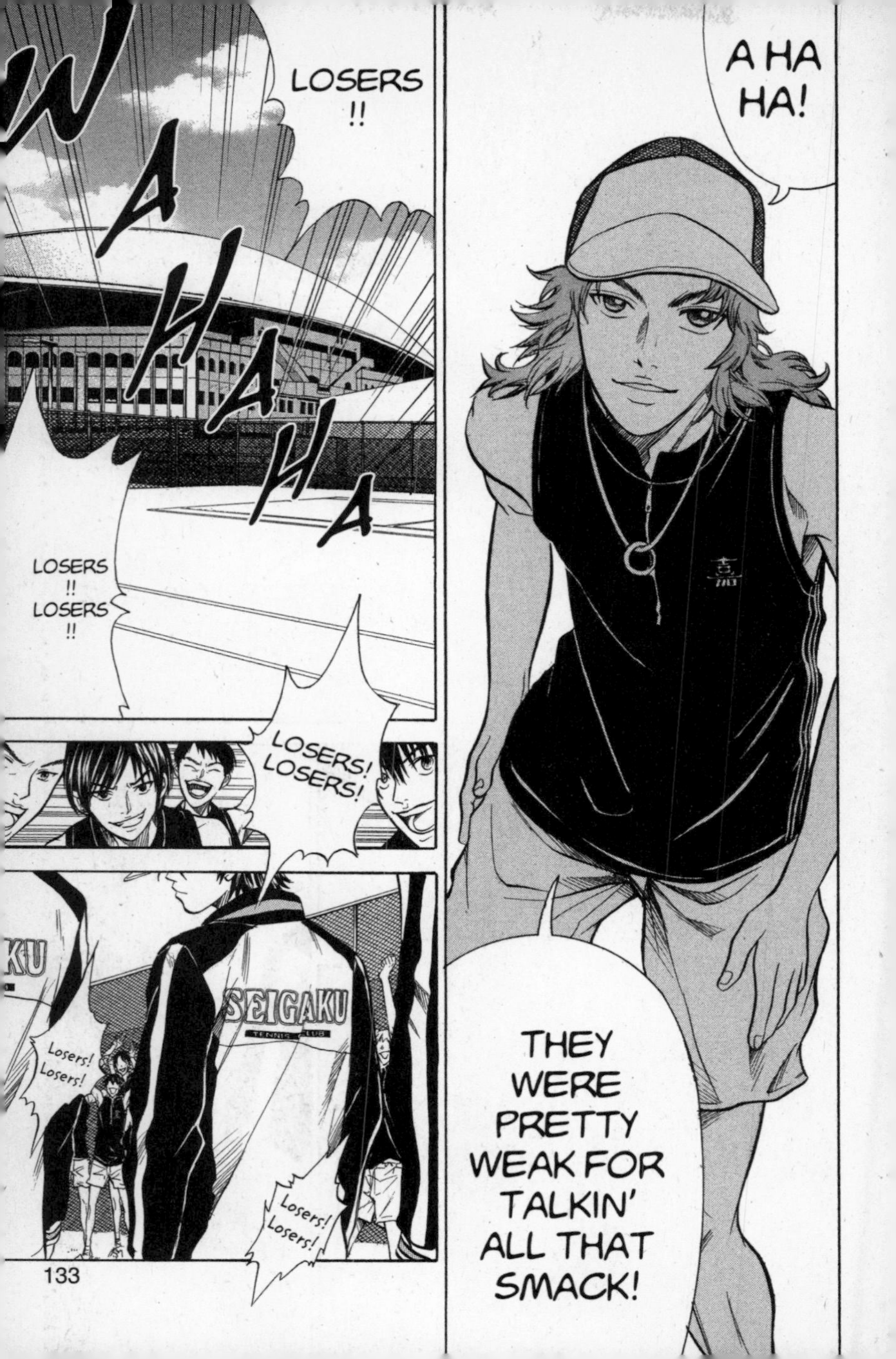
A HA HA!
THEY WERE PRETTY WEAK FOR TALKIN' ALL THAT SMACK!
LOSERS !!
WAHAHAHA
LOSERS !! LOSERS !!
LOSERS! LOSERS!
SEIGAKU
TENNIS CLUB
Losers! Losers!
Losers! Losers!

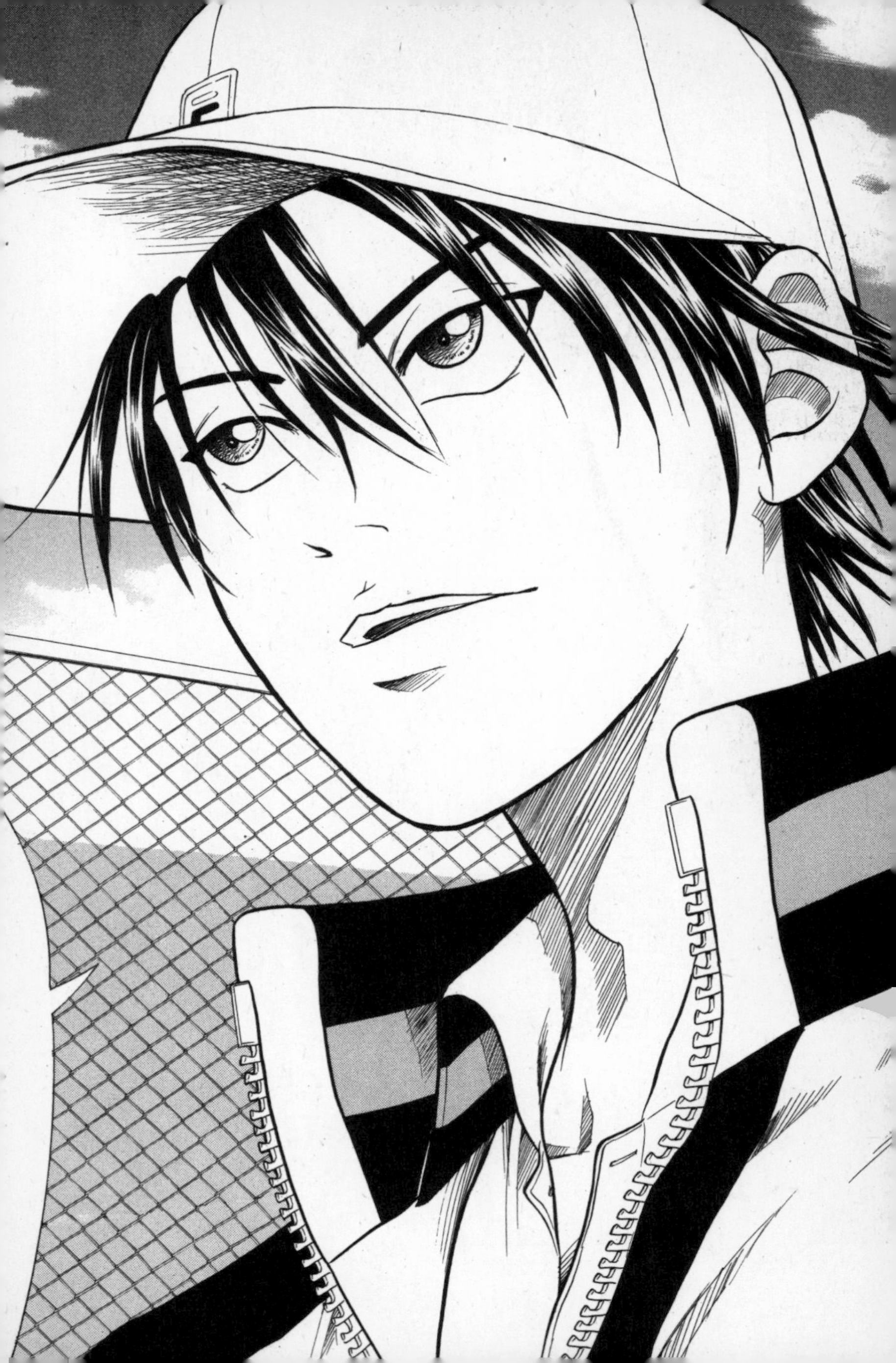

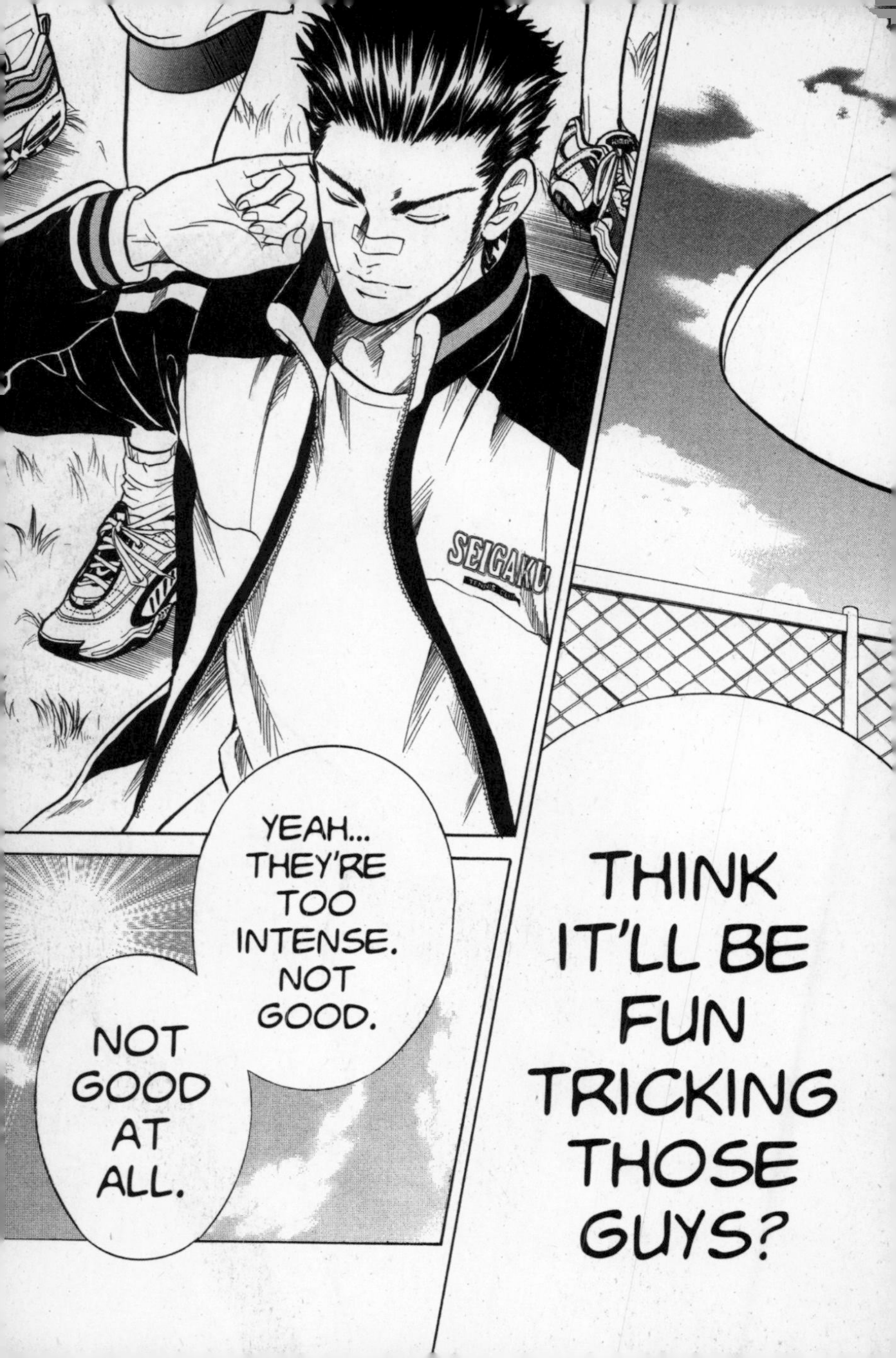
THINK IT'LL BE FUN TRICKING THOSE GUYS?
SEIGAKU
YEAH... THEY'RE TOO INTENSE. NOT GOOD.
NOT GOOD AT ALL.

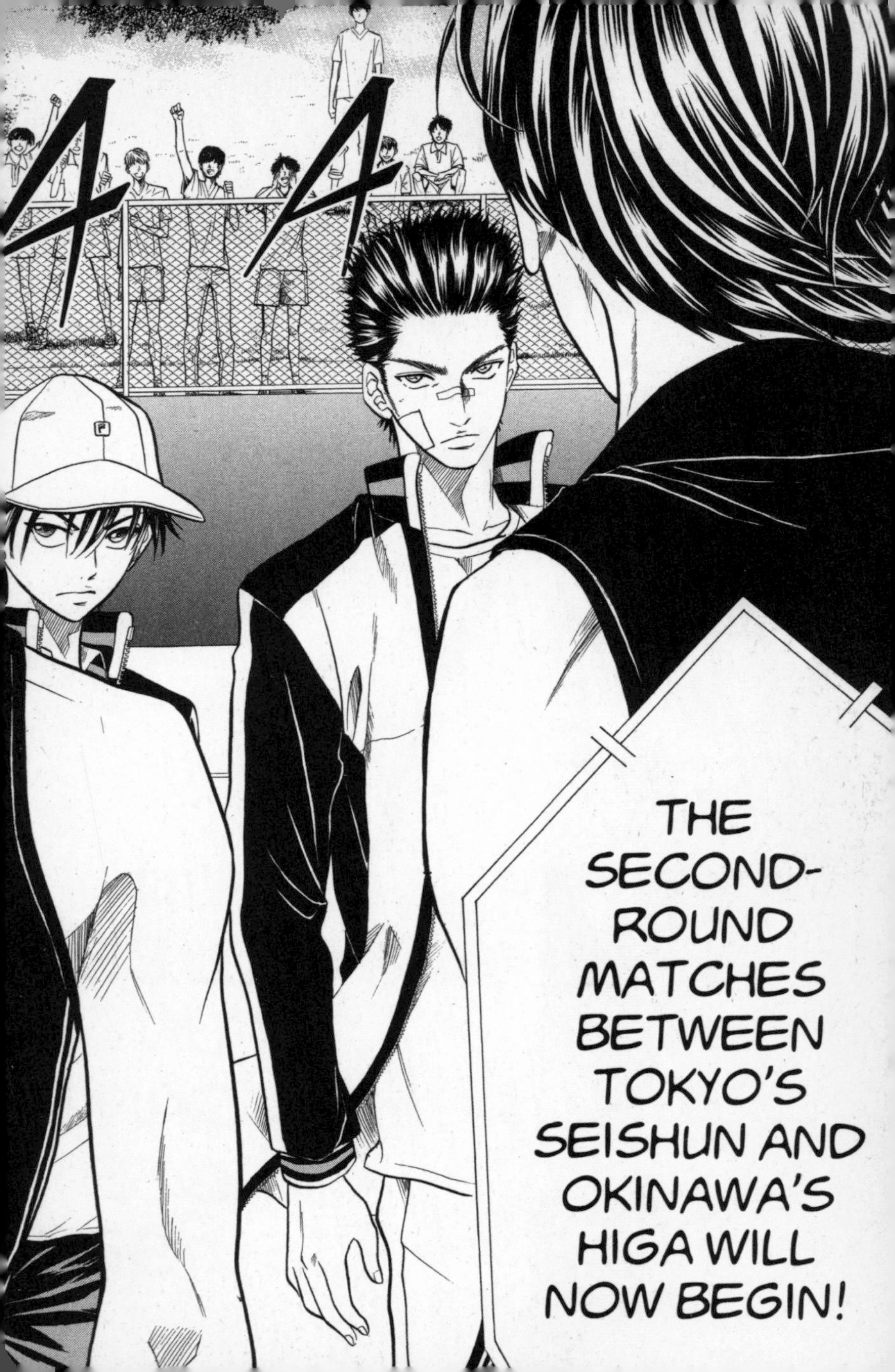
THE SECOND-ROUND MATCHES BETWEEN TOKYO'S SEISHUN AND OKINAWA'S HIGA WILL NOW BEGIN!

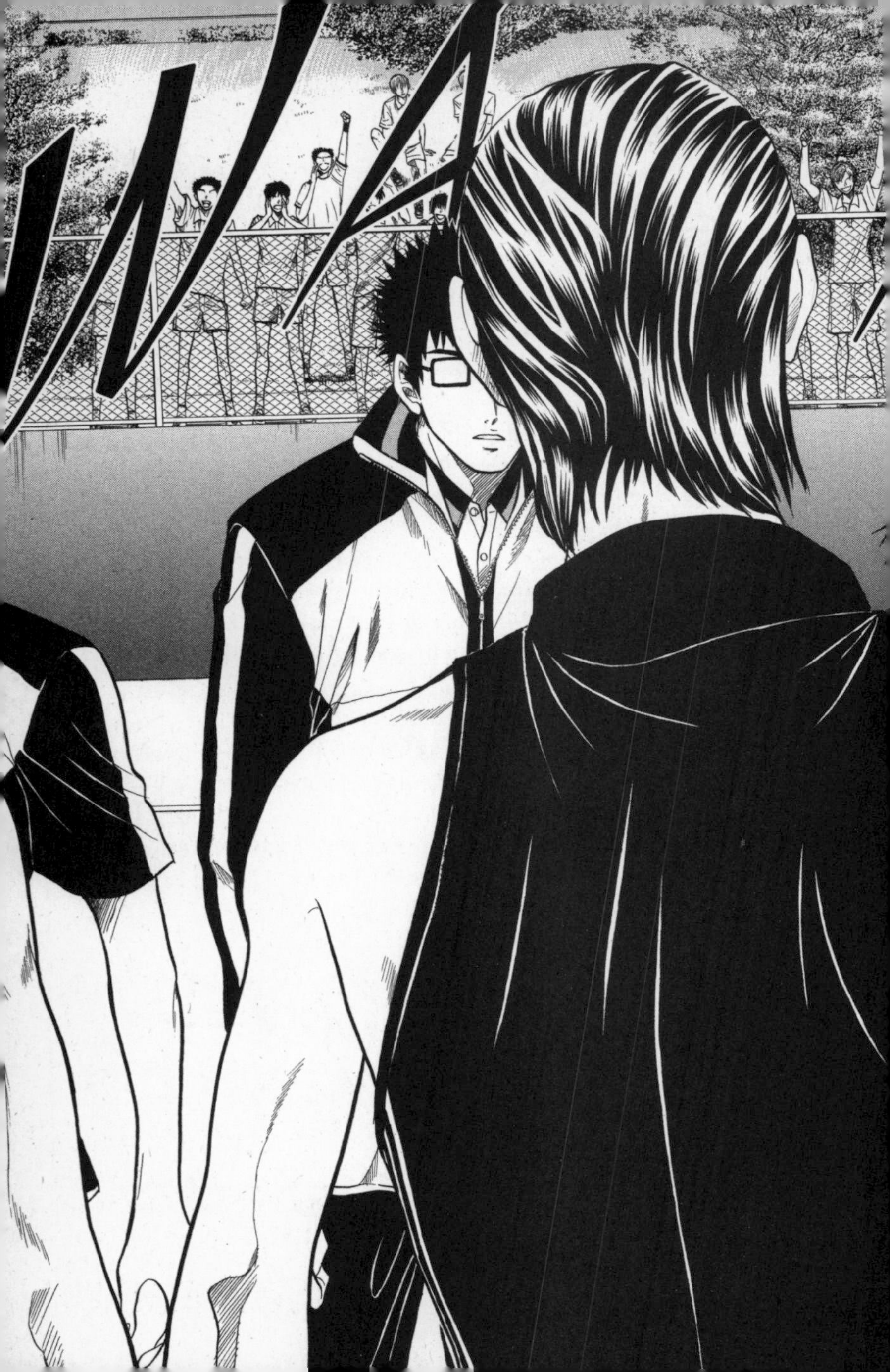
WA

テニスの王子様

THE PRINCE OF TENNIS

Thank you for reading *The Prince of Tennis*, volume 29.

Are you all sad the anime ended? Don't worry—you've still got a ways to go! Just between you and me, there are a few things in the works, so I may be able to give you some good news in the next volume.

Well... Volume 30 is coming up, isn't it? Speaking of volume 30 [smirk], I think you guys are in for a huge surprise. You'll just have to wait and see. And there are a lot of projects brewing starting this fall and continuing until next spring. Let's all keep *The Prince of Tennis* exciting!

They're right in the middle of playing Okinawa's Higa in this volume. I've received comments like "Don't make Okinawans look so bad," and "Okinawans don't talk like that." .... Sorry. I love Okinawa! I'm thinking about going when I have some time off, so if you see me on the beach, don't kick me!

Well then, see you in the next volume!

Keep supporting *The Prince of Tennis* and Ryoma!

KONOMI
2005. 6. 3

Send fan letters to: Takeshi Konomi, *The Prince of Tennis*, c/o VIZ Media LLC, P.O. Box 77010, San Francisco, CA 94107

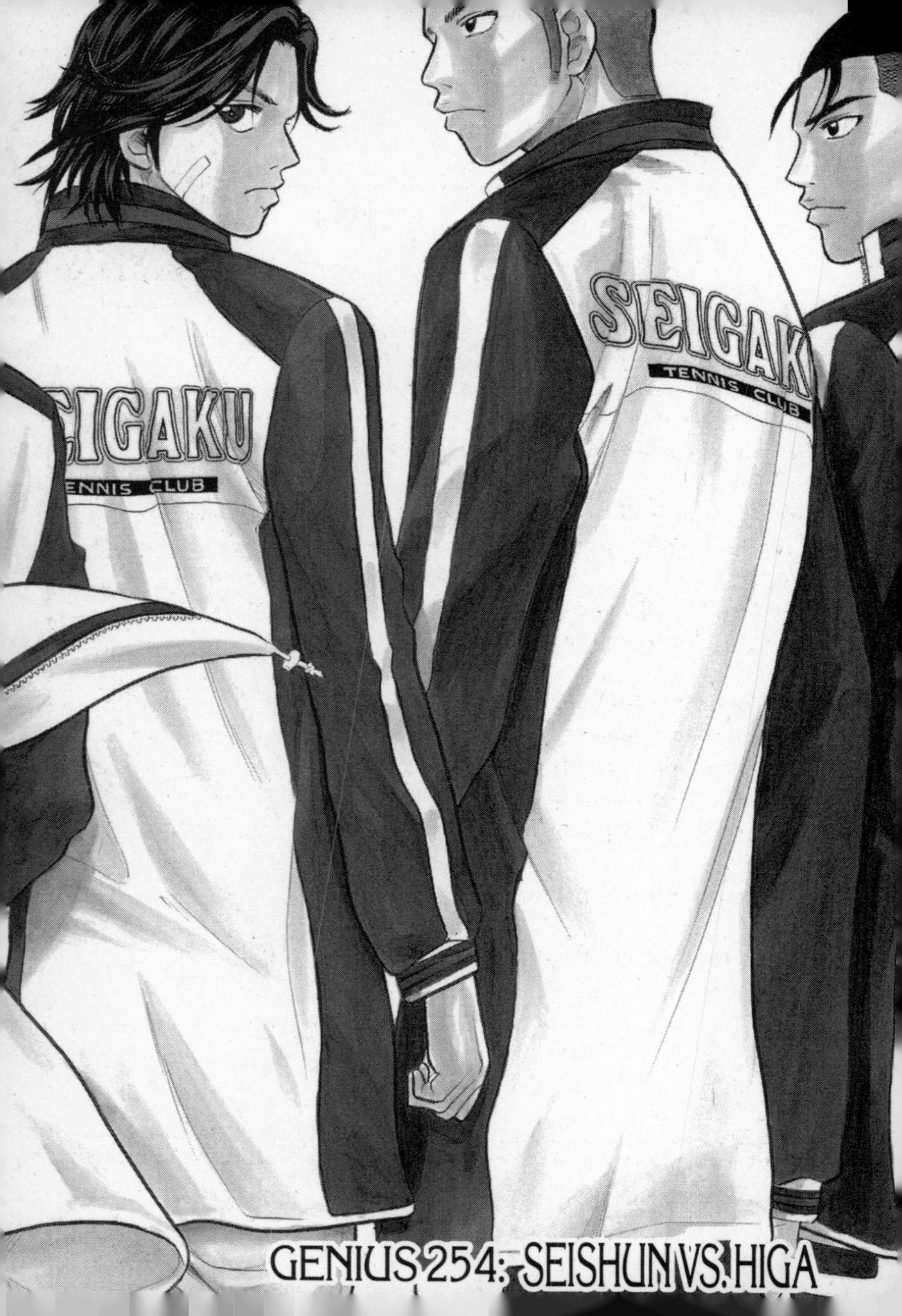
SEIGAKU
TENNIS CLUB
SEIGAKU
TENNIS CLUB
GENIUS 254: SEISHUN VS. HIGA

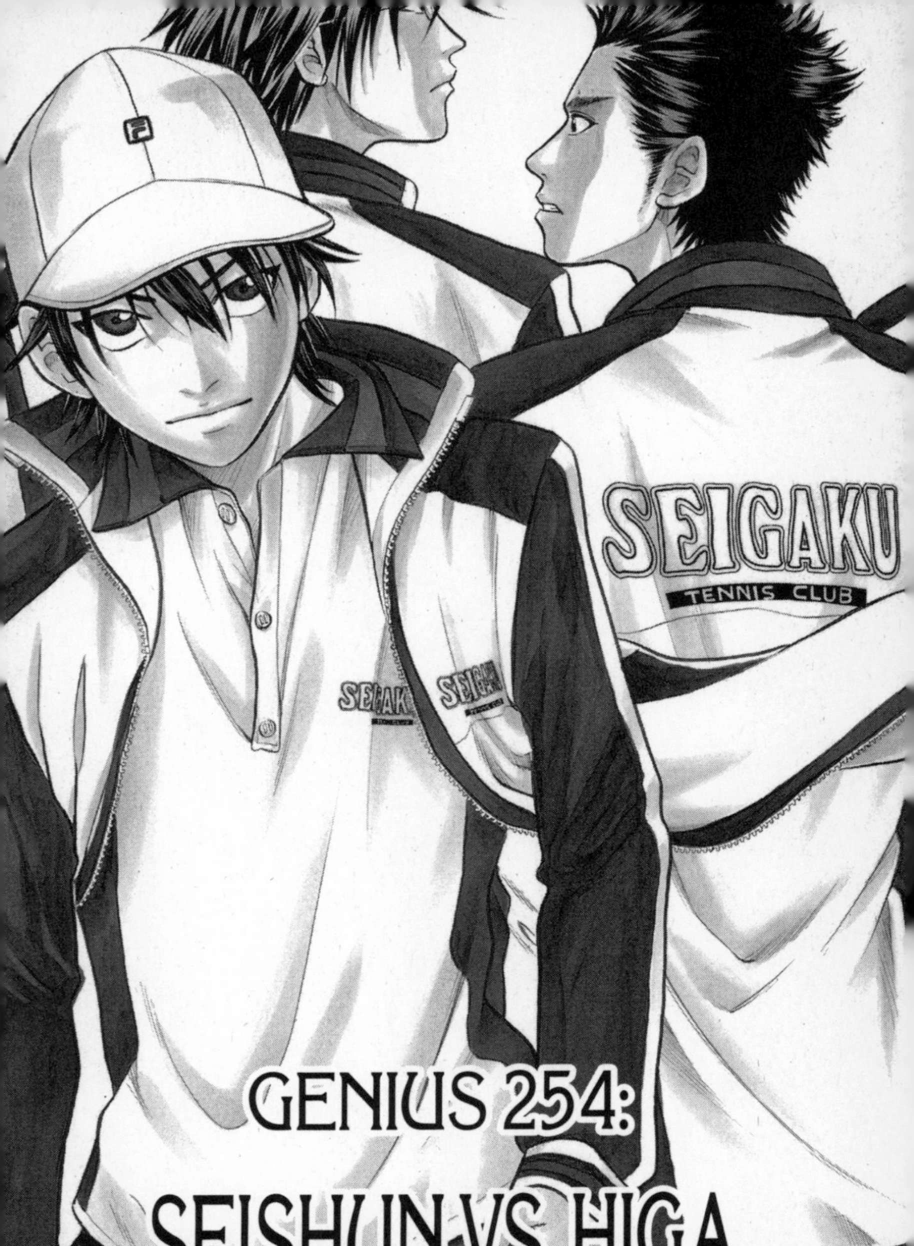
SEIGAKU
TENNIS CLUB
SEIGAKU
SEIGAKU
GENIUS 254:
SEISHUN VS. HIGA

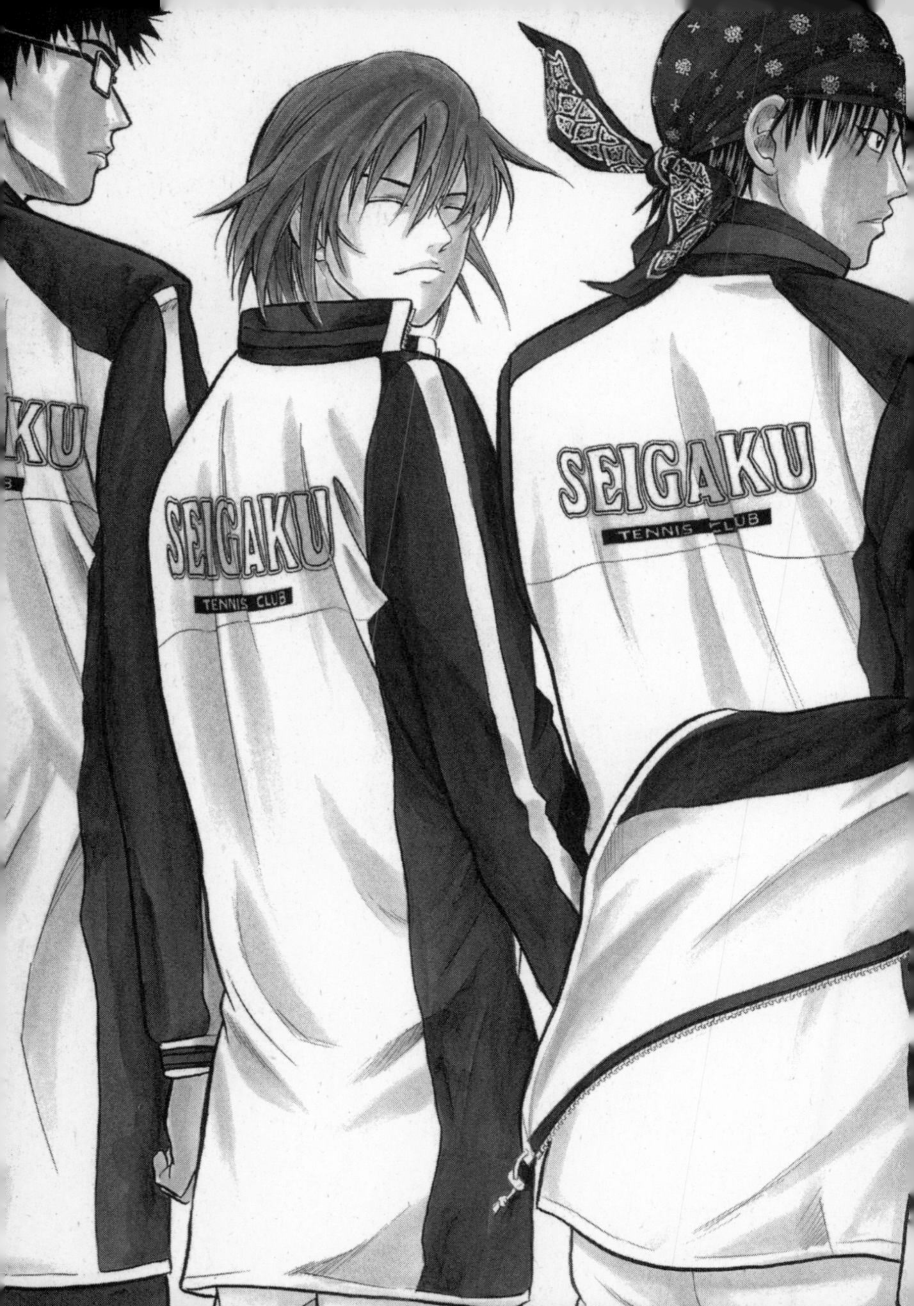
SEIGAKU
TENNIS CLUB
SEIGAKU
TENNIS CLUB

テニスの王子様

THE PRINCE OF TENNIS

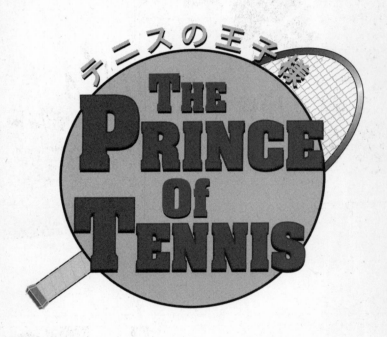

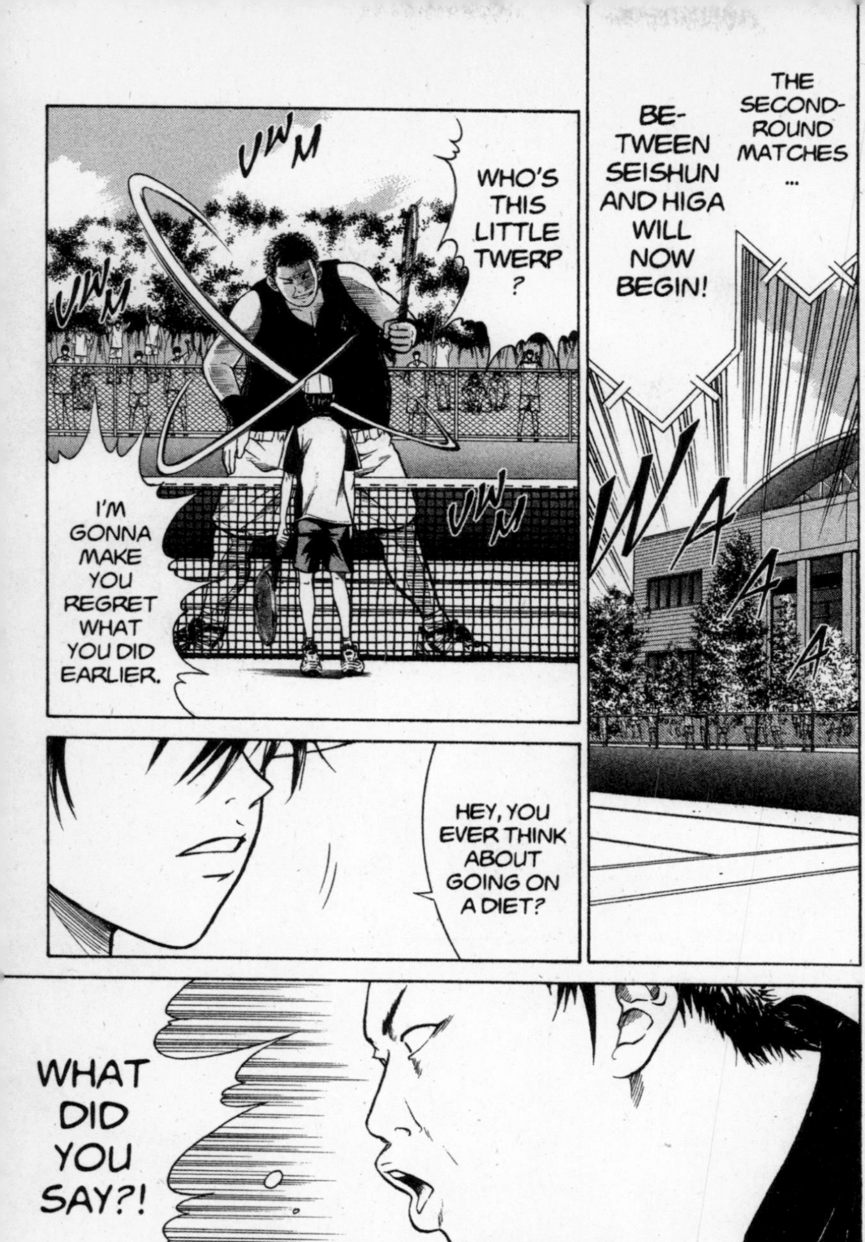
THE SECOND-ROUND MATCHES...
BE-TWEEN SEISHUN AND HIGA WILL NOW BEGIN!
WAAAA
WHO'S THIS LITTLE TWERP?
VWM
VWM
I'M GONNA MAKE YOU REGRET WHAT YOU DID EARLIER.
VWM
HEY, YOU EVER THINK ABOUT GOING ON A DIET?
WHAT DID YOU SAY?!

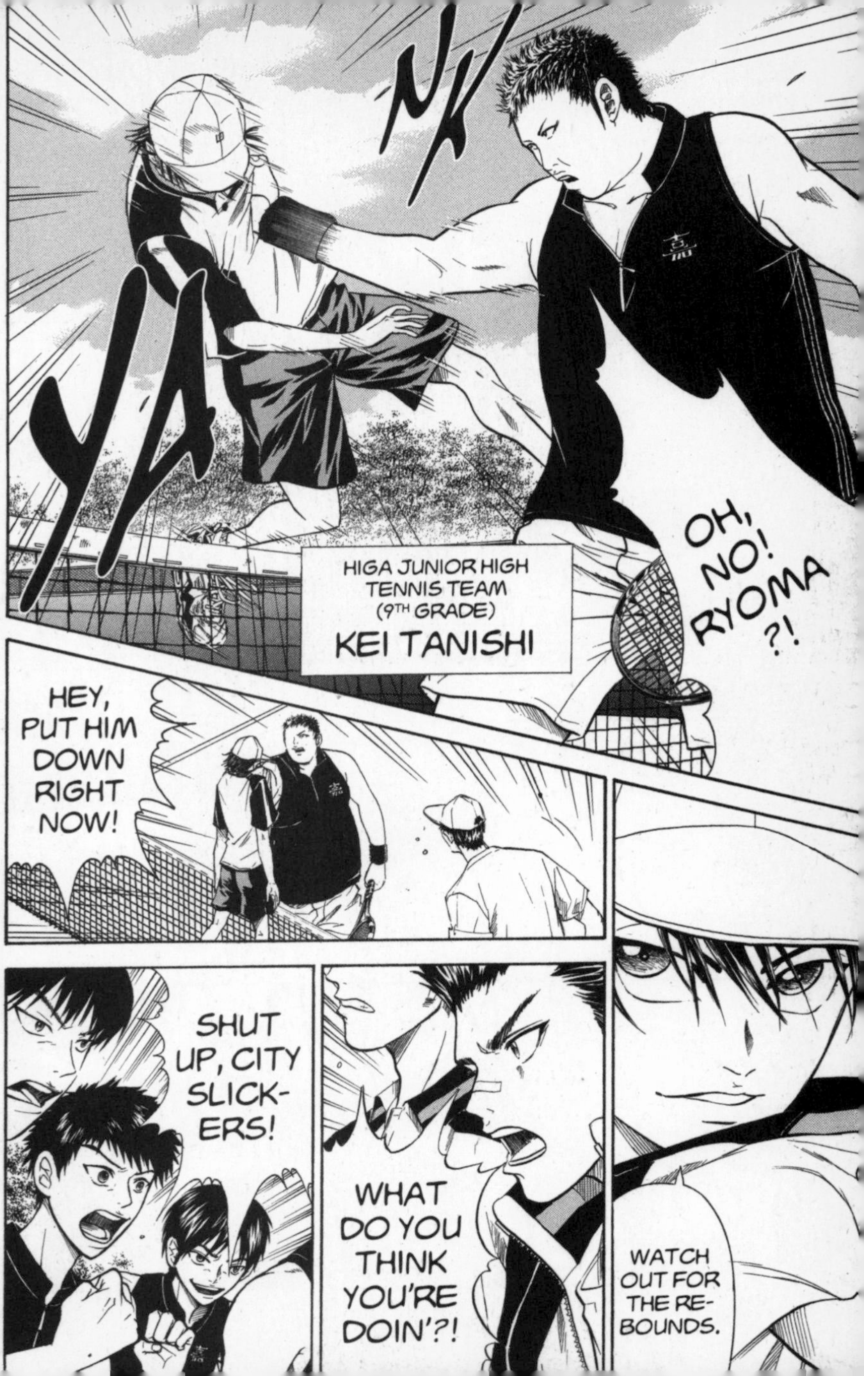

YANK
OH, NO! RYOMA ?!
HIGA JUNIOR HIGH TENNIS TEAM (9TH GRADE) KEI TANISHI
HEY, PUT HIM DOWN RIGHT NOW!
WHAT DO YOU THINK YOU'RE DOIN'?!
SHUT UP, CITY SLICK-ERS!
WATCH OUT FOR THE RE-BOUNDS.

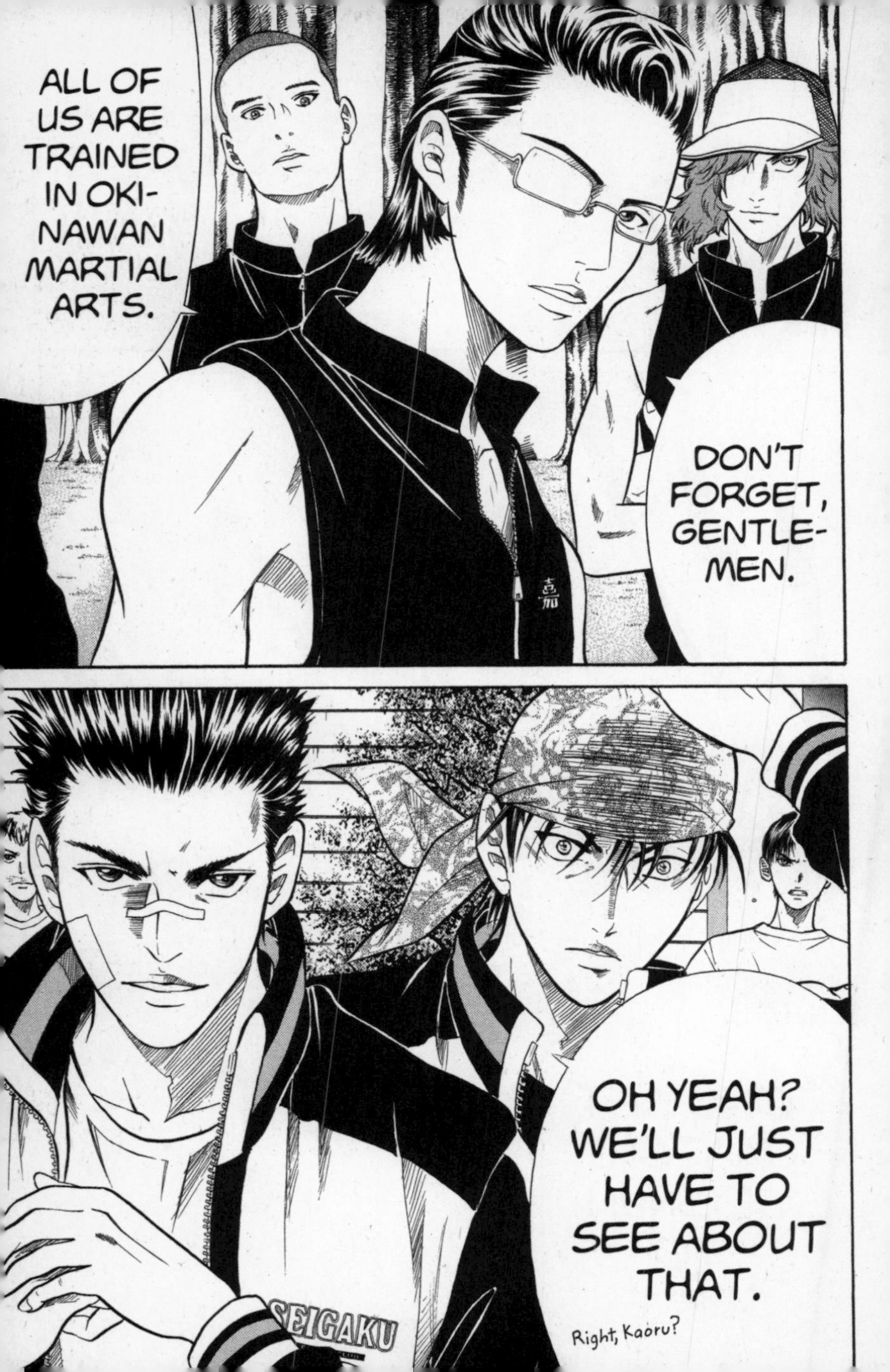
DON'T FORGET, GENTLE-MEN.
ALL OF US ARE TRAINED IN OKI-NAWAN MARTIAL ARTS.
OH YEAH? WE'LL JUST HAVE TO SEE ABOUT THAT.
Right, Kaoru?
SEIGAKU

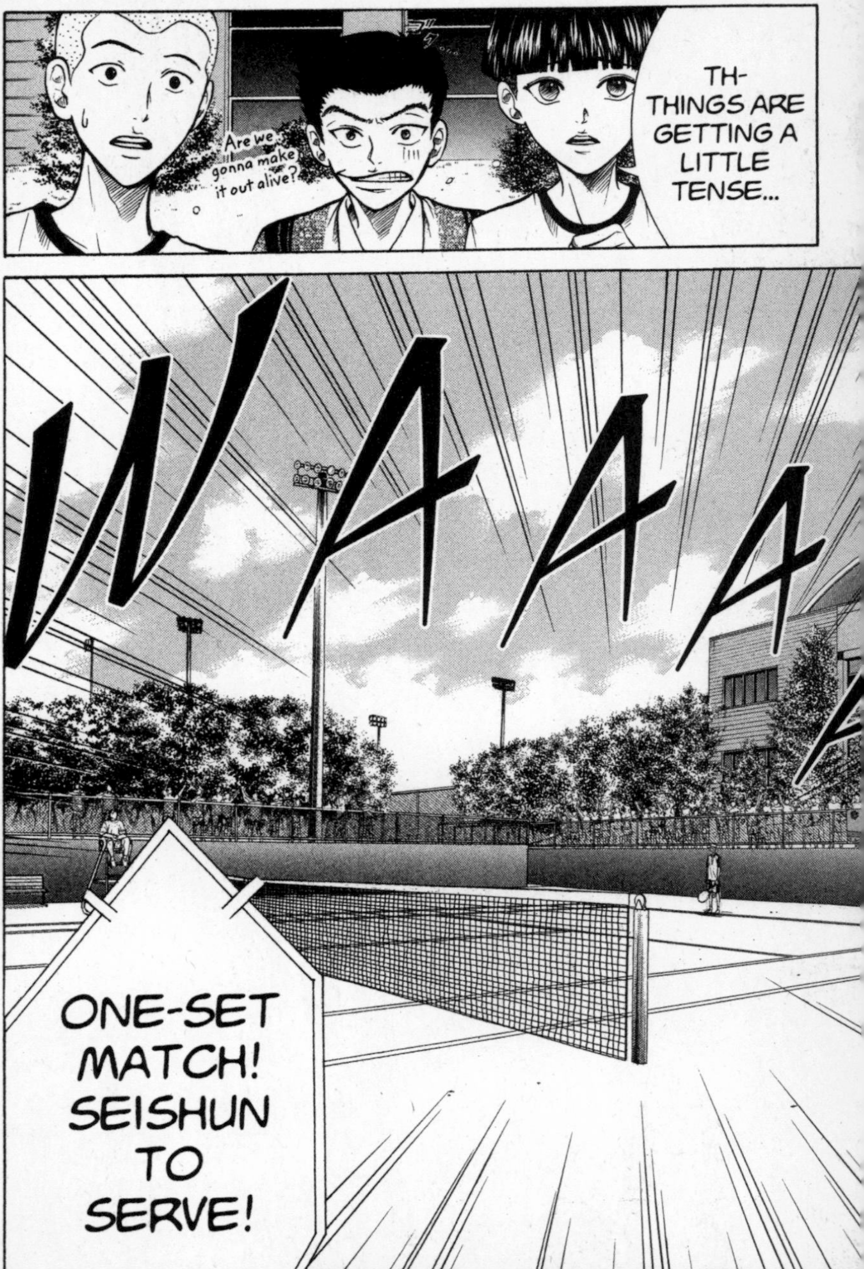
TH- THINGS ARE GETTING A LITTLE TENSE...
Are we gonna make it out alive?
WAAAA
ONE-SET MATCH! SEISHUN TO SERVE!

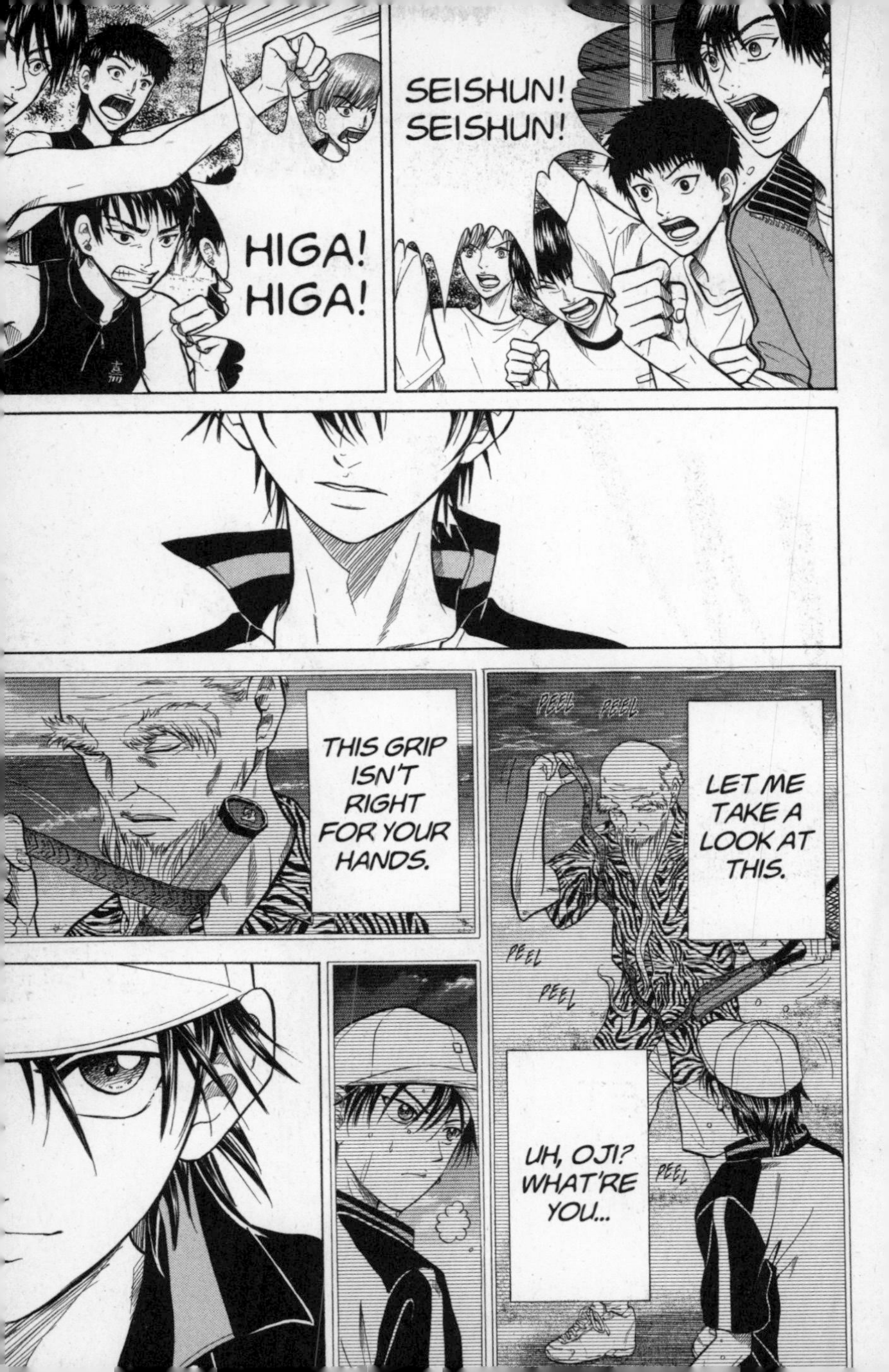
SEISHUN! SEISHUN!
HIGA! HIGA!
PEEL PEEL
LET ME TAKE A LOOK AT THIS.
PEEL
PEEL
UH, OJI? WHAT'RE YOU...
PEEL
THIS GRIP ISN'T RIGHT FOR YOUR HANDS.

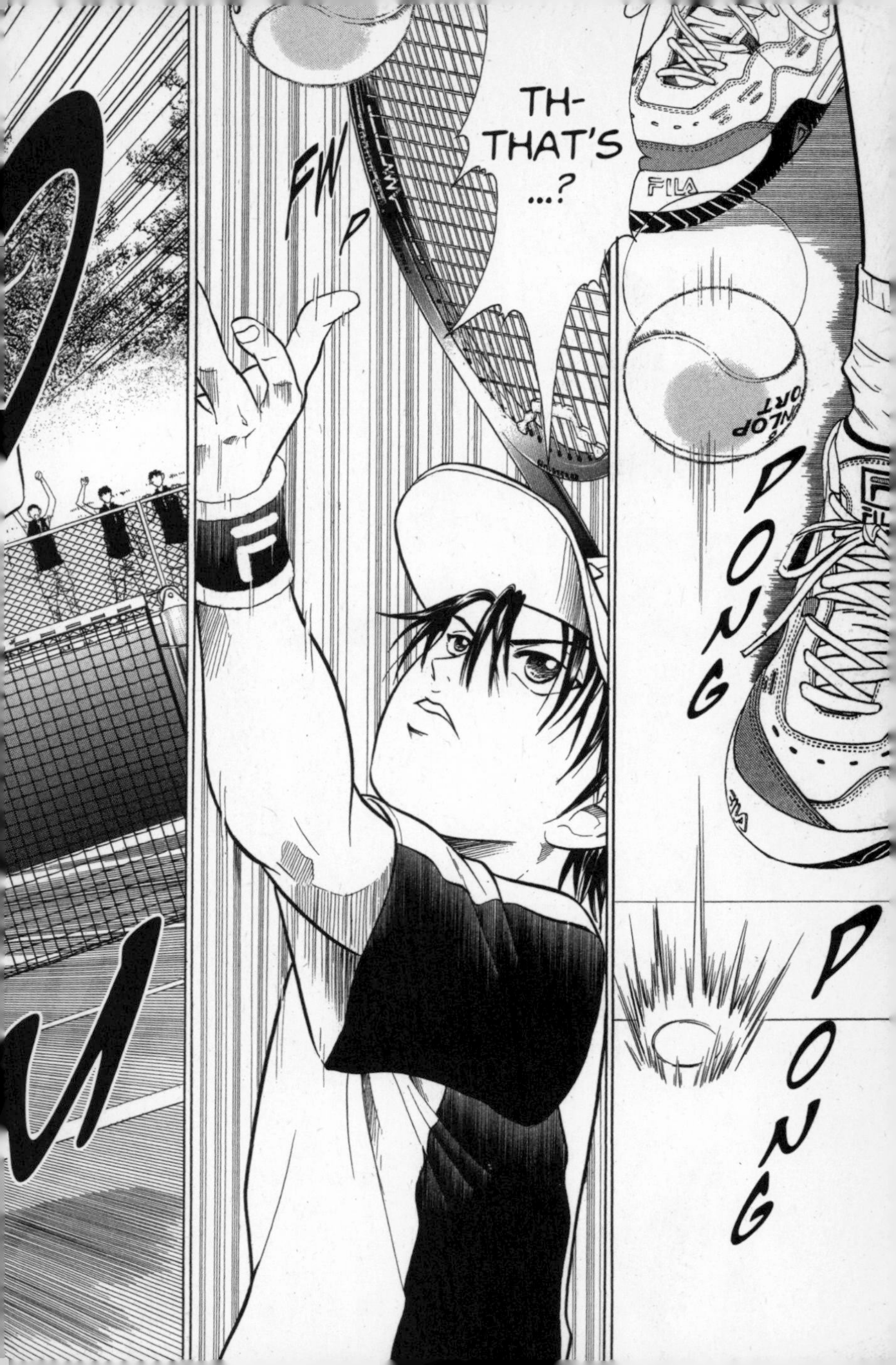
DOONG
DOONG
TH- THAT'S ...?
FWP

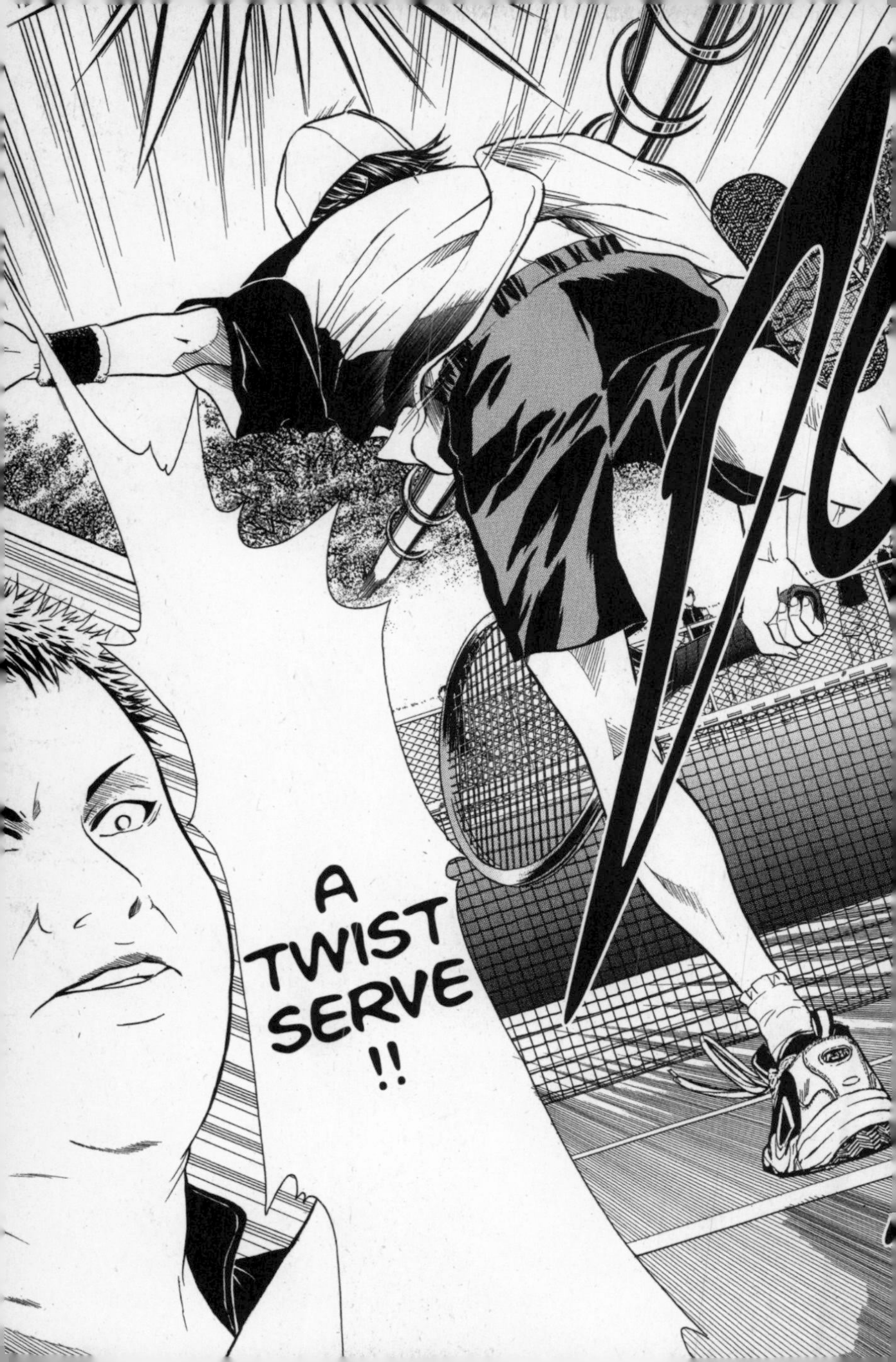
A TWIST SERVE !!

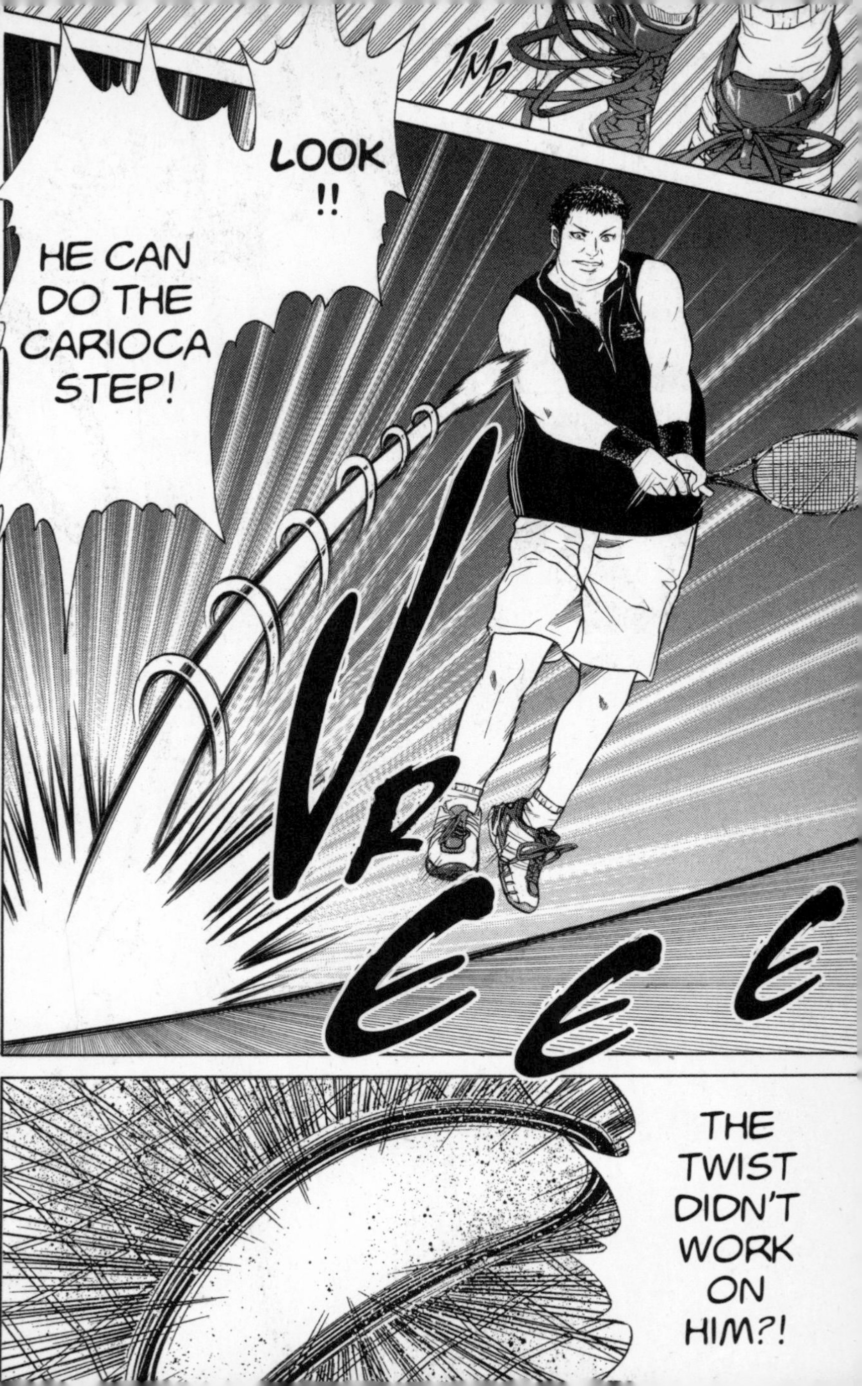
TMP
LOOK !!
HE CAN DO THE CARIOCA STEP!
VREEEE
THE TWIST DIDN'T WORK ON HIM?!

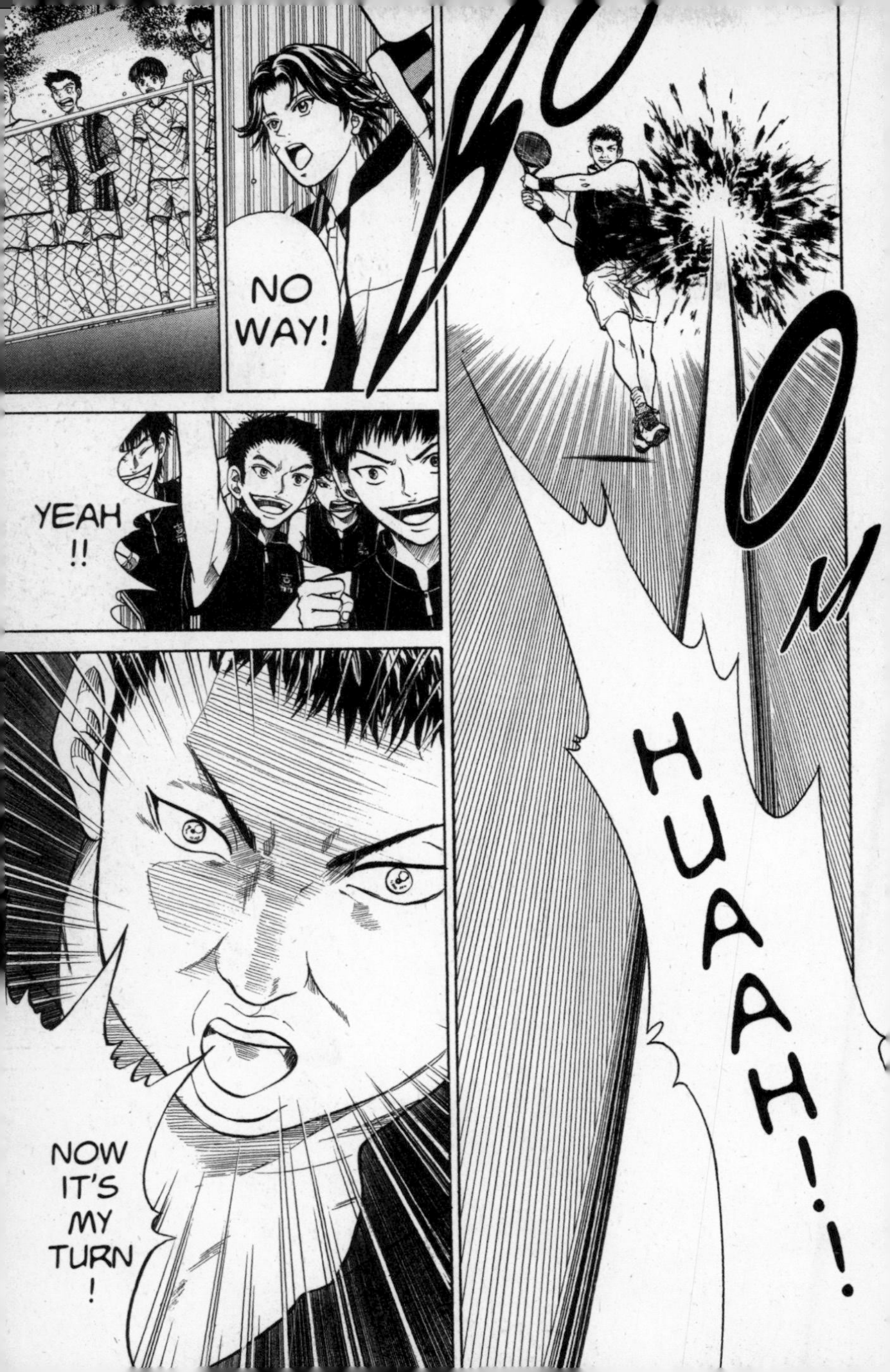
HUAAH!!!
NO WAY!
YEAH !!
NOW IT'S MY TURN !

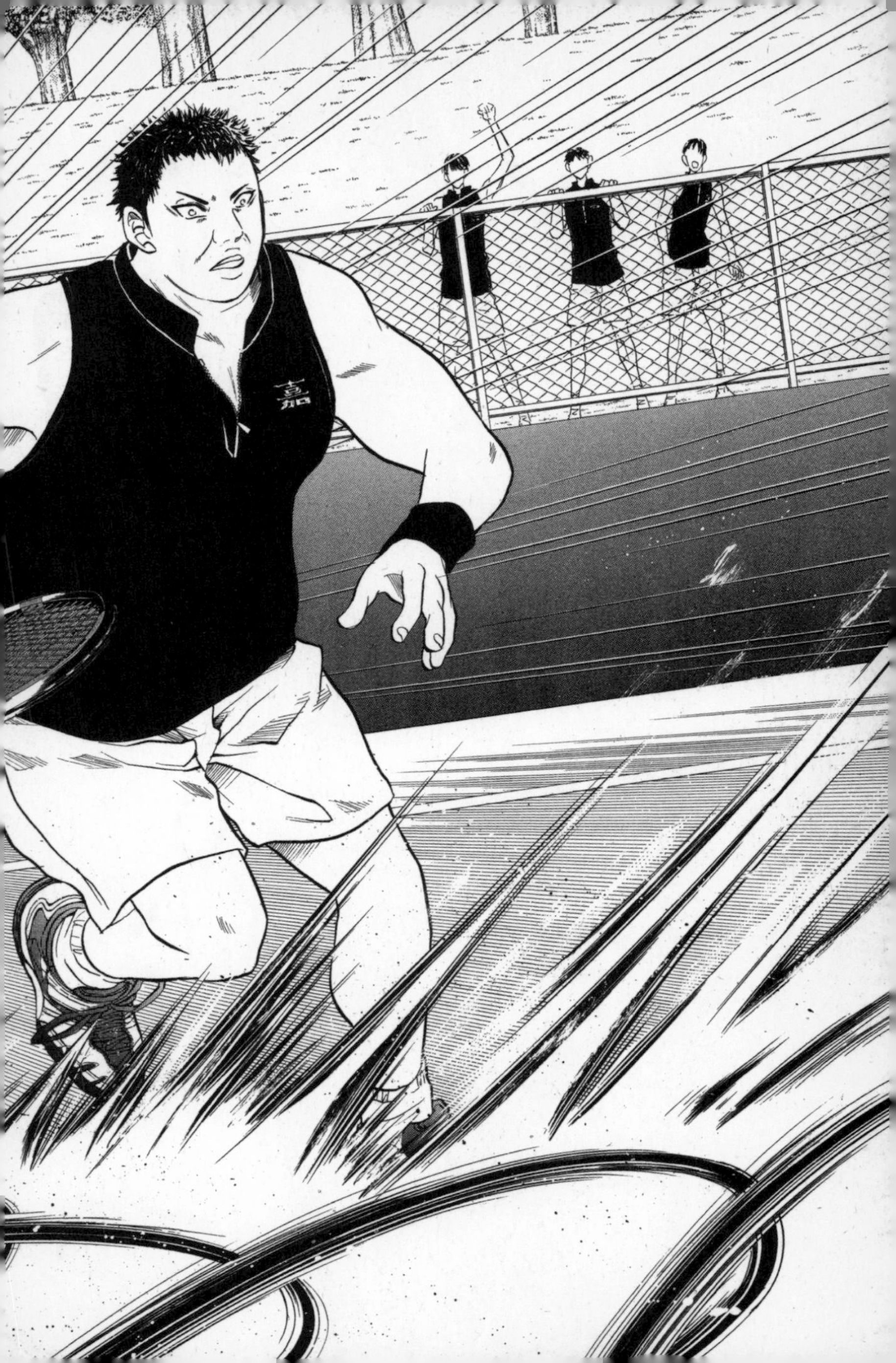
嘉

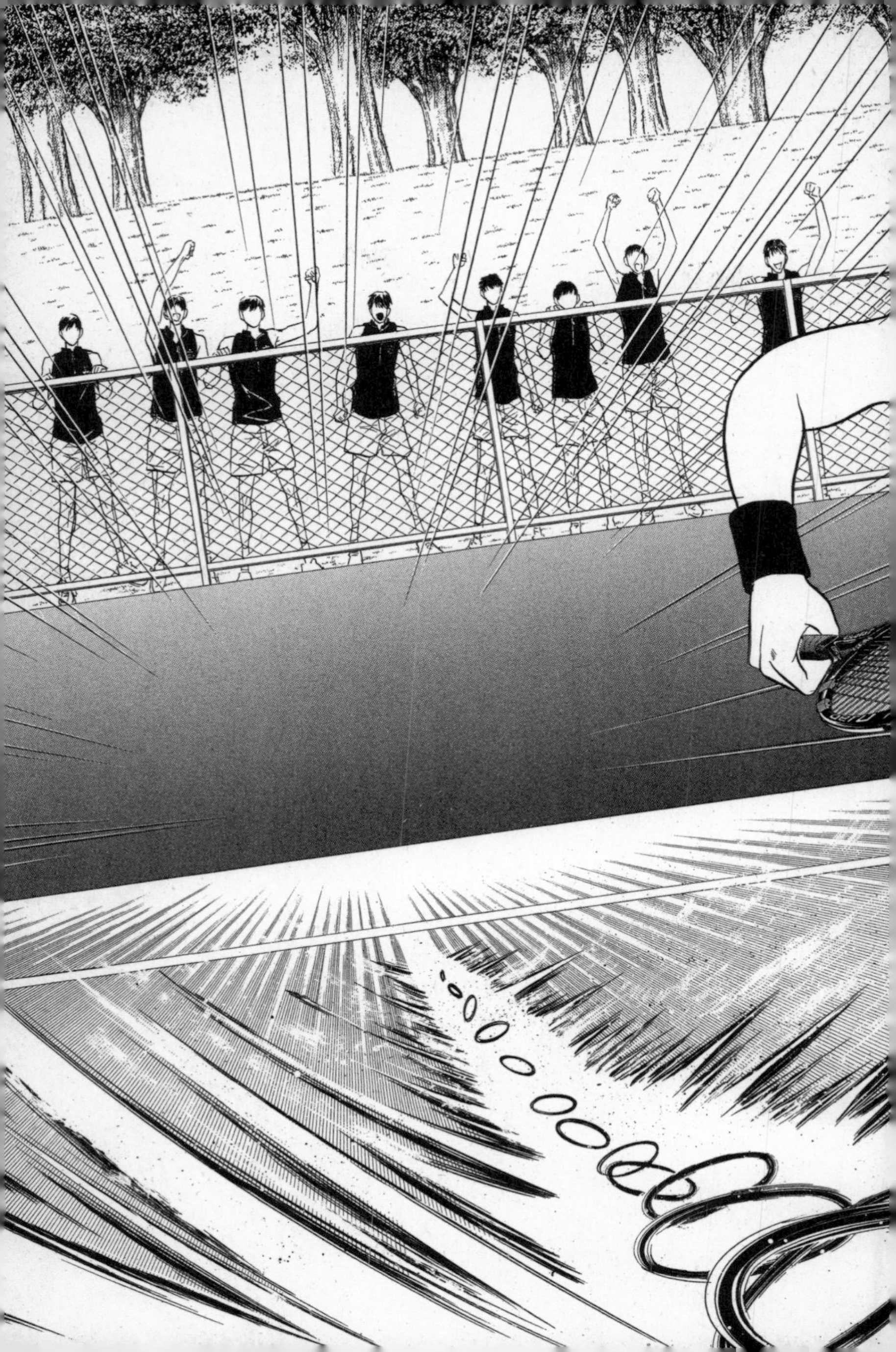

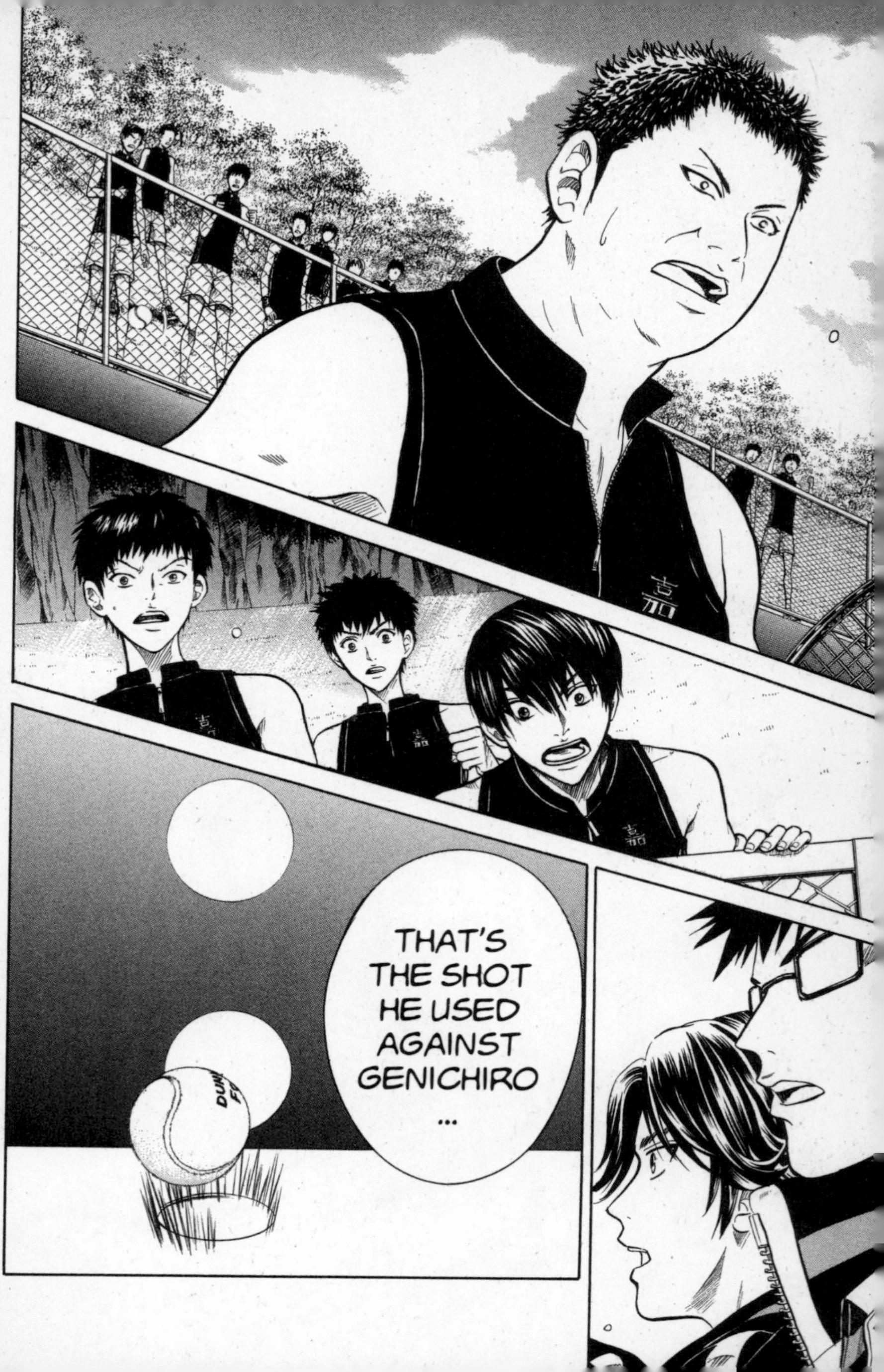
THAT'S THE SHOT HE USED AGAINST GENICHIRO ...

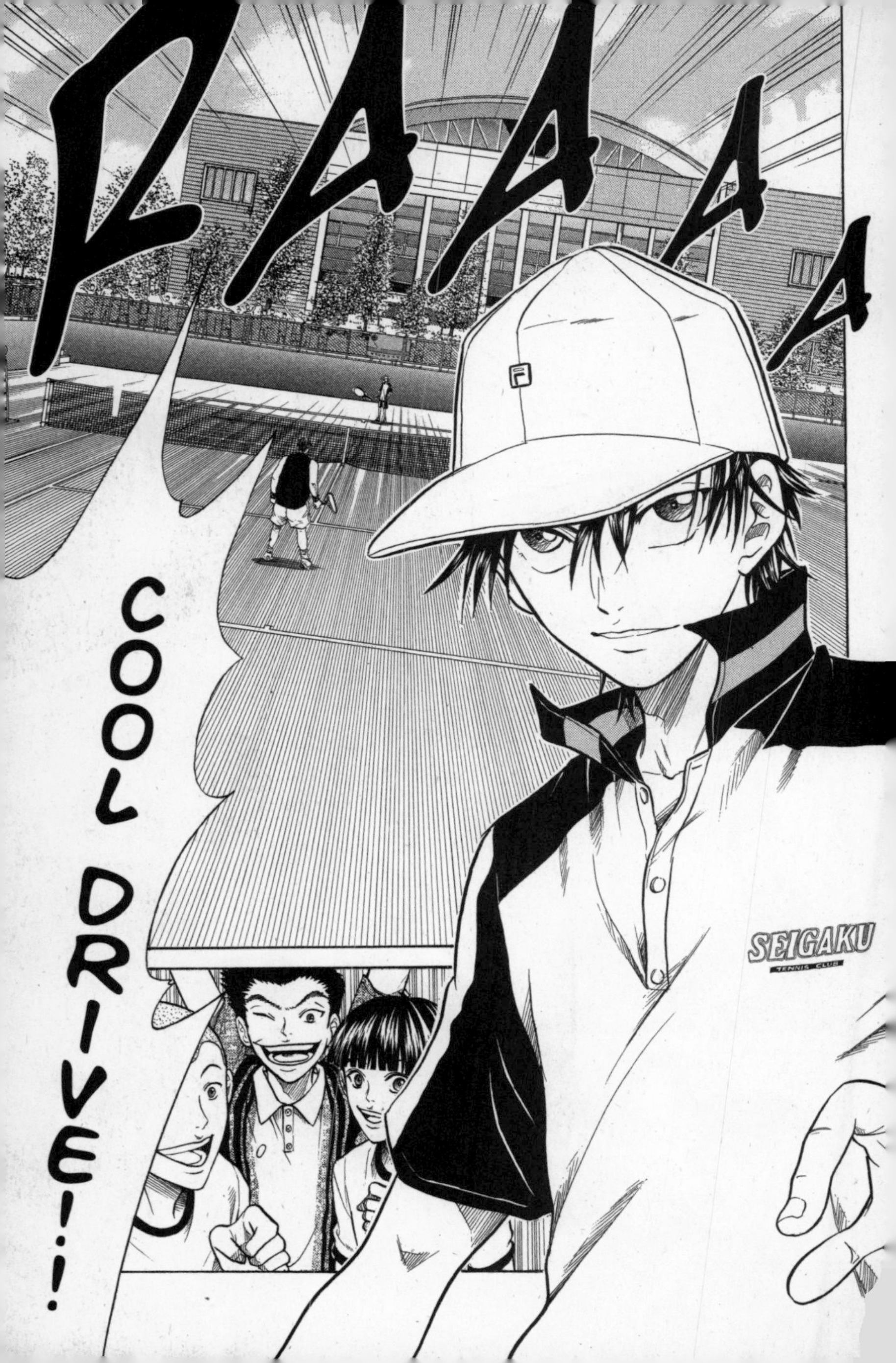
PAAAAA
COOL DRIVE!!!
SEIGAKU
TENNIS CLUB

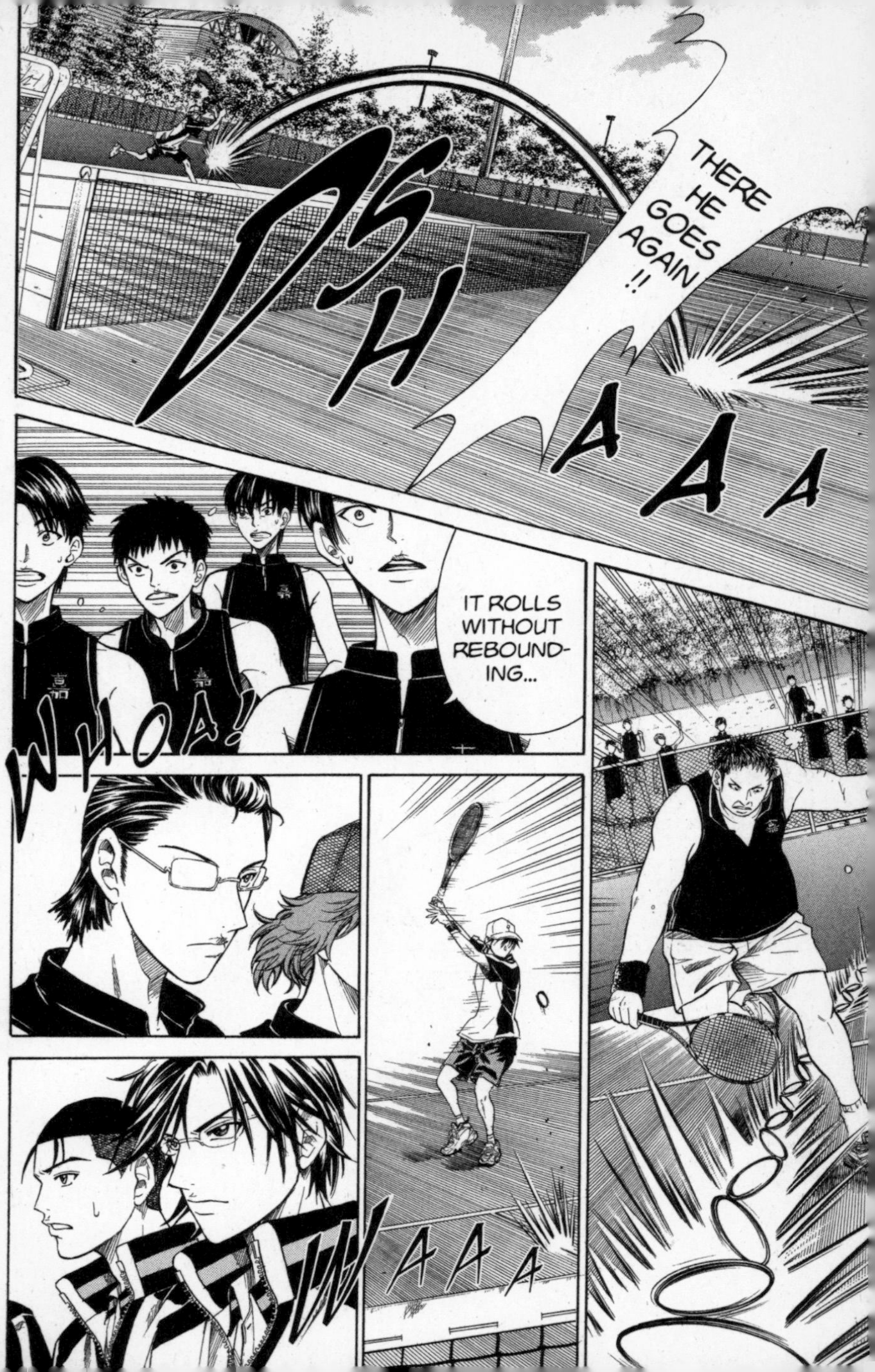

DOSH
THERE HE GOES AGAIN!!
AAA
IT ROLLS WITHOUT REBOUNDING...
WHOA!
WAAAA

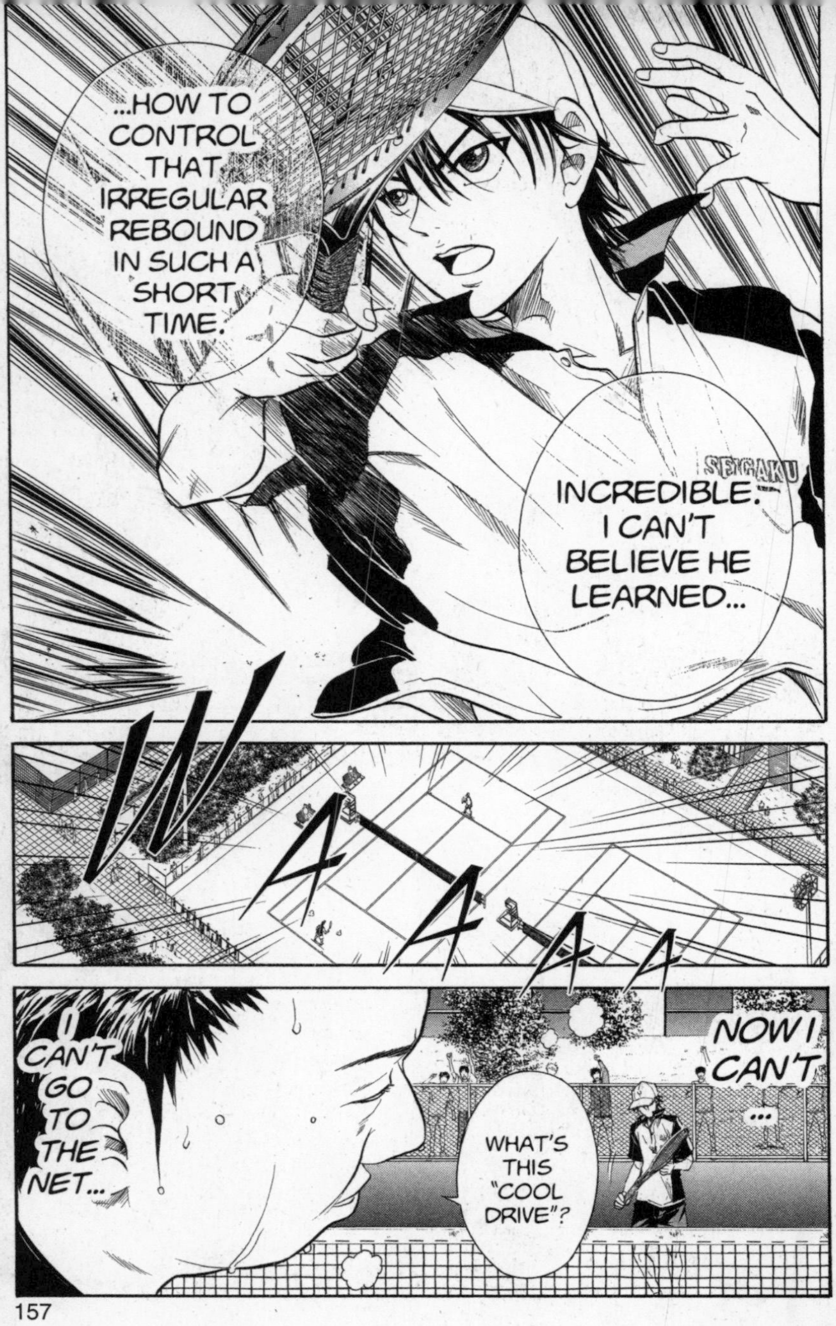
SEIGAKU
INCREDIBLE. I CAN'T BELIEVE HE LEARNED...
...HOW TO CONTROL THAT IRREGULAR REBOUND IN SUCH A SHORT TIME.
WAAAAA
NOW I CAN'T ...
WHAT'S THIS "COOL DRIVE"?
I CAN'T GO TO THE NET...

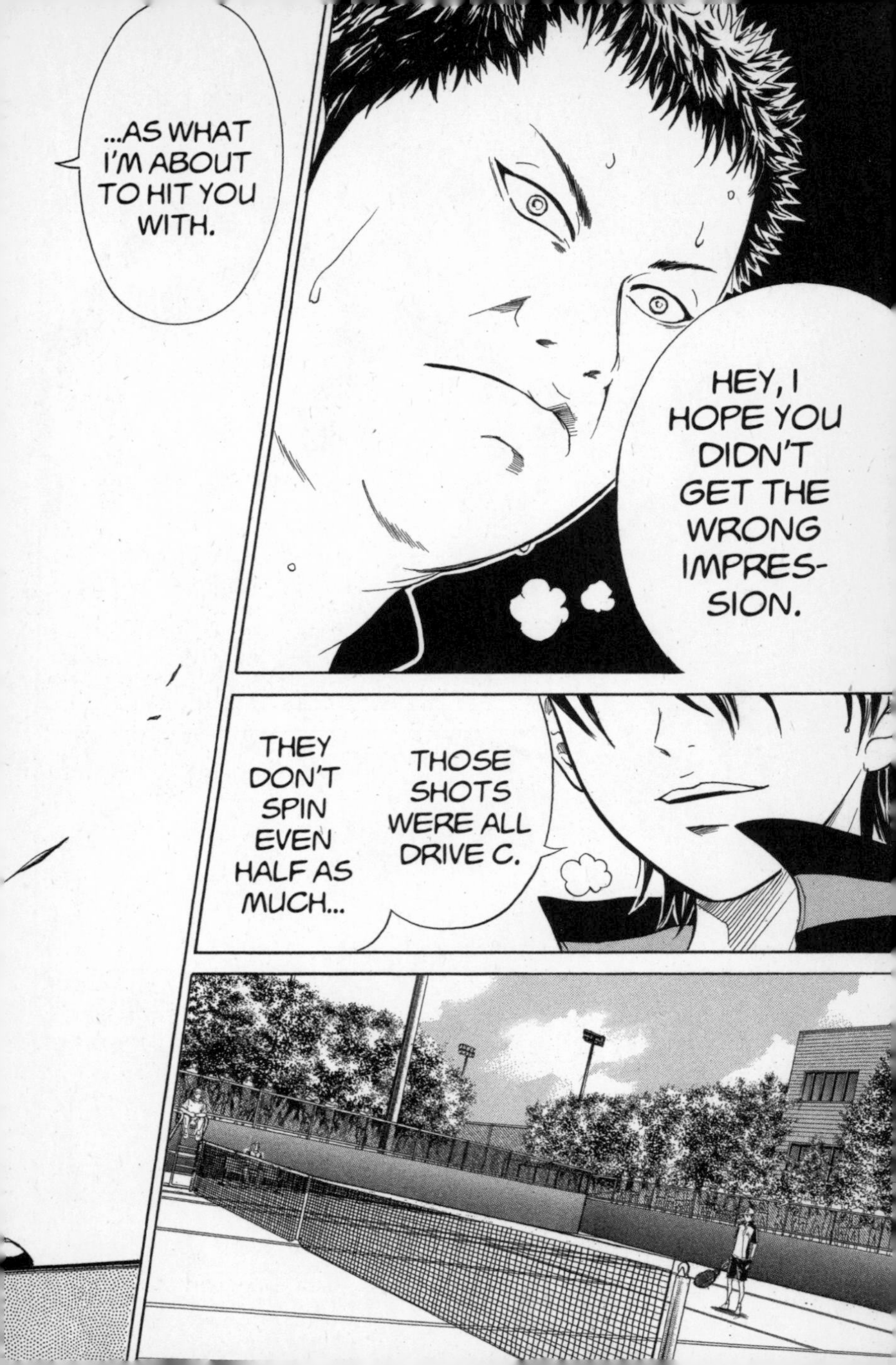
HEY, I HOPE YOU DIDN'T GET THE WRONG IMPRES-SION.
THOSE SHOTS WERE ALL DRIVE C.
THEY DON'T SPIN EVEN HALF AS MUCH...
...AS WHAT I'M ABOUT TO HIT YOU WITH.

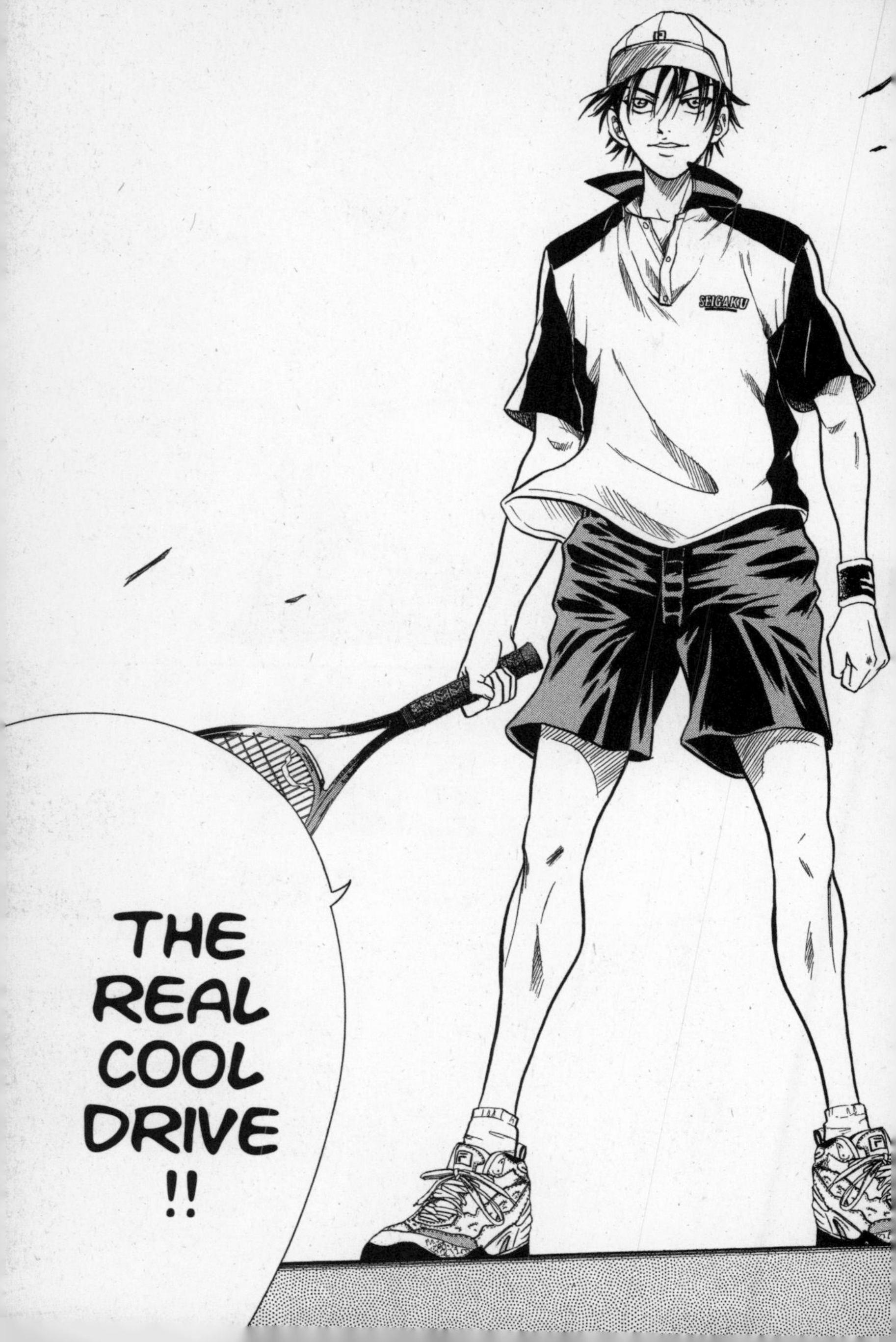

SEIGAKU
THE REAL COOL DRIVE !!

テニスの王子様

THE PRINCE OF TENNIS

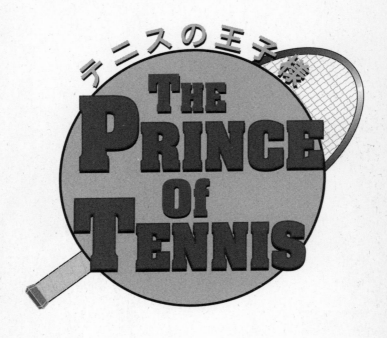

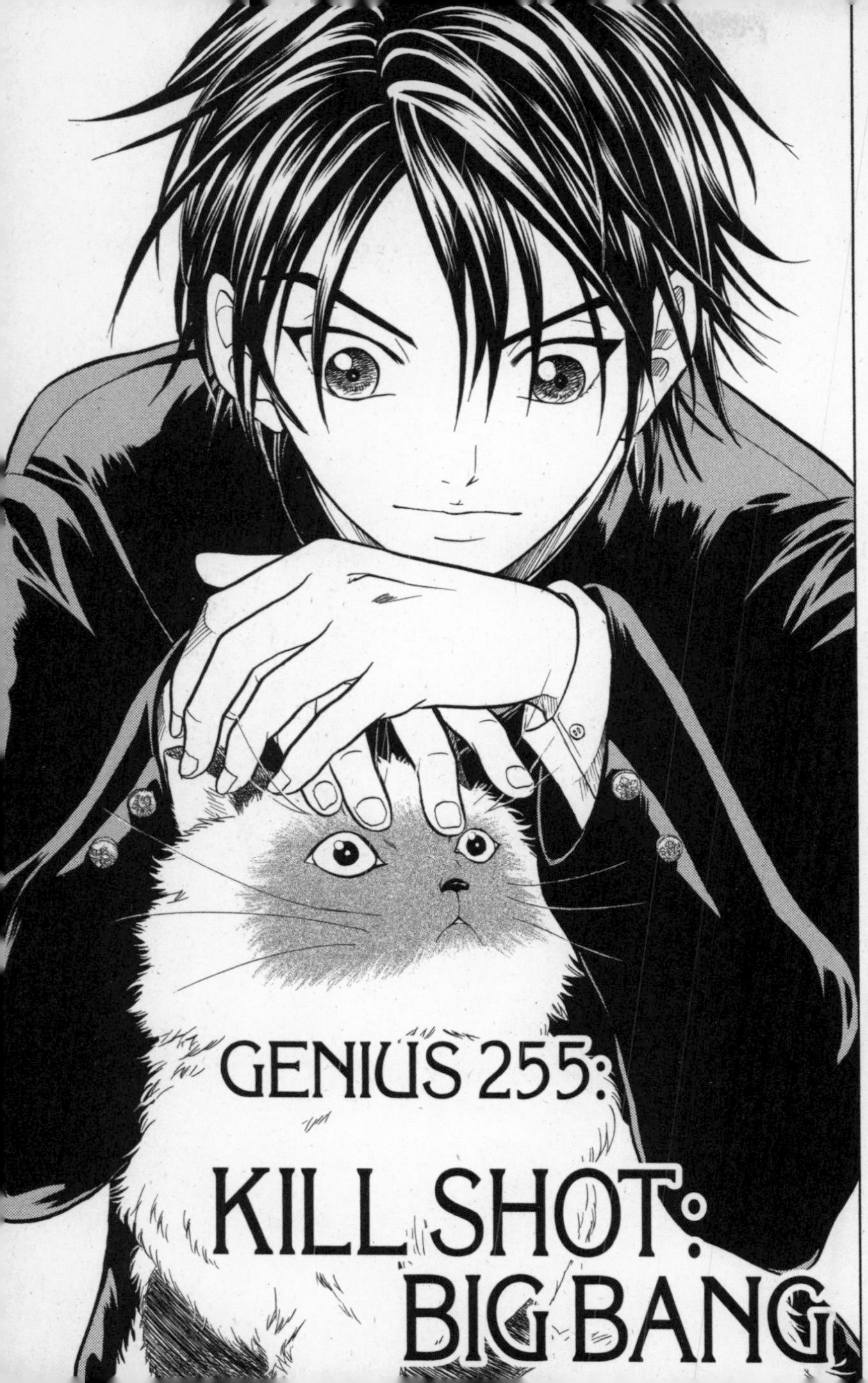
GENIUS 255:
KILL SHOT:
BIG BANG

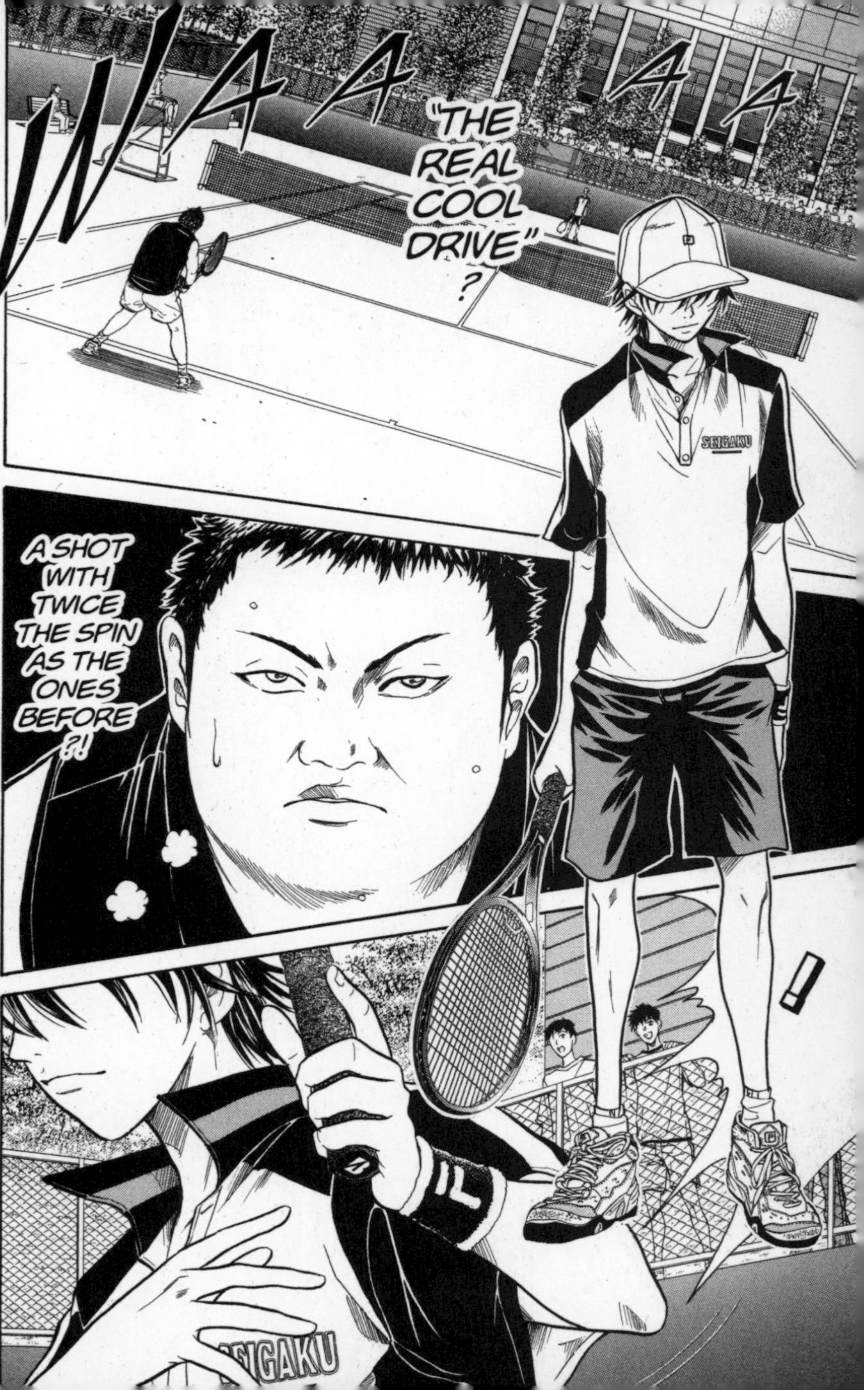
WAAAAA
"THE REAL COOL DRIVE" ?
A SHOT WITH TWICE THE SPIN AS THE ONES BEFORE ?!
!

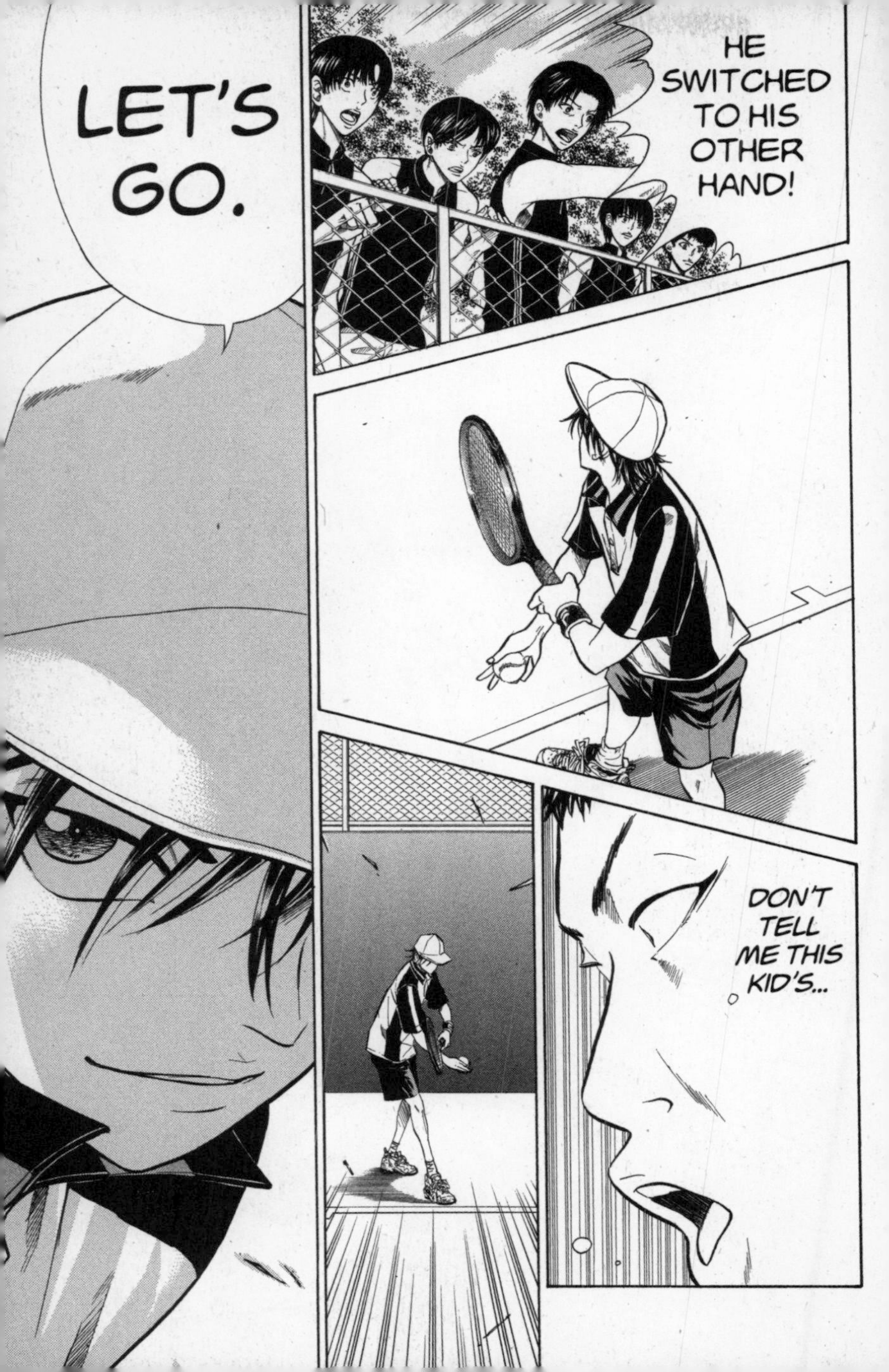
HE SWITCHED TO HIS OTHER HAND!
DON'T TELL ME THIS KID'S...
LET'S GO.

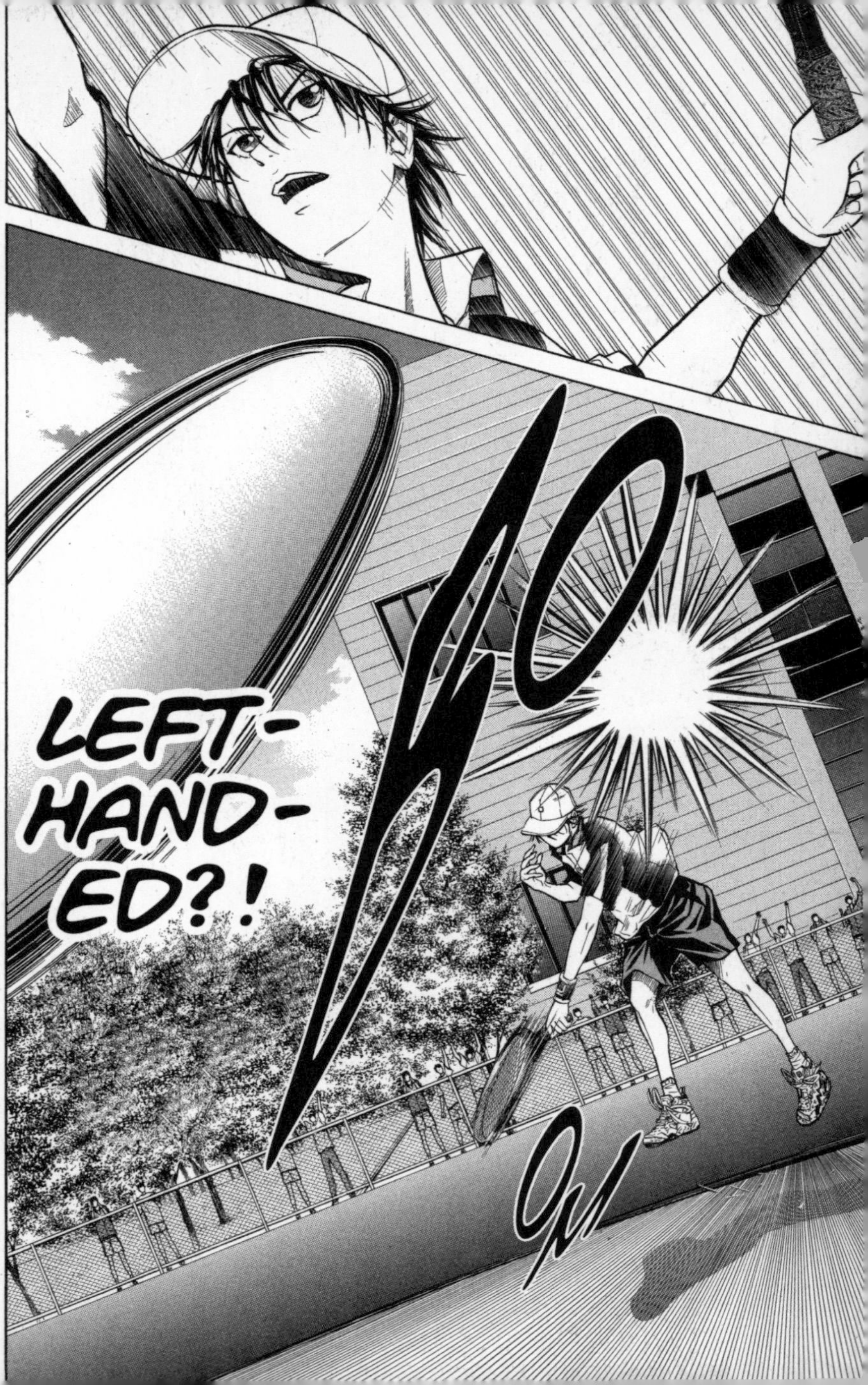
LEFT-HANDED?!

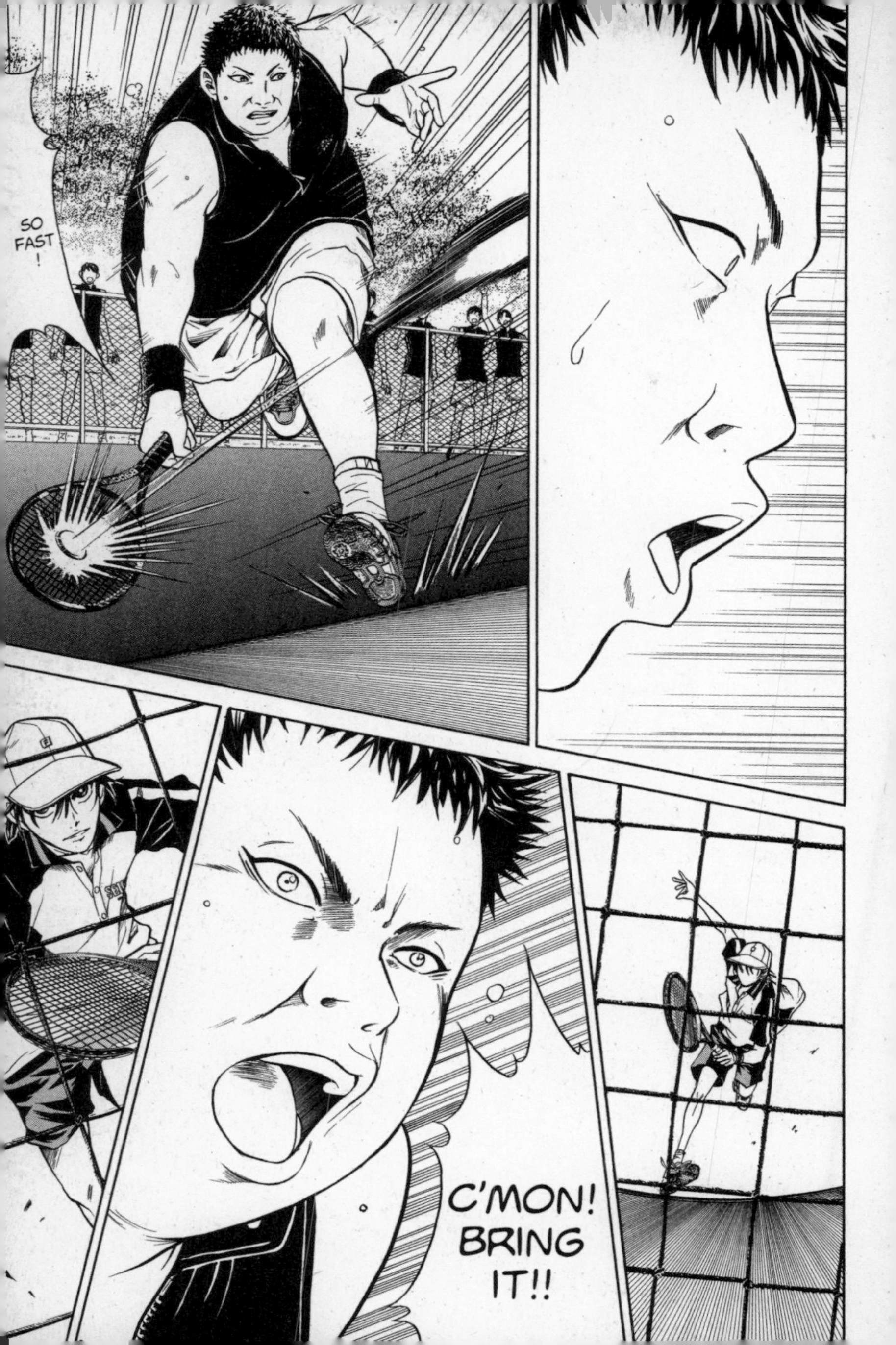
SO FAST!
C'MON! BRING IT!!

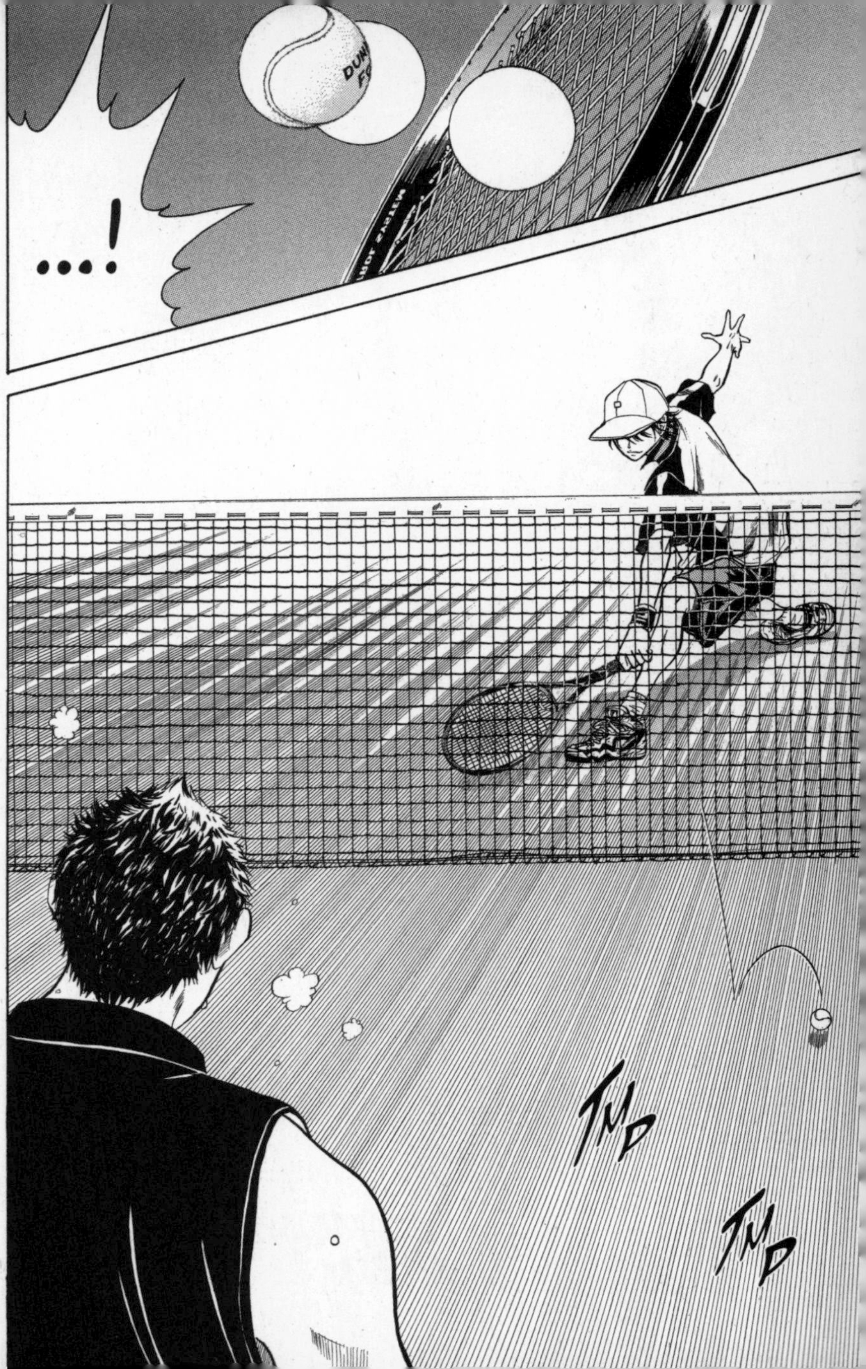
...!
TMP
TMP

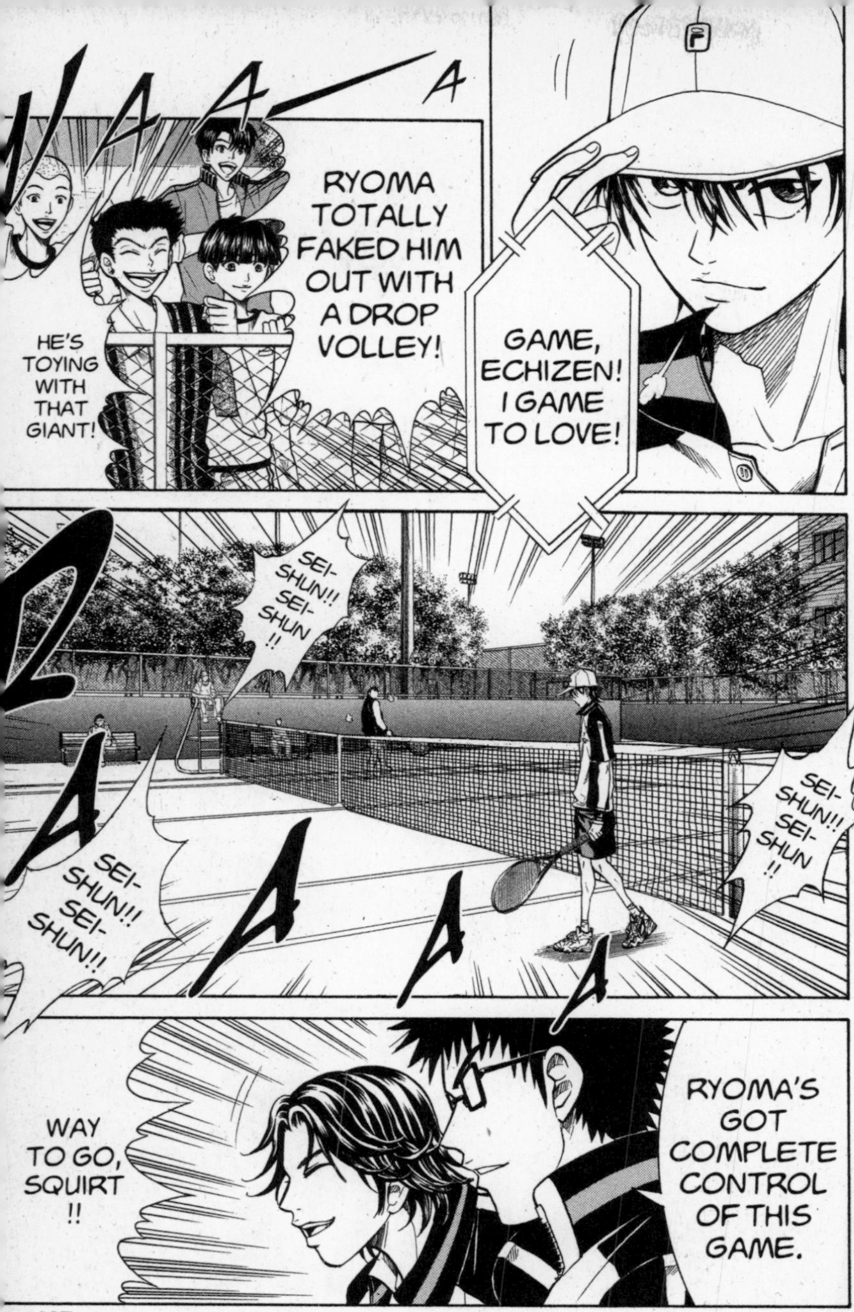
GAME, ECHIZEN! 1 GAME TO LOVE!
WAAAA
RYOMA TOTALLY FAKED HIM OUT WITH A DROP VOLLEY!
HE'S TOYING WITH THAT GIANT!
SEI-SHUN!! SEI-SHUN!!
SEI-SHUN!! SEI-SHUN!!
WAAAA
SEI-SHUN!! SEI-SHUN!!
RYOMA'S GOT COMPLETE CONTROL OF THIS GAME.
WAY TO GO, SQUIRT!!

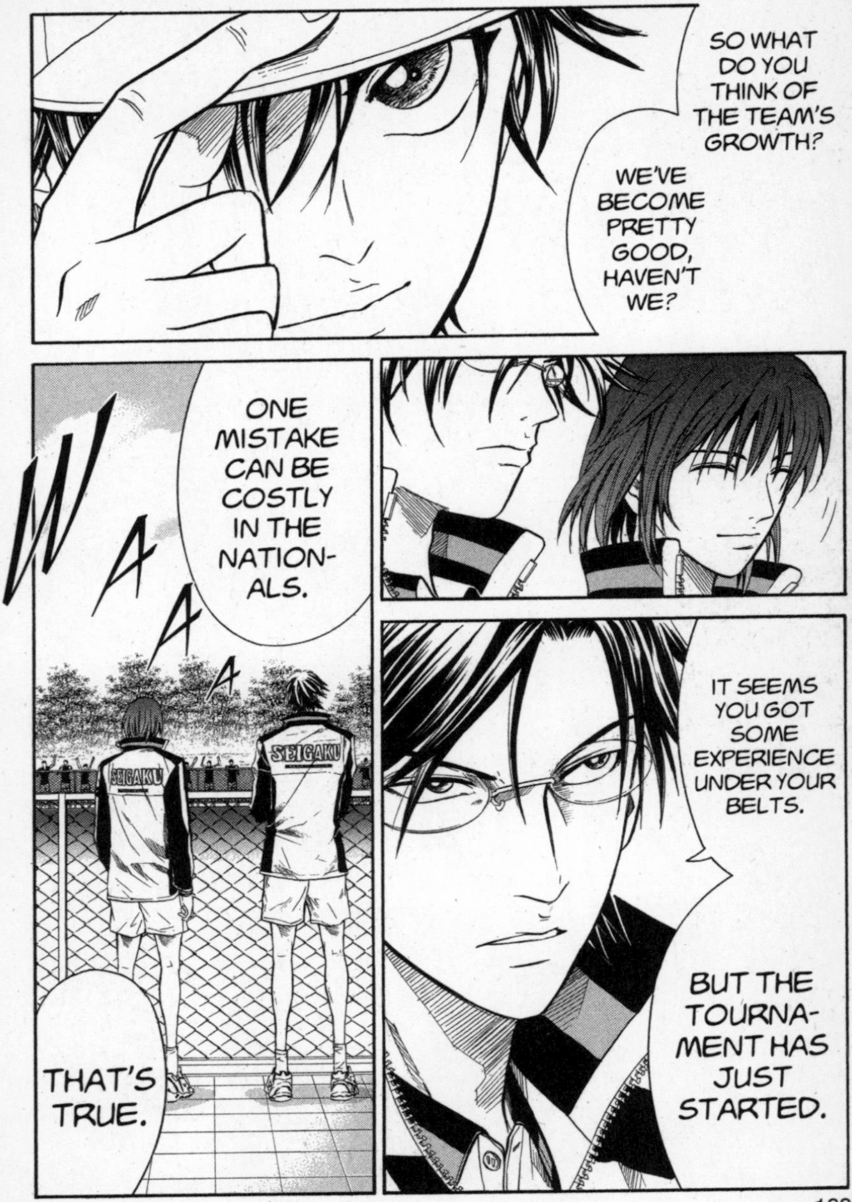
SO WHAT DO YOU THINK OF THE TEAM'S GROWTH?
WE'VE BECOME PRETTY GOOD, HAVEN'T WE?
IT SEEMS YOU GOT SOME EXPERIENCE UNDER YOUR BELTS.
BUT THE TOURNA-MENT HAS JUST STARTED.
WAAA
ONE MISTAKE CAN BE COSTLY IN THE NATION-ALS.
SEIGAKU
SEIGAKU
THAT'S TRUE.

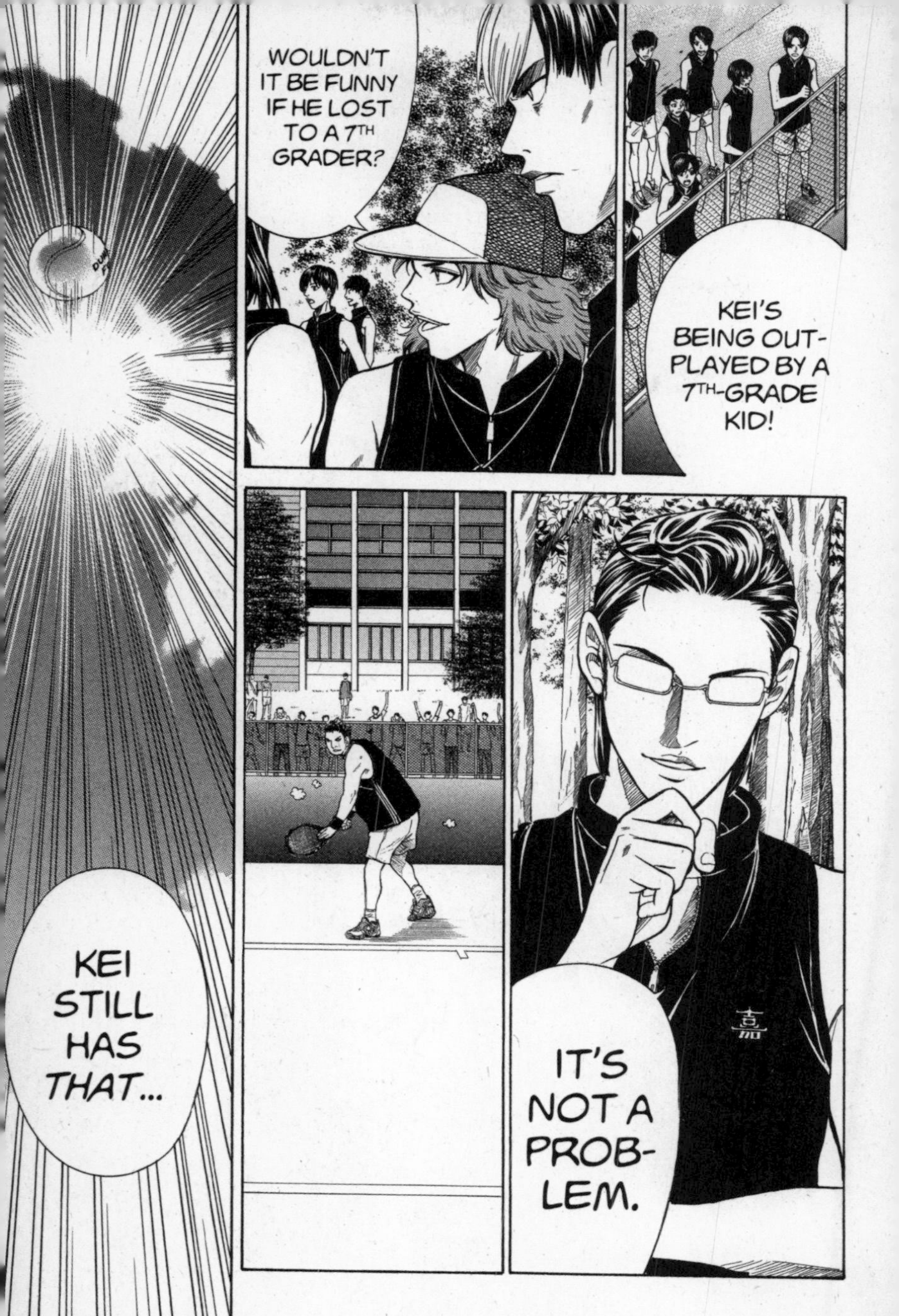
KEI'S BEING OUT-PLAYED BY A 7TH-GRADE KID!
WOULDN'T IT BE FUNNY IF HE LOST TO A 7TH GRADER?
IT'S NOT A PROB-LEM.
KEI STILL HAS THAT...

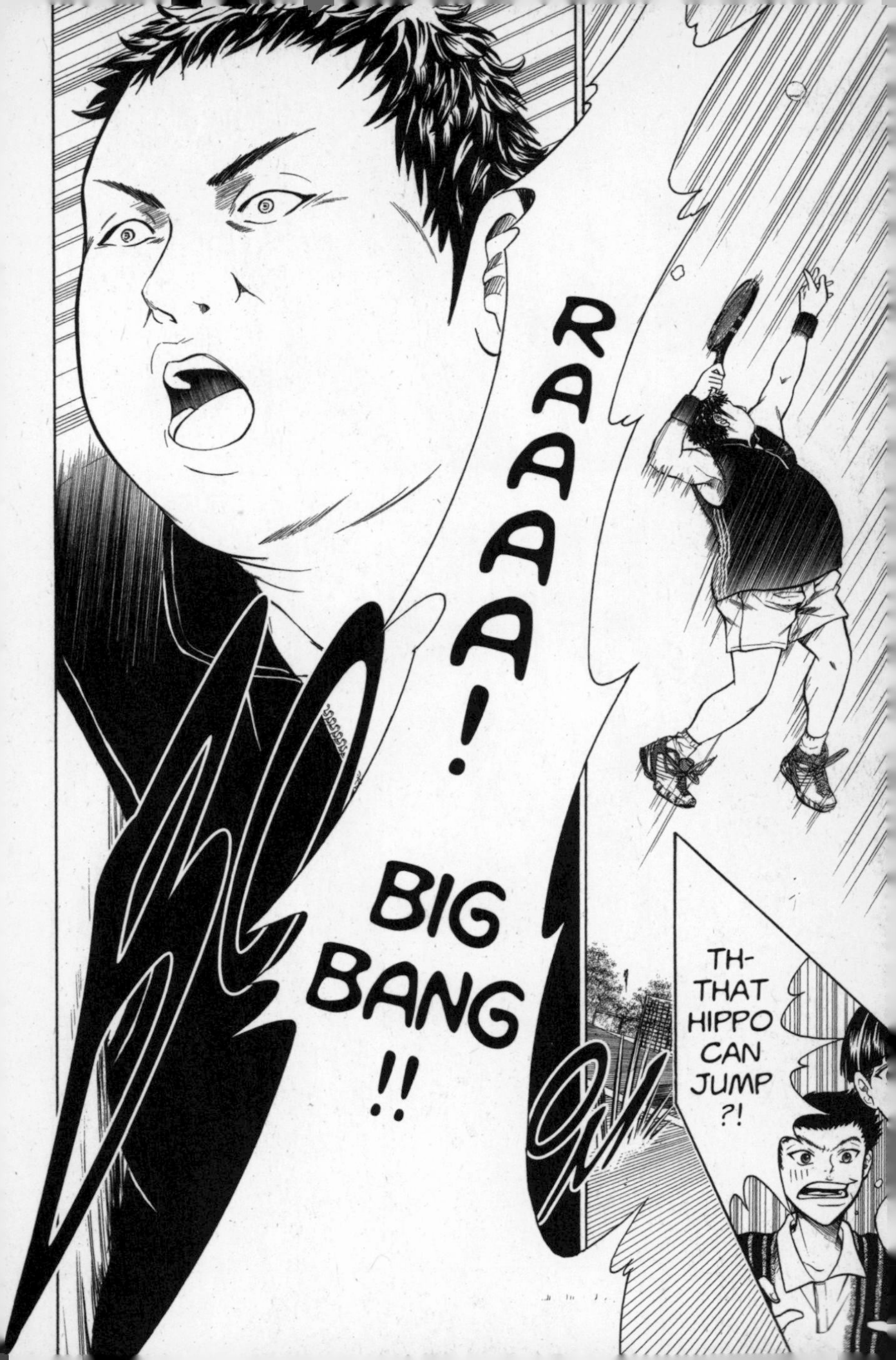
RAAAAAI!
BIG BANG!!
TH- THAT HIPPO CAN JUMP?!

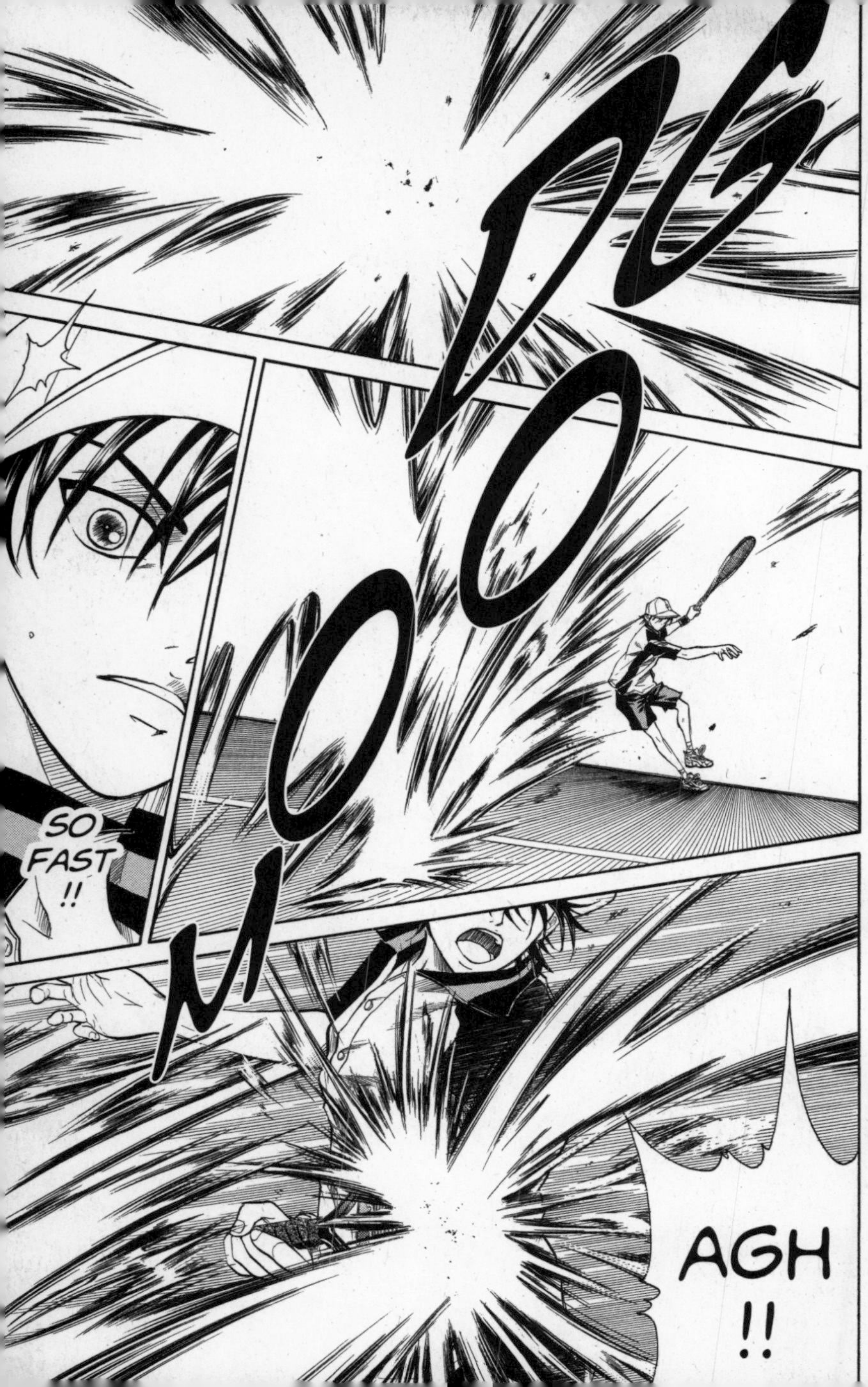
SO FAST !!
AGH !!

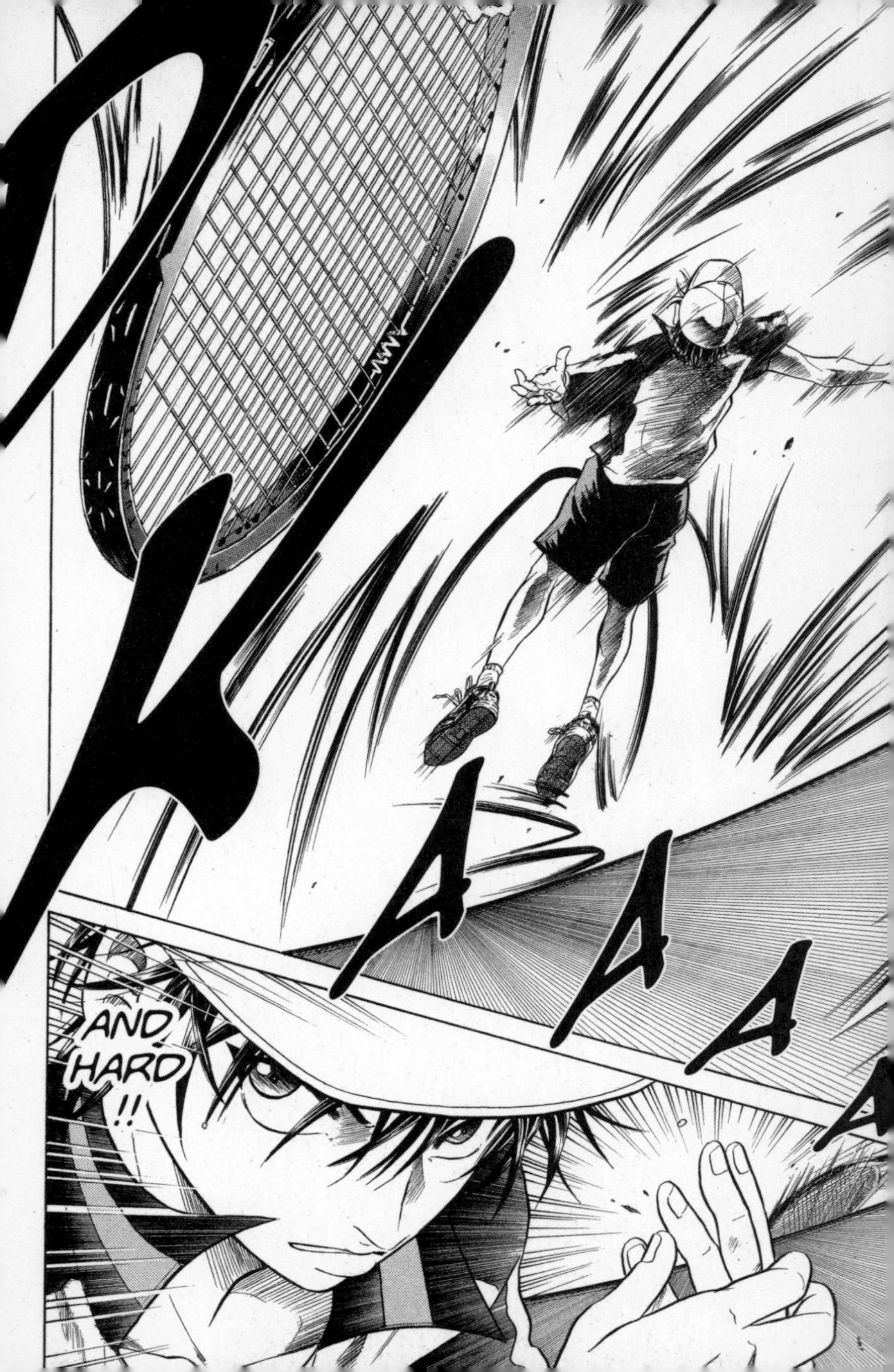
AND HARD!!

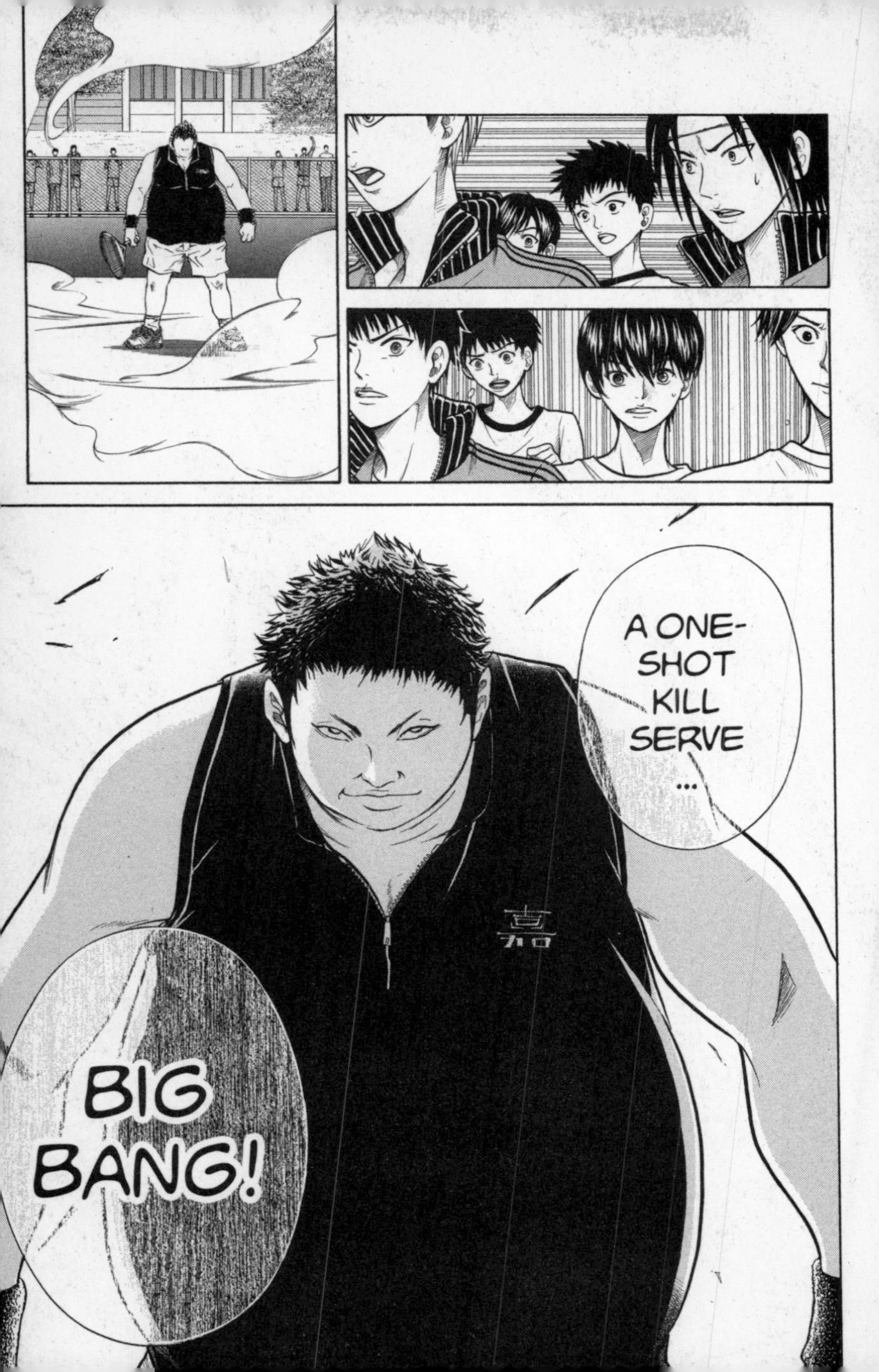
A ONE-SHOT KILL SERVE ...
BIG BANG!

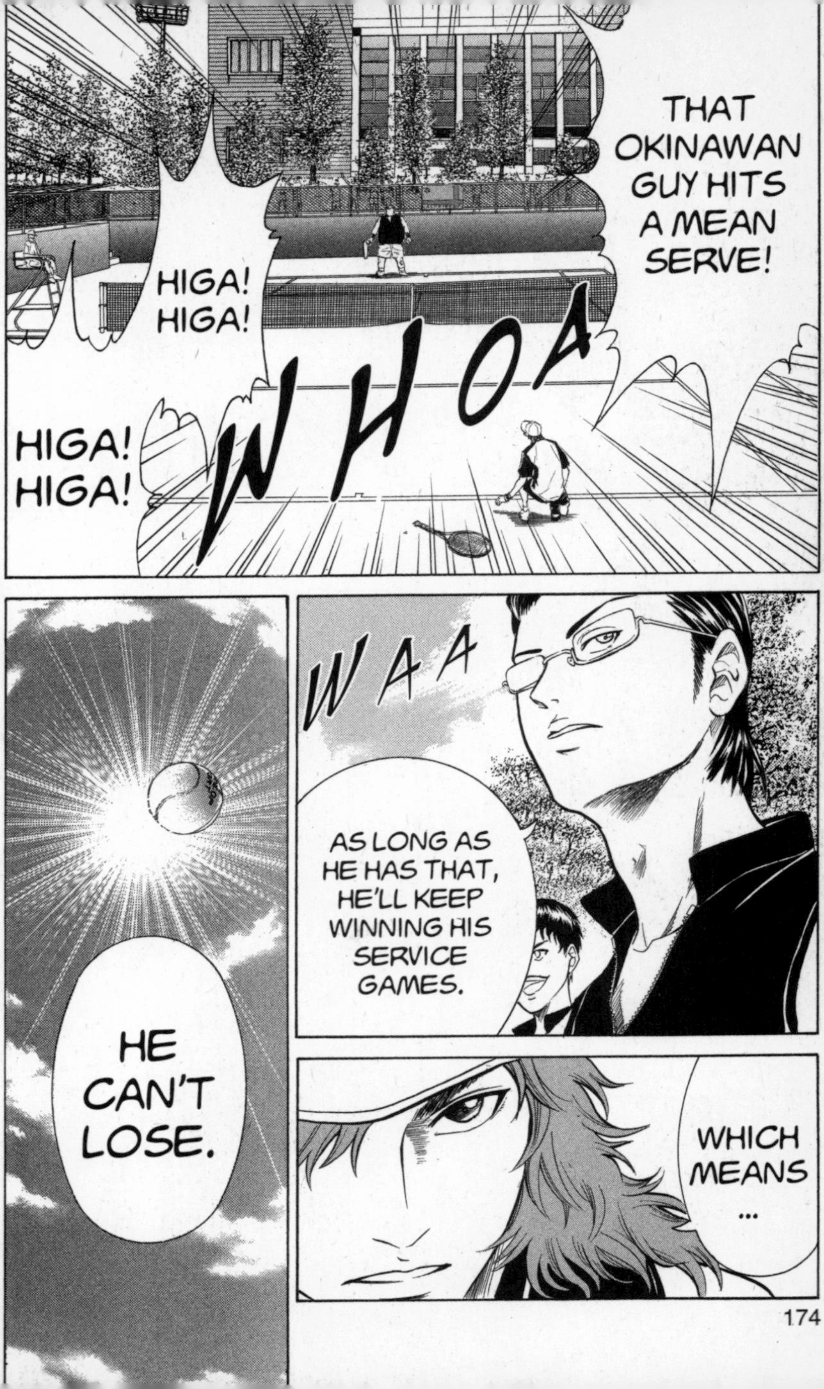
THAT OKINAWAN GUY HITS A MEAN SERVE!
HIGA! HIGA!
WHOA
HIGA! HIGA!
WAA
AS LONG AS HE HAS THAT, HE'LL KEEP WINNING HIS SERVICE GAMES.
WHICH MEANS ...
HE CAN'T LOSE.

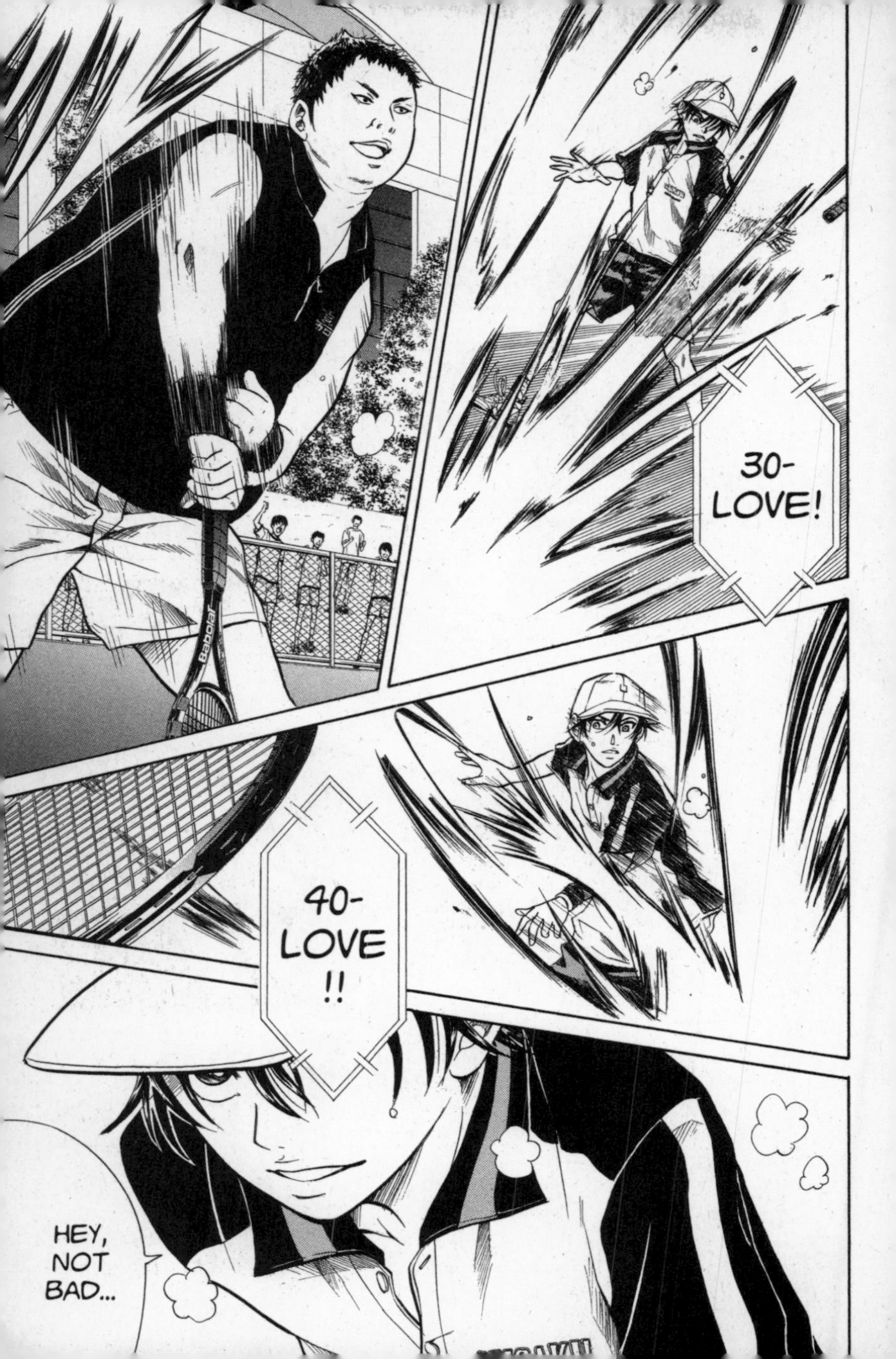
30-LOVE!
40-LOVE!!
HEY, NOT BAD...

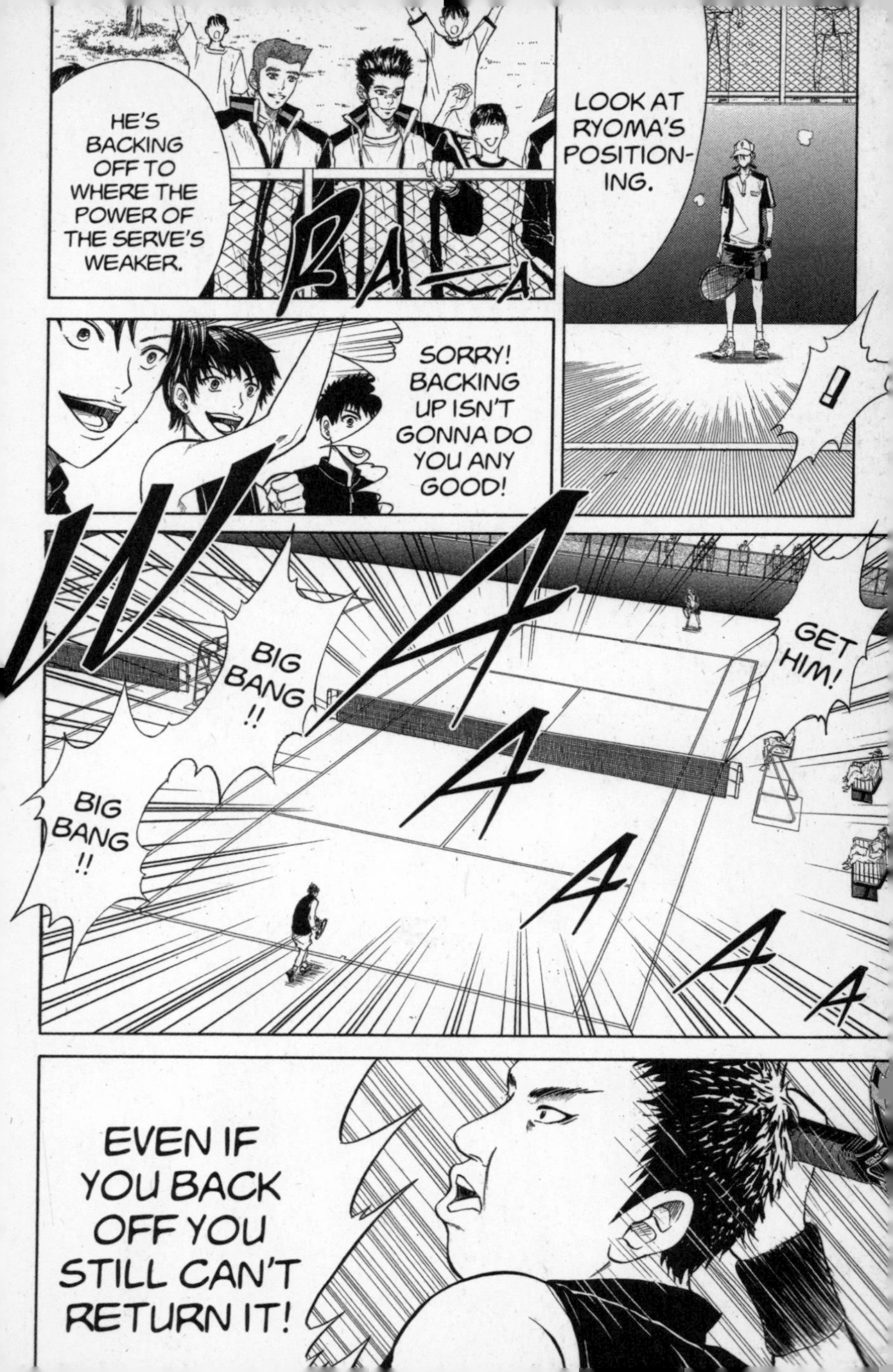
LOOK AT RYOMA'S POSITION-ING.
!
HE'S BACKING OFF TO WHERE THE POWER OF THE SERVE'S WEAKER.
SORRY! BACKING UP ISN'T GONNA DO YOU ANY GOOD!
GET HIM!
BIG BANG !!
BIG BANG !!
WAAAAAA
EVEN IF YOU BACK OFF YOU STILL CAN'T RETURN IT!

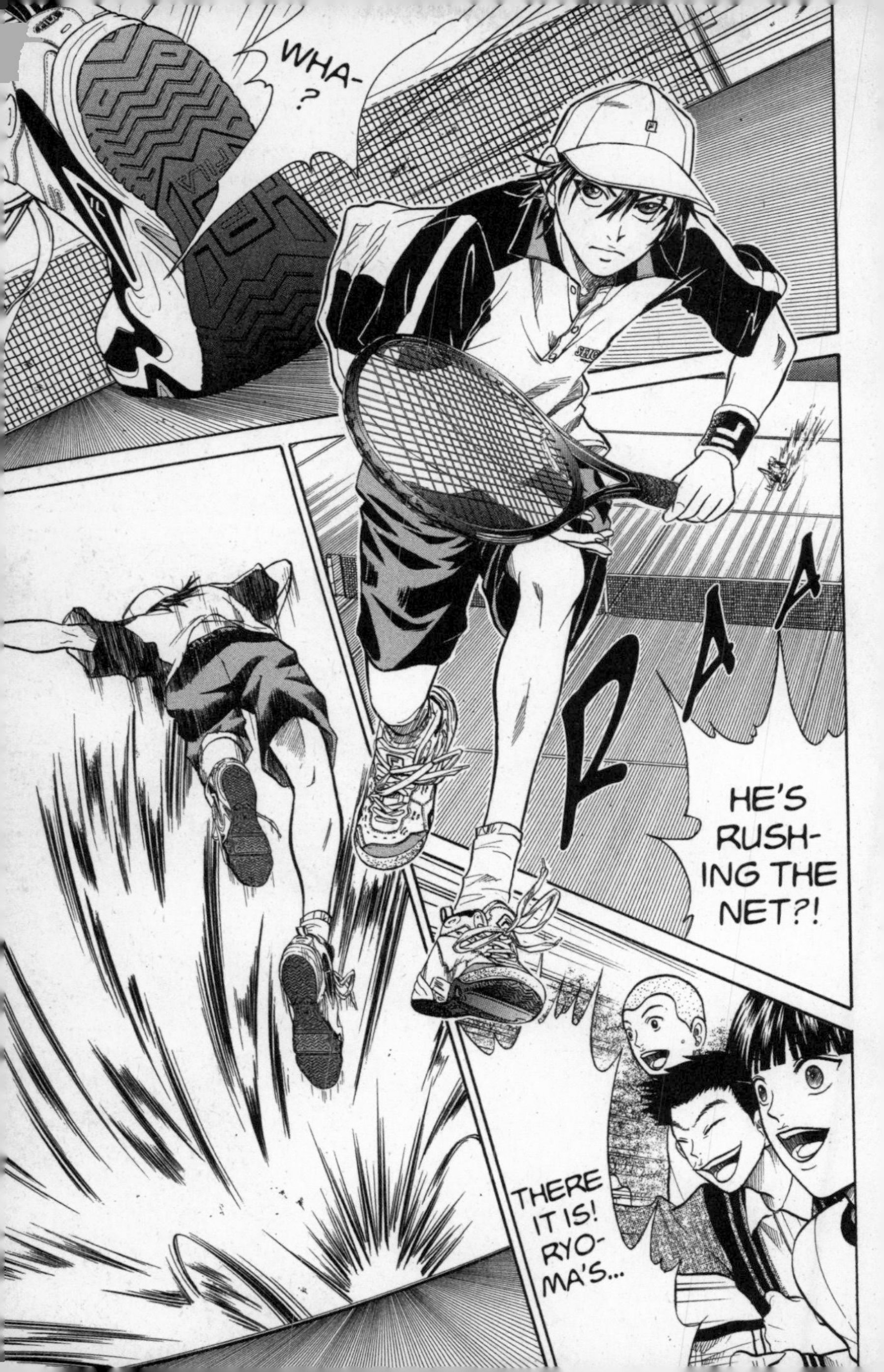
WHA-?
HE'S RUSHING THE NET?!
THERE IT IS! RYOMA'S...

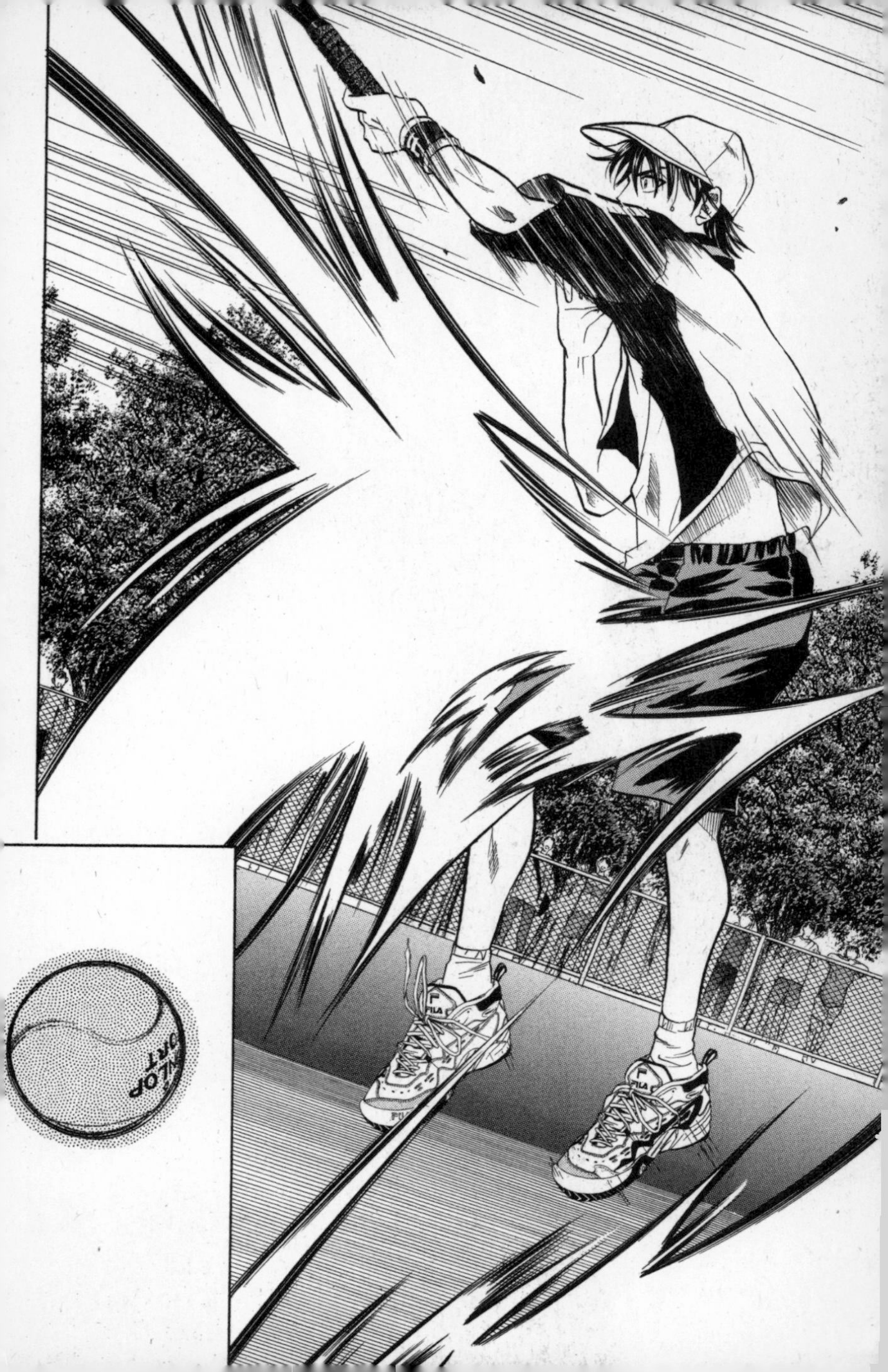
FILA

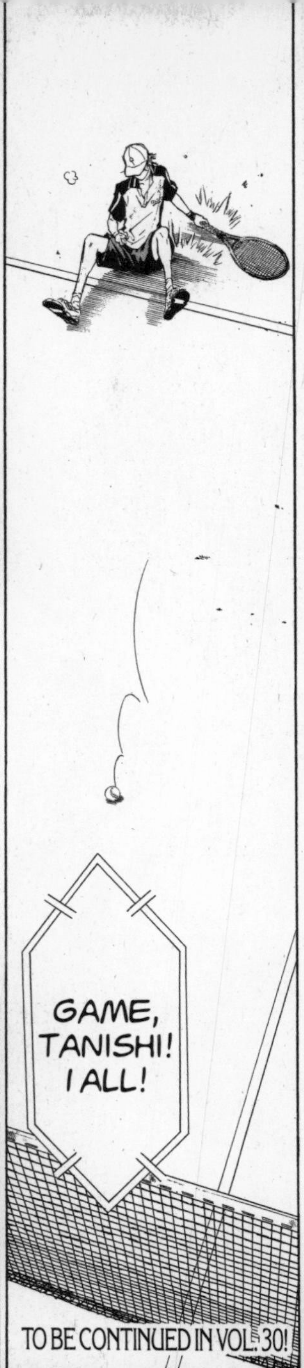
GAME, TANISHI! 1 ALL!
TO BE CONTINUED IN VOL. 30!
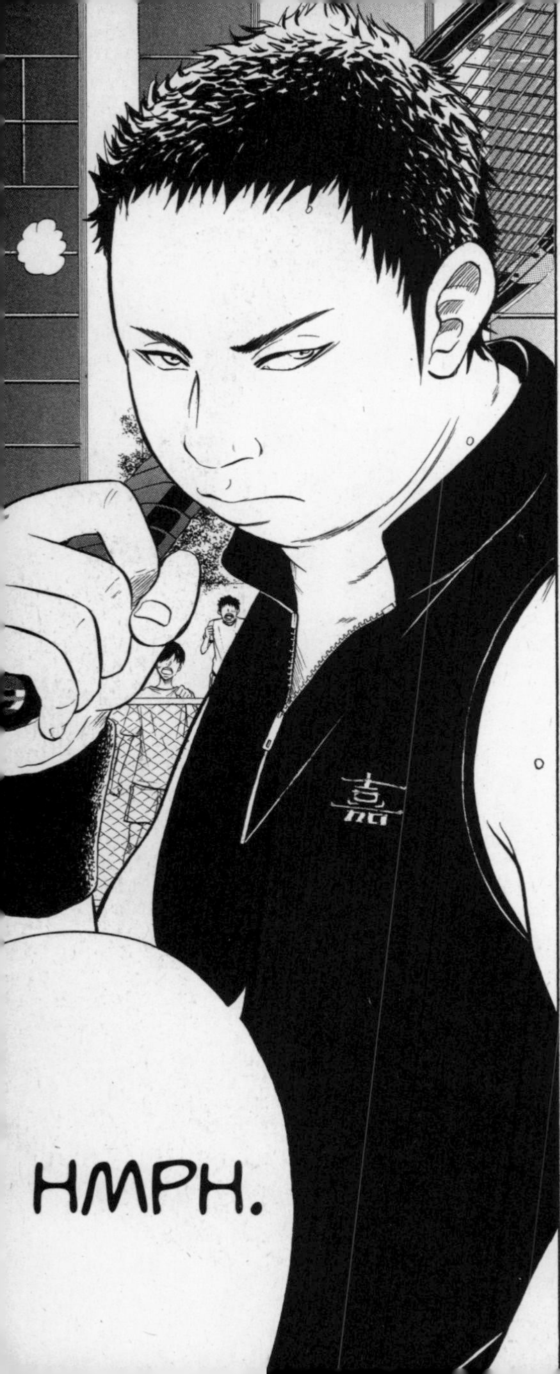
HMPH.

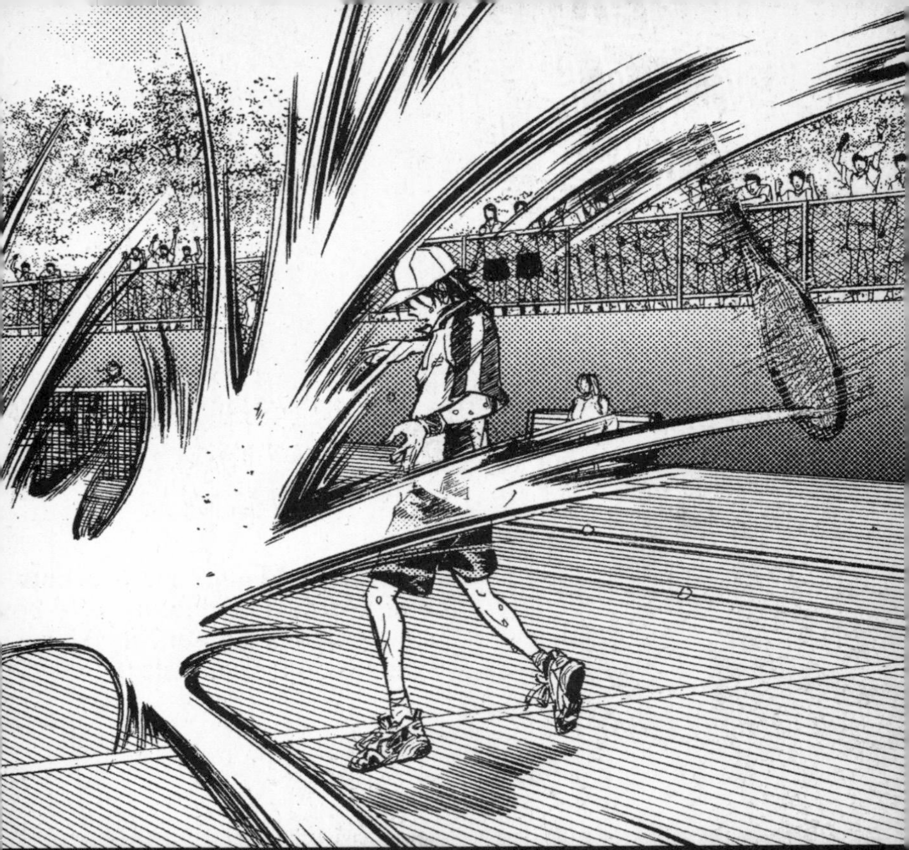

The Boys from Okinawa

As the match between Ryoma and Higa's giant Kei Tanishi continues, it's apparent to everyone that Tanishi is in control of the game—to everyone except Ryoma, that is. Higa continues to dominate in No. 2 Doubles, with Taka and Shusuke paired up against Hiroshi Chinen and Rin Hirakoba. Now Seishun's hopes rest on whether Shusuke can figure out how to effectively counter Rin's lethal "Habu" shot.

Available March 2009!

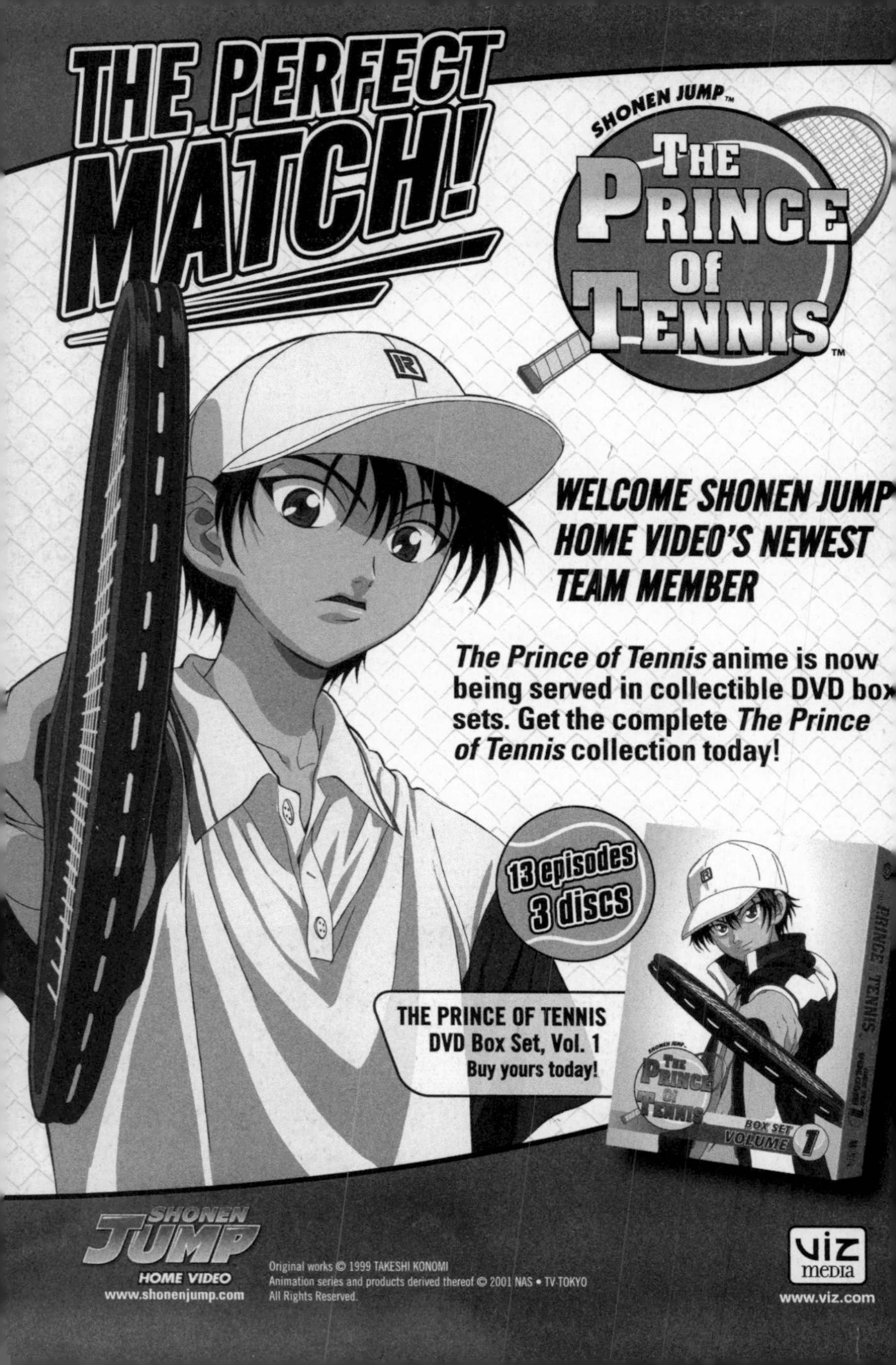

THE PERFECT MATCH!
SHONEN JUMP™
THE PRINCE OF TENNIS™
WELCOME SHONEN JUMP HOME VIDEO'S NEWEST TEAM MEMBER
The Prince of Tennis anime is now being served in collectible DVD box sets. Get the complete The Prince of Tennis collection today!
13 episodes 3 discs
THE PRINCE OF TENNIS DVD Box Set, Vol. 1 Buy yours today!
BOX SET VOLUME 1
SHONEN JUMP HOME VIDEO
www.shonenjump.com
Original works © 1999 TAKESHI KONOMI
Animation series and products derived thereof © 2001 NAS • TV-TOKYO
All Rights Reserved.
VIZ media
www.viz.com

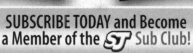

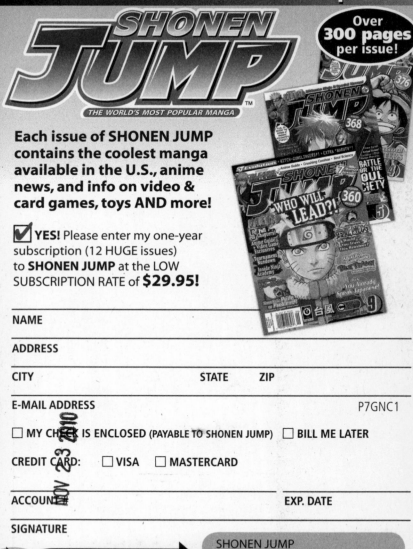